PA
6519
A2
1988

D0102460

CONTENTS

PREFACE TO THE SECOND EDITION

THIS second edition of volume VI of the Loeb Ovid continues the principles on which I have revised earlier volumes. Numerous alterations of the text and translation became imperative in view of much excellent work published in the last sixty years, foremost among which rank Georg Luck's editions. Moreover, especially since the Second World War, a juster appreciation of Ovid's exile poetry has won acceptance, and this is now reflected by the inclusion of various studies in a thoroughly revised *Bibliography*. Professor Wheeler's fine introduction has been left intact apart from a small amount of abbreviation at the end, but I have ventured to rewrite (without, however, suppressing his judgement) the note on the cause of Ovid's exile which originally appeared on pages xxiv f. Finally, I gratefully acknowledge several debts to a lecture by Professor John Richmond and even more to Dr. J. B. Hall, who at the proof stage of this second edition generously made available to me three unpublished articles of his on the textual criticism of these poems.

YALE UNIVERSITY   G. P. GOOLD
March 1988

OVID

VI

TRISTIA   EX PONTO

OVID

IN SIX VOLUMES

VI

TRISTIA · EX PONTO

WITH AN ENGLISH TRANSLATION BY

ARTHUR LESLIE WHEELER

ALUMNAE PROFESSOR OF LATIN, BRYN MAWR COLLEGE

Second edition, revised by G. P. Goold

CAMBRIDGE, MASSACHUSETTS

HARVARD UNIVERSITY PRESS

LONDON

WILLIAM HEINEMANN LTD

MCMLXXXVIII

American
ISBN 0-674-99167-2

British
ISBN 0 434 99151 1

First printed 1924
Reprinted 1939, 1953, 1959, 1965, 1975

Second Edition 1988

Printed in Great Britain by
St Edmundsbury Press Ltd, Bury St Edmunds, Suffolk

INTRODUCTION

Laeta fere laetus cecini, cano tristia tristis.
P. iii. 9. 35.

THE works of Ovid himself, and especially the auto-
biography (*T*. iv. 10), supply most of the material
for a sketch of his life. His fame, however, caused
him to be mentioned often by later writers, and
these, taken together, add not a little to the in-
formation derived from his own poems.

His full name was Publius Ovidius Naso, and he
was born on March twentieth, 43 B.C., at Sulmo, the
chief town of the Paeligni, about ninety miles by
road east of Rome. The family was of old equestrian
rank, and inscriptions prove that the name Ovidius
was common only in the region of Ovid's birthplace.
In Sulmo, now Sulmona, the tradition of the poet
still flourishes. The townspeople point out to the
infrequent tourist his statue in the court of the
Collegio Ovidio, the chief school of the town, and
the remains of his villa, the Villa Ovidio, on the slopes
of a neighbouring mountain. The main street of
the town, the Corso Ovidio, preserves his name,
and the letters S.M.P.E. ("Sulmo mihi patria est,"
T. iv. 10. 3) are inscribed on the façades of monu-
ments and at the head of public documents. In
folk-lore also and popular song his name survives.

But though the statue is mediaeval, though the
ruins are probably not connected with him, and the
traditions are fancy, the beautiful country on which

Ovid must have looked is true to his description. Sulmona lies in one of the loveliest vales of Italy, surrounded by towering mountains and watered, as Ovid himself says, by cold streams. As one views it from the mountain slopes the valley, carefully tilled and dotted with vineyards and fruit trees, is like a vast garden. Here lay those paternal fields of which the poet speaks, and here he passed the years of his boyhood.

Ovid's father, like the father of Horace, was ambitious for his sons and destined them for an oratorical career. While they were still very young Ovid and his brother, who was exactly one year older than the poet, were taken to Rome to receive a proper training. The brother displayed a decided gift for pleading, but Ovid found the legal grind distasteful. He tried to conform to his father's practical advice but the inborn impulse was too strong. "Whatever I tried to write," he says, "was verse," and the quaint anecdote told in one of the late *Lives* probably hits off the situation very well. Once when Ovid was being chastised by his angry father, says the *Life*, the squirming boy cried out (in verse!), "Parce mihi! numquam versificabo, pater!"

But though "he lisped in numbers," he nevertheless persisted half-heartedly in his preparation for a practical career until he held certain minor offices which were preliminary to the quaestorship. He became a *triumvir capitalis, i.e.* one of the board of three officials who had charged of prisons and executions and possessed judicial powers in petty cases. Ovid was probably not over twenty-one at this time. He also speaks of having been a member of

the centumviral court (which dealt with questions
of inheritance) and of having served as a single
judge, *i.e.* as a sort of referee in private lawsuits.
As a triumvir he was directly in line for the
quaestorship and seems to have had a right to
quaestoral privileges, but his tastes and frail con-
stitution led him to renounce a public career.

Ovid's thorough education under such distinguish-
ed teachers as the rhetoricians Arellius Fuscus and
Porcius Latro was not wasted, although it was not
applied to the end which his hard-headed father
had urged. Rhetoric and literature formed the
major part of the training of those who were qualify-
ing themselves for public life, and the young poet,
as we learn from Seneca the Elder, became a brilliant
declaimer. Poetry was much studied in the rhe-
torical schools of the day, and the training which
Ovid received undoubtedly laid the foundation of
that wide familiarity with myth and literature
which he displays in his work. In fact Seneca tells
us that Ovid transferred to his own verse many of
the pointed remarks of his teacher Latro. Even
his legal training was not entirely wasted, for there
are traces of it in his work.

Ovid studied at Athens, as Horace and many
other young Romans had done, and travelled in
Sicily and in Asia Minor. It is probable that his
sojourn in Athens occurred while he was still a
student, but it is not certain that the other journeys
belong to the same period.

Even before his education was finished he had
won fame as a poet of love. He was giving public
recitations of his *Amores*, he tells us, when his
"beard had been cut but once or twice" (*T*. iv.

10. 55 f.). Undoubtedly the popularity of these youthful poems did much to establish the conviction which he often expresses that his bent was erotic elegy; he considered himself the lineal successor of Gallus, Tibullus, and Propertius, and posterity has accepted him at his word. Thus the foundation of that fame which he was destined to deplore so bitterly was laid in his early youth.

In these youthful days Ovid made the acquaintance of many poets. His relations with Vergil and Tibullus were apparently not intimate, but he was only twenty-four when these poets died (19 B.C.), and it is probable that for some years before that date both had been in poor health and had seldom been seen in Rome. Ovid admired Horace but does not assert that he knew that poet personally. Propertius, however, he knew well, and he mentions him, together with Aemilius Macer, Ponticus, and Bassus, as a member of his own circle. He names besides a large number of fellow poets, many of whom were friends. To us they are hardly more than names, but they serve to illustrate the breadth of Ovid's literary interests, for these men worked in all departments of poetic composition. Ovid was always a generous critic, but in his remarks during his exile about these contemporaries there is the additional reason for generosity that he naturally wished to speak well of anybody who might help him.

Apart from literary men, professional or dilettanti, Ovid had a very wide acquaintance with Roman society in general. He came from a country town and he was not noble, but his rank was inherited and his fortune was considerable. With these ad-

vantages it was easy for a man of his brilliant talent
and agreeable personality to know everybody worth
knowing, and the poems from exile contain the
names of many statesmen, officials, and soldiers—
fewer, certainly, than he must have known since he is
careful not to name any to whom seeming connexion
with an exile might have brought offence. More-
over, many of those whom he must have known
in his youth had died before the period of his exile,
and these are mentioned as a rule only when they
are connected in some way with the living to whom
he made his appeals.

To the members of Rome's great families Ovid
stood rather in the relation of a client to patrons,
although this relation did not preclude intimacy.
Among these patrons the most distinguished man
was Marcus Valerius Messalla Corvinus, the states-
man, general, and orator, whose house was the centre
of a literary circle in which the most prominent
member was Tibullus. To this circle Ovid also
undoubtedly belonged. Messalla died not long
before Ovid was exiled, perhaps in the very year of
his exile (A.D. 8), and he had probably been in-
capacitated by illness for several years before his
death. It was Ovid's appeal to the great man's
sons that led him to mention the father. To the
house of Messalla he had been devoted from his
earliest years, and Messalla himself had been the
first to encourage him to publish his verse—un-
doubtedly some of those erotic poems which later
helped to ruin the poet. Messalla was, in Ovid's
phrase, "the guide of his genius," and the poet
wrote a tribute to him at his death.

Messalla had been one of Augustus' right-hand

men, but neither of his sons inherited his ability. Nevertheless both were prominent enough to attain the consulship. The elder, M. Valerius Messalla Corvinus or Messalinus (usually called merely Messalinus), had some reputation as a soldier and an orator, and was consul 3 B.C. Tacitus shows that he was guilty of fawning on Tiberius. Ovid addresses to him *P*. i. 7 and ii. 2, perhaps also *T*. iv. 4, and it is clear that the poet did not feel sure of the footing on which he stood with him. He has no doubts, however, of the loyalty of the younger son, who had been adopted by his maternal uncle and was called M. Aurelius Cotta Maximus or simply Maximus (or Cotta Maximus). He was born not earlier than 24 B.C. and became consul A.D. 20. He was something of a poet and an orator, but he is condemned by Tacitus for his luxurious and extravagant life and his servility. He seems, however, to have possessed good traits of character and he was loyal to Ovid; indeed he was rather a friend than a patron. Six of the *Pontic Epistles* are addressed to him (*P*. i. 5 and 9; ii. 3 and 8; iii. 2 and 5; *cf*. iv. 16. 41-44), and probably two *Tristia* (*T*. iv. 5 and v. 9).

Another Maximus—Paullus Fabius Maximus, a member of the famous Fabian family—is addressed *P*. i. 2 and iii. 3, possibly also iii. 8, *cf*. iv. 6, in which Ovid mourns his death. He was born not later than 45 B.C., and so was about Ovid's age. The poet's third wife had been a member of Fabius' household and intimate with Marcia, Fabius' wife. Ovid wrote a wedding-song for Fabius, had listened to his literary efforts, and had sat at his table, but his tone is more restrained in writing to him than

that which he adopts in his letters to Cotta Maximus.
Fabius was a good orator, held the consulship
11 B.C., and was a trusted friend of Augustus. Such
a man was in a position to make a plea for Ovid,
and the latter asserts that this was only prevented
by Fabius' death which occurred A.D. 14, not long
before that of Augustus.

Sextus Pompeius, who was descended from an
uncle of Pompey the Great, is addressed in four letters
of *P.* iv. (Nos. 1, 4, 5, and 15). He was consul A.D. 14,
was very wealthy, and Ovid assumes towards him
an attitude of extreme humility. Although he is
not addressed, so far as can be proved, before the
last book of the *Pontic Epistles*, he must have been
friendly to Ovid, for the poet thanks him for safe-
guarding his journey into exile. Ovid's hopes of
him were probably based on the fact that he was
a friend of Germanicus. Pompeius suffered death
at the hands of Caligula *c.* A.D. 39.

Three letters are addressed to P. Pomponius
Graecinus, who was *consul suffectus* beginning in
May A.D. 16 (*P.* i. 6, ii. 6, iv. 9), and one to his brother
L. Pomponius Flaccus who immediately succeeded
Graecinus as consul, January A.D. 17 (*P.* i. 10).
Graecinus was a soldier who took an interest in
literature. If, as seems probable, he is the Graecinus
mentioned *Amores* ii. 10, Ovid's acquaintance with
him was of long standing. The brother, Flaccus,
held some command in Moesia about A.D. 16 (*P.*
iv. 9. 75 ff.), and he was intimate with Tiberius.
Ovid probably did not know him well and addressed
him chiefly because he was Graecinus' brother.

With the exception of Cotta Maximus Ovid's
really intimate friends were naturally men of much

the same station in life as himself, and many of these are named in the *Pontic Epistles*. Since at the time Ovid was writing the *Tristia* he did not venture to name his friends, the question arises whether it is possible to identify any of the un-named recipients of the *Tristia* with friends who are named in the *Pontic Epistles*.[1] These are seventeen poems of the *Tristia* which are addressed to friends or patrons. Three of these, as the tone shows, are addressed to patrons, *i.e.* to men who were superior to Ovid in rank, twelve to friends of his own status or of such status that they were at least not his superiors, which in the case of two the tone supplies no good evidence for placing them in one class rather than the other. Now Ovid asserts several times that "only two or three" of his friends showed themselves really faithful at the time when disaster befell him (*T*. i. 5. 33, "vix duo tresve"; cf. iii. 5. 10; v. 4. 36, etc.). Examination of the *Pontic Epistles* shows that these few faithful ones were probably Brutus, Atticus, Celsus, and possibly Carus. To these we should add his patron-friend Cotta Maximus. By comparing the *Pontic Epistles* in which these men are addressed or named with the seventeen *Tristia* we may assign to Brutus *T*. iii. 4 (*cf. P*. i. 1, iii. 9, iv. 6); to Atticus *T*. v. 4 (*cf. P*. ii. 4 and 7); to Celsus *T*. i. 5, iii. 6 (*cf. P*. i. 9); to Carus *T*. iii. 5 (*cf. P*. iv. 13); to Cotta Maximus *T*. iv. 5, v. 9 (*cf. P*. i. 5 and 9, ii. 3 and 8, iii. 2 and 5, iv. 16. 41 ff.); to Messalinus *T*. iv. 4 (*cf. P*. i. 7, and ii. 3). The reproach, *T*. i. 8, is very possibly addressed to Macer (*cf. P*. ii. 10). Even if these identifications are accepted there remain eight

[1] *Cf.* G. Graeber, *Untersuchungen* (Part II), Elberfeld, 1884.

poems whose recipients have not been satisfactorily identified. Of these eight six (*T*. i. 7, iv. 7, v. 6, 7, 12, 13) are addressed to men who were apparently friends, two (*T*. i. 9, iii. 14) are uncertain, though the tone of *T*. i. 9 is perhaps better suited to a young man of rank, and that of *T*. iii. 14 to a poet-friend of greater age than Ovid.

Numerous other friends and acquaintances—poets, rhetoricians, officials, soldiers—appear in the *Pontic Epistles*, but among them there is nobody whom we may regard as the probable recipient of any poem among the *Tristia*. About some of them we know only what Ovid tells us, about others we can glean a few meagre facts from other sources. It is particularly unfortunate that, with the exception of Cotta Maximus, the poet's best friends, Celsus, Atticus, Brutus, and Carus, are known only from Ovid. All efforts to identify them with men of the same names mentioned elsewhere have proved unavailing.

There is no good evidence that Ovid had ever been intimate with any member of the imperial household. The approval of the Emperor to which he alludes (*T*. ii. 89 and 98, *cf*. 542) consisted merely in allowing Ovid to retain his rank as a knight. In his references to Augustus the poet assumes the tone of an abject suppliant appealing to a deity immeasurably removed. Even if there had been any former intimacy it would have been difficult to harmonize it with such an attitude as this and it would have been carefully suppressed. The references to Tiberius and his son Drusus, to Germanicus and his sons, permit the same general inference: that Ovid had probably never been intimate with any of them. The character of Germanicus was so affable and kindly that if Ovid had ever known him well one might expect a reference to the fact. But the passages in which Germanicus is addressed or mentioned show that Ovid's hopes in this direction were based upon the intercessions of mutual friends—Salanus (*P.* ii. 5), Sextus Pompey (*P.* iv. 5), Suillius (*P.* iv. 8), etc.

The method of appeal to the Empress Livia Augusta is similar. Ovid hoped to influence her through his wife and through Marcia, wife of Paullus Fabius Maximus, who was Augusta's close friend. Another possible approach to Augusta lay in the fact that Ovid's wife knew intimately the Emperor's maternal aunt, Atia Minor. This seems to have been the only real link between the poet's household and the palace.

At the time when Ovid was ordered into exile (A.D. 8) the only members of his immediate family who were in Rome were his wife and step-daughter. His own daughter, who must have been the daughter of his first or second wife, had married a second time and was absent in Libya, but we know neither her name nor that of her husband at the time. His only brother had died years before when he had just turned twenty, *i.e.* in 24 B.C. Both of the poet's parents also had passed away, his father at the advanced age of ninety.

Ovid himself was married three times. He speaks of his first wife whom he married when he was "almost a boy," as "unworthy and useless." The marriage lasted but a short time and may have ended in divorce. The second wife was "blameless," but this marriage also was broken off by death or divorce. The poet does not tell us the

xvi

names of these ladies, but he indicates that one of
them came from Falerii (*Am*. iii. 13. 1). Ovid's third
wife was "from the house" of the Fabii (*P*. i. 2.
136), but it is not certain that her name, which
Ovid does not give, was Fabia. She may have
been a poor relative (or a relative who had lost her
parents) who had lived in the protection of the
Fabian household. She was a widow (or divorced?)
with one daughter, Perilla, when Ovid married her,
but the marriage seems to have been childless.[1]
Upon her devolved the care of the poet's property
after he was exiled, and upon her efforts he rested
in large measure his hopes of pardon. Many
passages bear witness to his tender love for her;
he draws a most affecting picture of their mutual
despair at parting, and if at times after years of
exile he became somewhat peevish, we must pity
rather than condemn. The poor lady seems to have
been always faithful to his interests and no doubt she
did all within her power to secure a mitigation
of his sentence.

But neither family connexions nor influential
friends were able to save Ovid from his fate. After
more than thirty years of popularity, at the age of
fifty, he was suddenly ordered to leave that Rome
which was the very breath of life to men of his stamp
and take up his abode on the very edge of the
wilderness in a little town of which he had probably
never heard. The order emanated from the author-
ity of the Emperor and was never brought before the
Senate or a court. Ovid was not called an *exul*,

---

[1] Perilla married Suillius (*P*. iv. 8). In view of the absence
from *Tr*. of addressees' names, and of *Tr*. ii. 437, Perilla is
probably a pseudonym. (G.P.G.)

but was "relegated" (*relegatus*).[1] *Relegatio* was milder than the *exilium* of the late republic in that the poet's property was not confiscated and his civic rights were not taken from him, but it was harsher, in Ovid's case, in that he was ordered to stay in one designated locality. The *exul* of the republican period might wander where he would provided he kept beyond a prescribed radius from Rome. On the other hand, to judge from Cicero's case, the friends of an exile of that period subjected themselves to penalties if they aided him, whereas Ovid's friends freely assisted him and wrote to him. Even the fear of being publicly known as his friends, which prevailed at the time he was writing the *Tristia*, had vanished from the minds of all but one or two when the *Pontic Epistles* were written, and Ovid himself states openly (*P.* iii. 6. 11 f.) that the Emperor forbade neither mention of him nor correspondence with him.

The sins which led Augustus to banish Ovid have been endlessly discussed. The poet himself refers to them again and again, but his references are so vague that it is impossible to arrive at the whole truth, and of course the lips of his contemporaries were sealed. He was constantly hoping that his penalty might be revoked or at least mitigated by permission to change his place of exile, and he left no stone unturned to effect one or the other of these results. If we had his prose correspondence with friends in Rome and elsewhere—a correspondence to which he frequently refers—it would be easier to solve the problem, but in the poems from exile we have only such evidence as could be made public

[1] *T.* ii. 131 ff.; iv. 4. 45 f.; 9. 11 ff.; 5. 7; *P.* ii. 7. 56.

without injuring the exile's chances of pardon or involving his friends. In weighing this evidence it is necessary to allow for a double distortion—an over-emphasis on the charges which could be publicly argued and a corresponding reticence about those which it seemed impolitic to discuss in public. Moreover, the poet based his hope of pardon very largely on confession of guilt; he threw himself on the mercy of the court which consisted, in this case, of a single judge, the Emperor. Naturally, therefore, he did not argue his case as completely as he could have done if he had been free to use all the arguments at his disposal. He was aware that the mere presentation of evidence could avail him nothing. There was no appeal from the judge's verdict, but the judge himself might be induced to relent.

Ovid asserts that there were two charges against him, a poet and a mistake (*T*. ii. 207, "Duo crimina, carmen et error") of which the poem was the first in time. In many passages he makes the same distinction between his sins, and it will be advisable, even though they may have been connected, to discuss them separately in order to determine the poet's own attitude.

The poem was the *Ars Amatoria* which was published *c*. 1 B.C. This *Art*, as the poet often calls it, is no more immoral than other erotic works, among which Ovid mentions those of Tibullus and Propertius, but it is explicitly didactic. It gathers up and systematizes the erotic precepts which had gradually been developed (largely under Greek influence) by the Roman poets, especially Gallus, Tibullus, Propertius, and Ovid himself. It taught love explicitly, and Ovid became known as the chief erotic expert (*praeceptor amoris*). Erotic teaching had appeared often enough in Greek and Latin, but there had been no handbook like this. The *Art* was the culmination, the shining example, for it presented the subject as a didactic system, and it was this aspect of the book, not the erotic content *per se*, that angered Augustus. In his eyes and in the eyes of all those who hoped to regenerate Roman morals Ovid was the arch offender, and the *Art* was his chief sin. When the poet was exiled the *Art* was expelled from the public libraries and placed under a ban.

The charge of pernicious influence through the medium of the *Art* could be publicly discussed, and since Ovid presents his case in the second book of the *Tristia*, not to mention many other briefer passages, the discussion need not be repeated here. It is sufficient to say that he denied any intention of immoral influence, proving that the *Art* was explicitly restricted to affairs with courtesans, and that he was no more blameworthy than countless other writers if readers had made a perverse use of his work. He complained truly that he was the only erotic poet who had ever been punished for his compositions. In view of ancient standards in such matters it must be admitted that, so far as the *Art* was concerned, he was harshly treated. But whatever the merits of the case the poet bitterly regretted that he had ever written erotic verse, even at times that he had ever attempted verse of any kind. Augustus had condemned the *Art*, and Ovid had perforce to admit that he had sinned.

In Ovid's eyes then the *Art* was the earliest cause

of his exile and an important cause, but he says that there was a later cause which "had injured him more" (*P*. iii. 3. 72). Since the latter could not be discussed publicly, the poet speaks of it in very general terms. It was not a crime (*scelus*), not illegal, but rather a fault (*culpa*, *vitium*) which he admitted to be wrong (*peccatum*, *delictum*, *noxa*). He had not been guilty wittingly, but through chance (*fortuna*, *casus*). There had been no criminal action (*facinus*) on his part, but he had laboured under a misunderstanding, he had blundered (*error*). He had been stupid (*stultus*), thoughtless (*imprudens*, *non sapiens*), over ingenuous (*simplicitas*); he had been ashamed (*pudor*) and afraid (*timor*, *timidus*).[1]

From the passages in which he speaks most fully of this fault we infer that the affair with which it was connected had a considerable history, or at least that a full account of it would have been a long, one. It began with a misunderstanding on Ovid's part of something that he had seen by chance (*T*. iii. 6. 27 ff.; ii. 103 ff.), but he must soon have comprehended its import, for he began to be afraid. He harboured it as a secret when advice might have saved him.

He speaks of that which his eyes had seen as something wrong, but not as a crime. He had not at first considered it to be wrong, and perhaps his later confession that it was wrong is due to the fact that he was punished for it; at least confession of

[1] For these terms *cf*. *T*. i. 2. 100; iv. 4. 37 and 43 ff.; *P*. ii. 9. 71; *T*. i. 2. 64; iv. 8. 49; 4. 44; *P*. i. 7. 41; ii. 9. 72; *T*. ii. 105 f.; i. 2. 98 ff.; ii. 104; *P*. ii. 2. 17; *T*. i. 5. 42; iii. 6. 30; *P*. ii. 2. 17; *T*. iii. 6. 27; *P*. i. 6. 21; *T*. iv. 4. 38; iii. 6. 11 ff.; *P*. ii. 6. 7.

guilt was in this matter, as in the case of the *Ars Amatoria*, a necessary part of his appeal to Augustus.[1] It was necessary also for him to represent his friends, however sympathetic they were, as siding with Augustus, and so we hear that Cotta Maximus, Messalinus, and Graecinus condemned or reproved the poet's sins; they believed that Ovid had sinned but that his sin was rather foolish than criminal. The thing was an offence, a wound to Augustus, and he had used harsh words about it, but there is no proof that the wound concerned his private affairs. In fact the sin did not, according to Ovid, involve others but had ruined the poet alone. He advances his original error as a partial excuse, not as a defence, for his sin. This is his only plea, but it is fairly clear that if the question could have been argued he would have made a strong defence.

What had Ovid seen? Why, after he realized its import, had he been afraid to reveal his knowledge? To the second question one may answer that he was afraid of that which actually befell him, the Emperor's anger, for he must have been aware that he was disliked by Augustus. But to the first question there is with our present evidence no satisfactory answer although it has afforded a tempting field for surmise. Nevertheless such evidence as we have makes it possible to define approximately the nature of the thing, to say at least in some degree what it was not, and so to eliminate certain favourite hypotheses.

Ovid characterizes the affair as no crime, and we may accept this statement because he would not have ventured to misname it nor could he have

[1] *T.* ii. 103, 134, 209

misunderstood it if it had been criminal. Ovid himself could not discuss it because the case had been closed by the Emperor's verdict, but his statement is supported by the fact that he alludes to it many times without rebuke, that everybody knew it, and that the Emperor made no attempt to hush it up. It seems, therefore, very improbable that the evil of which he became cognizant was anything so heinous as the profligacy of the younger Julia, who was banished at about the same time as the poet. Ovid refers, it is true, to his fault as an offence against Augustus, as a "wound," an "injury" to him, but such phrases need not imply that the offence concerned the imperial household. Any offence against the state, or that which Augustus regarded as the interest of the state, was an injury to the ruler.

Augustus's own attitude, as shown by Ovid, indicates that the poet's sin was not a very heavy one. To say nothing of the comparatively mild conditions of Ovid's *relegatio*, which he himself urges as a proof of the Emperor's estimate, the poet and his friends were allowed to correspond freely, and he was allowed to publish poetry appealing openly to Augustus and to many others. It is plain that Augustus and after his death Tiberius, who continued so religiously the policies of his predecessor, were quite satisfied merely to have Ovid out of the way. Ovid's fault was serious enough to serve as a pretext, that is all. It was the exciting cause of his exile, and so he can speak of it as having "injured him more" than the *Ars Amatoria*, but the latter— all his erotic verse in fact—which had given him so great and unsavoury a reputation as the purveyor of wanton titbits, was the predisposing cause. His fault must have been something that enhanced the poet's pernicious influence by lowering his personal reputation. With the Emperor it was the final straw. Without it Ovid might never have been exiled, for he was turning to more dignified work, the *Metamorphoses*, the *Fasti*, but he could not escape the notoriety of that earlier work which was still so popular with his "host of readers."

Augustus himself was no prude. He had a weakness for mimes and he liked his little joke. It was not the content of the *Ars Amatoria* but rather its pernicious influence that angered him. If that work had merely been the talk of a day it would be impossible to understand why the Emperor allowed eight or nine years to pass before punishing its author. Everything indicates, however, that time only increased the vogue of the book, and when at an age that should have brought him wisdom the poet made that final stupid blunder, the Emperor became convinced that the question involved more than mere literature; it had passed into the sphere of public policy. In brief, from the point of view of Augustus, the ruler and reformer, Ovid had been a nuisance for many years and had given fresh proof of his incorrigibility by making a fool of himself. The thing was too much. "I am sick of this fellow," he decided. "Naviget!"[1]

---

[1] *Editor's note:* Professor Wheeler, impressed by Boissier, strongly held the opinions that "the chief cause of exile was the *Ars amat.* and that the *culpa* merely gave Augustus a pretext" and "the *culpa* could not have been *in itself* anything very serious" (a note at this point in the 1924 edition). These opinions are still held by many today. But no firm consensus exists, as a glance at Thibault's book will show; in particular the

xxiv

INTRODUCTION

When the blow fell Ovid was in Elba, probably in the suite of his friend Cotta Maximus, for the latter heard of Ovid's sin, and Ovid has described the interview in which he stammeringly confessed to Cotta that the report was true. This must have been in the summer or early autumn of A.D. 8. Ovid returned to Rome and arranged his affairs as best he could. In his despair he contemplated suicide, but he was not of the stuff of which suicides are made. Moreover, he cherished hopes of pardon, and he prevailed on his wife to remain behind to work for this object. His parting from her and the events of his dismal journey are described in *Tristia* i., all of which, save possibly the proem, was written before he reached Tomis. The account of the journey does not begin until he has boarded ship, at which time we find him storm-tossed on the Adriatic, and so it is uncertain whether he followed the Appian Way to Capua and its extension to Brundisium, the customary route for travellers bound to the East, or whether he embarked at some port nearer Rome, for example, Ostia. At any rate he sailed to Corinth, crossed the Isthmus from Lechaeum to Cenchreae and boarded a second ship which carried him to Imbros and Samothrace. This ship completed her voyage to Tomis, but the poet preferred to cross from Samothrace to Tempyra near the Thracian coast and so to finish his journey

---

notion that the *culpa* was not a serious matter seems an unwarranted paradox. Specific suggestions mostly focus on involvement in the adultery of the younger Julia (also banished in A.D. 8: the *Ars* would then be a supporting charge) or in a political plot to rehabilitate Agrippa Postumus. See further the articles of G. P. Goold and Peter Green. (G.P.G.)

by land. He must have journeyed slowly, for he received news from home on the way, and it is probable that he did not cross the Thracian mountains to Tomis until the spring or summer of A.D. 9, since he alludes to no discomfort from cold, although after his arrival in Tomis this is a hardship on which he dwells insistently.

Tomis! Outlandish name! With what bitterness the storm-tossed poet speaks of "the Tomitans, situated in some corner of the world"! We cannot expect from a poet, much less from an exiled poet, an adequate description of the town. It was his interest to paint a gloomy picture. And yet if we allow for his exaggeration of the hardships there are details enough with which to form a fairly good conception of the poet's hostelry of calamity.

Tomis[1] (the modern Constantza) lay on an elevated and rocky part of the coast, about sixty-five miles south-west of the nearest mouth of the Danube, in that part of Roumania now called the Dobrudja. The townspeople were a mixed crowd of half-breed Greeks and full-blooded barbarians. The latter were in the majority and were chiefly of Getic, hence Indo-European, stock. They dressed in skins, wore their hair and beards long, and went about armed. They were fine horsemen and experts with the bow. Apart from trade the chief occupation of the region was grazing, for border warfare made agriculture difficult. It was a rude community. Latin was almost never heard and the people spoke some hybrid Greek, but Getic and Sarmatian were

[1] Tomis, not Tomi, is indicated by the manuscripts and is the older form of the name.

so much in use that Ovid was forced to learn these languages. He even wrote a poem in Getic.

The coastal region is often called by Ovid "Pontus" after the Pontus Euxinus, the modern Black Sea, which washed its shores. Sometimes he speaks of it as Pontus Laevus or Sinister, "Pontus-on-the-Left" (as one enters the Black Sea), to distinguish it from the kingdom of Pontus in Asia Minor, but at times these epithets seem to mean "ill-omened." Tomis itself was an ancient colony of Miletus and was in ancient as in modern times an important port. Because of the silt in the outlets of the Danube much freight passed to and from the river, in ancient times, by way of Tomis. The country about the town is in general flat and treeless, often marshy. Ovid often speaks of this and also of the bad water which, together with the rough fare, may have caused the frequent illnesses which he mentions. He suffered from indigestion, fever, insomnia, "an aching side." He dwells on the extreme cold. Snow lies all winter, the Danube and the sea are frozen hard, even wine freezes in the jar and is served in pieces! The hair of the barbarians "tinkles with ice." This picture, as modern evidence proves, is not overdrawn. Although the latitude of Tomis is about the same as that of Florence, the winters are very severe. The temperature in the flat country sinks at times to 20° or even 30° below zero (Fahrenheit), and the Danube is sometimes ice-bound for three months. Violent winds, as Ovid also observed, are prevalent.

Since Tomis was a border town it was subject to raids by the wild tribes from across the Danube, and this constant peril was in Ovid's eyes one of his worst misfortunes. The shepherds wore helmets as they tended their flocks. When the barbarians swooped down they destroyed or carried away everything that could not be brought within the walls. Poisoned arrows fell thickly within the town and even the elderly poet was called upon to aid in the defence. We are reminded of the tales of colonial America and the warfare of the settlers against the savages.

Such is the picture that Ovid paints. No wonder that he regarded Tomis as "the worst element in his cruel lot," for it would be difficult to conceive of a place more distasteful to a man of his type. And yet even in his account there are some bright spots. The people were rough but they were kind to him. They realized how hard it was for such a man to live a virtual prisoner among them. They honoured him by a decree exempting him from taxation and they listened sympathetically when he told them of his appeals to be restored to his native land. For all this the poet was grateful, and when his wild hosts became aware of his attacks upon their land and showed their indignation, he was almost in despair. They could hardly be expected to accept the distinction that he made between his gratitude to them and his detestation of their country.

There was nothing of Roman sternness about Ovid. Physically he was not strong and, even if the portrait which he draws of himself in exile— his emaciation, his pallor and whitening hair, his frequent illness—is exaggerated, it is clear that he was not one who cared for the strenuous life.

INTRODUCTION

His tastes were all against it. He did not care for exercises in arms, though he professes that he had to don a helmet to aid in the defence of Tomis. Archery, the favourite sport of the barbarians, had no attractions for him. In fact the only form of outdoor occupation that he cared for was gardening. This he had practised in Italy and he would have liked to continue it at Tomis if such a thing had been possible. He liked the ordinary inactive amusements, dice-playing, etc., as little as he did physical exercises. "Games," he said, "are wont to waste that precious thing, our time!"

He was abstemious. Eating and drinking as mere pleasures did not appeal to him; "You know," he writes to Flaccus, "that water is almost my only drink." In his younger days his heart had not been impregnable to Cupid's darts, although he asserts that no scandal had ever been attached to his name, but advancing years and the sorrows of exile had removed this susceptibility.

There was little of the philosopher or the scientist in Ovid and nothing at all of the explorer. What a chance he had during his long residence at Tomis to study the geography and ethnology of that almost unknown region! What a chance for excursions into the wild country and among tribes still wilder! Probably such excursions would not have been contrary to the decree of *relegatio*. But he was not a Varro or a Pliny, and his only attempt at science (aside from his effort to explain the freezing of the Pontus) seems to have been his *Halieutica*, a disquisition, of which only a fragment remains, on the fishes and animals of the Pontus. Nowhere in all his verses is there an adequate description of the many interesting barbarian tribes with which he became so familiar. Such details as he gives are almost always part of his effort to paint his lot in the darkest colours.

But we cannot reproach him for the lack of qualities which he did not possess. His interests were in that humanity whose life centred in the great metropolis. His feeling was that of Catullus, "that is my settled abode, there do I pluck the blooms of life," or of Cicero, "I am gripped by a marvellous love of the city." But unlike his two great predecessors he was forced to doubt whether he was ever to behold that loved city again. No wonder that the longing to return became with him an obsession, no wonder that to a man of his tastes Tomis was the hardest element in his fate.

A few congenial companions would have greatly lightened the tedium of his exile. He had been a brilliant declaimer and undoubtedly an equally brilliant conversationalist. If there had only been some friend with whom he could have whiled away the lagging hours in those endless talks which he recalls so pleasantly! But he was forced to talk with his friends by letter and in imagination. Cut off thus from his friends and from everything that he held dear, unable to find or to create for himself any real interest in his surroundings, he found his chief solace in writing. Poetry had ruined him, but he could not lightly abandon his very nature and the practice of a lifetime. He was a born poet and he felt an irresistible impulse to write. Poetic composition not only comforted him and hastened the dragging hours, but although it had injured him he had hoped that, perhaps, like Telephus of

old, he would be healed by the very weapon that
had wrought him harm; he sought no fame, but
poetry was the best means in his power of making
a personal effort in his own behalf. Therefore he
wrote, and the verse of this period, apart from its
references to others, throws interesting lights upon
his own work and his own methods.

Ovid was a very careful artist, severe in self-
criticism, although he was a generous critic of
others. Occasionally he speaks of hurried com-
position, but his habit was quite the opposite. He
toiled over his work, and his verse smells of the lamp.
Before his exile he had followed the practice, common
at the time, of reading his poetry to discerning
friends in order to profit by their advice, and to
revise it carefully before publication. In Tomis he
complains that there was nobody to whom he could
read it; he had to be his own critic, and he shrank
from the task of revision. Moreover, all the condi-
tions favourable for good work were lacking—an
untroubled mind, peaceful surroundings, abundant
books, the stimulus of an audience (P. iv. 2. 29 ff.).
He has so little opportunity to speak Latin that he
fears lest barbarisms creep into his work. His
talent is broken and the stream of his inspiration is
dried up. He recognizes the faults of his work
and admits that it is poor stuff, not better than
his lot. Again and again he asks indulgence for it.

Poetry written by such a man amid such surround-
ings was inevitably monotonous and aroused criti-
cism. The almost unvarying sadness of its tone, the
constant repetition of the same appeal were criticiz-
ed. He admits the charge; his poetry is conditioned
by his lot and by his purpose, and he regards possible

advantage to himself as preferable to fame; if he could be restored to his home he would be gay as of old, though he would never again attempt wanton verse.[1]

And yet, although his work of necessity fell short of his ideals, he was conscious that it was good enough to be read, for the host of readers of which he boasts must have included many who were not interested solely in the work of his happier years. His great reputation also must have interested many in the poetry of a fallen idol, even if from mere curiosity to discover how that idol comported himself in exile. He affirms, moreover, that to be named in his verse was to receive fame. This affirmation was not mere convention, nor was it entirely for the purpose of propaganda that he published these poems. He believed that they were worth publishing. And he was right. They are too pervasively gloomy, although the reader will find not a few exceptions to the rule, and their purpose is too obviously pressed. Nevertheless as human documents they possess great interest in spite of the author's weakness and slavish fawning.

Their chief interest, however, lies in their art. Ovid possessed remarkable powers over language: he was a great phrase-maker. He was also one of the greatest of metricians. These are high qualities, and in the poems from exile they are scarcely impaired at all, in spite of the fact that here as elsewhere in Ovid they often degenerate into mere juggling with words. But when the poet is at his best there is the old skill in the use of a remarkably simple vocabulary, the old simplicity of structure, the

[1] *T.* v. 1.

same limpid clearness and skilful arrangement, the same sweetness and melody in the verse. No translation can hope to render all this. It cannot be separated from the Latin. But the translator can at least use simple English; he can try to be clear and to hint at the beauties of the order. He can do little else. Ovid destroyed much that he wrote, he tells us, and the *Tristia* and *Epistulae ex Ponto* are the cream of his years of exile. Considering the fact that they represent eight or nine years of work their bulk is not great. Because of the monotony of their content and tone and the almost constant obtrusion of mere rhetorical trickery they will never be popular, and yet they contain much that is admirable. To those who can be patient with Ovid, who like good writing for its own sake, the poems from exile will always make a strong appeal.

Chronology and Publication

In *P*. iv. 6. 16 there is a reference to the death of Augustus together with the statement (v. 5) that Ovid has passed an Olympiad of five years in Scythia. Augustus died August 19, A.D. 14. Therefore *P*. iv. 6 was written in the autumn of A.D. 14, and the poet had been in Tomis since A.D. 9 (probably summer at least). The poems of *T*. i. were all written during his journey into exile (*T*. i. 11. 1 ff.), and since he refers in his book to December and winter (*T*. i. 11. 3 ff., 39, etc.), but mentions no discomforts of a winter journey through the Thracian mountains, and since he travelled so leisurely that he received news from home (*T*. i. 6. 8 ff., i. 9. 39 f.), it is very probable that he left Rome in the autumn or early

winter of A.D. 8. Moreover, *T*. iv. 10. 95 f. implies
that he was fifty when he was ordered into exile (cf.
Ibis 1). If he is speaking at all precisely, we may
infer that the order came after March 20, A.D. 8, his
fiftieth birthday. On this basis we may establish the
following table:

T. i.   Composed during the winter, A.D. 8-9.

T. ii.   Composed A.D. 9. Tiberius is still warring
in Pannonia, and Ovid has not heard of the
close of the war and of Tiberius's transfer to
Germany after the defeat of Varus (*cf.* vv. 177,
225 ff.).

T. iii.   Composed A.D. 9-10. Germany has rebel-
led(*cf.* iii. 12. 47 ff.). The defeat of Varus
occurred in the late summer or autumn A.D. 9.

T. iv.   Composed A.D. 10-11. Tiberius is cam-
paigning against the Germans (A.D. 10, *cf.*
iv. 2. 2). Ovid has passed two summers
away from home (*i.e.* autumn of A.D. 10, *cf.* iv.
6. 19), and two winters (*i.e.* the spring of either
A.D. 10 or 11 is meant, according as we
interpret the passage to refer to two winters
since the poet left Rome, or two passed in
Tomis, *cf.* iv. 7. 1 f.).

T. v.   Composed A.D. 11-12, *cf.* v. 10. 1 (after three
winters or in the third winter in Pontus, *i.e.*
in the winter, *cf.* A.D. 11-12, or spring of A.D.
12). Also Ovid has not yet heard of the
triumph of Tiberius, January 16, A.D. 13,[1] *i.e.*
he is writing before that date.

---

[1] *Cf.* H. Schulz, *Quaestiones Ovid.*, 1883, p. 15, and
Mommsen, *Provinces* (Engl. transl.), i. p. 55.

INTRODUCTION

P. i.-iii. were *published* as a unit, *cf.* the proem (i. 1) and the epilogue (iii. 9) to Brutus.

P. i.-iii. Composed A.D. 12-13. The triumph is expected, *i.e.* before January 16, A.D. 13, and therefore late in A.D. 12, *cf.* iii. 3. 86. Other references to the triumph imply that Ovid is writing not long before it or not long after it, *i.e.* in the latter part of A.D. 12 or the early part of A.D. 13, *cf.* ii. 1. 1 and 46; ii. 2. 75; ii. 5. 27; iii. 1. 136; iii. 4. 3 ff. Also Ovid is in Tomis for the fourth winter, *i.e.* the winter of 12-13 A.D., *cf.* i. 2. 26, and for the fourth autumn, *i.e.* the autumn of A.D. 12, *cf.* i. 8. 27. Lastly iv. 4 was sent to Sex. Pompey before he entered on his consulship in A.D. 14, *i.e.* this poem of the fourth book was written in the latter part of A.D. 13. It is quite possible that some of the letters which cannot be dated may have been written before some of the later *Tristia*.

P. iv. Composed A.D. 13-16. *P*. iv. 4 belongs to A.D. 13 (see above), iv. 5 to A.D. 14, since it was written after Pompey became consul. Iv. 6 was written after Augustus's death, *i.e.* in the autumn A.D. 14. The sixth summer (iv. 10. 1) and the sixth winter (iv. 13. 40) in Tomis are mentioned, *i.e.* the summer of A.D. 14 and the winter of A.D. 14-15. The latest reference is that to the consulship of Graecinus (iv. 9. 4), and since he was *consul suffectus* A.D. 16, and the letter was intended to reach him on the day he took office in May, it was probably written early in A.D. 16.

Thus the letters of *P.* iv., so far as they can be dated, were composed A.D. 13-16, but some of the letters which cannot be dated may have been written a little before or a little after this period. Since the book has no proem and several of the letters are addressed to persons not mentioned before, it is probable that Ovid did not himself collect these letters for publication in book form. Perhaps, on the other hand, he was preparing to do so, for iv. 16 has the air of having been written as an epilogue. It is a variation on that assertion of fame which was a convention with Augustan poets, only, since Ovid regarded himself as already dead to the world, Horace's *non omnis moriar* becomes here a *non omnis mortuus sum*.

The internal evidence already cited shows that it was Ovid's custom to send each letter separately to its recipient, and when enough letters had accumulated to collect them from publication in book form. At the time of publication it is possible that he excluded some letters which had been sent separately; certainly he added the introductory and perhaps some of the closing poems. Each book, save *T.* ii., which is one long composition, and *P.* iv. (see above), is provided with such poems, and the same is true of *P.* i.-iii., which for purposes of publication formed a unit. With this exception each book also was published separately (*cf. T.* v. 1. 1 f.).

The arrangement of letters within the books is not chronological. This is proved for the *Pontic Epistles* by the chronological references which they contain, and by Ovid's statement that the pieces of *P.* i.-iii. were collected "without order" (*P.* iii.

9. 53), which refers primarily if not exclusively to chronological order, and it is probable for the *Tristia*, since at least the proems do not owe their positions to considerations of chronology. We should make an exception to this general principle when pairs of letters to the same person occur within a book. Such pairs seem to be in chronological order. The letters are therefore not arranged chronologically but so as to present as much variety as possible.

As Ovid himself states (*P.* i. 1. 15 ff.), the *Tristia* do not differ essentially from the *Pontic Epistles* except that, so far as the epistolary form is concerned, the recipients of the *Tristia* are not addressed by name. The term *epistula* is in fact used of one of the *Tristia* (*T.* v. 4. 1). In the *Tristia* only the members of the imperial house are addressed by name[1]; in the *Pontic Epistles* all the persons addressed are named save two enemies (*P.* iv. 3 and 16) and one friend who was still afraid to be connected so openly with the exile (*P.* iii. 6).

Saint Jerome, in his continuation of the *Chronicle of Eusebius* says, under the year A.D. 16 or (according to some manuscripts) 17, that Ovid died in exile and was buried near Tomis. The dates agree well with the latest datable reference in the poems from exile—the consulship of Graecinus, A.D. 16. The date A.D. 18, which is often given, is based on *Fasti* i. 223-226, a reference to the restoration of the temple of Janus, near the theatre of Marcellus, which was completed by Tiberius in that year. But this restoration was begun by Augustus, and Ovid's words do not certainly imply that the work was completed at the time he was writing.

[1] Except (the probably pseudonymous) Perilla (*T.* iii. 7).

INTRODUCTION

A smaller share of the fame which Ovid often prophesies for his verse fell to the poems from exile than to other parts of his work, especially the *Metamorphoses*, and yet there is abundant evidence that this poetry of his declining years has been read almost continuously from his own time to ours. During the centuries of the Empire it is constantly mentioned and often imitated by the poets, both pagan and Christian, although the prose writers contain few references. From early in the second century to the first half of the fourth there is a period of silence, but the references then begin once more and continue through the Carlovingian Age and the Middle Ages to the Renaissance.

The great vogue of the *Tristia*, and in less degree the *Pontic Epistles*, came in the twelfth and thirteenth centuries. They were used for the construction of fanciful lives of the poet and even introduced into schools. They were much imitated and pillaged; in the fourteenth century Alberto Mussato, the friend of Dante, composed a cento from the *Tristia*, and Dante himself made use of the *Tristia* together with the other works of Ovid. To this interest we own the numerous manuscripts which date from this period, and the careful study devoted to the poet is manifest in the throng of interpolations, showing knowledge of the verse technique, with which these manuscripts are filled.

THE MANUSCRIPTS

Tristia

The textual tradition of the *Tristia* is not good. We have no early manuscript of, say, the ninth century; a striking error at 1. 11. 12 shows that the whole tradition may on occasion be interpolated; and none of the 60-odd manuscripts available inspires special confidence in its readings or permits us to ignore them. The mss fall into three groups.

(i) **Tr:** fragmentum Trevirense, 10th century, containing 1. 11. 1-31, 33-2. 21 ; 4. 4. 35-65, 67-4. 5. 9.

    M: Florentinus Laur., olim Marcianus 223, late 11th c., cont. 1. 5. 11-3. 7. 1 ; 4. 1. 12-4. 7. 5 (Owen's *L*).

    Tr and *M* are related and contain variant readings, but though the text they exhibit is generally superior, it is marked by blunders.

(ii) **A:** Marcianus Politiani, 12th c., now lost and known only from Politian's collation.

    G: Guelferbytanus, Gud. lat. 192, 13th c.

    H: Brit. Lib. Add. 49368, olim Holkhamicus 322, 13th c.

    P: Vaticanus Pal. lat. 910, *c.*1476.

    V: Vaticanus lat. 1606, 13th c.

    This group (Luck's *N*) provides the staple of the *Tristia* text, but may anywhere be infected by interpolation.

(iii) **D:** Gothanus membr. II 122, 13th c., lacks 3. 2. 6-3. 12.50.

    G^2: The second and coeval hand of *G*.

    K: Leidensis, B.P.L. 177, late 13th c.

    T: Turonensis Bibl. Mun. 879, early 13th c.

    This third group (Luck's *S*) sometimes

> preserves the truth where the second group is interpolated, but in general is less trustworthy.

All three groups go back to a medieval archetype, but readings in later mss and medieval anthologies suggest that genuine variants may occasionally have been handed down independently of the main tradition.

Epistulae ex Ponto

The transmission of the *Epistulae ex Ponto* shows no special relationship to that of the *Tristia*.

   (i) **G:** fragmentum Guelferbytanum, 6th c., a palimpsest, contains only 4. 9. 101-108, 127-133 and 4. 12. 15-19, 41-44. It is not the archetype of the other mss, but derived from it.

   (ii) **A:** Hamburgensis 52, 9th c., contains the work as far as 3. 2. 67, omitting however 1. 3; it seems to represent a unique branch of the tradition and, though often wrong, preserves many good readings.

   (iii) **B:** Monacensis 384, 12th c.

   C: Monacensis 19476, 12th c.

   D: Gothanus membr. II 121, 13th c.

   S: Argentoratensis, 12th c., destroyed by fire in 1870 and now known only from Korn's apparatus; its text ended at 3. 5. 34.

   T: Turonensis Bibl. Mun. 879, early 13th c. (=*T* in *Trist.*).

   Tarrant notes that the clearest division is between *BC* and *DT*, with the latter showing a greater propensity to interpolation.

The brief critical notes aim only at showing where the tradition has been abandoned in favour of a scholar's emendation and at giving a selection of those places where one well attested variant has been preferred to another. For more details the reader is directed to Owen's large edition of the *Tristia* and André's of the *Ex Ponto*.

xl

SELECT BIBLIOGRAPHY

Editions and commentaries

Editiones principes : Rome and Bologna, 1741.

N. Heinsius : Amsterdam, 1661.

P. Burman : Volume III of his great variorum edition, Amsterdam, 1727.

S. G. Owen : *Tristia, Ibis, Ex Ponto, Halieutica* (OCT), Oxford, 1915.

R. Ehwald–F. Levy : *Tristia, Ibis, Ex Ponto* (Teubner), Leipzig, 1922.

Georg Luck : *Briefe aus der Verbannung* (Artemis : text and notes ; German translation by Wilhelm Willige), Zürich/Stuttgart, 1963 (review by M. v. Albrecht, *Gnomon* 37 [1965] 491-6).

S. G. Owen : *Tristia* (large critical edition), Oxford, 1889.

G. Némethy : *Tristia* (comm. exegeticus), Budapest, 1913.

S. G. Owen : *Tristia II* (elaborate introduction ; text, translation, and copious commentary), Oxford, 1924, repr. 1967.

J. T. Bakker : *Tristia V* (with comm.), Amsterdam, 1946.

T. J. De Jonge : *Tristia IV* (with comm.), Groningen, 1951.

Georg Luck : *Tristia* (2 vols), Heidelberg (I : Text, app. crit. and German translation, 1967 ; II : Commentary, 1977).

Jacques André : *Tristes* (Budé, i.e. introd., text, app. crit., notes, and French translation), Paris, 1968.

O. Korn : *Ex Ponto libri IV* (comm.), Leipzig, 1868.

G. Némethy : *Ex Ponto* (comm. exegeticus), Budapest, 1915.

A. Scholte : *Ex Ponto I* (with comm.), Amersfort, 1933.

xli

SELECT BIBLIOGRAPHY

U. Staffhorst: *Ex Ponto III 1-3* (comm.), Diss. Würzburg,
1965.
Jacques André: *Pontiques* (Budé), Paris, 1977.

General

Hermann Fränkel: *Ovid: A Poet between Two Worlds* (Sather
Classical Lectures, No. 18), Berkeley & Los Angeles, 1945,
repr. 1956.
L. P. Wilkinson: *Ovid Recalled*, Cambridge, 1955.

Text

D. R. Shackleton Bailey: "Notes on Ovid's Poems from
Exile," *CQ* 32 (1982) 390-398.
James Diggle: "Notes on Ovid's Tristia, Books I-II," *CQ* 30
(1980) 401-419.
A. E. Housman: "Ovidiana," *CQ* 10 (1916) 130-150 (= *Collec-
ted Papers* III, pp. 917-939).
Georg Luck: "Notes on the Language and Text of Ovid's
Tristia," *HSCP* 65 (1961) 243-261.
Georg Luck: *Untersuchungen zur Textgeschichte Ovids*, Heidel-
berg, 1969 (a speculative attempt to reconstruct the
archetype of the Ovidian corpus).
R. J. Tarrant in *Texts and Transmission* (ed. L. D. Reynolds),
Oxford, 1983 (the transmission of *Ex Ponto*: 262-5; of the
Tristia: 282-4).

Concordance

R. J. Deferrari, I. Barry, and R. P. McGuire: *A Concordance of
Ovid*, Washington, 1939, repr. 1968.

SELECT BIBLIOGRAPHY

On Ovid's Exile

Gaston Boissier : *L'Opposition sous les Césars*, Paris, 1909 (pp. 106-159 on Ovid's exile).

G. P. Goold : "The Cause of Ovid's Exile," *ICS* 8 (1983) 94-107 (complicity in the adultery of the younger Julia).

Peter Green: "Carmen et Error," *Classical Antiquity* 1 (1982) 202-220 (complicity in a treasonable plot).

J. C. Thibault: *The Mystery of Ovid's Exile*, Berkeley & Los Angeles, 1964.

Thomas Wiedemann : "Political Background to *Tristia* 2," *CQ* 25 (1975) 264–271.

On the Exile Poems

R. J. Dickinson : "The *Tristia* : Poetry in Exile," pp. 154-190 in J. W. Binns (ed.), *Ovid*, London, 1973.

Harry B. Evans: *Publica Carmina : Ovid's Books from Exile*, Lincoln, Nebraska, 1983.

B. R. Fredericks (= Nagle): "*Tristia* 4. 10," *TAPA* 106 (1976) 139-154.

H. H. Froesch : *Ovids Epistulae ex Ponto I-III als Gedichtsammlung*, Diss. Bonn, 1967.

H. H. Froesch : *Ovid als Dichter des Exils*, Bonn, 1976.

E. J. Kenney : "The Poetry of Ovid's Exile," *PCPhS* 11 (1965) 37-49.

A. G. Lee : "An Appreciation of *Tristia* III. viii," *Greece & Rome* 18 (1949) 113-120.

R. G. M. Nisbet : "Great and Lesser Bear" (Ovid, *Tristia* 4. 3), *JRS* 72 (1982) 49-56.

Ronald Syme : *History in Ovid*, Oxford, 1978 (mostly on *Ex Ponto*).

SELECT BIBLIOGRAPHY

Bibliographical

Walther Kraus: RE XVIII² (1942) cols 1910-1986 (repr. in *Wege zu Ovid* 269-294, ed. M. v. Albrecht and E. Zinn, Darmstadt, 1968).

Anzeiger für die Altertumswissenschaft, Innsbruck: 11 (1958) 129 ff.; 16 (1963) 1 ff.; 18 (1965) 193 ff. by Walther Kraus; *ibid.* 25 (1972) 55 ff., 267 ff.; 26 (1973) 129 ff. by M. v. Albrecht.

R. J. Gariepy: *CW* 64 (1970) 37-56.

John Barsby: *Ovid (Greece & Rome*: New Surveys in the Classics, No. 12), Oxford, 1978.

OVID'S TRISTIA

TRISTIUM LIBER PRIMUS

I.

Parve—nec invideo—sine me, liber, ibis in urbem,
    ei mihi, quo [1] domino non licet ire tuo !
vade, sed incultus, qualem decet exulis esse ;
    infelix habitum temporis huius habe.
5 nec te purpureo velent vaccinia fuco—
    non est conveniens luctibus ille color—
nec titulus minio, nec cedro charta notetur,
    candida nec nigra cornua fronte geras.
felices ornent haec instrumenta libellos ;
10   fortunae memorem te decet esse meae.
nec fragili geminae poliantur pumice frontes,
    hirsutus passis [2] ut videare comis.
neve liturarum pudeat ; qui viderit illas,
    de lacrimis factas sentiet esse meis.
15 vade, liber, verbisque meis loca grata saluta :
    contingam certe quo licet illa pede.
siquis, ut in populo, nostri non inmemor illic, [3]
    siquis, qui, quid agam, forte requirat, erit,

---

[1] cum *vel* quod   [2] sparsis   [3] illi

---

[1] The order of the poems is not chronological.   (See Introd.
p. xxxvi.)

OVID'S TRISTIA—BOOK I

I. The Poet to his Book [1]

LITTLE book, you will go without me—and I
grudge it not—to the city, whither alas your master
is not allowed to go! Go, but go unadorned,
as becomes the book of an exile; in your misfortune
wear the garb that befits these days of mine. You
shall have no cover dyed with the juice of purple
berries—no fit colour is that for mourning; your
title shall not be tinged with vermilion nor your
paper with oil of cedar; and you shall wear no
white bosses upon your dark edges.[2] Books of good
omen should be decked with such things as these;
'tis my fate that you should bear in mind. Let no
brittle pumice polish your two edges; I would have
you appear with locks all rough and disordered.
Be not ashamed of blots; he who sees them will
feel that they were caused by my tears.

[15] Go, my book, and in my name greet the loved
places: I will tread them at least with what foot [3] I
may. If, as is natural in so great a throng, there
shall be any there who still remembers me, any who
may perchance ask how I fare, you are to say

[2] In Ovid's time the Roman book was a roll. The ends of the
rod (bosses, knobs) were called *cornua* (" horns ").

[3] *i.e.* metrical foot.

3

vivere me dices, salvum tamen esse negabis ;
20 id quoque, quod vivam, munus habere dei.
atque ita tu tacitus—quaerenti plura legendum—
ne, quae non opus est, forte loquare, cave !
protinus admonitus repetet mea crimina lector,
et peragar populi publicus ore reus.
25 tu cave defendas, quamvis mordebere dictis ;
causa patrocinio non bona maior [1] erit.
invenies aliquem, qui me suspiret ademptum,
carmina nec siccis perlegat ista genis,
et tacitus secum, ne quis malus audiat, optet,
30 sit mea lenito Caesare poena levis.
nos quoque, quisquis erit, ne sit miser ille, precamur,
placatos miseris qui volet esse deos ;
quaeque volet, rata sint, ablataque principis ira
sedibus in patriis det mihi posse mori.
35 ut peragas mandata, liber, culpabere forsan
ingeniique minor laude ferere mei.
iudicis officium est ut res, ita tempora rerum
quaerere.   quaesito tempore tutus eris.
carmina proveniunt animo deducta sereno ;
40 nubila sunt subitis pectora [2] nostra malis.
carmina secessum scribentis et otia quaerunt ;
me mare, me venti, me fera iactat hiems.
carminibus metus omnis obest [3] ; ego perditus ensem
haesurum iugulo iam puto iamque meo.
45 haec quoque quod facio, iudex mirabitur aequus,
scriptaque cum venia qualiacumque leget.

---

[1] peior *s*   [2] tempora *corr. Heinsius*
[3] abest *corr. Francius*

that I live, yet not in health and happiness; that even the fact of life I hold to be the gift of a god. Except for this be silent—for he who requires must read more—and take care that you chance not to say what you should not; forthwith, if but a reminder be given, the reader will recall my sins, and I shall still be convicted by the people's voice as a public criminal. Do you take care to make no defence though attacked with biting words; my case is not a good one, and will prove too difficult for advocacy. You are to find one who sighs over my exile, reading your lines with cheeks that are not dry, one who will utter a silent prayer unheard by any ill-wisher, that through the softening of Caesar's anger my punishment may be lightened. On my part I pray that whoever he may be, suffering may not come to him who wishes the gods to be kind to suffering. May his wish be fulfilled! May the removal of the Prince's wrath grant me the power to die at home in my country!

³⁵ Though you should carry out my directions you will be criticized perchance, my book, and regarded as beneath the glory of my genius 'Tis a judge's duty to investigate both the circumstances and the time of an act. If they ask the time you will be secure. Poetry comes fine spun from a soul at peace; my mind is clouded with unexpected woes. Poetry requires the writer to be in privacy and ease; I am harassed by the sea, by gales, by wintry storms. Poetry is injured by any fear; I in my ruin am ever and ever expecting a sword to pierce my throat. Even the making of such verse as this will surprise a fair-minded critic and he will read these verses with indulgence, how-

5

da mihi Maeoniden et tot circumice [1] casus,
    ingenium tantis excidet omne malis.
denique securus famae, liber, ire memento,
50   nec tibi sit lecto displicuisse pudor.
non ita se praebet nobis Fortuna secundam,
    ut tibi sit ratio laudis habenda tuae.
donec eram sospes, tituli tangebar amore,
    quaerendique mihi nominis ardor erat.
55 carmina nunc si non studiumque, quod obfuit, odi,
    sit satis; ingenio sic fuga parta meo.
tu tamen i pro me, tu, cui licet, aspice Romam.
    di facerent, possem nunc meus esse liber!
nec te, quod venias magnam peregrinus in urbem,
60   ignotum populo posse venire puta.
ut titulo careas, ipso noscere colore;
    dissimulare velis, te liquet esse meum.
clam tamen intrato, ne te mea carmina laedant;
    non sunt ut quondam plena favoris erant.
65 siquis erit, qui te, quia sis meus, esse legendum
    non putet, e gremio reiciatque suo,
"inspice" dic "titulum.   non sum praeceptor
       Amoris;
    quas meruit, poenas iam dedit illud opus."
forsitan expectes, an in alta Palatia missum
70   scandere te iubeam Caesareamque domum.
ignoscant augusta mihi loca dique locorum!
    venit in hoc illa fulmen ab arce caput.

---

[1] circumice *Heinsius* : circumspice

ever poor they are. Pray bring the Maeonian[1]
and cast just as many dangers about him; all his
genius will fall away in the presence of such great
ills.

[49] Take heed, then, my book, to go untroubled
about fame, and be not ashamed that your readers
gain no pleasure. Fortune is not now so favourable
to me that you should take account of your
praise. In the time of my security I was touched by
the love of renown, and I burned to win a
name. Now let it be enough if I do not hate poetry
and the pursuit which has injured me; through that
my own wit has brought me exile. But do you go in
my stead, do you, who are permitted to do so, gaze on
Rome! Would that the gods might grant me now to
be my book!—and think not, because you enter into
the great city as one from foreign lands, that you can
come as a stranger to the people. Though you
should lack a title, your very style will bring
recognition; though you should wish to play the
deceiver, it is clear that you are mine. And yet enter
secretly, that my verses may not harm you; they are
not popular as once they were. If there shall be
anybody who thinks you unworthy to be read for the
reason that you are mine and repels you from his
breast, say to him, "Examine the title. I am not
Love's teacher; that work[2] has already paid its
deserved penalty."

[69] Perchance you are waiting to see if I shall send
you to the lofty Palatine and bid you mount to
Caesar's house. May those places of awe and the
gods of those places grant me pardon! It was from
that citadel that the bolt fell upon this head

---

[1] Homer.   [2] A reference to *Ars amatoria* 1.17f.

esse quidem memini mitissima sedibus illis
    numina, sed timeo qui nocuere deos.
75 terretur minimo pennae stridore columba,
    unguibus, accipiter, saucia facta tuis.
nec procul a stabulis audet discedere, siqua
    excussa est avidi dentibus agna lupi.
vitaret caelum Phaëthon, si viveret, et quos
80   optarat stulte, tangere nollet equos.
me quoque, quae sensi, fateor Iovis arma timere:
    me reor infesto, cum tonat, igne peti.
quicumque Argolica de classe Capherea fugit,
    semper ab Euboicis vela retorquet aquis;
85 et mea cumba semel vasta percussa procella
    illum, quo laesa est, horret adire locum.
ergo cave, liber, et timida circumspice mente,
    ut satis a media sit tibi plebe legi.
dum petit infirmis nimium sublimia pennis
90   Icarus, aequoreis nomina fecit aquis.[1]
difficile est tamen hinc, remis utaris an aura,
    dicere: consilium resque locusque dabunt.
si poteris vacuo tradi, si cuncta videbis
    mitia, si vires fregerit ira suas,
95 siquis erit, qui te dubitantem et adire timentem
    tradat, et ante tamen pauca loquatur, adi.
luce bona dominoque tuo felicior ipse
    pervenias illuc et mala nostra leves.
namque ea vel nemo, vel qui mihi vulnera fecit
100   solus Achilleo tollere more potest.

---

[1] aequoreas nomine fecit aquas

of mine. There are, I know, in those shrines deities of exceeding mercy, but I still fear the gods who have wrought me harm. The least rustle of a feather brings dread upon the dove that thy talons, O hawk, have wounded. Nor does any lamb, once wrested from the teeth of a ravenous wolf, venture to go far from the fold. Phaëthon would avoid the sky if he were alive; the steeds which in his folly he desired, he would refuse to touch. I too admit—for I have felt it—that I fear the weapon of Jupiter: I believe myself the target of a hostile bolt whenever the thunder roars. Every man of the Argive fleet who escaped the Capherean rocks always turns his sails away from the waters of Euboea; and even so my bark, once shattered by a mighty storm, dreads to approach that place where it was wrecked. Therefore be careful, my book, and look all around with timid heart, so as to find content in being read by ordinary folk. By seeking too lofty heights on weak wings Icarus gave a name to waters of the sea. Yet from this position of mine 'tis hard to say whether you should use the oars or the breeze. You will be advised by the time and the place. If you can be handed to him[1] when he is at leisure, if you see everything kindly disposed, if his anger has lost its keenness, if there is anybody, while you are hesitating in fear to approach, who will hand you to him, introducing you with but a few brief words—then approach him. On a lucky day and with better fortune than your master may you arrive there and lighten my misfortunes. For either nobody can remove them or, in the fashion of Achilles, that man only who

[1] The Emperor.

tantum ne noceas, dum vis prodesse, videto—
    nam spes est animi nostra timore minor—
quaeque quiescebat, ne mota resaeviat ira
    et poenae tu sis altera causa, cave !
105 cum tamen in nostrum fueris penetrale receptus,
    contigerisque tuam, scrinia curva, domum,
aspicies illic positos ex ordine fratres,
    quos studium cunctos evigilavit idem.
cetera turba palam titulos ostendet apertos,
110   et sua detecta nomina fronte geret ;
tres procul obscura latitantes parte videbis,—
    sic quoque,[1] quod nemo nescit, amare docent.
hos tu vel fugias, vel, si satis oris habebis,
    Oedipodas facito Telegonosque voces.
115 deque tribus, moneo, si qua est tibi cura parentis,
    ne quemquam, quamvis ipse docebit, ames.
sunt quoque mutatae, ter quinque volumina, formae,
    nuper ab exequiis carmina rapta meis.
his mando dicas, inter mutata referri
120   fortunae vultum corpora posse meae.
namque ea dissimilis subito est effecta priori,
    flendaque nunc, aliquo tempore laeta fuit.
plura quidem mandare tibi, si quaeris, habebam,
    sed vereor tardae causa fuisse morae[2] ;
125 et si quae subeunt, tecum, liber, omnia ferres,
    sarcina laturo magna futurus eras.

---

[1] hi qui *vel* hi quoque : sic quoque *Bentley*
[2] viae

---

[1] See Index, *s.v.* Telephus.

wounded me.[1]   Only see that you do no harm in your
wish to help—for my hope is smaller than my fear—
and that slumbering wrath !—take care that it be not
roused to renewed fierceness and that you be not to
me a second cause of punishment.

[105] But when you find refuge in my sanctuary,
reaching your own home, the round book-cases, you
will behold there brothers arranged in order—
brothers whom the same craftmanship produced
with toil and waking.   The rest of the band will
display their titles openly, bearing their names on
their exposed edges, but three at some distance
will strive to hide themselves in a dark place, as
you will notice—even so, as everybody knows,
they teach how to love.   These you should either
avoid or, if you have the assurance, give them the
names of Oedipus or of Telegonus.[2]   And I warn you,
if you have any regard for your father, love not any
one of the three, though he himself teach you. There
are also thrice five rolls about changing forms,[3] poems
recently saved from the burial of my fortunes.   To
these I bid you say that the aspect of my own fate can
now be reckoned among those metamorphosed
figures.   For that aspect has on a sudden become
quite different from what it was before—a cause of
tears now, though once of joy.   More directions for
you, if you ask me, I have been keeping, but I fear to
be the cause of lingering delay ; and if you were
to carry with you, my book, all that occurs to
me, 'tis likely you would be a heavy burden to him
who shall bear you.   The road is long.   Make

[2] Both were parricides, and so, like Ovid's book, destroyed
the author of their being.

[3] The *Metamorphoses* in fifteen books.

11

OVID

longa via est, propera ! nobis habitabitur orbis
    ultimus, a terra terra remota mea.

II.

Di maris et caeli—quid enim nisi vota supersunt ?—
    solvere quassatae parcite membra ratis,
neve, precor, magni subscribite Caesaris irae !
    saepe premente deo fert deus alter opem.
5 Mulciber in Troiam, pro Troia stabat Apollo ;
    aequa Venus Teucris, Pallas iniqua fuit.
oderat Aenean propior Saturnia Turno ;
    ille tamen Veneris numine tutus erat.
saepe ferox cautum petiit Neptunus Ulixem ;
10   eripuit patruo saepe Minerva suo.
et nobis aliquod, quamvis distamus ab illis,
    quis vetat irato numen adesse deo ?
verba miser frustra non proficientia perdo.
    ipsa graves spargunt ora loquentis aquae,
15 terribilisque Notus iactat mea dicta, precesque
    ad quos mittuntur, non sinit ire deos.
ergo idem venti, ne causa laedar in una,
    velaque nescio quo votaque nostra ferunt.
me miserum, quanti montes volvuntur aquarum !
20   iam iam tacturos sidera summa putes.
quantae diducto subsidunt aequore valles !
    iam iam tacturas Tartara nigra putes.
quocumque aspicio, nihil est, nisi pontus et aër,
    fluctibus hic tumidus, nubibus ille minax.

12

haste! I shall continue to dwell at the edge of the world, a land far removed from my own.

II. Storm and Prayer

O gods of sea and sky—for what but prayer is left?—break not the frame of our shattered bark and second not, I implore, the wrath of mighty Caesar! Oft when a god presses hard another god brings succour. Mulciber was opposed to Troy, but in Troy's defence stood Apollo; Venus favoured the Teucrians, Pallas favoured them not. There was hate for Aeneas on the part of Saturnia who stood closely by Turnus; yet that hero was safe through Venus' power. Ofttimes unruly Neptune assailed the wily Ulysses; ofttimes Minerva saved him from her own uncle. And different though I am from them, who forbids a divine power from being of some avail to me against the angry god?

[13] But, wretch that I am, to no purpose am I wasting profitless words. My very lips as I speak are sprayed by the heavy waves, and dread Notus hurls away my words nor suffers my prayers to reach the gods to whom they are directed. So the same winds, that I be not punished in one way only, are driving—I know not whither—both my sails and my prayers. Wretched me! what vast mountains of water heave themselves aloft! Now, now, you think, they will touch the highest stars. What mighty abysses settle beneath us as the flood yawns apart! Now, now you think they will touch black Tartarus. Wherever I gaze there is naught but sea and air—sea swollen with billows, air athreat

13

25 inter utrumque fremunt inmani murmure venti.
    nescit, cui domino pareat, unda maris.
nam modo purpureo vires capit Eurus ab ortu.
    nunc Zephyrus sero vespere missus adest,
nunc sicca gelidus Boreas bacchatur ab Arcto,
30   nunc Notus adversa proelia fronte gerit.
rector in incerto est nec quid fugiatve petatve
    invenit : ambiguis ars stupet ipsa malis.
scilicet occidimus, nec spes est ulla salutis,
    dumque loquor, vultus obruit unda meos.
35 opprimet hanc animam fluctus, frustraque precanti
    ore necaturas accipiemus aquas.
at pia nil aliud quam me dolet exule coniunx :
    hoc unum nostri scitque gemitque mali.
nescit in inmenso iactari corpora ponto,
40   nescit agi ventis, nescit adesse necem.
o bene, quod non sum mecum conscendere passus,
    ne mihi mors misero bis patienda foret !
at nunc, ut peream, quoniam caret illa periclo,
    dimidia certe parte superstes ero.
45 ei mihi, quam celeri micuerunt nubila flamma !
    quantus ab aetherio personat axe fragor !
nec levius tabulae laterum feriuntur ab undis,
    quam grave ballistae moenia pulsat onus.
qui venit hic fluctus, fluctus supereminet omnes :
50   posterior nono est undecimoque prior.
nec letum timeo ; genus est miserabile leti.
    demite naufragium, mors mihi munus erit.
est aliquid, fatove suo ferrove [1] cadentem
    in solida [2] moriens ponere corpus humo,

---

[1] fatove . . . ferrove *Heinsius* : fatoque . . . ferroque
        [2] solita : solida *s*

---

[1] The ancient "siege gun," which hurled stones.

14

with clouds ; and between are the hum and roar of the cruel winds. The waves of ocean know not what master to obey. For now Eurus storms mightily from the red east, now Zephyrus comes rushing from the realm of late evening, now Boreas raves from the dry pole-star, now Notus battles with opposing brow. The helmsman is confused nor can he find what to avoid or what to seek ; his very skill is numbed by the baffling perils. We are surely lost, there is no hope of safety, and as I speak, the waters overwhelm my face. The billows will crush this life of mine, and with lips that pray in vain I shall drink in the destroying water.

[37] But my loyal wife grieves for naught save my exile—that is the only ill of mine she knows and bemoans. She knows not that I am buffeted about on the vast sea, knows not that I am harried by the winds, knows not that death is near me. Ah, well it was that I suffered her not to board ship with me, else I, poor wretch, should now be forced to suffer a double death ! But as it is, even though I perish, in her freedom from peril at least I shall half survive. Alas ! what a swift glitter of flame from the clouds ! What a mighty crash roars from the zenith ! And no lighter blow falls upon her planks from the billows than the heavy pounding of the ballista[1] upon a wall. Here comes a wave that o'ertops them all—the wave after the ninth and before the eleventh. I fear not death ; 'tis the form of death that I lament. Save me from shipwreck and death will be a boon. 'Tis something worth if falling by fate[2] or by the steel one rests in death upon the solid ground, utters some parting words to friends,

[2] *i.e.* natural death.

15

55 et mandare suis aliqua et sperare sepulcrum
   et non aequoreis piscibus esse cibum.
fingite me dignum tali nece, non ego solus
   hic vehor.   inmeritos cur mea poena trahit ?
pro superi viridesque dei, quibus aequora curae,
60   utraque iam vestras sistite turba minas,
quamque dedit vitam mitissima Caesaris ira,
   hanc sinite infelix in loca iussa feram.
si quam commerui,[1] poenam me pendere[2] vultis,
   culpa mea est ipso iudice morte minor.
65 mittere me Stygias si iam voluisset in undas
   Caesar, in hoc vestra non eguisset ope.
est illi nostri non invidiosa cruoris
   copia ; quodque dedit, cum volet, ipse feret.
vos modo, quos certe nullo, puto, crimine laesi,
70   contenti nostris iam, precor, este malis !
nec tamen, ut cuncti miserum servare velitis,
   quod periit, salvum iam caput esse potest.
ut mare considat ventisque ferentibus utar,
   ut mihi parcatis, non minus exul ero.
75 non ego divitias avidus sine fine parandi
   latum mutandis mercibus aequor aro,
nec peto, quas quondam petii studiosus, Athenas,
   oppida non Asiae, non loca visa prius,
non ut Alexandri claram delatus ad urbem
80   delicias videam, Nile iocose, tuas.
quod faciles[3] opto ventos,—quis credere possit[4] ?—
   Sarmatis est tellus, quam mea vela petunt.
obligor, ut tangam laevi fera litora Ponti ;
   quodque sit a patria tam[5] fuga tarda, queror.

[1] quoque quam merui
[2] poena me perdere
[3] facile est : faciles *Heinsius*   [4] posset   [5] iam *corr. s*

[1] Possibly *laevi* here means " propitious," "favouring," *cf.*

16

and looks forward to a tomb—not to be the food of
fishes in the sea. Suppose me deserving of such a
death, yet I am not here the only passenger. Why
does my punishment involve the innocent? O ye
gods above and ye of the green flood, who rule the
waters,—stay ye now, both hosts of you, your
threats. The life that Caesar's merciful wrath has
granted, let me carry, unhappy man that I am, to the
appointed place. If ye wish me to pay the penalty
which I have deserved, my fault even in my judge's
eyes merits not death. If ere now Caesar had wished
to send me to the waters of the Styx, he had not
needed your aid in this. He has a power over my life
which ye may not begrudge; and what he has granted
he will take away when he shall wish. But ye, whom
surely no crime of mine has wronged, be content by
now with my woes. And yet, though ye be all willing
to save a wretch, that life which is lost cannot now be
safe. Even should the sea grow calm and favouring
breezes bear me on—even should ye spare me—I
shall be not less an exile. Not in greed of limitless
wealth do I plough the sea to trade my wares nor am I
on my way to Athens as once I was while a student,
nor to the cities of Asia, nor the places I have seen
before, nor am I sailing to Alexander's famous city to
see thy pleasures, merry Nile. The reason of my
prayers for favouring winds (who could believe it?) is
the Sarmatian land, the object of my voyage. I am
making vows to reach the wild shores of ill-omened [1]
Pontus, and I complain that my journey into exile
from my native land is so slow! That

ὁ Εὐώνυμος Πόντος, "Pontus of the fair name." Or Ovid
means "Pontus-on-the-left" (see Introd. p. xxvii).

85 nescio quo videam positos ut in orbe Tomitas,
   exilem facio per mea vota viam.
   seu me diligitis, tantos conpescite fluctus,
   pronaque sint nostrae numina vestra rati ;
   seu magis odistis, iussae me advertite terrae :
90   supplicii pars est in regione mei.[1]
   ferte—quid hic facio ?—rapidi mea carbasa[2] venti !
   Ausonios fines cur mea vela volunt ?
   noluit hoc Caesar. quid, quem fugat ille, tenetis ?
   aspiciat vultus Pontica terra meos.
95 et iubet et merui ; nec, quae damnaverit ille,
   crimina defendi fasque piumque puto.
   si tamen acta deos numquam mortalia fallunt,
   a culpa facinus scitis abesse mea.
   immo ita si scitis, si me meus abstulit error,
100   stultaque mens nobis, non scelerata fuit,
   quamlibet in minimis, domui si favimus illi,
   si satis Augusti publica iussa mihi,
   hoc duce si dixi felicia saecula, proque
   Caesare tura pius Caesaribusque dedi,—
105 si fuit hic animus nobis, ita parcite divi !
   si minus, alta cadens obruat unda caput !
   fallor, an incipiunt gravidae vanescere nubes,
   victaque mutati frangitur ira maris ?
   non casu, vos sed sub condicione vocati,
110   fallere quos non est, hanc mihi fertis opem.

III.

Cum subit illius tristissima noctis imago,
   quod[3] mihi supremum tempus in urbe fuit,

---

[1] mori: mei *s*   [2] corpora   [3] quo *vel* quae

---

[1] The grandsons and adopted sons of Augustus.

18

I may see the Tomitans, situate in some corner of the world, I am trying to shorten the road by prayer!

[87] If it be that you love me, restrain these mighty billows, and let your powers favour my bark; or if you detest me, turn me towards the ordained land; a part of my punishment consists in the place of it. Drive on my ship, swift winds! What have I to do here? Why do my sails crave the Ausonian land? This was not Caesar's will. Why do you detain one whom he drives forth? Let the land of Pontus behold my face. He commands it and I have deserved it; nor do I account it lawful and righteous to defend the sins that he has condemned. Yet if human acts never deceive the gods, ye know that no guilty deed is connected with my fault. Nay, if such your knowledge, if a mistake of mine has carried me away, if stupid was my mind, not criminal, if in matters however small I have supported that house with favour, if the public commands of Augustus were in my eyes sufficient; if under his lead I have sung of a happy age, and for Caesar and his house[1] have loyally offered incense;—if such has been my spirit, then spare me, gods! If not, may a towering wave fall and whelm my head!

[107] Am I wrong or do the heavy clouds begin to melt away and is the frenzy of the changing sea being conquered and subdued? It is no chance, but ye, summoned to hear my pledge, ye whom we cannot deceive, are bringing me this succour!

III. The Night of Exile

When steals upon me the gloomy memory of that night which marked my latest hours in the

19

cum repeto noctem, qua tot mihi cara reliqui,
    labitur ex oculis nunc quoque gutta meis.
5 iam prope lux aderat, qua me discedere Caesar
    finibus extremae iusserat Ausoniae.
nec spatium nec mens fuerat satis apta parandi :
    torpuerant dempta [1] pectora nostra mora.
non mihi servorum, comitis non cura legendi,
10   non aptae profugo vestis opisve fuit.
non aliter stupui, quam qui Iovis ignibus ictus
    vivit et est vitae nescius ipse suae.
ut tamen hanc animi nubem dolor ipse removit,
    et tandem sensus convaluere mei,
15 adloquor extremum maestos abiturus amicos,
    qui modo de multis unus et alter erant.
uxor amans flentem flens acrius ipsa tenebat,
    imbre per indignas usque cadente genas.
nata procul Libycis aberat diversa sub oris,
20   nec poterat fati certior esse mei.
quocumque aspiceres, luctus gemitusque sonabant,
    formaque non taciti funeris intus erat.
femina virque meo, pueri quoque funere maerent,
    inque domo lacrimas angulus omnis habet.
25 si licet exemplis in parvo [2] grandibus uti,
    haec facies Troiae, cum caperetur, erat.
iamque quiescebant voces hominumque canumque,
    Lunaque nocturnos alta regebat equos.
hanc ego suspiciens et ad hanc [3] Capitolia cernens,
30   quae nostro frustra iuncta fuere Lari,
"numina vicinis habitantia sedibus," inquam,
    "iamque oculis numquam templa videnda meis,

[1] longa *corr. Sh. Bailey*   [2] parvis   [3] ab hac

city—when I recall that night on which I left so many things dear to me, even now from my eyes the teardrops fall.

[5] Already the morning was close at hand on which Caesar had bidden me to depart from Ausonia's furthest bounds. No time had there been or spirit to prepare what might suit best; my mind had become numb with delay denied me. I took no thought to select my slaves or a companion or the clothing and outfit suited to an exile. I was as dazed as one who, smitten by the fire of Jove, still lives and knows not that he lives. But when my very pain drove away the cloud upon my mind and at length my senses revived, I addressed for the last time as I was about to depart my sorrowing friends of whom, just now so many, but one or two remained. My loving wife was in my arms as I wept, herself weeping more bitterly, tears raining constantly over her innocent cheeks. My daughter was far separated from us on the shores of Libya, and we could not inform her of my fate. Wherever you had looked was the sound of mourning and lamentation, and within the house was the semblance of a funeral with its loud outcries. Men and women, children too, grieved at this funeral of mine; in my home every corner had its tears. If one may use in a lowly case a lofty example, such was the appearance of Troy in the hour of her capture.

[27] Now the voices of men and dogs were hushed and the moon aloft was guiding her steeds through the night. Gazing up at her, and by her light at the Capitol, which, all in vain, adjoined my home, I prayed: "Ye deities that dwell near by and ye temples never henceforth to be seen by my eyes,

21

dique relinquendi, quos urbs habet alta Quirini,
    este salutati tempus in omne mihi.
35 et quamquam sero clipeum post vulnera sumo,
    attamen hanc odiis exonerate fugam,
caelestique viro, quis me deceperit error,
    dicite, pro culpa ne scelus esse putet,
ut, quod vos scitis, poenae quoque sentiat auctor.
40   placato possum non miser esse deo.''
hac prece adoravi superos ego, pluribus uxor,
    singultu medios impediente sonos.
illa etiam ante Lares [1] passis adstrata capillis
    contigit extinctos [2] ore tremente focos,
45 multaque in aversos effudit verba Penates
    pro deplorato non valitura viro.
iamque morae spatium nox praecipitata negabat,
    versaque ab axe suo Parrhasis Arctos erat.
quid facerem ? blando patriae retinebar amore,
50   ultima sed iussae nox erat illa fugae.
a ! quotiens aliquo dixi properante '' quid urges ?
    vel quo festinas ire, vel unde, vide.''
a ! quotiens certam me sum mentitus habere
    horam, propositae quae foret apta viae.
55 ter limen tetigi, ter sum revocatus, et ipse
    indulgens animo pes mihi tardus erat.
saepe '' vale '' dicto rursus sum multa locutus,
    et quasi discedens oscula summa dedi.
saepe eadem mandata dedi meque ipse fefelli,
60   respiciens oculis pignora cara meis.

---

    [1] Lares] aras   [2] extinctos] aeternos

---

  [1] *i.e.* had revolved about the pole-star, which is practically
the axis of the constellation, *cf.* 2, 190 ; iii. 2. 2.

ye gods of this lofty city of Quirinus, whom I must leave, receive from me this my salutation for all time! And although too late I take up the shield when wounded, yet disburden of hatreds this banishment of mine; tell to that man divine what error beguiled me, that he may not think a fault to be a crime and that what you know he too, the author of my punishment, may feel. If the god be appeased I cannot be wretched."

[41] With such prayer as this I appealed to the gods, my wife with many more, the sobs interrupting her cries half uttered. She even cast herself with flowing hair before the Lares, touching the cold hearth with quivering lips and pouring forth to the estranged Penates many words not destined to avail the spouse she mourned.

[47] Now night hurrying to her close refused me time for lingering, and the Parrhasian bear had wheeled about her axis.[1] What was I to do? The enthralling love of country held me, yet that was the last night before the exile that had been decreed. Alas! how many times did I say, as somebody hastened by, "Why do you hurry me? Consider whither you are hastening or whence!" Alas! how many times did I falsely say that I had a definite hour suited to my intended journey. Thrice I touched the threshold, thrice did something call me back, and my very feet moved slowly to gratify my inclination. Oft when I had said farewell once again I uttered many words, and as if I were in the act of setting forth I gave the final kisses. Oft I gave the same parting directions, thus beguiling myself, with backward look at the objects of my

23

denique " quid propero ? Scythia est, quo mittimur,"
   inquam,
   " Roma relinquenda est.   utraque iusta mora.
uxor in aeternum vivo mihi viva negatur,
   et domus et fidae dulcia membra domus,
65 quosque ego dilexi fraterno more sodales,
   o mihi Thesea pectora iuncta fide !
dum licet, amplectar : numquam fortasse licebit
   amplius.   in lucro est quae datur hora mihi."
nec mora, sermonis verba imperfecta relinquo,
70   complectens animo proxima quaeque meo.
dum loquor et flemus, caelo nitidissimus alto,
   stella gravis nobis, Lucifer ortus erat.
dividor haud aliter, quam si mea membra relinquam,
   et pars abrumpi corpore visa suo est.
75 sic doluit Mettus [1] tum cum in contraria versos
   ultores habuit proditionis equos.
tum vero exoritur clamor gemitusque meorum,
   et feriunt maestae pectora nuda manus.
tum vero coniunx umeris abeuntis inhaerens
80   miscuit haec lacrimis tristia verba meis :
" non potes avelli.   simul ah ! simul ibimus," inquit,
   " te sequar et coniunx exulis exul ero.
et mihi dicta[2] via est, et me capit ultima tellus :
   accedam profugae sarcina parva rati.
85 te iubet e patria discedere Caesaris ira,
   me pietas.   pietas haec mihi Caesar erit."
talia temptabat, sicut temptaverat ante,
   vixque dedit victas utilitate manus.

---

[1] Priamus   [2] facta *corr. Hall*

---

[1] *She remained in Rome to work for the poet's recall.*

love. At last I said, "Why hasten? 'Tis Scythia whither I am going, 'tis Rome that I must leave. Both are good reasons for delay. My wife lives and I live, but she is being denied me forever and my home and the sweet inmates of that faithful home, and the comrades I have loved with a brother's love, O hearts knit to me with Theseus' faith! Whilst I may I will embrace you. Never more perhaps shall I have the chance. The hour granted me is so much gain."

[69] No longer delaying I left my words unfinished and embraced each object dearest to my heart. During my talk and our weeping, bright in the lofty sky Lucifer had arisen, to me a baneful star. I was torn asunder as if I were leaving my limbs behind—a very half seemed broken from the body to which it belonged. Such was the anguish of Mettus when the steeds were driven apart, punishing his treachery. Then in truth arose the cries and laments of my people; sorrowing hands beat upon naked breasts. Then in truth my wife, as she hung upon my breast at parting, mingled these sad words with my tears, "I cannot suffer you to be torn away. Together, together we will go; I will follow you and be an exile's exiled wife. For me too the journey has been commanded, for me too there is room in the faraway land. My entrance will add but a small freight to your exile ship. You are commanded to flee your country by Caesar's wrath, I by my loyal love. This love shall be for me a Caesar."

[87] Such was her attempt, as it had been before, and with difficulty did she surrender her resolve for my profit.[1] I set forth—if it was not rather

25

egredior, sive illud erat sine funere ferri,
90   squalidus inmissis hirta per ora comis.
illa dolore amens tenebris narratur obortis
    semianimis media procubuisse domo,
utque resurrexit foedatis pulvere turpi
    crinibus et gelida membra levavit humo,
95 se modo, desertos modo complorasse Penates,
    nomen et erepti saepe vocasse viri,
nec gemuisse minus, quam si nataeque meumque
    vidisset structos corpus habere rogos,
et voluisse mali [1] moriendo ponere sensum,[2]
100   respectuque tamen non potuisse mei.
vivat, et absentem, quoniam sic fata tulerunt,
    vivat ut,[3] auxilio sublevet usque suo.

IV.

Tinguitur oceano custos Erymanthidos ursae,
    aequoreasque suo sidere turbat aquas.
nos tamen Ionium non nostra findimus aequor
    sponte, sed audaces cogimur esse metu.
5 me miserum!   quantis increscunt aequora ventis,
    erutaque ex imis fervet harena fretis!
monte nec inferior prorae puppique recurvae
    insilit et pictos verberat unda deos.
pinea texta sonant pulsu,[4] stridore rudentes,
10   ingemit et nostris ipsa carina malis.
navita confessus gelidum pallore timorem,
    iam sequitur victus, non regit arte ratem.
utque parum validus non proficientia rector
    cervici rigidae frena remittit equi[5],

[1] mori: *Madrig*   [2] -us: *Luck*   [3] et: *Salmasius*   [4] -si: *Rothmaler*
[5] cervicis ... equo *corr. Hall*

[1] Boötes.   [2] The figures painted or carved on the stern.

being carried forth to burial without a funeral—unkempt, my hair falling over my unshaven cheeks. She, frenzied by grief, was overcome, they say, by a cloud of darkness, and fell half dead in the midst of our home. And when she rose, her tresses fouled with unsightly dust, raising her body from the cold ground, she lamented now her deserted self, now the deserted Penates, and often called the name of her ravished husband, groaning as if she had seen the bodies of her daughter and myself resting on the high-built pyre ; she wished by dying to lay aside all feeling of pain, yet from regard for me she could not die. May she live and ever with her aid bring succour to her husband far away (since thus the fates have willed) that he too may live !

IV. On the Deep

The guardian [1] of the Erymanthian bear dips in ocean and with his setting stars makes stormy the waters of the sea. Yet I am cleaving the Ionian waves not of my own will but forced to boldness through fear. Wretched me ! what mighty winds swell the waters, casting up the seething sand from the lowest depths ! Mountain-high upon prow and out-curving stern leaps the billow lashing the painted gods. [2] The pine planks resound from the battering, the ropes from the shrieking wind, and the very keel groans over my woes. The sailor confessing by his pale face a chilling fear now in defeat humours the craft, no longer skilfully guiding her. As a rider who is not strong enough lets the ineffective reins fall loose upon the stubborn neck of his horse,

15 sic non quo voluit, sed quo rapit impetus undae,
  aurigam video vela dedisse rati.
quod nisi mutatas emiserit Aeolus auras,
  in loca iam nobis non adeunda ferar.
nam procul Illyriis laeva de parte relictis
20 interdicta mihi cernitur Italia.
desinat in vetitas quaeso contendere terras,
  et mecum magno pareat aura deo.
dum loquor, et timeo pariter cupioque [1] repelli.
  increpuit quantis viribus unda latus!
25 parcite caerulei, vos parcite numina ponti,
  infestumque mihi sit satis esse Iovem.
vos animam saevae fessam subducite morti,
  si modo, qui periit, non periisse potest.

V.

O mihi post nullos umquam memorande sodales,
  et cui praecipue sors mea visa sua est,
attonitum qui me, memini, carissime, primus
  ausus es adloquio sustinuisse tuo,
5 qui mihi consilium vivendi mite dedisti,
  cum foret in misero pectore mortis amor,
scis bene, quem [2] dicam, positis pro nomine signis,
  officium nec te fallit, amice, tuum.
haec mihi semper erunt imis infixa medullis,
10 perpetuusque animae debitor huius ero,
spiritus in vacuas prius hic evanidus [3] auras
  ibit, et in tepido deseret ossa rogo,

---

[1] timeo cupio nimiumque *vel* cupio pariter timeoque
[2] cui *corr. Diggle*   [3] tenuandus in *corr. M², Luck*

so not where he wishes but where the billow's power carries him our charioteer, I see, has given the ship her head. And unless Aeolus changes the winds he sends forth, I shall be driven to a region that I must not now approach, for Illyria's shores are far behind on the left and forbidden Italy is beginning to appear. I pray the wind may cease its striving towards a forbidden land and may unite with me in obedience to the mighty god.[1] Whilst I speak, at once afraid and eager to be driven back, with what mighty power the waves have set her beam to creaking! Mercy, ye gods of the dark sea, mercy! Let it suffice that Jupiter[1] is angered against me. Save ye my weary life from cruel death, if only 'tis possible for one already dead[2] not to die!

V. To a Faithful Friend

You who shall never be named after any of my comrades, you who above all made my lot your own, who were the first, dearest one, I remember, to dare to support me with words of comfort after the bolt had struck, who gave me the gentle counsel to live when my wretched breast was filled with the love of death, —you will recognize whom I mean by means of these symbols substituted for your name, nor are you unaware, my friend, of your own service. These things shall ever remain fixed in my inmost heart and I will be an everlasting debtor for this life of mine, my spirit shall disappear into the empty air leaving my bones on the warm

[1] Augustus.
[2] Ovid often likens his exile to death.

quam subeant animo meritorum oblivia nostro,
   et longa pietas excidat ista die.
15 di tibi sint faciles, et opis nullius egentem
   fortunam praestent dissimiliemque meae.
si tamen haec navis vento ferretur amico,
   ignoraretur forsitan ista fides.
Thesea Pirithous non tam sensisset amicum,
20   si non infernas vivus adisset aquas.
ut foret exemplum veri Phoceus amoris,
   fecerunt furiae, tristis Oresta, tuae.
si non Euryalus Rutulo cecidisset in hoste, [1]
   Hyrtacidae Nisi gloria nulla foret.
25 scilicet ut fulvum spectatur in ignibus aurum,
   tempore sic duro est inspicienda fides.
dum iuvat et vultu ridet Fortuna sereno,
   indelibatas cuncta sequuntur opes :
at simul intonuit, fugiunt, nec noscitur ulli,
30   agminibus comitum qui modo cinctus erat.
atque haec, exemplis quondam collecta priorum,
   nunc mihi sunt propriis cognita vera malis.
vix duo tresve mihi de tot superestis amici ;
   cetera Fortunae, non mea turba fuit.
35 quo magis, o pauci, rebus succurrite laesis,
   et date naufragio litora tuta meo,
neve metu falso nimium trepidate, timentes,
   hac offendatur ne pietate deus !
saepe fidem adversis etiam laudavit in armis,
40   inque suis amat hanc Caesar, in hoste probat.
causa mea est melior, qui non contraria fovi
   arma, sed hanc merui simplicitate fugam.

---

[1] Rutulos . . . hostes corr. *Madvig*

---

[1] Pylades.
[2] On the causes of Ovid's exile see Introd. pp. xviii ff.

pyre ere forgetfulness of your deserving steals into my heart and that loyalty of yours falls away from it through length of time. May the gods be gracious to you and grant you a lot that lacks naught, a lot unlike mine.

[17] And yet if this bark of mine were being borne on by a friendly breeze, perchance that loyalty of yours would be unknown. Theseus' friendship would not have been so keenly felt by Pirithous if he had not gone while still alive to the waters below. That the Phocean[1] was a model of sincere love was due to thy madness, gloomy Orestes. If Euryalus had not fallen against the Rutulian foe, Hyrtacian Nisus would have had no renown. 'Tis clear that as tawny gold is tested in the flames so loyalty must be proved in times of stress. While Fortune aids us and a smile is upon her calm face, all things follow our unimpaired resources. But at the first rumble of the thunder they flee, and nobody recognizes him who but now was encircled with troops of comrades. This, which once I inferred from the examples of former men, now I know to be true from my own woes. Scarce two or three of you, my friends, once so many, remain to me; the rest were Fortune's following, not mine. And so, few though ye are, run all the more to aid my injured state and provide a secure shore for my shipwreck. Tremble not over much with false fear lest this loyalty give offence to our god. Ofttimes faith even among his enemies in arms has been praised by Caesar; when it exists among his own, he loves it; in an enemy he approves it. My case is still more favourable since I did not nurse strife against him, but earned this exile by my simplicity.[2] Do you,

    invigiles igitur nostris pro casibus, oro,
       deminui siqua [1] numinis ira potest.
45 scire meos casus siquis desiderat omnes,
       plus, quam quod fieri res sinit, ille petit.
    tot mala sum passus, quot in aethere sidera lucent
       parvaque quot siccus corpora pulvis habet;
    multaque credibili tulimus maiora ratamque,
50   quamvis acciderint, non habitura fidem.
    pars etiam quaedam mecum moriatur oportet,
       meque velim possit dissimulante tegi.
    si vox infragilis, pectus mihi firmius aere, [2]
       pluraque cum linguis pluribus ora forent,
55 non tamen idcirco complecterer omnia verbis,
       materia vires exsuperante meas.
    pro duce Neritio docti mala nostra poetae
       scribite: Neritio nam mala plura tuli.
    ille brevi spatio multis erravit in annis
60   inter Dulichias Iliacasque domos:
    nos freta sideribus totis distantia mensos
       detulit in Geticos Caesaris ira [3] sinus.
    ille habuit lectamque [4] manum sociosque fideles:
       me profugum comites deseruere mei.
65 ille suam laetus patriam victorque petebat:
       a patria fugi victus et exul ego.
    nec mihi Dulichium domus est Ithaceve Sameve,
       poena quibus non est grandis abesse locis,
    sed quae de septem totum circumspicit orbem
70   montibus, imperii Roma deumque locus.
    illi corpus erat durum patiensque laborum:
       invalidae vires ingenuaeque mihi.
    ille erat assidue saevis agitatus in armis:
       adsuetus studiis mollibus ipse fui.

         [1] q nunc *L*   [2] heret *vel* esset *corr.* ς
    [3] Sarmatis ora *vel* Sarmaticosque   [4] fidamque *corr. Hall*

then, watch on behalf of my fortunes, I beg of you, if in any way the wrath of the deity can be lessened.

[45] If anyone desires to know all my fortunes he seeks more than the circumstances permit. I have endured woes as many as the stars that shine in heaven, or the grains that the dry dust holds; many have I borne too great to be believed and not destined to find credence, although they have really befallen me. A part, too, might well perish with me, and I wish that, since I would veil them, they might be hidden. If I had a tireless voice, lungs stronger than brass, and many mouths with many tongues, not even so could I embrace them all in words, for the theme surpasses my strength. Ye learned poets, write of my evils instead of the Neritian hero's [1]! for I have borne more than the Neritian. He wandered over but a narrow space in many years—between the homes of Dulichium and Ilium; I, after traversing seas whole constellations apart, have been banished by Caesar's anger to the bays of the Getae. He had a picked band of true companions; I in my flight have been abandoned by my comrades. He was seeking his native land in joy and victory; I have fled mine, vanquished and an exile. My home is not Dulichium or Ithaca or Same, places from which absence is no great punishment, but Rome, that gazes about her from her seven hills upon the whole world,—Rome, the place of empire and the gods. He had a frame sturdy and enduring of toil; I have but the frail strength of one gently nurtured. He had been constantly engaged in fierce warfare; I have been used to

[1] Odysseus, so-called from Mount Neritus in Ithaca.

75 me deus oppressit, nullo mala nostra levante :
    bellatrix illi diva ferebat opem.
cumque minor Iove sit tumidis qui regnat in undis,
    illum Neptuni, me Iovis ira premit.
adde, quod illius pars maxima ficta laborum,
80   ponitur in nostris fabula nulla malis.
denique quaesitos tetigit tandem [1] ille Penates,
    quaeque diu petiit, contigit arva tamen :
at mihi perpetuo patria tellure carendum est,
    ni fuerit laesi mollior ira dei.

VI.

Nec tantum Clario est Lyde dilecta poëtae,
    nec tantum Coo Bittis [2] amata suo est,
pectoribus quantum tu nostris, uxor, inhaeres,
    digna minus misero, non meliore viro.
5 tea mea supposita veluti trabe fulta ruina est :
    siquid adhuc ego sum, muneris omne tui est.
tu facis, ut spolium non sim, nec nuder ab illis,
    naufragii tabulas qui petiere mei.
utque rapax stimulante fame cupidusque cruoris
10   incustoditum captat ovile lupus,
aut ut edax vultur corpus circumspicit ecquod
    sub nulla positum cernere possit humo,
sic mea nescio quis, rebus male fidus acerbis
    in bona venturus, si paterere, fuit.
15 hunc tua per fortis virtus summovit amicos,
    nulla quibus reddi gratia digna potest.
ergo quam misero, tam vero teste probaris,
    hic aliquod pondus si modo testis habet.

---

[1] tamen *corr. Wassenbergh*   [2] *battis corr. Merkel*

[1] Pallas Athene (Minerva).

softer pursuits.   I was crushed by a god and nobody
lightened my sorrows; to him the goddess[1] of war
brought aid.   And though the king of the swelling
waves is inferior to Jove, he was oppressed by
Neptune's wrath, I by that of Jove.   Moreover, the
largest part of his labours is fiction; in my woes no
myth resides.   And finally—he did reach the home of
his quest, attaining the fields he long had sought.
But I must be forever deprived of my native land,
unless the wrath of the injured god be softened.

VI. To His Wife

Not so great was the love of the Clarian bard[2] for
Lyde or that of her own Coan[3] for Bittis as the love
that clings in my heart for thee, my wife, for thee who
art worthy of a less wretched, not a better,
husband.   Upon thee as upon a supporting pillar my
ruins rest; if even now anything of me exists, it is all
thy gift.   'Tis thy doing that I am not plundered nor
stripped bare by those who have attacked the timbers
of my wreckage.   As the wolf ravening under the
goad of hunger and eager for blood strives to catch
the sheepfold unguarded, or as the hungry vulture
peers about for the possible sight of some unburied
corpse, so there was one, treacherous
in my bitter fortune, who, hadst thou suffered
it, would have come into my wealth.   Him thy
courage has repelled with the aid of spirited friends
whom I can never thank as they deserve.   Thus
thou art approved by a witness as sincere as he is
wretched,—if only such a witness carries any

[2] Antimachus.   [3] Philetas.

nec probitate tua prior est aut Hectoris uxor,
20   aut comes extincto Laodamia viro.
tu si Maeonium vatem sortita fuisses,
      Penelopes esset fama secunda tuae:
33 prima locum sanctas heroidas inter haberes,
34   prima bonis animi conspicerere tui,
23 sive tibi hoc debes, nullo pia facta magistro,
      cumque nova mores sunt tibi luce dati,
25 femina seu princeps omnes tibi culta per annos
      te docet exemplum coniugis esse bonae,
adsimilemque sui longa adsuetudine fecit,
      grandia si parvis adsimilare licet.
ei mihi, non magnas quod habent mea carmina vires,
30   nostraque sunt meritis ora minora tuis!
siquid et in nobis vivi fuit ante vigoris,
32   extinctum longis occidit omne malis!
35 quantumcumque tamen praeconia nostra valebunt,
      carminibus vives tempus in omne meis.

VII.

Siquis habes nostri similes in imagine vultus,
      deme meis hederas, Bacchica serta, comis.
ista decent laetos felicia signa poëtas:
      temporibus non est apta corona meis.
5 hoc tibi dissimula, senti tamen, optime, dici,
      in digito qui me fersque refersque tuo,

      [1] 33f *post* 22 *ed. Ven. 1486*

---

      [1] Andromache.
      [2] Livia, wife of Augustus, is here called *princeps femina*, as
her husband was called *princeps (civitatis)*.
      [3] Possibly Brutus.   See Introd. p. xv.
      [4] The first four lines are a general injunction to all who

weight. In uprightness neither Hector's wife [1] excels thee, nor Laodamia, companion of her husband in death. If fate had allotted thee the Maeonian bard, Penelope's fame would be second to thine : then thou wouldst hold first place amid the revered heroines, first wouldst thou be looked upon because of thy qualities of heart: whether thou owest this to thyself, schooled to loyalty by no teacher, and such character was given thee with life's earliest dawn, or whether that first of women,[2] reverenced by thee through all the years, teaches thee to be the model of a good wife and by long training has made thee like herself—if 'tis lawful to liken great things to small. Alas that great power lies not in my song and my lips cannot match thy merits! If ever in former times I had aught of quickening vigour, all has been extinguished by my long sorrows! Yet so far as my praise has power, thou shalt live for all time in my song.

VII. THE METAMORPHOSES

Whoever you [3] may be who possess a portrait of my features, remove from my locks the ivy, the chaplet of Bacchus. Such fortunate symbols are suited to happy poets; a wreath becomes not my temples.[4] Hide the fact—yet feel it, too,—that this is said to you, my best of friends, who carry me about on your finger, and, clasping my image

possessed likenesses of the poet such as, for example, crowned busts (*imagines*) which were a common ornament of libraries. Vv. 5 ff. are addressed directly to the recipient of this letter.

effigiemque meam fulvo complexus in auro
    cara relegati, qua potes, ora vides.
quae quotiens spectas, subeat tibi dicere forsan
10   "quam procul a nobis Naso sodalis abest!"
grata tua est pietas. sed carmina maior imago
    sunt mea, quae mando qualiacumque legas,
carmina mutatas hominum dicentia formas,
    infelix domini quod fuga rupit opus.
15 haec ego discedens, sicut bene multa meorum,
    ipse mea posui maestus in igne manu.
utque cremasse suum fertur sub stipite natum
    Thestias et melior matre fuisse soror,
sic ego non meritos mecum peritura libellos
20   imposui rapidis viscera nostra rogis:
vel quod eram Musas, ut crimina nostra, perosus,
    vel quod adhuc crescens et rude carmen erat.
quae quoniam non sunt penitus sublata, sed extant—
    pluribus exemplis scripta fuisse reor—
25 nunc precor ut vivant et non ignava legentum [1]
    otia delectent admoneantque mei.
nec tamen illa legi poterunt patienter ab ullo,
    nesciet his summam siquis abesse manum.
ablatum mediis opus est incudibus illud,
30   defuit et scriptis ultima lima meis.
et veniam pro laude peto, laudatus abunde,
    non fastiditus si tibi, lector, ero.
hos quoque sex versus, in primi [2] fronte libelli
    si praeponendos esse putabis, habe:
35 "orba parente suo quicumque volumina tangis,
    his saltem vestra detur in urbe locus.

---

[1] legentem *corr. Scaliger*   [2] prima *corr. Heinsius*

---

[1] The *Metamorphoses.*   [2] Althaea. See Index.
[3] *i.e.* Rome, where *you* can still live.

on the tawny gold, see the dear face—in such fashion
as you can—of an exile. Whenever you gaze upon
it, you may perchance feel prompted to say, "How
far away is our comrade Naso!" There is comfort in
your love. But my verses are a more striking
portrait, and these I bid you read however poor they
are—the verses that tell of the changed forms of
men,[1] the work broken off by the unfortunate exile of
their master.

[15] These verses upon my departure, like so much
that was mine, in sorrow I placed with my own hand
in the fire. Just as Thestius' daughter[2] burned her
own son, they say, in burning the branch, and proved
a better sister than mother, so I placed the innocent
books consigned with me to death, my very
vitals, upon the devouring pyre, because I had come
to hate the Muses as my accusers or because the
poem itself was as yet half grown and rough. These
verses were not utterly destroyed; they still exist—
several copies were made, I think—and now I pray
that they may live, and that they may delight the
industrious leisure of readers and remind them of
me. And yet they cannot be read in patience by
anybody who does not know that they lack the final
hand. That work was taken from me while it
was on the anvil and my writing lacked the last
touch of the file. Indulgence, then, instead of praise
I ask; I shall have abundance of praise if you do
not disdain me, reader. Receive these six lines
also, if you think them worthy to be placed at the
head of the first book:—

[35] "All you who touch these rolls bereft of their
father, to them at least let a place be granted in your[3]
city! And your indulgence will be all the

quoque magis faveas, haec non sunt edita ab ipso,
    sed quasi de domini funere rapta sui.
quicquid in his igitur vitii rude carmen habebit,
40   emendaturus, si licuisset, erat."[1]

VIII.

In caput alta suum labentur ab aequore retro
    flumina, conversis Solque recurret equis :
terra feret stellas, caelum findetur aratro,
    unda dabit flammas, et dabit ignis aquas,
5 omnia naturae praepostera legibus ibunt,
    parsque suum mundi nulla tenebit iter,
omnia iam fient, fieri quae posse negabam,
    et nihil est, de quo non sit habenda fides.
haec ego vaticinor, quia sum deceptus ab illo,
10   laturum misero quem mihi rebar opem.
tantane te, fallax, cepere oblivia nostri,
    afflictumque fuit tantus adire timor,
ut neque respiceres nec solarere iacentem,
    dure, nec exequias prosequerere meas ?
15 illud amicitiae sanctum et venerabile nomen
    re tibi pro vili sub pedibusque iacet ?
quid fuit, ingenti prostratum mole sodalem
    visere et adloquii parte levare tui,[2]
inque meos si non lacrimam demittere casus,
20   pauca tamen ficto verba dolore loqui,[3]
idque, quod ignoti, "factum male" dicere[4] saltem,
    et vocem populi publicaque ora sequi,—
denique lugubres vultus numquamque videndos
    cernere supremo dum licuitque die,

[1] eram
[2] alloquiis . . . tuis
[3] pati   [4] faciunt vale *corr. Rothmaler*

greater because these were not published by their master, but were rescued from what might be called his funeral. And so whatever defect this rough poem may have he would have corrected, had it been permitted him."

VIII. To a Traitorous Friend

To their sources shall deep rivers flow, back from the sea, and the sun, wheeling his steeds, shall hurry backwards; the earth shall support stars and the sky shall be cloven by the plough, water shall produce flame and flame water; all things shall proceed reversing nature's laws and no part of the universe shall keep its path; everything that I once called impossible shall now take place, and there is nothing that one ought not to believe. All this I prophesy because I have been deceived by that man who I thought would bring aid to me in my wretchedness.

[11] Treacherous one, did you forget me so utterly or were you so afraid to approach me in my misfortune that you did not regard or comfort me in my downfall, cruel man, or become one of my funeral escort? Does the sacred and revered name of friendship lie, a cheap thing, beneath your feet? What trouble was it to visit a comrade overwhelmed by a mighty disaster, to encourage him with your share of comfort, and if not to let fall a tear at my misfortune, yet to utter a few words of feigned sorrow and, as strangers do, at least to say "Hard luck!," to copy the people's speech, the public phrases—in fine to look upon my sad features never to be seen again, on the last

41

25 dicendumque semel toto non amplius aevo
    accipere, et parili reddere voce " vale " ?
at fecere alii nullo mihi foedere iuncti,
    et lacrimas animi signa dedere sui.
quid, nisi convictu causisque valentibus essem
30   temporis et longi iunctus amore tibi ?
quid, nisi tot lusus et tot mea seria nosses,
    tot nossem lusus seriaque ipse tua ?
quid, si dumtaxat Romae mihi cognitus esses,
    ascitus totiens in genus omne loci ?
35 cunctane in aerios [1] abierunt irrita ventos ?
    cunctane Lethaeis mersa feruntur aquis ?
non ego te genitum placida reor urbe Quirini,
    urbe, meo quae iam non adeunda pede est,
sed scopulis, Ponti quos haec habet ora sinistri,
40   inque feris Scythiae Sarmaticisque iugis :
et tua sunt silicis circum praecordia venae,
    et rigidum ferri semina pectus habet,
quaeque tibi quondam tenero ducenda palato
    plena dedit nutrix ubera, tigris erat :
45 aut mala nostra minus quam nunc aliena putares,
    duritiaeque mihi non agerere reus.
sed quoniam accedit fatalibus hoc quoque damnis,
    ut careant numeris tempora prima suis,
effice, peccati ne sim memor huius, et illo
50   officium laudem, quo queror, ore tuum.

IX.

Detur inoffenso vitae tibi tangere metam,
    qui legis hoc nobis non inimicus opus.

---

[1] aequoreos *corr. Riese*

[1] The conjecture that this friend was Carus is improbable.
See Introd. p. xv.

day, whilst you might, and to hear the " Farewell "
never more to be uttered in all time and to return it to
me in a like tone ?   Others did this who were bound
to me by no tie, and wept in token of their
feeling.   What if in our common life there were not
strong reasons for our union, and in our long
continued love ?   What if you had not known so
many of my gay and serious moments, and I so many
of yours ?   What if you had known me merely at
Rome—you who have so often been my comrade in
all sorts of places ?   Have all these things been in
vain, vanishing into the winds that blow over the
sky ?   Are they all carried away, drowned in Lethe's
waters ?   You were not born, I think, in Quirinus'
peaceful city, the city that my feet must enter
nevermore, but of the crags which stand upon this
coast of the ill-omened Pontus, or in the cruel
mountains of Scythia and Sarmatia.   Your heart
also is girt with veins of flint, and seeds of iron are
implanted in your unyielding breast.   She who once
nursed you, offering full udders to be drained by your
tender throat, was a tigress ; or else you would think
my woes less foreign to you than you now do, nor
would you stand accused by me of hardheartedness.

[47] But since this also has been added to my fated
ills, that those early years fall short of consum-
mation, see to it that I forget this sin and praise your
service with the same lips with which I now complain.

IX. To a Steadfast Friend [1]

Be it your lot to reach life's goal without stumbling
—you who read this work of mine in no unfriendly

atque utinam pro te possint mea vota valere,
    quae pro me duros non tetigere deos!
5 donec eris sospes,[1] multos numerabis amicos:
    tempora si fuerint nubila, solus eris.
aspicis, ut veniant ad candida tecta columbae,
    accipiat nullas sordida turris aves.
horrea formicae tendunt ad inania numquam:
10   nullus ad amissas ibit amicus opes.
utque comes radios per solis euntibus umbra est,
    cum latet hic pressus nubibus, illa fugit,
mobile sic sequitur Fortunae lumina vulgus:
    quae simul inducta nocte teguntur, abit.
15 haec precor ut semper possint tibi falsa videri;
    sunt tamen eventu vera fatenda meo.
dum stetimus, turbae quantum satis esset, habebat
    nota quidem, sed non ambitiosa domus.
at simul impulsa est, omnes timuere ruinam,
20   cautaque communi terga dedere fugae.
saeva neque admiror metuunt si fulmina, quorum
    ignibus adflari proxima quaeque solent.
sed tamen in duris remanentem rebus amicum
    quamlibet [2] inviso Caesar in hoste probat,
25 nec solet irasci—neque enim moderatior alter—
    cum quis in adversis, siquid amavit, amat.
de comite Argolici [3] postquam cognovit Orestae,
    narratur Pyladen ipse probasse Thoas.
quae fuit Actoridae cum magno semper Achille,
30   laudari solita est Hectoris ore fides.
quod pius ad Manes Theseus comes iret amico,
    Tartareum dicunt indoluisse deum.

[1] felix   [2] qualibet *vel* quolibet *corr.* ς
[3] argolico *corr. Heinsius*

spirit.   Would that in your behalf my prayers may
prevail which in my own did not affect the cruel
gods !   So long as you are secure you will count many
friends ; if your life becomes clouded you will be
alone.   You see how the doves come to a white
dwelling, how an unclean tower harbours no
birds.   Ants seek a granary, but an empty one
never : no friend will approach when wealth is
lost.   As a shadow accompanies those who pass
through the rays of the sun, but when the sun is
hidden, hemmed in by clouds, the shadow vanishes,
so the fickle crowd follows the light of good fortune,
but, when once the veil of darkness covers it, the
crowd is gone.   I pray this may always seem untrue
to you, yet from my fate its truth must be admitted.
Whilst I stood upright, my house, well known indeed
but courting no honours, found enough to throng
it.   Yet, as soon as shock came all men feared its fall
and discreetly turned their backs in common
flight.   I wonder not if they dread the fierce
lightnings whose flames are wont to blast everything
nearby ; nevertheless a friend who is steadfast
in times of stress is approved by Caesar in the case
of an enemy, however he may hate him, and he
is not wont to be angry—for no other shows greater
restraint—when one continues in adversity to
love whatever he has loved before.   After hearing
the tale of Argive Orestes' comrade, even Thoas,
they say, approved of Pylades.   The unwavering
loyalty of Actor's grandson [1] for mighty Achilles
was wont to be praised by Hector's lips.   When
loyal Theseus accompanied his friend to the shades,
they say the god [2] of Tartarus was grieved.   When

---

[1] Patroclus.   [2] Pluto.

Euryali Nisique fide tibi, Turne, relata
　　credibile est lacrimis inmaduisse genas.
35 est etiam miseris pietas, et in hoste probatur.
　　ei mihi, quam paucos haec mea dicta movent!
　is status, haec rerum nunc est fortuna mearum,
　　debeat ut lacrimis nullus adesse modus.
　at mea sunt, proprio quamvis maestissima casu,
40　pectora processu facta serena tuo.
　hoc eventurum iam tum, carissime, vidi,
　　ferret adhuc istam cum minor [1] aura ratem.
　sive aliquod morum seu vitae labe carentis
　　est pretium, nemo pluris emendus erat:
45 sive per ingenuas aliquis caput extulit artes—
　　quaelibet eloquio fit bona causa tuo.
　his ego commotus dixi tibi protinus ipsi
　　"scaena manet dotes grandis, amice, tuas."
　haec mihi non ovium fibrae tonitrusve sinistri,
50　linguave servatae pennave dixit avis:
　augurium ratio est et coniectura futuri:
　　hac divinavi notitiamque tuli.
　quae quoniam vera est, tota tibi mente mihique
　　gratulor, ingenium non latuisse tuum.
55 at nostrum tenebris utinam latuisset in imis!
　　expediit studio lumen abesse meo.
　utque tibi prosunt artes, facunde, severae,
　　dissimiles illis sic nocuere mihi.
　vita tamen tibi nota mea est.　scis artibus illis
60　auctoris mores abstinuisse sui:
　scis vetus hoc iuveni lusum mihi carmen, et istos,
　　ut non laudandos, sic tamen esse iocos.

[1] ista . . . minus

---

[1] The *Ars amatoria*.

they told you, Turnus, of the fidelity of Nisus and
Euryalus, we may believe that your cheeks were
moist with tears. There is loyalty even for the
unfortunate and it finds approval even in an
enemy. Ah me! how few do these words of mine
affect! Such is my condition, such is now the state
of my affairs that there should be no measure to my
tears. Yet my heart, in the depths of grief from its
own disaster, has been calmed by your
advancement. This I saw approaching, dear one, as
early as the time when as yet a lesser breeze was
bearing onward that bark of yours. If there is a
reward for character or for a life without blemish,
nobody was more highly to be prized; or if anyone has
by liberal arts achieved prominence, you have
eloquence which renders every cause a good
one. Moved by this I said at once to you, "A mighty
stage awaits thy gifts." This was told me by no
sheep's liver or thunder on my left or the note or wing
of a bird I had observed; it is an augury and inference
of the future based on reason: by this I made my
divination and gained my knowledge.

[53] Since this proves true, with my whole heart I
congratulate you and myself that your ability has not
been obscured. But mine! would it had been
obscured in the depths of darkness! It had been
best that light had failed my pursuit. And just
as you are aided, my eloquent friend, by serious
arts, so arts unlike them have injured me. Yet
my life is well known to you; you know that
with those arts their author's character had no con-
nexion; you know that this poem [1] was written long
ago, an amusement of my youth, and that those
jests, though not deserving praise, were still mere

47

ergo ut defendi nullo mea posse colore,
    sic excusari crimina posse puto.
65 qua potes, excusa, nec amici desere causam :
    qua bene coepisti, sic bene semper eas.

X.

Est mihi sitque, precor, flavae tutela Minervae,
    navis et a picta casside nomen habet.
sive opus est velis, minimam bene currit ad auram,
    sive opus est remo, remige carpit iter.
5 nec comites volucri contenta est vincere cursu,
    occupat egressas quamlibet ante rates,
et pariter flatus [1] fert ac salientia [2] longe
    aequora, nec saevis victa fatiscit [3] aquis.
illa, Corinthiacis primum mihi cognita Cenchreis,
10   fida manet trepidae duxque comesque fugae,
perque tot eventus et iniquis concita ventis
    aequora Palladio numine tuta fuit.
nunc quoque tuta, precor, vasti secet ostia Ponti,
    quasque petit, Getici litoris intret aquas.
15 quae simul Aeoliae mare me deduxit in Helles,
    et longum tenui limite fecit iter,
fleximus in laevum cursus, et ab Hectoris urbe
    venimus ad portus, Imbria terra, tuos.

---

[1] *fluctus corr. Hall*
[2] *ferit atque silentia corr. Vogel*   [3] madescit

---

[1] The stern of Ovid's ship was apparently adorned with a figure of Minerva clad in armour. Such a figure was called a *tutela*, "protecting emblem."

[2] Ovid reached Corinth by way of the Adriatic and the Corinthian Gulf. He crossed the Isthmus and boarded this ship at Cenchreae whence he continued his voyage to Samothrace. There he left the ship (which continued to

jests. So then although my crimes can be defended
by no plea however brilliant, yet an excuse can be
made for them, I think. As far as you can, make
that excuse; do not abandon the cause of a
friend. On this condition may you ever travel
happily along the road upon which you have happily
set out.

X. The Exile's Journey

I have, and pray that I may always have, the
protection of golden-haired Minerva, and my bark
draws her name from an emblazoned[1] helmet. If
sails be needed, she runs well at the touch of the
lightest breeze, or if oars, the rowers speed her on her
way. She is not content to outstrip in winged course
her companions: she overhauls the craft that set out
no matter how long before; alike she bears the
gales and the far-leaping billows; she is no leaky
craft overwhelmed by the raging seas. Her I knew
first at Corinthian Cenchreae[2] and she remained the
faithful guide and comrade of my anxious flight, safe
through the power of Pallas amid so many fortunes,
amid waves roused by the cruel gales. Now too I
pray she may safely cut her path through the gates of
the wide Pontus and reach the waters of her goal by
the Getic shore.

[15] As soon as she brought me to the sea of the
Aeolian Helle,[3] cleaving her long journey with slender
furrow, I turned my course to the left, away from
Hector's city, and came to thy port, land of Imbros,

Tomis, vv. 24–42) and took another for Tempyra, near the
Thracian coast, whence he passed by land to Tomis.

[3] The Hellespont.

inde, levi vento Zerynthia litora nacta,
20   Threïciam tetigit fessa carina Samon.
saltus ab hac contra brevis est Tempyra petenti:
      hac dominum tenus est illa secuta suum.
nam mihi Bistonios placuit pede carpere campos :
      Hellespontiacas illa relegit [1] aquas
25 Dardaniamque petit, auctoris nomen habentem,
      et te ruricola, Lampsace, tuta deo,
quodque per angustas vectae male virginis undas
      Seston Abydena separat urbe fretum,
inque Propontiacis haerentem Cyzicon oris,
30   Cyzicon, Haemoniae nobile gentis opus,
quaeque tenent Ponti Byzantia litora fauces :
      hic locus est gemini ianua vasta maris.
haec, precor, evincat, propulsaque fortibus Austris
      transeat instabilis strenua Cyaneas
35 Thyniacosque sinus, et ab his per Apollinis urbem
      arta [2] sub Anchiali moenia tendat iter.
inde Mesembriacos portus et Odeson et arces
      praetereat dictas nomine, Bacche, tuo,
et quos Alcathoi memorant e moenibus ortos
40   sedibus his profugos constituisse Larem.
a quibus adveniat Miletida sospes ad urbem,
      offensi quo me detulit ira dei.
haec si contigerint, meritae cadet agna Minervae :
      non facit ad nostras hostia maior opes.

[1] reliquit: relegit *s*
[2] apta *vel* alta *vel* vecta : arta *s*

---

[1] Samothrace, on the north side of which was the Zerynthian cave of Hecate.   [2] Priapus.   [3] Helle.

[4] Founded by the Argonaut Aeneus of Haemonia.

[5] 'Double sea' : Housman explains from Strabo (2.5.22), for whom the Pontus was divided into two by the facing promontories of the Crimea and Carambis (modern Kerempe).

whence reaching the Zerynthian shore with a light breeze my wearied keel touched the Thracian Samos.[1] From here 'tis but a short leap for one who seeks Tempyra on the opposite coast : thus far only did my bark attend her master. For it was my resolve to pick my way on foot through the Bistonian land ; she coasted back through the waters of the Hellespont seeking Dardania, bearing the name of its founder, and thee, Lampsacus, secure through the protection of the country-loving god,[2] and the strait of that maiden[3] all too insecurely carried through the narrow waters—the strait that separates Sestos from Abydos' town—and Cyzicos clinging to the shores of Propontis, Cyzicos, the famed work of the Haemonian race,[4] and Byzantium's shores, that hold the entrance to the Pontus, the huge portal to a double sea[5]. Through all these may she win her way, and driven by the sturdy breeze may she have power to pass the shifting Cyaneae, and the Thynian bay, and after may she hold her course past Apollo's city[6] and close beneath the narrow walls of Anchialus. Thence may she pass the port of Mesembria and Odesos, and the citadel[7] called after thy name, Bacchus, and those exiles from Alcathous' walls, who, so 'tis said, placed on this site their home. From their land may she come in safety to the Milesian city[8] whither the wrath of an angered god has dispatched me.

[43] If this but happen, a lamb shall fall in sacrifice to deserving Minerva ; a larger victim ill becomes

[6] Apollonia, on the west coast of the Pontus, where lay also the other towns mentioned in vv. 35–40.

[7] Probably Dionysopolis. The exiles from Alcathous' walls settled at Callatis.

[8] Tomis, a colony of Miletus, *cf. Tr.* iii. 9.

45 vos quoque, Tyndaridae, quos haec colit insula, fratres,
    mite, precor, duplici numen adeste [1] viae !
altera namque parat Symplegadas ire per artas,
    scindere Bistonias altera puppis aquas.
vos facite ut ventos, loca cum diversa petamus,
50   illa suos habeat, nec minus illa suos.

XI.

Littera quaecumque est toto tibi lecta libello,
    est mihi sollicitae tempore facta viae.
aut haec me, gelido tremerem cum mense Decembri,
    scribentem mediis Hadria vidit aquis ;
5 aut, postquam bimarem cursu superavimus Isthmon,
    alteraque est nostrae sumpta carina fugae,
quod facerem versus inter fera murmura ponti,
    Cycladas Aegaeas obstipuisse puto.
ipse ego nunc [2] miror tantis animique marisque
10   fluctibus ingenium non cecidisse meum.
seu stupor huic studio sive est insania nomen,
    omnis ab hac cura cura levata [3] mea est.
saepe ego nimbosis dubius iactabar ab Haedis,
    saepe minax Steropes sidere pontus erat,
15 fuscabatque diem custos Azanidos [4] Ursae,
    aut Hyadas seris hauserat Auster aquis,
saepe maris pars intus erat ; tamen ipse trementi
    carmina ducebam qualiacumque manu.

[1] adesse   [2] ego nunc] etenim
[3] cura levata] mens relevata   [4] Atlantidos *corr. Alton*

[1] Castor and Pollux, worshipped by sailors.   Ovid writes in Samothrace.
[2] Ovid means that he wrote mechanically as one dazed (*stupor*).   [3] Boötes.
[4] Ovid seems to mean that rainy Auster combined with the

my poor resources. Ye too, brother Tyndaridae,[1] whom this isle worships, attend in propitious power our twofold way; for one craft makes ready to pass through the narrow Symplegadae, the other to plough Bistonia's waters. Make ye the winds, though different the places we seek, favour the one and no less favour the other!

XI. Epilogue

Every letter that you have read in my whole book was formed by me during the troubled days of my journey. Either the Adriatic saw me writing these words in the midst of his waters, while I shivered in cold December, or when I had passed in my course the Isthmus with its two seas and had taken the second ship of my journey into exile, my writing of verses amid the wild roar of the sea brought wonder, I think, to the Aegean Cyclades. I myself now marvel that amid such turmoil of my soul and of the sea my powers did not fail. But whether "trance"[2] or "madness" be the name for this pursuit, 'twas by such pains that all my pain was lightened. Often my perilous tossing was caused by the storm-bringing Kids, often the constellation of Sterope made the sea to threaten, or the day was darkened by the guardian[3] of the Arcadian bear, or Auster had drawn from the Hyades an autumnal flood.[4] Often part of the sea was within our ship; nevertheless, with shaking hand I continued to spin my verses such as they were.

setting Hyades (in November, a time of rain) to produce a downpour.

53

nunc quoque contenti stridunt Aquilone rudentes,
20 inque modum cumuli concava surgit aqua.
ipse gubernator tollens ad sidera palmas
    exposcit votis, inmemor artis, opem.
quocumque aspexi, nihil est nisi mortis imago,
    quam dubia timeo mente timensque precor.
25 attigero portum, portu terrebor ab ipso :
    plus habet infesta terra timoris aqua.
nam simul insidiis hominum pelagique laboro,
    et faciunt geminos ensis et unda metus.
ille meo vereor ne speret sanguine praedam,
30 haec titulum nostrae mortis habere velit.
barbara pars laeva est avidaeque adsueta rapinae,[1]
    quam cruor et caedes bellaque semper habent,
cumque sit hibernis agitatum fluctibus aequor,
    pectora sunt ipso turbidiora mari.
35 quo magis his debes ignoscere, candide lector,
    si spe sint, ut sunt, inferiora tua.
non haec in nostris, ut quondam, scripsimus[2] hortis,
    nec, consuete, meum, lectule, corpus habes.
iactor in indomito brumali luce profundo
40 ipsaque caeruleis charta feritur aquis.
improba pugnat hiems indignaturque quod ausim
    scribere se rigidas incutiente minas.
vincat hiems hominem ! sed eodem tempore, quaeso,
    ipse modum statuam carminis, illa sui.

---

[1] ad ethera penne *vel* substrata (substracta *vel* subtracta *etc.*)
rapinae : adsueta rapinae *Haupt*
[2] scribimus

Now too the ropes drawn taut by Aquilo are shrieking, and like a hill swells the curving surge. The very helmsman lifts his hands to the stars imploring aid with prayer and forgetful of his skill. Wherever I gaze there is naught but the presentment of death that with wavering mind I fear and pray for in my fear. Should I reach the harbour, the very harbour will affright me: there is more to dread upon the land than on the hostile sea. For the snares of men and of the sea unite in causing my woe; the sword and the waves produce twin fears. The one may look for booty through my blood, I fear, whilst the other may wish to win renown from my death. Wild is the shore on my left, accustomed to the greed of robbers, ever filled with bloodshed and murder and war, and though the sea is shaken by stormy billows my breast is more turbulent than the sea.

[35] And so, kindly reader, you should grant me the more indulgence should these verses be—as they are—poorer than your hopes. They were not written, as of old, in my garden or while you, my familiar couch, supported my frame. I am tossing of a winter's day on the stormy deep, and my paper is sprayed by the dark waters. The vicious storm battles, indignant that I dare to write whilst he is brandishing against me his stern threats. Let the storm vanquish the man; but at the same time that I end my verse, let him, I pray, reach his own end.

LIBER SECUNDUS

Quid mihi vobiscum est, infelix cura, libelli,
   ingenio perii qui miser ipse meo ?
cur modo damnatas repeto, mea crimina, Musas ?
   an semel est poenam commeruisse parum ?
5 carmina fecerunt, ut me cognoscere vellet
   omine non fausto femina virque meo :
carmina fecerunt, ut me moresque notaret
   iam demi iussa [1] Caesar ab Arte mea.
deme mihi studium, vitae quoque crimina demes ;
10   acceptum refero versibus esse nocens.
hoc pretium curae vigilatorumque laborum
   cepimus : ingenio est poena reperta meo.
si saperem, doctas odissem iure sorores,
   numina cultori perniciosa suo.
15 at nunc—tanta meo comes est insania morbo—
   saxa malum refero rursus ad icta pedem :
scilicet ut victus repetit gladiator harenam,
   et redit in tumidas naufraga puppis aquas.
forsitan, ut quondam Teuthrantia regna tenenti,
20   sic mihi res eadem vulnus opemque feret,
Musaque, quam movit, motam quoque leniet iram ;
   exorant magnos carmina saepe deos.

[1] demum visa

---

[1] The *Ars amatoria*, which had been removed from the public
libraries.   But the text is not certain.
[2] The Muses.   [3] Telephus. See Index.

BOOK II

The Poet's Plea

What have I to do with you, ye books, ill-starred
object of my toil,—I, ruined and wretched through
my own talent? Why I return to the Muses I have
just denounced, the causes of my guilt? Or is one
well-earned penalty not enough? Verse gave men
and women a desire to know me, but 'twas no good
omen for me; verse caused Caesar to brand me and
my ways by commanding that my "Art"[1] be
forthwith taken away. Take away from me my
pursuit and you will take away from my life also the
charges against it. I lay the charge of guilt against
my verse. This is the reward I have received for my
work and my wakeful toil: a penalty has been found
for my talent. Were I wise I should justly hate the
learned sisters,[2] the deities fatal to their own
votary. But as it is—such madness accompanies
my disease—I am once more returning my luckless
foot to the stone it has struck, just as the vanquished
gladiator seeks again the arena or the battered ship
returns to the surging sea.
  [19] Perchance, as once for him who ruled the
Teuthrantian kingdom,[3] the same object will both
wound and cure me, and the Muse who aroused the
wrath will also soften it; song often prevails

57

ipse quoque Ausonias Caesar matresque nurusque
    carmina turrigerae dicere iussit Opi.
25 iusserat et Phoebo dici, quo tempore ludos
    fecit, quos aetas aspicit una semel.
his precor exemplis tua nunc, mitissime Caesar,
    fiat ab ingenio mollior ira meo.
illa quidem iusta est, nec me meruisse negabo—
30   non adeo nostro fugit ab ore pudor—
sed nisi peccassem, quid tu concedere posses ?
    materiam veniae sors tibi nostra dedit.
si, quotiens peccant homines, sua fulmina mittat
    Iuppiter, exiguo tempore inermis erit ;
35 nunc ubi detonuit strepituque exterruit orbem,
    purum discussis aëra reddit aquis.
iure igitur genitorque deum rectorque vocatur,
    iure capax mundus nil Iove maius habet.
tu quoque, cum patriae rector dicare paterque,
40   utere more dei nomen habentis idem.
idque facis, nec te quisquam moderatius umquam
    imperii potuit frena tenere sui.
tu veniam parti superatae saepe dedisti,
    non concessurus quam tibi victor erat.
45 divitiis etiam multos et honoribus auctos
    vidi, qui tulerant in caput arma tuum;
quaeque dies bellum, belli tibi sustulit iram,
    parsque simul templis utraque dona tulit ;
utque tuus gaudet miles, quod vicerit hostem,
50   sic victum cur se gaudeat, hostis habet.
causa mea est melior, qui nec contraria dicor
    arma nec hostiles esse secutus opes.

---

[1] The Secular Games.   See Index.   [2] Augustus.

on the mighty gods. Caesar himself bade the
mothers and daughters of Ausonia chant a hymn to
turret-bearing Ops. He commanded a hymn to
Phoebus also when he celebrated those games [1] which
each age views but once. Such precedents now form
the basis of my prayer, O merciful Caesar, that my
poetic gift may assuage thy wrath. Just indeed it
is—I will not deny that I have deserved it, for shame
has not so utterly fled my lips. But had I not sinned,
what leniency were it possible for thee to
display? My fate has given thee the means of
mercy. If at every human error Jupiter should hurl
his thunderbolts, he would in a brief space be
weaponless. But as it is, when the roll of his thunder
has died away, affrighting the world with its roar, he
scatters the rain-clouds and clears the air. Just it is,
then, to call him the father and ruler of the gods, just
it is that in the spacious universe there is naught
mightier than Jove. Do thou [2] also, seeing thou art
called ruler and father of our native land, follow
the way of the god who has the same title. And that
thou dost; no one has ever been able to hold
the reins of his power with more restraint. Thou
hast often granted indulgence to a conquered
foe which he would not have granted to thee
had he been victor. Many even who had been
enhanced in riches and in honours have I seen direct
their arms against thee, and the day that ended the
battle ended for thee also the wrath of battle; both
sides together made their gifts to the temples; and
as thy soldiery rejoice to have vanquished the
enemy, so the enemy has reason to rejoice at his
defeat. My cause is a better one, for none assert
that I have followed arms opposed to thee, or hostile

59

per mare, per terras, absentia [1] numina, iuro,
    per te praesentem conspicuumque deum,
55 hunc animum favisse tibi, vir maxime, meque,
    qua sola potui, mente fuisse tuum.
optavi, peteres caelestia sidera tarde,
    parsque fui turbae parva precantis idem,
et pia tura dedi pro te, cumque omnibus unus
60   ipse quoque adiuvi publica vota meis.
quid referam libros, illos quoque, crimina nostra,
    mille locis plenos nominis esse tui ?
inspice maius opus, quod adhuc sine fine reliqui,[1]
    in non credendos corpora versa modos :
65 invenies vestri praeconia nominis illic,
    invenies animi pignora certa mei.
non tua carminibus maior fit gloria, nec quo,
    ut maior fiat, crescere possit, habet.
fama Iovi superest : tamen hunc sua facta referri
70   et se materiam carminis esse iuvat,
cumque Gigantei memorantur proelia belli,
    credibile est laetum laudibus esse suis.
te celebrant alii, quanto decet ore, tuasque
    ingenio laudes uberiore canunt :
75 sed tamen, ut fuso taurorum sanguine centum,
    sic capitur minimo turis honore deus.
a ! ferus et nobis nimium crudeliter [2] hostis,
    delicias legit qui tibi cumque meas,
carmina de nostris cum [3] te venerantia libris
80   iudicio possint candidiore legi.
esse sed irato quis te mihi posset amicus ?
    vix tunc ipse mihi non inimicus eram.

    [1] per tertia *corr. Hall*   [2] *crudelior omnibus*   [3] *ne n. quae*

---

[1] See *Metam.* xv. 857 ff.

power. By the unseen gods of the earth and sea I swear, by thee, a present and manifest deity, that this soul of mine favoured thee, mightiest of men, and that, wherein alone I could, in heart I have been thine. I prayed that thou mightest make thy way late to the stars of heaven, and I was an humble member of the throng that uttered the same prayer; loyal incense I offered in thy behalf and with all the rest I too aided the prayers of the state with my own.

[61] Why should I say that my books, even those which are my accusers, in a thousand passages hold thy name? Examine the greater work, which I have left unfinished, the book of figures transformed in ways unbelievable; thou wilt find praises of thy name there,[2] thou wilt find sure pledges of my loyalty. Thy glory is not made mightier by song, nor has it room wherein to grow so as to be made mightier. Jupiter has more than enough of glory: yet is he pleased to have his deeds related and himself become the theme of song, and when the battles of his war with the Giants are told, we may believe that he finds pleasure in his praises. Thou art praised by others in a lofty style that befits thee; they sing thy praise with richer gifts than mine; but though a god be won by the out-poured blood of a hundred bulls, yet is he also won by the humblest offering of incense.

[77] Alas! harsh was he and too cruelly an enemy of mine, who read to thee my playful verse, when other poems from my oeuvre doing thee homage might have been read with fairer judgment. But when thou wert angry, who could have been friendly to me? Scarce could I at that time refrain from being an enemy to myself. When once

61

cum coepit quassata domus subsidere, partes
   in proclinatas omne recumbit onus,
85 cunctaque fortuna rimam faciente dehiscunt,
   ipsa suoque eadem [1] pondere tracta ruunt.
ergo hominum quaesitum odium mihi carmine, quosque
   debuit, est vultus turba secuta tuos.
at, memini, vitamque meam moresque probabas
90   illo, quem dederas, praetereuntis equo.
quod si non prodest et honesti gratia [2] nulla
   redditur, at nullum crimen adeptus eram.[3]
nec male commissa est nobis fortuna reorum
   lisque [4] decem deciens inspicienda viris.
95 res quoque privatas statui sine crimine iudex,
   deque mea fassa est pars quoque victa fide.
me miserum! potui, si non extrema nocerent,
   iudicio tutus non semel esse tuo.
ultima me perdunt, imoque sub aequore mergit
100   incolumem totiens una procella ratem.
nec mihi pars nocuit de gurgite parva, sed omnes
   pressere hoc fluctus oceanusque caput.
cur aliquid vidi? cur noxia lumina feci?
   cur imprudenti cognita culpa mihi?
105 inscius Actaeon vidit sine veste Dianam:
   praeda fuit canibus non minus ille suis.
scilicet in superis etiam fortuna luenda est,
   nec veniam laeso numine casus habet.
illa nostra die, qua me malus abstulit error,
110   parva quidem periit, sed sine labe domus:

---

[1] suo quondam *corr. Binsfield*   [2] gloria
[3] eram] erit   [4] usque: lisque *Heinsius*

---

[1] In the annual procession of the knights.

a battered house has begun to settle, the whole weight leans upon the yielding parts,—when accident makes a crack, the whole gapes apart and crashes in ruins, dragged by its own weight. So my verse has won me men's dislike; the crowd, as was right, have only guided themselves by the expression of thy face.

[89] And yet, I remember, thou wert wont to approve my life and my ways when I passed before thee with the steed thou hadst granted me.¹ If that avails me not, if no credit for what is honourable is granted me, at least I had suffered no impeachment. Nor was fate of those on trial wrongfully entrusted to me, suits to be examined by the centumvirs. Private cases also I brought to settlement, acting without criticism as referee; and even the defeated side admitted my good faith. Wretched me! were it not for the injury caused me by recent events, I might be secure through more than one judgment of thine. These last events ruin me; one blast sends to the bottom of the sea the craft that has so many times been safe. 'Tis no small part of the flood that has wrought me harm, but all the billows of ocean have fallen upon my head.

[103] Why did I see anything? Why did I make my eyes guilty? Why was I so thoughtless as to harbour the knowledge of a fault? Unwitting was Actaeon when he beheld Diana unclothed; none the less he became the prey of his own hounds. Clearly, among the gods, even ill-fortune must be atoned for, nor is mischance an excuse when a deity is wronged. On that day when my ruinous mistake ravished me away, my house, humble but stainless,

63

sic quoque parva tamen, patrio dicatur ut aevo
    clara nec ullius nobilitate minor,
et neque divitiis nec paupertate notanda,
    unde sit in neutrum conspiciendus eques.
115 sit [1] quoque nostra domus vel censu parva vel ortu,
    ingenio certe non ladet illa meo ;
quo videar quamvis nimium iuvenaliter usus,
    grande tamen toto nomen ab orbe fero,
turbaque doctorum Nasonem novit et audet
120   non fastiditis adnumerare viris.
corruit haec igitur Musis accepta sub uno
    sed non exiguo crimine lapsa domus :
atque ea sic lapsa est, ut surgere, si modo laesi
    ematuruerit Caesaris ira, queat,
125 cuius in electu [2] poenae clementia tanta est,
    venerit ut nostro lenior illa metu.
vita data est, citraque necem tua constitit ira,
    o princeps parce viribus use tuis !
insuper accedunt, te non adimente, paternae,
130   tamquam vita parum muneris esset, opes.
nec mea decreto damnasti facta senatus,
    nec mea selecto iudice iussa fuga est.
tristibus invectus verbis—ita principe dignum—
    ultus es offensas, ut decet, ipse tuas.
135 adde quod edictum, quamvis immite minaxque,
    attamen in poenae nomine lene fuit :
quippe relegatus, non exul, dicor in illo,
    privaque fortunae sunt ibi verba meae.
nulla quidem sano gravior mentisque potenti
140   poena est, quam tanto displicuisse viro ;

[1] sit] si *vel* sic   [2] eventu *corr. Palmer*

[1] If the test is right, Ovid means that the language of the

was destroyed—humble indeed, but in our ancestors' time 'tis said to have been illustrious and inferior in fame to none, though noted neither for wealth nor poverty, so that from it spring knights conspicuous for neither. But even if our house be small in wealth and in origin, at least my genius does not suffer it to be obscure. This I may have employed in too youthful exuberance, yet my name is great throughout the world; a throng of the cultured are well acquainted with Naso and venture to count him with those whom they do not despise.

[121] Fallen then is my house, though pleasing to the Muses, beneath one charge albeit no small one—yet so fallen that it can rise again, if only time shall mellow the wrath of injured Caesar whose leniency in the choice of my penalty is such that the penalty is milder than I feared. Life was granted me; thy wrath halted ere it achieved my death: O sire, with what restraint hast thou used thy power! Then too there is added—for thou takest it not away—my inherited wealth, as if life were too small a gift. Thou didst not condemn my deeds through a degree of the senate nor was my exile ordered by a special court. With words of stern invective—worthy of a prince—thou didst thyself, as is fitting, avenge thine own injury. And thy command, though severe and threatening, was yet mild in naming my punishment, for it calls me *relegatus*, not exile, and thou dost use therein language especially adapted to my fate.[1]

[139] No punishment indeed is heavier to one in command of his senses than the displeasure of so

edict was not that which was customarily used but was peculiar, especially in calling him *relegatus* (Introd. p. xviii).

sed solet interdum fieri placabile numen :
    nube solet pulsa candidus ire dies.
vidi ego pampineis oneratam vitibus ulmum,
    quae fuerat saevi fulmine tacta Iovis.
145 ipse licet sperare vetes, sperabimus usque [1] ;
    hoc unum fieri te prohibente potest.
spes mihi magna subit, cum te, mitissime princeps,
    spes mihi, respicio cum mea facta, cadit.
ac veluti ventis agitantibus aequora non est
150   aequalis rabies continuusque furor,
sed modo subsidunt intermissique silescunt,
    vimque putes illos deposuisse suam :
sic abeunt redeuntque mei variantque timores,
    et spem placandi dantque negantque tui.
155 per superos igitur, qui dent tibi longa dabuntque
    tempora, Romanum si modo nomen amant,
per patriam, quae te tuta et secura parente est,
    cuius, ut in populo, para ego nuper eram,—
sic tibi, quem semper factis animoque mereris,
160   reddatur gratae debitus urbis amor ;
Livia sic tecum sociales compleat annos,
    quae, nisi te, nullo coniuge digna fuit,
quae si non esset, caelebs te vita deceret,
    nullaque, cui posses esse maritus, erat ;
165 sospite sic te sit [2] natus quoque sospes, et olim
    imperium regat hoc cum seniore senex ;
ut faciuntque tui, sidus iuvenale, nepotes,
    per tua perque sui facta parentis eant ;
sic adsueta tuis semper Victoria castris
170   nunc quoque se praestet notaque signa petat,

       [1] utque *vel* atque : usque *Heinsius*
            [2] sit tecum

---

     [1] Tiberius ; *cf.* also 171 ff.
     [2] Germanicus and Drusus the Younger.

mighty a man as thou; yet 'tis common for a deity to be appeased at times; 'tis common for clouds to scatter and the bright daylight to return. I have seen an elm laden with the tendrils of a vine even after it had been blasted by the thunderbolt of angry Jove. Though thou dost thyself forbid me to hope, I shall hope constantly; this one thing can be done in spite of thy command. Strong hope comes upon me when I regard thee, most merciful of princes, but hope fails me when I regard my own needs. As in the winds that buffet the seas there is no steady, no constant madness, but now they decrease or are lulled to silence so that one would suppose they had laid aside their power, in this wise my fears depart, return, or change, giving me or denying me hope of appeasing thee.

[155] Wherefore by the gods above, who must and will give thee long years, if only they love the Roman race; by our native land which is safe and secure under thy fatherly care, of which I as one among the people was recently part:—as surely as there may be duly paid thee by a grateful city that debt of love which thy constant deeds and spirit deserve; as in union with thee Livia may fill out her years—she whom no husband but thou deserved, but for whose existence an unwedded life would befit thee and there were none other whom thou couldst espouse; as together with thy safety thy son [1] may too be safe, and one day rule this empire, an old man with one still older; and thy grandsons,[2] stars of the youth, may still hold their course, as now they do, through thy deeds and those of their own sire; as Victory, always at home in thy camp, may now also present herself, seeking the

Ausoniumque ducem solitis circumvolet alis,
    ponat et in nitida laurea serta coma,
per quem bella geris, cuius nunc corpore pugnas,
    auspicium cui das grande deosque tuos,
175 dimidioque tui praesens dum respicis [1] urbem,
    dimidio procul es saevaque bella geris ;
hic tibi sic redeat superato victor ab hoste,
    inque coronatis fulgeat altus equis,—
parce, precor, fulmenque tuum, fera tela, reconde,
180   heu nimium misero cognita tela mihi !
parce, pater patriae, nec nominis inmemor huius
    olim placandi spem mihi tolle tui !
non precor ut redeam, quamvis maiora petitis
    credibile est magnos saepe dedisse deos ;
185 mitius exilium si das propiusque roganti,
    pars erit ex poena magna levata mea.
ultima perpetior medios eiectus in hostes,
    nec quisquam patria longius exul abest.
solus ad egressus missus septemplicis Histri
190   Parrhasiae gelido virginis axe premor
[Ciziges et Colchi Tereteaque [2] turba Getaeque
    Danuvii mediis vix prohibentur aquis] [3]
cumque alii causa tibi sint graviore fugati,
    ulterior nulli, quam mihi, terra data est.
195 longius hac nihil est, nisi tantum frigus et hostes,
    et maris adstricto quae coit unda gelu.
hactenus Euxini pars est Romana sinistri :
    proxima Basternae Sauromataeque tenent.

[1] et respicis *corr. Luck*
[2] metereaque *corr. Ellis*   [3] 191 f *del. Bentley*

---

[1] A different people from the Colchi who dwelt east of the
Pontus.   Perhaps 191–192 should be transposed after 198, *cf.*
Owen, *Trist.*, 1889, pp. xcv–xcvi.

standards so well known to her, hovering with
familiar wings about the Ausonian leader and placing
the laurel wreath upon the shining hair of him
through whom thou dost wage wars, in whose person
thou art now doing battle, to whom thou dost grant
thy lofty auspices and thy gods, and whilst half
present thou watchest o'er Rome, thou art half far
away and wagest savage wars ; as he may return to
thee after conquering the foe, and be seen in radiance
high on a garlanded car—so spare me, I pray, and
hide away thy thunderbolt, cruel weapon, alas ! but
too well known to wretched me ! Spare me, father of
our country ! Do not, forgetful of this name, take
from me the hope that sometime I may appease
thee ! I pray not for return, even though we may
believe that more than the prayer has oft been
granted by the mighty gods. Grant me a milder and
a nearer place of exile, and a large part of my
punishment will be lightened.

   [187] I am now enduring the extreme, thrust forth
into the midst of enemies ; no exile is farther from his
native land. I alone have been sent to the mouths of
the seven-streamed Hister, I am crushed beneath the
Parrhasian virgin's icy pole [The Ciziges, the Colchi,[1]
the hordes of Teretei, and the Getae are scarce fended
off by the interposition of the Danube's waters.]
Though others have been exiled for weightier
cause, a more remote land has been assigned to
no one ; nothing is farther away than this land
except only the cold and the enemy and the sea
whose waters congeal with the frost. Here is the
end of Rome's domain on the ill-omened Euxine's
shore ; hard by the Basternae and Sauromatae
hold sway. This land comes last of all beneath

haec est Ausonio sub iure novissima vixque
200   haeret in imperii margine terra tui.
    unde precor supplex ut nos in tuta releges,
      ne sit cum patria pax quoque dempta mihi,
    neu timeam gentes, quas non bene summovet Hister,
      neve tuus possim civis ab hoste capi.
205 fas prohibet Latio quemquam de sanguine natum
      Caesaribus salvis barbara vincla pati.
    perdiderint cum me duo crimina, carmen et error,
      alterius facti culpa silena mihi:
    nam non sum tanti, renovem ut tua vulnera, Caesar,
210   quen nimio plus est indoluisse semel.
    altera pars superest, qua turpi carmine factus
      arguor obsceni doctor adulterii.
    fas ergo est aliqua caelestia pectora falli,
      et sunt notitia multa minora tua;
215 utque deos caelumque simul sublime tuenti
      non vacat exiguis rebus adesse Iovi,
    de te pendentem sic dum circumspicis orbem,
      effugiunt curas inferiora tuas.
    scilicet imperii princeps statione relicta
220   imparibus legeres carmina facta modis?
    non ea te moles Romani nominis urget,
      inque tuis umeris tam leve fertur onus,
    lusibus ut possis advertere numen ineptis,
      excutiasque oculis otia nostra tuis.
225 nunc tibi Pannonia est, nunc Illyris ora domanda,
      Raetica nunc praebent Thraciaque arma metum,
    nunc petit Armenius pacem, nunc porrigit arcus
      Parthus eques timida captaque signa manu,

---

[1] The *Ars amatoria*.

Ausonian law, clinging with difficulty to the very edge of thy empire.

²⁰¹ And so I offer a suppliant's prayer that thou wilt banish me to a safe abode—that together with my fatherland peace also be not taken from me, that I may not fear the tribes which the Hister holds insecurely in check, that I, thy subject, be not within an enemy's power to capture. Right forbids that anyone of Latin blood should suffer barbarian bondage while Caesars live.

²⁰⁷ Though two crimes, a poem [1] and a blunder have brought me ruin, of my fault in the one I must keep silent, for my worth is not such that I may reopen thy wounds, O Caesar; 'tis more than enough that thou shouldst have been pained once. The other remains: the charge that by an obscene poem I have taught foul adultery. 'Tis possible then, somehow, for divine minds to be deceived, for many things to be beneath thy notice. As Jove who watches at once o'er the gods and the lofty heaven has not leisure to give heed to small things, so whilst thou dost gaze about upon the world that depends upon thee, things of less moment escape thy care. Shouldst thou, forsooth, the prince of the world, abandon thy post and read songs of mine set to unequal measure? That weight of the Roman name does not lay so light a burden upon thy shoulders that thou canst direct thy divine attention to silly trifles, examining with thine own eye the product of my leisure hours. Now Pannonia, now the Illyrian shore must be subdued by thee, now the wars in Raetia or Thrace bring thee anxiety; now the Armenian seeks peace, now the Parthian horseman extends to thee with timorous hand his

71

nunc te prole tua iuvenem Germania sentit,
230   bellaque pro magno Caesare Caesar obit;
denique, ut in tanto, quantum non extitit umquam,
    corpore pars nulla est, quae labet, imperii.
urbs quoque te et legum lassat tutela tuarum
    et morum, similes quos cupis esse tuis.
235 nec tibi contingunt, quae gentibus otia praestas,
    bellaque cum vitiis inrequieta geris.
mirer in hoc igitur tantarum pondere rerum
    te numquam nostros evoluisse iocos?
at si, quod mallem, vacuum tibi forte [2] fuisset,
240   nullum legisses crimen in Arte mea.
illa quidem fateor frontis non esse severae
    scripta, nec a tanto principe digna legi:
non tamen idcirco legum contraria iussis
    sunt ea Romanas eruduntque nurus.
245 nerve, quibus scribam, possis dubitare, libellos,
    quattuor hos versus e tribus unus habet:
"este procul, vitae tenues, insigne pudoris,
    quaeque tegis medios instita longa pedes!
nil nisi legitimum concessaque furta canemus,
250   inque meo nullum carmine crimen erit."
ecquid ab hac omnes rigide summovimus Arte,
    quas stola contingi vittaque sumpta vetat?
"at matrona potest alienis artibus uti,
    quodque [3] trahat, quamvis non doceatur, habet."
255 nil igitur matrona legat, quia carmine ab omni
    ad delinquendum doctior esse potest.

---

[1] multis *corr. Bentley*   [2] tibi forte] fortasse   [3] quoque

---

[1] Tiberius.
[2] See *Ars amat.* i. 31–34. The verses are almost identical.
[3] The *instita* was a border or ruffle woven to the lower edge of
the matron's dress (*stola*).

bow and the standards once he seized; now through
thy son[1] Germany feels thy youthful vigour, and a
Caesar wars for a mighty Caesar. In fine, though
the body of the empire is vaster than has ever ex-
isted, no part is weak. The city also wearies thee,
and the guardianship of thy laws and of the morals
which thou dost desire to be like thine own, nor to
thy lot falls that repose thou bestowest upon the
nations, for thou art waging unremitting war
against vice.

[237] Can I wonder, then, that under this weight of
great affairs thou hast never unrolled the volume of
my jests ? Yet if, as I could wish, thou hadst
changed to have the leisure, thou wouldst have read
no crimes in my " Art." That poem, I admit, has
no serious mien, it is not worthy to be read by so
great a prince; but not for that reason is it opposed
to the commandments of the law, nor does it
offer teaching to the daughters of Rome. And that
thou may'st not doubt for whom I write the books,
one of the three has these four verses :[2] "Far from
me! ye narrow fillets, badge of modesty! and thou,
long ruffle[3] covering half the feet! I shall sing of
naught but what is lawful, of loves which men
allow. There shall be in my song no sin " Have I
not strictly excluded from this "Art" all women
whom the assumption of the robe and fillet of wedlock
protect ?

[253] But, thou mayst say, the matron can use arts
intended for others and has something to tempt her,
though she be not herself the pupil. Let the
matron read nothing then, for from every song
she can gain wisdom for sin. From whatever

quodcumque attigerit, siqua est studiosa sinistri,
    ad vitium mores instruet inde suos.
sumpserit Annales—nihil est hirsutius illis—
260   facta sit unde parens Ilia, nempe leget.
sumpserit Aeneadum genetrix ubi prima, requiret,
    Aeneadum genetrix unde sit alma Venus.
persequar inferius, modo si licet ordine ferri,
    posse nocere animis carminis omne genus.
265 non tamen idcirco crimen liber omnis habebit :
    nil prodest, quod non laedere possit idem.
igne quid utilius ? siquis tamen urere tacta
    comparat, audaces instruit igne manus.
eripit interdum, modo dat medicina salutem,
270   quaeque iuvet, monstrat, quaeque sit herba nocens.
et latro et cautus praecingitur ense viator ;
    ille sed insidias, hic sibi portat opem.
discitur innocuas ut agat facundia causas ;
    protegit haec sontes, inmeritosque premit.
275 sic igitur carmen, recta si mente legatur,
    constabit nulli posse nocere meum.
atque ortum vitium quicumque hinc [1] concipit, errat,
    et nimium scriptis arrogat ille meis.
ut tamen hoc fatear, ludi quoque semina praebent
280   nequitiae : tolli tota theatra iube !
peccandi causam quam multis saepta [2] dederunt,
    Martia cum durum sternit harena solum !
tollatur Circus ! non tuta licentia Circi est :
    hic sedet ignoto iuncta puella viro.

---

[1] at quasdam vitio ... hoc *corr. Madrig*   [2] saepe *corr.*
                          Damsté

---

[1] Probably the *Annals* of Ennius.
[2] The opening words of Lucretius' *De rerum natura*.
The Romans often refer to a work by citing the first words.

she touches, be she inclined to wrongdoing, she
will equip her character for vice. Let her take
up the *Annals* [1]—naught is ruder than they—she will
surely read by whom Ilia became a mother.
So soon as she takes up the "Aeneadum genetrix," [2]
she will ask by whom fostering Venus became the
mother of the Aeneadae. I will show later, if only I
may present it in order, that it is possible for the
soul to be injured by every kind of poem. Yet not
on that account shall every book be guilty. Nothing
is useful which cannot at the same time be injurious.
What more useful than fire? Yet whoever is making
ready to burn a house arms his criminal hands with
fire. Medicine sometimes removes, sometimes be-
stows safety, showing what plant is healthful, what
harmful. Both the brigand and the cautious way-
farer gird on a sword, but the one carries it for
treacherous attack, the other for his own
defence. Eloquence is learned for the conduct of
just causes; yet it protects the guilty and crushes the
innocent. So then with verse: if it be read with
upright mind, it will be established that it can injure
nobody—even though it be mine.

[277] Whoever believes that this has resulted
in depravity is mistaken and attributes too
much to my works. Even should I admit this
charge, the games also furnish the seeds of wrong
doing; order the abolition of all the theatres! To
how many have the voting enclosures proved a cause
of sin when the hard earth is covered with the sand of
Mars [3]! Abolish the Circus! The license of the
Circus is not safe, for here a girl may sit close to a

[3] *i.e.* the arena in which gladiatorial displays, etc.,
occurred.

75

OVID

285 cum quaedam spatientur in hoc,[1] ut amator eodem [2]
    conveniat, quare porticus ulla patet ?
quis locus est templis augustior ? haec quoque vitet,
    in culpam siqua est ingeniosa suam.
cum steterit Iovis aede, Iovis succurret in aede
290   quam multas matres fecerit ille deus.
proxima adoranti Iunonis templa subibit
    paelicibus multis hanc doluisse deam.
Pallade conspecta, natum de crimine virgo
    sustulerit quare, quaeret, Ericthonium.
295 venerit in magni templum, tua munera, Martis,
    state Venus Ultori iuncta, vir ante fores.
Isidis aede sedens, cur hanc Saturnia, quaeret,
    egerit Ionio Bosphorioque mari.
in Venerem Anchises, in Lunam Latmius heros,
300   in Cererem Iasion, qui referatur, erit.
omnia perversas possunt corrumpere mentes ;
    stant tamen ipsa[3] suis omnia tuta locis.
et procul a scripta solis meretricibus Arte
    summovet ingenuas pagina prima manus.
305 quaecumque irrupit, quo non sinit ire sacerdos,
    protinus huic[4] dempti criminis ipsa rea est.
nec tamen est facinus versus evolvere mollis ;
    multa licet castae non facienda legant.
saepe supercilii nudas matrona severi
310   et veneris stantis ad genus omne videt.
corpora Vestales oculi meretricia cernunt,
    nec domino poenae res ea causa fuit.

        [1] hac   [2] eadem   [3] illa *corr. Diggle*
               [4] haec : huic *Rothmaler*

---

   [1] After the battle of Actium Augustus built a temple to Mars,
the Avenger.
   [2] This probably refers to the statues of Venus Genetrix and
Mars by Arcesilaus. The goddess was depicted fully clothed,
perhaps a man's armour, and Cupid was shown gliding

strange man. Since certain women stroll in them, intent on meeting a lover there, why does any portico stand open ? What place more dignified than the temples ? But these too should be avoided by any woman whose nature inclines to fault. When she stands in Jupiter's temple, in Jupiter's temple it will occur to her how many that god has caused to be mothers.

[291] As she worships in the neighbouring temple of Juno, the thought will come upon her that many rivals have caused this goddess wrath. When she has looked on Pallas, she will ask why the virgin brought up Erichthonius, the child of sin. If she enters the temple of mighty Mars, thine own gift,[1] Venus stands close to the Avenger, in the guise of a man before the door.[2] If she sit in Isis' fane, she will ask why she was driven by Saturnia over the Ionian sea and the Bosporus. Anchises will remind her of Venus, the Latmian hero[3] of Luna, Iasion of Ceres. All things can corrupt perverted minds, yet all things stand harmless in their own proper places. Far from the "Art," written for courtesans alone, its first page warns the hands of upright women. Any woman who rushes into a place forbidden by a priest, forthwith removes from him the sin and becomes herself guilty. Nevertheless it is no crime to read tender verse ; the chaste may read much that they should not do. Often matrons of serious brow behold women nude, ready for every kind of lust. The eyes of Vestals behold the bodies of courtesans nor has that been the cause of punishment to their owner.

down in such a way as to form a bond (*iuncta*) between the divinities.　　　　　　　　[3] Endymion.

at cur in nostra nimia est lascivia Musa,
    curve meus cuiquam suadet amare liber ?
315 nil nisi peccatum manifestaque culpa fatenda est.
    paenitet ingenii iudiciique mei.
cur non Argolicis potius quae concidit armis
    vexata est iterum carmine Troia meo ?
cur tacui Thebas et vulnera mutua fratrum,
320   et septem portas, sub duce quamque suo ?
nec mihi materiam bellatrix Roma negabat,
    et pius est patriae facta referre labor.
denique cum meritis impleveris omnia, Caesar,
    pars mihi de multis una canenda fuit,
325 utque trahunt oculos radiantia lumina solis,
    traxissent animum sic tua facta meum.
arguor inmerito.   tenuis mihi campus aratur ;
    illud erat magnae fertilitatis opus.
non ideo debet pelago se credere, siqua
330   audet in exiguo ludere cumba lacu.
forsan—et hoc dubito—numeris levioribus aptus
    sim satis, in parvos sufficiamque modos :
at si me iubeas domitos Iovis igne Gigantes
    dicere, conantem debilitabit onus.
335 divitis ingenii est immania Caesaris acta
    condere, materia ne superetur opus.
et tamen ausus eram ; sed detrectare videbar,
    quodque nefas, damno viribus esse tuis.
ad leve rursus opus, iuvenalia carmina, veni,
340   et falso movi pectus amore meum.
non equidem vellem.   sed me mea fata trahebant,
    inque meas poenas ingeniosus eram.
ei mihi, quod didici ! cur me docuere parentes
    litteraque est oculos ulla morata meos ?

---

[1] Eteocles and Polynices.

³¹³ Yet why is my muse so wanton ?   Why does my book advise anybody to love ?   There is naught for me but confession of my error and my obvious fault : I repent of my talent and my tastes.   Why rather did I not harass once again in my song Troy, which fell before the Argive arms ?   Why was I silent of Thebes and the mutual wounds of the brothers,¹ and the seven gates each under command of its own leader ?   Warlike Rome did not refuse me a subject, and 'tis a pious task to tell the story of one's native land.   In fine, since thou hast filled the world with thy great deeds, Caesar, some one part of those many should have been the theme of my song, and as the glittering rays of the sun attract the eye, so thy exploits would have drawn forth my powers.   Undeservedly am I blamed. Poor is the field I plough ; that was a theme mighty and fruitful.   A skiff ought not to trust itself to the sea just because it ventures to disport itself in a little pool.   Perhaps (but even this I doubt) I am well enough suited to lighter verse, capable of humble measures ; but if thou shouldst bid me sing of the Giants conquered by Jove's lightning, the burden will weaken me in the attempt.   Only a rich mind can tell the tale of Caesar's mighty deeds if the theme is not to surpass the work.   Even so I made the venture, but methought I impaired the theme and—an impious thing—wrought injury to thy might.

³²⁹ I returned once more to my light task, the songs of youth, stimulating my breast with fictitious love.   Would that I had not !   But my fate drew me on to be clever to my own hurt.   Alas that I ever acquired learning !   Why did my parents teach me ?   Why did any letter ever beguile my eyes ?

345 haec tibi me invisum lascivia fecit, ob artes,
    quas ratus es vetitos sollicitare toros.
  sed neque me nuptae didicerunt furta magistro,
    quodque parum novit, nemo docere potest.
  sic ego delicias et mollia carmina feci,
350   strinxerit ut nomen fabula nulla meum.
  nec quisquam est adeo media de plebe maritus,
    ut dubius vitio sit pater ille meo.
  crede mihi, distant mores a carmine nostri—
    vita verecunda est, Musa iocosa mea—
355 magnaque pars mendax operum est et ficta meorum :
    plus sibi permisit compositore suo.
  nec liber indicum est animi, sed honesta voluptas [1];
    plurima mulcendis auribus apta feret.
  Accius esset atrox, conviva Terentius esset,
360   essent pugnaces quo fera bella canunt.
  denique composui teneros non solus amores :
    composito poenas solus amore dedi.
  quid, nisi cum multo Venerem confundere vino
    praecepit lyrici Teïa Musa senis ?
365 Lesbia quid docuit Sappho, nisi amare, puellas ?
    tuta tamen Sappho, tutus et ille fuit.
  nec tibi, Battiade, nocuit, quod saepe legenti
    delicias versu fassus es ipse tuas.
  fabula iucundi nulla est sine amore Menandri,
370   et solet hic pueris virginibusque legi.
  Ilias ipsa quid est aliud nisi adultera, de qua
    inter amatorem pugna virumque fuit ?
  quid prius est illic flamma Briseidos, utque
    fecerit iratos rapta puella duces ?

[1] voluntas

---

[1] 359–360 are the conclusion of a condition, "if this were not
true," implied in 357–358.

This wantonness has caused thee to hate me on account of the arts which thou didst think disturbed unions that all were forbidden to attack. But no brides have learned deceptions through my teaching; nobody can teach that of which he knows too little. I have composed songs of pleasure and love but in such fashion that no scandal has ever touched my name. No husband exists even amid the common people who doubts his fatherhood through sin of mine. I assure you, my character differs from my verse (my life is moral, my muse is gay), and most of my work, unreal and fictitious, has allowed itself more licence than its author has had. A book is not evidence of the writer's mind, but respectable entertainment; it will offer many things suited to charm the ear. Else [1] would Accius be cruel, Terence a reveller, or those would be quarrelsome who sing of fierce war.

[361] Moreover, not I alone have written tales of tender love, but for writing of love I alone have been punished. What but the union of love and lavish wine was the teaching of the lyric muse of the aged Tean bard [2]? What did Lesbian Sappho teach the girls if not love? Yet Sappho was secure, the Tean also was secure. It did not injure thee, scion of Battus,[3] that thou didst often in verse confess to the reader thy wanton pleasures. No play of charming Menander is free from love, yet he is wont to be read by boys and girls. The very *Iliad*—what is it but an adulteress about whom her lover and her husband fought? What occurs in it before the flaming passion for Briseis and the feud between the chiefs due to the seizure of the girl? What is

[2] Anacreon.   [3] Callimachus.

81

375 aut quid Odyssea est nisi femina propter amorem,
    dum vir abest, multis una petita procis ?
quis nisi Maeonides, Venerem Martemque ligatos
    narrat, in obsceno corpora prensa toro ?
unde nisi indicio magni sciremus Homeri
380   hospitis igne duas incaluisse deas ?
omne genus scripti gravitate tragoedia vincit :
    haec quoque materiam semper amoris habet.
num quid [1] in Hippolyto, nisi caecae flamma novercae ?
    nobilis est Canace fratris amore sui.
385 quid ? non Tantalides, agitante Cupidine currus,
    Pisaeam Phrygiis vexit eburnus equis ?
tingueret ut ferrum natorum sanguine mater,
    concitus a laeso fecit amore dolor.
fecit amor subitas volucres cum paelice regem,
390   quaeque suum luget nunc quoque mater Ityn.
si non Aëropen frater sceleratus amasset,
    aversos Solis non legeremus equos.
impia nec tragicos tetigisset Scilla cothurnos,
    ni patrium crinem desecuisset amor.
395 qui legis Electran et egentem mentis Oresten,[2]
    Aegisthi crimen Tyndaridosque legis.
nam quid de tetrico referam domitore Chimaerae,
    quem leto fallax hospita paene dedit ?
quid loquar Hermionen, quid te, Schoeneïa virgo,
400   teque, Mycenaeo Phoebas amata duci ?

---

       [1] namquid   [2] orestem

            [1] Penelope.
     [2] Circe and Calypso, who loved Ulysses.
             [3] Phaedra.
    [4] Pelops, who had an ivory shoulder.
     [5] Medea.   [6] Tereus.
   [7] *i.e.* would never have become a theme for tragedy.

the *Odyssey* except the story of one woman [1] wooed in her husband's absence for love's sake by many suitors ? Who but the Maeonian tells of Venus and Mars caught in bonds of unseemly love ? On whose evidence but that of great Homer should we know of two goddesses [2] on fire with passion for a guest ?

[381] Every kind of writing is surpassed in seriousness by tragedy, but this also constantly deals with the theme of love. Is there aught in the *Hippolytus* except the blind passion of a stepmother [3] ? Canace's fame is due to her love for her brother. Again, did not the ivory scion [4] of Tantalus, while Cupid drove the car, bear away the Pisan maiden with his Phrygian horses ? The mother [5] who stained her sword with the blood of her children was roused to the deed by the anger of slighted love. Love suddenly transformed into birds the king [6] with his paramour, and that mother who still mourns her son Itys. If her accused brother had not loved Aërope we should not read about the horses of the Sun turning aside. Wicked Scylla would never have touched the tragic buskin [7] had not love caused her to cover her father's lock. You who read of Electra and crazed Orestes are reading of the guilt of Aegisthus and Tyndareus' daughter.[8] Why should I tell of the dread conqueror [9] of the Chimaera whom a deceitful hostess brought near to death ? Why speak of Hermione, why of thee, maiden daughter [10] of Schoeneus, and of thee,[11] priestess of Phoebus, beloved by the Mycenean

[8] Clytaemestra. [9] Bellerophon.
[10] Atalanta. [11] Cassandra.

quid Danaën Danaësque nurum matremque Lyaei
    Haemonaque et noctes cui coiere duae ?
quid Peliae generum, quid Thesea, quique [1] Pelasgum
    Iliacam tetigit de rate primus humum ?
405 huc Iole Pyrrhique parens, huc Herculis uxor,
    huc accedat Hylas Iliacusque puer.
tempore deficiar, tragicos si persequar ignes,
    vixque meus capiet nomina nuda liber.
est et in obscenos commixta [2] tragoedia risus,
410   multaque praeteriti verba pudoris habet ;
nec nocet auctori, mollem qui fecit Achillem,
    infregisse suis fortia facta modis.
iunxit Aristides Milesia crimina secum,
    pulsus Aristides nec tamen urbe sua est.
415 nec qui descripsit corrumpi semina matrum,
    Eubius, impurae conditor historiae,
nec qui composuit nuper Sybaritica, fugit,
    nec qui concubitus non tacuere suos.
suntque ea doctorum monumentis mixta [3] virorum,
420   muneribusque ducum publica facta patent.
neve peregrinis tantum defendar ab armis,
    et Romanus habet multa iocosa liber.
utque suo Martem cecinit gravis Ennius ore—
    Ennius ingenio maximus, arte rudis—
425 explicat ut causas rapidi Lucretius ignis,
    casurumque triplex vaticinatur opus,

[1] quidve *vel* quisve *corr. Ehwald*
[2] deflexa   [3] saxa *vel* texta

---

[1] Agamemnon.   [2] Andromeda.
[3] Semele, mother of Bacchus.
[4] Alcmena.   [5] Admetus.
[6] Protesilaus.   [7] Deidamia.
[8] Deianira.   [9] Ganymede.

leader [1] ?   Why of Danaë and of Danaë's daughter-in-law,[2] of the mother [3] of Lyaeus, of Haemon, and of her [4] for whom two nights combined ?   Why speak of Pelias' son-in-law,[5] of Theseus, and of him [6] who first of the Pelasgians touched the soil of Ilium ?   To these add Iole, and the mother [7] of Pyrrhus, the wife [8] of Hercules, Hylas, and the Ilian boy.[9]   Time will fail if I tell all the loves of tragedy, and my book will scarce hold the bare names.

[409] There is too a tragedy involved in coarse laughter, containing many terms of shamelessness ; and the author [10] who depicted Achilles tender with love does not suffer for having weakened by his verses deeds of valour.   Aristides connected the vices of Miletus with himself, yet Aristides was not driven from his own city.   Neither Eubius, who described the destruction of the mother's seed, the composer of a foul tale, nor he [11] who recently wrote the *Sybaritica*, were exiled, nor those who have not concealed their own erotic adventures.   And those things exist among the memorials of learned men and through the gifts of our leaders have become public property open to all.[12]

[421] And I need not defend myself with foreign arms only, for Roman books also contain much that is frivolous.   Though Ennius lent his lips to the serious strains of war—Ennius mighty in genius, rude in art—though Lucretius sets forth the causes of scorching flame and prophesies the destruction of

[10] Unknown.   The theme was probably Achilles' love for Patroclus.
[11] Hemitheon.
[12] *i.e.* such compositions may be found in the public libraries.

sic sua lascivo cantata est saepe Catullo
 femina, cui falsum Lesbia nomen erat ;
nec contentus ea, multos vulgavit amores,
430 in quibus ipse suum fassus adulterium est.
par fuit exigui similisque licentia Calvi,
 detexit variis qui sua furta modis.
quid referam Ticidae, quid Memmi carmen, apud
  quos
 rebus adest nomen nominibusque pudor ?
435 Cinna quoque his comes est, Cinnaque procacior
  Anser,
 et leve Cornifici parque Catonis opus.
et quorum libris modo dissimulata Perillae [1]
 nomine, nunc legitur dicta Metella suo.[2]
is quoque, Phasiacas Argo qui duxit in undas,
440 non potuit Veneris furta tacere suae.
nec minus Hortensi, nec sunt minus improba Servi
 carmina. quis dubitet nomina tanta sequi ?
vertit Aristiden Sisenna, nec obfuit illi
 historiae turpis inseruisse iocos.
445 non fuit opprobrio celebrasse Lycorida Gallo,
 sed linguam nimio non tenuisse mero.
credere iuranti durum putat esse Tibullus,
 sic etiam de se quod neget illa viro.
fallere custodes idem [3] docuisse fatetur,
450 seque sua miserum nunc ait arte premi.
saepe, velut gemmam dominae signumve probaret,
 per causam meminit se tetigisse manum ;

---

[1] per illos : Perillae *s*   [2] Metelle tuo *corr. Heinsius*
   [3] custodem tandem (*vel* demum) *corr. Francius*

---

[1] One of these was Ticidas, *cf.* Apuleius, *Apol.* 10.
[2] See Index *s.v.* Perilla.

three elements, yet wanton Catullus sang oft of her who was falsely called Lesbia, and not content with her he noised abroad many other loves in which he admitted his own intrigues. Equal in degree and of the same kind was the licence of diminutive Calvus, who revealed his own love adventures in various metres. Why allude to the verse of Ticidas or of Memmius, in whom things are named—with names devoid of shame ? With them Cinna too belongs and Anser, more wanton than Cinna, and the light poems of Cornificius and of Cato, and those [1] in whose books Metella is now disguised beneath the name of Perilla [2] and now referred to with her own. He,[3] too, who guided the Argo to the waters of Phasis, could not keep silent about his own adventures in love. Hortensius' verses and those of Servius are not less wanton. Who would hesitate to imitate these mighty names? Sisenna translated Aristides and was not harmed for writing lewd jests side by side with his histories. It was no reproach to Gallus that he gave fame to Lycoris, but that from too much wine he did not restrain his tongue. Tibullus [4] thinks it hard to believe his lady under oath because she makes the same denials about himself to her lord. He admits, too, teaching her how to deceive her guard, saying that he is now in his wretchedness overcome by his own ruse. Often on the pretext of trying the gem and seal of his mistress he recalls that he touched her hand; he

---

[3] Varro of Atax, who wrote an *Argonautica*.

[4] In this passage (through v. 460) Ovid paraphrases parts of Tibull. i. 5 and i. 6 in which the poet becomes the victim at the hands of his faithless Delia of the very deceits he had taught her.

utque refert, digitis saepe est nutuque locutus,
    et tacitam mensae duxit in orbe notam ;
455 et quibus e sucis abeat de corpore livor,
    impresso fieri qui solet ore, docet :
denique ab incauto nimium petit ille marito,
    se quoque uti servet, peccet ut illa minus.
scit, cui latretur, cum solus obambulet, ipsas [1]
460   cur [2] totiens clausas excreet ante fores,
multaque dat furti talis praecepta docetque
    qua nuptae possint fallere ab arte viros.
non fuit hoc illi fraudi, legiturque Tibullus
    et placet, et iam te principe notus erat.
465 invenies eadem blandi praecepta Properti :
    destrictus minima nec tamen ille nota est.
his ego successi, quoniam praestantia candor
    nomina vivorum dissimulare iubet.
non timui, fateor, ne, qua tot iere carinae,
470   naufraga servatis omnibus una foret.
sunt aliis scriptae, quibus alea luditur, artes :—
    hoc erat ad nostros non leve crimen avos—
quid valeant tali, quo possis plurima iactu

----

    [1] ipse *corr. Owen*   [2] cui *vel* qui : cur *s*

----

  [1] Perhaps *quis* for *cur* (ALW) : "who is coughing, etc."
Cf. Tib. i. 5. 74 f.
  [2] *i.e.* Tibullus was expert in detecting the presence of a
rival.
  [3] About 26 B.C.
  [4] Lines 471–482 are obscure because Ovid, writing
for readers familiar with the subject, uses technical terms and
gives only a hint or two to indicate each game. Even
with the help of the full evidence which has been collected
in such handbooks as Marquardt's *Privatleben der Römer*,
ii. pp. 855 ff., and Becker-Göll, *Gallus*, iii. pp. 455–480,
these games are far from being fully understood. Moreover

tells how ofttimes he spoke by means of his fingers or
by nods and drew inarticulate marks upon the table's
round; and he teaches what lotions cause to vanish
from the body the bruises which are often caused by
the mouth's imprint: at last he prays her all too
careless partner to watch him also that so her sins
may be less frequent. He knows who causes the
barking, as a man strolls alone before the house,
why [1] there is so much coughing just before the closed
door.[2] He gives teachings of many sorts for such an
intrigue, showing brides by what arts ladies can
deceive their lords. This did not injure him, for
Tibullus is still read with favour; he was famous when
thou wert first called prince.[3]

[465] Thou wilt find the same teachings in alluring
Propertius; yet not the least shame has touched
him. I was their successor, for generosity bids me
withhold the names of prominent living men. I
feared not, I admit, that where so many barks plied,
one only would be wrecked while all the rest were
safe.

[471] Others have written of the arts of playing at
dice [4]—this was no light sin in the eyes of our
ancestors—what is the value of the *tali*,[5] with what

the text is not certain in vv. 474, 479. I have appended notes
based on such information as we have.

[5] Roman dice were of two sorts: the *tali*, made from
bones of small animals and other materials, with four long
faces, two of which were broad (numbered 3, 4), two narrow
(1, 6); and the *tesserae*, cubical and marked in the same
way as our dice. The highest throw with the *tali* was the
Venus (1, 3, 4, 6), the lowest the *Canis* (four aces.) Three
(or two) *tesserae*, were usually employed, but we have no
trustworthy information concerning the highest and lowest
throws.

OVID

figere,[1] damnosos effugiasque canes;
475 tessera quos habeat numeros, distante vocato
mittere quo deceat, quo dare missa modo;
discolor ut recto grassetur limite miles,
cum medius gemino calculus hoste perit,
ut dare bella [2] sequens [3] sciat et revocare priorem,
480 nec tuto fugiens incomitatus eat;
parva sit ut ternis [4] instructa tabella lapillis,
in qua vicisse est continuasse suos;
quique alii lusus—neque enim nunc persequar
omnes—
perdere, rem caram, tempora nostra solent.

[1] fingere
[2] mare (vel mage vel male) velle corr. Landi   [3] sequi
  [4] sed uternis (vel internis vel interius) corr. Ehwald

---

[1] This probably refers to the game called πλειστοβολίνδα
(cf. plurima iactu and valeant) in which the highest throw
depended on the total number of units, cf. Pollux, ix. 95 and
117. Figere (fingere?) is a technical term not occurring
elsewhere.

[2] Numeros seems to refer, not to the numbers of the dice,
but to the significance of these numbers in the game—the
"count."

[3] In 475–476 some scholars (e.g. Göll, Gallus, p. 475)
find a reference to the game called duodecim scripta, which
was in some respects like backgammon. It was played
on a board with 12 lines (duodecim scripta) with 15 pieces
on a side which were moved forwards and backwards accord-
ing to the throws of the dice. But it is more probable that
this couplet (and also Ars amat. iii. 355–356) refer to a game
in which there were several sides or contestants. Each
player had to decide at the throw of the dice which side or
player to "join" (subire), which to "challenge" (=vocare,
provocare), cf. Brandt on Ars amat. 353 f., 205. As in
duod. script. the moves were conditioned by the throws

90

throw one can make the highest point,[1] avoiding the
ruinous dogs ; how the *tessera* is counted,[2] and when
the opponent is challenged, how it is fitting to throw,
how to move according to the throws ;[3] how the
variegated soldier steals to the attack along
the straight path when the piece between two
enemies is lost, and how he understands warfare by
pursuit and how to recall the man before him and
to retreat in safety not without escort ;[4] how a
small board is provided with three men on a side
and victory lies in keeping one's men abreast ;[5] and
the other games—I will not now describe them
all—which are wont to waste that precious thing,
our time.

(*dare missa*). I take *distante vocato*, a phrase which has given
rise to many conjectures, as referring to the " challenging " of
an adversary or side.

[4] Vv. 477-480 refer to the *ludus latrunculorum*, a game in
some respects resembling chess but on the whole more like
draughts. It was played with 30 pieces on each side on a board
marked in squares. At least two kinds of pieces can
be distinguished : *latrones* (*bellatores, milites* ?), " officers," and
others called collectively *mandra*, " herd," " drive," *i.e.*
" pawns " (?). Some scholars consider the *milites* to have been
different from the *latrones*. The pieces or men were white,
black, or (more commonly in the case of the *latrones*)
variegated. Some (the *latrones* ?) had greater freedom of
movement (*vagi*) than others (*ordinarii*) but the only moves
definitely known were straight forward and backward. Some
pieces could be checkmated and these were then called *inciti*,
and men could be " taken " by being caught between two
opponents. It was important to advance men in pairs so as to
support each other.

[5] This game seems to have resembled a game of draughts
played with few men. It is mentioned also in *Ars amat.* iii. 365
f. and Isidor. *Orig.* xviii. 64. In the German *Mühlespiel* (a sort
of draughts) the detail of keeping three men close together in a
line is also present.

485 ecce canit formas alius iactusque pilarum,
    hic artem nandi praecipit, ille trochi.
composita est aliis fucandi cura coloris;
    hic epulis leges hospitioque dedit;
alter humum, de qua fingantur pocula, monstrat,
490   quaeque, docet, liquido testa sit apta mero.
talia luduntur fumoso mense Decembri,
    quae damno nulli composuisse fuit.
his ego deceptus non tristia carmina feci,
    sed tristis nostros poena secuta iocos.
495 nempe (nec invideo) [1] tot de scribentibus unus,
    quem sua perdiderit Musa, repertus ego.
quid, si scripsissem mimos obscena iocantes,
    qui semper vetiti crimen amoris habent,
in quibus assidue cultus procedit adulter,
500   verbaque dat stulto callida nupta viro?
nubilis hos virgo matronaque virque puerque
    spectat, et ex magna parte senatus adest.
nec satis incestis temerari vocibus aures;
    adsuescunt oculi multa pudenda pati:
505 cumque fefellit amans aliqua novitate maritum,
    plauditur et magno palma favore datur;
quoque [2] minus prodest, scaena [3] est lucrosa poetae,
    tantaque non parvo crimina praetor emit.
inspice ludorum sumptus, Auguste, tuorum:
510   empta tibi magno talia multa leges.
haec tu spectasti spectandaque saepe dedisti—
    maiestas adeo comis ubique tua est—

[1] denique nec video *corr. Diggle*
[2] quodque   [3] poena : scaena *Heumann*

---

[1] The officials in charge of the games (aediles, praetors) paid most of the expenses.

⁴⁸⁵ See, another tells in verse of the various forms of balls and the way they are thrown; this one instructs in the art of swimming, that in the art of the hoop. Others have composed works on tinting the complexion, another has laid down rules for feasts and entertaining; still another describes the clay from which bowls are fashioned, teaching what jar is adapted to the clear wire. Such playful verses as these are written in smoky December, but nobody had been ruined for composing them. Beguiled by such as these I wrote verse lacking in seriousness, but a serious penalty has befallen my jests. Truly, I am the only one singled out from so many writers (and I bear them no ill-will) to be ruined by his muse.

⁴⁹⁷ What if I had written foul-jesting mimes which always contain the sin of forbidden love, in which constantly a well-dressed adulterer appears and the artful wife fools her stupid husband? These are viewed by the marriageable maiden, the wife, the husband, and the child; even the senate in large part is present. Nor is it enough that the ear is outraged with impure words; the eyes grow accustomed to many shameful sights, and when the lover has deceived the husband by some novel trick, there is applause and he is presented amid great favour with the palm. The more the stage is immoral, it is profitable to the poet, and these great immoralities are bought at no small price by the praetor.¹ Run over the expenses of thine own games, Augustus, and thou wilt read of many things of this sort that cost thee dear. These thou hast thyself viewed and oft presented to the view of others—so benign is thy majesty everywhere—

luminibusque tuis, totus quibus utitur orbis,
    scaenica vidisti lentus adulteria.
515 scribere si fas est imitantes turpia mimos,
    materiae minor est debita poena meae.
an genus hoc scripti faciunt sua pulpita tutum,
    quodque licet, mimis scaena licere dedit ?
et mea sunt populo saltata poemata saepe,
520   saepe oculos etiam detinuere tuos.
scilicet in domibus nostris [1] ut prisca virorum
    artificis fulgent corpora picta manu,
sic quae concubitus varios venerisque figuras
    exprimat, est aliquo parva tabella loco.
525 utque sedet vultu fassus Telamonius iram,
    inque oculis facinus barbara mater habet,
sic madidos siccat digitis Venus uda capillos
    et modo maternis tecta videtur aquis.
bella sonat alii telis instructa cruentis,
530   parsque tui generis, pars tua facta canunt.
invida me spato natura coercuit arto,
    ingenio vires exiguasque dedit.
et tamen ille tuae felix Aeneidos auctor
    contulit in Tyrios arma virumque toros,
535 nec legitur pars ulla magis de corpore toto,
    quam non legitimo foedere iunctus amor.
Phyllidis hic idem teneraeque Amaryllidis ignes
    bucolicis iuvenis luserat ante modis.
nos quoque iam pridem scripto peccavimus isto :
540   supplicium patitur non nova culpa novum ;
carminaque edideram, cum te delicta notantem
    praeterii totiens irrevocatus [2] eques.

---

[1] vestris *corr.* s   [2] inrequietus *corr. Bentley*

---

[1] Ajax.   [2] Medea.
[3] Apelles' famous picture of Venus rising from the sea.

and with thine eyes, by which the whole world profits, thou hast gazed undisturbed at these adulteries of the stage. If 'tis right to compose mimes that copy vice, to my themes a smaller penalty is due.

[517] Can it be that this type of writing is rendered safe by the stage to which it belongs—that the licence of the mimes has been granted by the theatre ? My poems too have often been presented to the people with dancing, often they have even beguiled thine own eyes. Surely in our houses, even as figures of old heroes shine, painted by an artist's hand, so in some place a small tablet depicts the varying unions and forms of love ; there sits not only the Telamonian [1] with features confessing wrath and the barbarian mother [2] with crime in her eyes, but Venus as well, wringing her damp hair with her hands and seeming barely covered by her maternal waves.[3] Some sing of the roar of war and its bloody weapons, some of the deeds of thy race, and some of thine own. As for me—grudging nature has confined me within a narrow space, granting me but meagre powers. And yet the blessed author of thy *Aeneid* brought his "arms and the man" to a Tyrian couch, and no part of the whole work is more read than that union of illicit love. The same man had written as a youth playful verse of the passion of Phyllis and tender Amaryllis—all in pastoral strains.[4] Long ago I too sinned in that style of composition—thus a fault not new is suffering a new penalty—and I had published verse when thou wert censuring our sins and I passed thee so many times, a knight uncriticized.[5]

---

[4] The *Eclogues*.   [5] *Cf.* v. 90.

ergo quae iuvenis mihi non nocitura putavi
   scripta parum prudens, nunc nocuere seni.
545 sera redundavit veteris vindicta libelli,
   distat et a meriti tempore poena sui.
ne tamen omne meum credas opus esse remissum,
   saepe dedi nostrae grandia vela rati.
sex ego Fastorum scripsi totidemque libellos,
550   cumque suo finem mense volumen habet,
idque tuo nuper scriptum sub nomine, Caesar,
   et tibi sacratum sors mea rupit opus ;
et dedimus tragicis sceptrum regale tyrannis,[1]
   quaeque gravis debet verba cothurnus habet ;
555 dictaque sunt nobis, quamvis manus ultima coeptis
   defuit, in facies corpora versa novas.
atque utinam revoces animum paulisper ab ira,
   et vacuo iubeas hinc tibi pauca legi,
pauca, quibus prima surgens ab origine mundi
560   in tua deduxi tempora, Caesar, opus !
aspicies, quantum dederis mihi pectoris ipse,
   quoque favore animi teque tuosque canam.
non ego mordaci destrinxi carmine quemquam,
   nec meus ullius crimina versus habet.
565 candidus a salibus suffusis felle refugi :
   nulla venenato littera mixta ioco est.
inter tot populi, tot scriptis, milia nostri,
   quem mea Calliope laeserit, unus ego.
non igitur nostris ullum gaudere Quiritem
570   auguror, at multos indoluisse malis ;
nec mihi credibile est, quemquam insultasse iacenti
   gratia candori si qua relata meo est.

---

[1] scriptum r. cothurnis *corr. Housman*

---

[1] We must infer that Ovid drafted all twelve books, but
brought only six to a state fit for publication ; these he
dedicated in exile to Germanicus.

Thus the writings which in my youth all thoughtless I supposed would harm me not, have harmed me now that I am old.   Late and overfull is the vengeance for that early book, distant is the penalty from the time of the sin.

[547] Yet think not all my work trivial; oft have I set grand sails upon my bark. Six books of *Fasti* and as many more have I written, each containing its own month.   This work did I recently compose, Caesar, under thy name, dedicated to thee,[1] but my fate has broken it off.   I have also given to the kings of tragedy their royal sceptre and speech suited to the buskin's dignity.[2]   I sang also, though my attempt lacked the final touch, of bodies changed into new forms.[3]   Would that thou mightest recall thy temper awhile from wrath and bid a few lines of this be read to thee when thou art at leisure, the few lines[4] in which after beginning with the earliest origin of the world I have brought the work to thy times, Caesar!   Thou wilt see how much heart thou hast thyself given me, with what warmth I sing of thee and thine.   I have never injured anybody with a mordant poem, my verse contains charges against nobody.   Ingenuous I have shunned wit steeped in gall not letter of mine is dipped in poisoned jest.   Amid all the myriads of our people, many as are my writings, I am the only one whom my own Calliope has injured.   No citizen then, I feel sure, rejoices in my woes, but many grieve.   Nor can I believe that anyone has mocked my fall, if any indulgence has been granted to my open heart.

[2] The *Medea*, a tragedy, not extant. [3] The *Metamorphoses*.
[4] *Cf. Metam.* xv. 745–870, where Julius Caesar and Augustus are praised.

97

his, precor, atque aliis possint tua numina flecti,
    o pater, o patriae cura salusque tuae !
575 non ut in Ausoniam redeam, nisi forsitan olim,
    cum longo poenae tempore victus eris ;
tutius exilium pauloque quietius oro,
    ut par delicto sit mea poena suo.

May this, I pray, and other things have power to bend
thy will, O father, O protector and salvation of thy
native land : not that I may return to Ausonia, unless
perchance some day thou shalt be overborne by the
length of my punishment ; I only beg a safer, a more
peaceful place of exile, slight though the change be,
that the punishment may match my wrongdoing.

LIBER TERTIUS

I.

" Missus in hanc venio timide liber exulis urbem :
    da placidam fesso, lector amice, manum ;
neve reformida, ne sim tibi forte pudori :
    nullus in hac charta versus amare docet.
5 haec domini fortuna mei est, ut debeat illam
    infelix nullis dissimulare iocis.
id quoque, quod viridi quondam male lusit in aevo,
    heu nimium sero damnat et odit opus !
inspice quid portem : nihil hic nisi triste videbis,
10   carmine temporibus conveniente suis.
clauda quod alterno subsidunt carmina versu,
    vel pedis hoc ratio, vel via longa facit ;
quod neque sum cedro flavus [1] nec pumice levis,
    erubui domino cultior esse meo ;
15 littera suffusas quod habet maculosa lituras,
    laesit opus lacrimis ipse poeta suum.
siqua videbuntur casu non dicta Latine,
    in qua scribebat, barbara terra fuit.
dicite, lectores, si non grave, qua sit eundum,
20   quasque petam sedes hospes in urbe liber.''

[1] fulvus

---

[1] The *Ars amatoria.*
[2] The elegiac couplet is often spoken of as " lame " because of
the unequal length of the verses.

100

BOOK III

I. Proem

"Though sent to this city I come in fear, an exile's book. Stretch forth a kindly hand to me in my weariness, friendly reader, and fear not that I may perchance bring shame upon you; not a line on this paper teaches love. Such is my master's fate that the wretched man ought not to conceal it with any jests. Even that work [1] which once was his ill-starred amusement in the green of youth, too late, alas! he condemns and hates. Examine what I bring: you will see nothing here except sadness, and the verse befits its own state. If the lame couplets halt in alternate verses, 'tis due to the metre's nature [2] or to the length of the journey; if I am not golden with oil of cedar nor smoothed with the pumice, 'tis because I blushed to be better dressed than my master; if the letters are spotted and blurred with erasures, 'tis because the poet with tears has injured his own work. If any expressions perchance shall seem not Latin, the land wherein he wrote was a barbarian land. Tell me, readers, if it is not a trouble, whither I ought to go, what abode I, a book from foreign lands, should seek in the city."

101

haec ubi sum furtim lingua titubante locutus,
    qui mihi monstraret, vix fuit unus, iter.
"di tibi dent, nostro quod non tribuere poetae,
    molliter in patria vivere posse tua.
25 duc age! namque sequar, quamvis terraque marique
    longinquo referam lassus ab orbe pedem."
paruit, et ducens "haec sunt fora Caesaris," inquit,
    "haec est a sacris quae via nomen habet,
hic locus est Vestae, qui Pallada servat et ignem,
30   haec fuit antiqui regia parva Numae."
inde petens dextram "porta est" ait "ista Palati,
    hic Stator, hoc primum condita Roma loco est."
singula dum miror, video fulgentibus armis
    conspicuos postes tectaque digna deo,
35 et "Iovis haec" dixi "domus est?" quod ut esse
      putarem,
    augurium menti querna corona dabat.
cuius ut accepi dominum, "non fallimur," inquam,
    "et magni verum est hanc Iovis esse domum.
cur tamen opposita [1] velatur ianua lauro,
40   cingit et augustas arbor opaca fores [2]?
num quia perpetuos meruit domus ista triumphos,
    an quia Leucadio semper amata deo est?
ipsane quod festa est, an quod facit omnia festa?
    quam tribuit terris, pacis an ista nota est?

---

      [1] apposita.   [2] comas.

---

    [1] The Sacred Way.
    [2] The temple of Vesta contained the Palladium (image of Pallas) which fell from heaven at Troy.
    [3] Jupiter Stator.
    [4] The oaken wreath was given to Augustus as saviour of the citizens, but the oak was also sacred to Jove.
    [5] Augustus' house was (by a degree of the senate) kept

[21] When thus I had spoken timidly, with hesitant tongue, I found with difficulty just one to show me the way.

[23] "May the gods grant you what they have not vouchsafed our poet, the power to live at ease in your native land—come, lead me ; I will follow, though by land and sea I come in weariness from a distant world."

[27] He obeyed, and as he guided me, said, "This is Caesar's forum ; this is the street named from the sacred rites.[1] This is the place of Vesta guarding Pallas [2] and the fire, here was once the tiny palace of ancient Numa. Then turning to the right, "That," he said, "is the gate of the Palatium. Here is Stator[3] ; on this spot first was Rome founded." While I was marvelling at one thing after another, I beheld doorposts marked out from others by gleaming arms and a dwelling worthy of a god !

[35] "Is this also Jove's abode," I said, and for such thought an oaken wreath [4] gave to my mind the augury. And when I learned its master, I said, "No error is mine ; it is true that this is the home of mighty Jove. But why is the door screened by the laurels before it, their dark foliage surrounding the august portals ? Can it be because that home has deserved unending triumph or because it has always been loved by the Leucadian [5] god ? Is it because the house itself is full of joy or because it fills all things with joy ? Is it a mark of that peace which it has given to the world ? And as

continually adorned with oak and laurel, triumphal insignia. His victory at Actium occurred near the temple of Leucadian Apollo and he honoured Apollo above all other gods.

45 utque viret semper laurus nec fronde caduca
   carpitur, aeternum sic habet illa decus ?
   causa superpositae scripto est testata coronae :
   servatos cives indicat huius ope.
   adice servatis unum, pater optime, civem,
50   qui procul extremo pulsus in orbe latet,
   in quo poenarum, quas se meruisse fatetur,
   non facinus causam, sed suus error habet.
   me miserum ! vereorque locum vereorque potentem,
   et quatitur trepido littera nostra metu.
55 aspicis exsangui chartam pallere colore ?
   aspicis alternos intremuisse pedes ?
   quandocumque, precor, nostro placere parenti
   isdem et ¹ sub dominis aspiciare domus ! ''
   inde tenore pari gradibus sublimia celsis
60   ducor ad intonsi candida templa dei,
   signa peregrinis ubi sunt alterna columnis,
   Beïides et stricto barbarus ense pater,
   quaeque viri docto veteres cepere novique
   pectore, lecturis inspicienda patent.
65 quaerebam fratres, exceptis scilicet illis,
   quos suus optaret non genuisse pater.
   quaerentem frustra custos me ² sedibus illis
   praepositus sancto iussit abire loco.
   altera templa peto, vicino, iuncta theatro :
70   haec quoque erant pedibus non adeunda meis.

---

¹ et *om. codd. add. Itali*   ² e *corr. Heinsius*

---

¹ *i.e.* Augustus and his family.
² In the portico of the temple of Apollo on the Palatine
(built by Augustus) were the figures of Danaus and his
daughters.
³ Augustus had established a library in the temple of
Apollo.
⁴ The other works of Ovid.

the laurel is ever green with no withering leaves to be plucked away, so does that house possess an eternal glory?

[47] The reason for the crowning wreath is shown by an inscription: it declares that by his aid citizens have been saved. Add, O best of fathers, to those whom thou hast saved one citizen who far on the world's edge lies in forgotten exile, the cause of whose punishment, which he admits that he has deserved, is not a deed, but his own mistake. Wretched me! I fear the spot, I fear the man of power, my script wavers with shuddering dread. See you my paper pale with bloodless colour? See you each alternate foot tremble? Sometime, I pray, mayst thou, O palace, be reconciled with him who fathered me, and may it be his lot to behold thee under the same masters[1]!"

[59] Then with even pace up the lofty steps I was conducted to the shining temple of the unshorn god, where alternating with the columns of foreign marble stand the figures of the Belids,[2] the barbarian father with a drawn sword, and all those things which the men of old or of modern times conceived in their learned souls are free for the inspection of those who would read[3] I was seeking my brothers,[4] save those indeed whom their father would he had never begot, and as I sought to no purpose, from the abode the guard who presides over the holy place commanded me to depart.[5] A second temple I approached, one close to a theatre:[6] this too might not be visited by my feet.

[5] Ovid's works had been placed under the ban, cf. v. 79.

[6] Augustus had founded another library in the *porticus Octavia*, near the theatre of Marcellus.

nec me, quae doctis patuerunt prima libellis,
    atria Libertas tangere passa sua est.
in genus auctoris miseri fortuna redundat,
    et ferimus [1] nati, quam tulit ipse, fugam.
75 forsitan et nobis olim minus asper et illi
    evictus longo tempore Caesar erit.
    di, precor, atque adeo—neque enim mihi turba
       roganda est—
    Caesar, ades voto, maxime dive, meo!
interea, quoniam statio mihi publica clausa est,
80   privato liceat delituisse loco.
    vos quoque, si fas est, confusa pudore repulsae
    sumite plebeiae carmina nostra manus.

II.

Ergo erat in fatis Scythiam quoque visere nostris,
    quaeque Lycaonio terra sub aze iacet;
nec vos, Pierides, nec stirps Letoïa, vestro
    docta sacerdoti turba tulistis opem.
5 nec mihi, quod lusi vero sine crimine, prodest,
    quodque magis vita Musa iocata [2] mea est,
plurima sed pelago terraque pericula passum
    ustus ab assiduo frigore Pontus habet.
quique fugax rerum securaque in otia natus,
10   mollis et inpatiens ante laboris eram,
ultima nunc patior, nec me mare portubus orbum
    perdere, diversae nec potuere viae;
suffecitque [3] malis animus; nam corpus ab illo
    accepit vires vixque ferenda tulit.

---

    [1] patimur *corr. Hall*   [2] *iocosa*   [3] *sufficit atque*

    [1] The library in the temple of Liberty was founded by Asinius
Pollio.

Nor did Liberty allow me to touch her halls, the first that were opened to learned books.[1]   The fate of our unfortunate sire overflows upon his offspring, and we suffer at our birth the exile which he has borne. Perhaps sometime both to us and to him Caesar conquered by long years will be less severe.   O gods, or rather (for it is not meet that I should pray to a throng), Caesar, mightiest of gods, hearken to my prayer !   In the meanwhile, since a public resting-place is closed to me, may it be granted me to lie hidden in some private spot.   You too, hands of the people, receive, if you may, our verses dismayed by the shame of their rejection.

II. Better Death than Exile

So then 'twas fated for me to visit even Scythia, the land that lies beneath the Lycaonian pole ; neither you, ye learned throng of Pierians, nor you, O son of Leto, have aided your own priest.   It avails me not that without real guilt I wrote playful verse, that my Muse was merrier than my life, but many are the perils by land and sea that I have undergone, and now the Pontus shrivelled with constant frost possesses me.   I, who once shunned affairs, who was born for a care-free life of ease, who was soft and incapable of toil, am now suffering extremes ; no harbourless sea, no far journeys by land have been able to destroy me.   And my spirit has proved equal to misfortune ; for my body, borrowing strength from that spirit, has endured things scarce endurable.

107

15 dum tamen et terris dubius iactabar et undis,
  fallebat curas aegraque corda labor :
ut via finita est et opus requievit eundi,
  et poenae tellus est mihi tacta meae,
nil nisi flere libet, nec nostro parcior imber
20 lumine, de verna quam nive manat aqua.
Roma domusque subit desideriumque locorum,
  quicquid et amissa restat in urbe mei.
ei mihi, quod [1] totiens nostri pulsata sepulcri
  ianua sub nullo tempore aperta fuit !
25 cur ego tot gladios fugi totiensque minata
  obruit infelix nulla procella caput ?
di, quos experior nimium constanter iniquos,
  participes irae quos deus unus habet,
exstimulate, precor, cessantia fata meique
30 interitus clausas esse vetate fores !

III.

Haec mea si casu miraris epistula quare
  alterius digitis scripta sit, aeger eram.
aeger in extremis ignoti partibus orbis,
  incertusque meae nempe [2] salutis eram.
5 quem mihi nunc animum dira regione iacenti
  inter Sauromatas esse Getasque putes ?
nec caelum patior, nec aquis adsuevimus istis,
  terraque nescio quo non placet ipsa modo.
non domus apta satis, non hic cibus utilis aegro,
10 nullus, Apollinea qui levet arte malum,
non qui soletur, non qui labentia tarde
  tempora narrando fallat, amicus adest.

---

  [1] quo   [2] paene *corr. Hall*

  [1] *Augustus.*

[15] Yet while I was being driven through the perils of land and wave, there was beguilement for my cares and my sick heart in the hardship; now that the way has ended, the toil of journeying is over, and I have reached the land of my punishment, I care for naught but weeping; from my eyes comes as generous a flood as that which pours from the snow in springtime. Rome steals into my thought, my home, and the places I long for, and all that part of me that is left in the city I have lost. Ah me! that I have knocked so often upon the door of my own tomb but it has never opened to me! Why have I escaped so many swords? Why has not one of those gales that threatened so often overwhelmed an ill-starred head? Ye gods, whom I have found too steadily cruel, sharers in a wrath that one god[1] feels, goad on my laggard fate, I beseech ye; forbid the door of my destruction to be closed!

III. To his Wife

If haply you wonder why this letter of mine is written by another's fingers, I am ill—ill at the ends an unknown world, and in fact I was unsure of my recovery. What spirit can you think is now mine, lying sick in a hideous land among Sauromatae and Getae? The climate I cannot endure, and I have not become used to such water, and even the land, I know not why, pleases me not. There is no house here well suited to a sick man, no beneficial food for him, none to relieve, with Apollo's art, his pain, no friend to comfort, none to beguile with talk the slow-moving hours. Aweary I lie among

lassus in extremis iaceo populisque locisque,
    et subit adfecto nunc mihi, quicquid abest.
15 omnia cum subeant, vincis tamen omnia, coniunx,
    et plus in nostro pectore parte tenes.
te loquor absentem, te vox mea nominat unam ;
    nulla venit sine te nox mihi, nulla dies.
quin etiam sic me dicunt aliena locutum,
20   ut foret amenti nomen in ore tuum.
sit iam deficiens [1] suppressaque lingua palato
    vix instillato restituenda mero,
nuntiet huc aliquis dominam venisse, resurgam,
    spesque tui nobis causa vigoris erit.
25 ergo ego sum dubius vitae, tu forsitan istic
    iucundum nostri nescia tempus agis ?
non agis, adfirmo.   liquet hoc, carissima, nobis,
    tempus agi sine me non nisi triste tibi.
si tamen inplevit mea sors, quos debuit, annos,
30   et mihi vivendi tam cito finis adest,
quantum erat, o magni, morituro parcere, divi,
    ut saltem patria contumularer humo ?
vel poena in tempus mortis dilata fuisset,
    vel praecepisset mors properata fugam.
35 integer hanc potui nuper bene reddere lucem ;
    exul ut occiderem, nunc mihi vita data est.
tam procul ignotis igitur moriemur in oris,
    et fient ipso tristia fata loco ;
nec mea consueto languescent corpora lecto,
40   depositum nec me qui fleat, ullus erit ;
nec dominae lacrimis in nostra cadentibus ora
    accedent animae tempora parva meae ;

[1] si . . . deficiam *corr. Luck*

these far-away peoples in this far-away place, and thoughts come to me in my weakness of everything that is not here. All things steal into my mind, yet above all, you, my wife, and you hold more than half my heart. You I address though you are absent, you alone my voice names; no night comes to me without you, no day. Nay more, they say that when I talked strange things, 'twas so that your name was on my delirious lips. If my tongue were now to fail and cleaving to my palate were scarcely to be revived by drops of wine, let someone announce that my lady has come, I'll rise, and the hope of you will be the cause of my strength. Am I then uncertain of life, but are you perhaps passing happy hours yonder forgetful of me? You are not; I assert it. This is clear to me, dearest, that without me you pass no hour that is not sad.

[29] Still if my lot has filled out its destined years and if the end of living is come so quickly upon me, how small a thing, ye mighty gods, to show mercy to one on the eve of death so that at least I might have been covered with my native soil! Would that the penalty had been postponed to the hour of my death or that quick death had anticipated my exile! In full possession of my rights, as I was but recently, I could have been content to give up this light of day; to die an exile—for that has life now been granted me. So far away, then, on a strange shore I shall die, and the very place shall render harsh my fate; neither shall my body grow weak upon the familiar couch, nor when I am at the point of death shall there be any to weep, nor shall my lady's tears fall upon my face adding brief

111

nec mandata dabo, nec cum clamore supremo
 labentes oculos condet amica manus;
45 sed sine funeribus caput hoc, sine honore sepulcri
 indeploratum barbara terra teget!
ecquid, ubi audieris, tota turbabere mente,
 et feries pavida pectora fida manu?
ecquid, in has frustra tendens tua brachia partes,
50 clamabis miseri nomen inane viri?
parce tamen lacerare genas, nec scinde capillos:
 non tibi nunc primum, lux mea, raptus ero.
cum patriam amisi, tunc me periisse putato:
 et prior et gravior mors fuit illa mihi.
55 nunc, si forte potes—sed non potes, optima con-
 iunx—
 finitis gaude tot mihi morte malis.
quod potes, extenua forti mala corde ferendo,
 ad quae iam pridem non rude pectus habes.
atque utinam pereant animae cum corpore nostrae,
60 effugiatque avidos pars mihi nulla rogos!
nam si morte carens vacua volat altus in aura
 spiritus, et Samii sunt rata dicta senis,
inter Sarmaticas Romana vagabitur umbras,
 perque feros manes hospita semper erit.
65 ossa tamen facito parva referantur in urna:
 sic ego non etiam mortuus exul ero.
non vetat hoc quisquam: fratrem Thebana
 peremptum
 supposiut tumulo rege vetante soror.
atque ea cum foliis et amomi pulvere misce,
70 inque suburbano condita pone solo;
quosque legat versus oculo properante viator,
 grandibus in tumuli marmore caede notis:

---

¹ Pythagoras.   ² Antigone.

moments to my life; nor shall I utter parting words, nor with a last lament shall a loved hand close my fluttering eyes, but without funeral rites, without the honour of a tomb, this head shall lie unmourned in a barbarian land!

[47] Will not your whole heart be shaken, when you hear this? Will you not beat with trembling hand your loyal breast? Will you not stretch forth your arms all in vain towards this region and call upon the empty name of your wretched husband? Yet mar not your cheeks nor tear your hair: not now for the first time, light of mine, shall I have been torn from you. When I lost my native land, then must you think that I perished; that was my earlier and harder death. Now, if perchance you have the power (but you have it not, best of wives), rejoice that so many misfortunes are ended for me by death. For this you have power: lighten by bearing them with a brave soul woes in which for a long time now your heart is not untrained.

[59] O that our souls might perish with the body and that so no part of me might escape the greedy pyre! For if the spirit flits aloft deathless in the empty air, and the words of the Samian sage [1] are true, a Roman will wander among Sarmatian shades, a stranger forever among barbarians. But my bones—see that they are carried home in a little urn: so shall I not be an exile even in death. This nobody forbids: the Theban sister [2] laid her slain brother beneath the tomb though the king forbade; and mingling with my bones the leaves and powder of the nard lay them to rest in soil close to the city, and on the marble tomb carve lines for the wayfarer to read with hasty eye, lines in large characters:

HIC · EGO · QVI · IACEO · TENERORVM · LVSOR · AMORVM
INGENIO · PERII · NASO · POETA · MEO
75 AT · TIBI · QVI · TRANSIS · NE · SIT · GRAVE · QVISQVIS · AMASTI
DICERE · NASONIS · MOLLITER · OSSA · CVBENT

hoc satis in titulo est.   etenim maiora libelli
  et diuturna magis sunt monimenta mihi,
quos ego confido, quamvis nocuere, daturos
80   nomen et auctori tempora longa suo.
tu tamen extincto feralia munera semper
  deque tuis lacrimis umida serta dato.
quamvis in cinerem corpus mutaverit ignis,
  sentiet officium maesta favilla pium.
85 scribere plura libet : sed vox mihi fessa loquendo
  dictandi vires siccaque lingua negat.
accipe supremo dictum mihi forsitan ore,
  quod, tibi qui mittit, non habet ipse, " vale."

IV.

O mihi care quidem semper, sed tempore duro
  cognite, res postquam procubuere meae,
usibus edocto si quicquam credis amico,
  vive tibi et longe nomina magna fuge.
5 vive tibi, quantumque potes praelustria vita :
  saevum praelustri fulmen ab acre venit.
nam quamquam soli possunt prodesse potentes,
  non prosit ¹ potius, siquis ² obesse potest.
effugit hibernas demissa antemna procellas,
10   lataque plus parvis vela timoris habent.

----

¹ prodest *vel* prosunt   ² siquis] plurimum

----

¹ Ovid often plays on the literal meaning of *valere*, " to be
strong," " to be in health."

I, WHO LIE HERE, WITH TENDER LOVES ONCE PLAYED,
NASO, THE BARD, WHOSE LIFE HIS WIT BETRAYED.
GRUDGE NOT, O LOVER, AS THOU PASSEST BY,
A PRAYER : "SOFT MAY THE BONES OF NASO LIE!"

This for the inscription ; my books are a greater and
more enduring memorial. These I have sure trust,
although they have injured him, will give a name and
a long enduring life to their author. Yet do you ever
give to the dead the funeral offerings and garlands
moist with your own tears. Although the fire
change my body to ashes, the sorrowing dust shall
feel the pious care.

[85] More would I write, but my voice worn out with
speaking and my parched tongue deny the strength
for dictation. Receive the last word perhaps my lips
shall utter, a word which is not true [1] of the sender :
"Farewell!"

IV. To a Friend—in Warning

O thou who wast ever dear to me, but whom I
really came to know in the cruel hour when my
fortunes fell in ruins, if thou dost in anything believe
a friend who has been taught by experience, live for
thyself, flee afar from great names! Live for thyself,
and to thine utmost power shun glittering renown ;
cruel is the bolt that falls from the glittering citadel
of renown. For though the powerful alone can
help, rather would such a one not help if he can
harm! [2] The lowered yard-arm escapes the
blast of the storm, broad sails bring more fear than

[2] The text of vv. 7–8 is uncertain.

aspicis ut summa cortex levis innatet unda,
 cum grave nexa simul retia mergat onus.
haec ego si monitor monitus prius ipse fuissem,
 in qua debebam forsitan urbe forem.
15 dum mecum ¹ vixi, dum me levis aura ferebat,
 haec mea per placidas cumba cucurrit aquas.
qui cadit in plano—vix hoc tamen evenit ipsum—
 sic cadit, ut tacta surgere possit humo ;
at miser Elpenor tecto delapsus ab alto
20 occurrit regi debilis umbra suo.
quid fuit, ut tutas agitarit ² Daedalus alas,
 Icarus inmensas nomine signet aquas ?
nempe quod hic alte, demissius ille volabat ;
 nam pennas ambo non habuere suas.
25 crede mihi, bene qui latuit bene vixit, et intra
 fortunam debet quisque manere suam.
non foret Eumedes orbus, si filius eius
 stultus Achilleos non adamasset equos ;
nec natum in flamma vidisset, in arbore natas,
30 cepisset genitor si Phaëthonta Merops.
tu quoque formida nimium sublimia semper,
 propositique, precor, contrahe vela tui.
nam pede inoffenso spatium decurrere vitae
 dignus es et fato candidiore frui.
35 quae pro te ut voveam, miti pietate mereris
 haesuraque fide tempus in omne mihi.
vidi ego te tali vultu mea fata gementem,
 qualem credibile est ore fuisse meo.
nostra tuas vidi lacrimas super ora cadentes,
40 tempore quas uno fidaque verba bibi.
nunc quoque summotum studio defendis amicum,
 et mala vix ulla parte levanda levas.

¹ tecum *corr. Faber*   ² agitaret

small. Thou seest how the light cork floats atop the wave when the heavy burden sinks with itself the woven nets. If I who warn thee now had once myself been warned of this, perchance I should now be in that city in which I ought to be. Whilst I lived for myself, whilst the light breeze wafted me on, this bark of mine sped through calm waters. Who falls on level ground—though this scarce happens—so falls that he can rise from the ground he has touched, but poor Elpenor who fell from the high roof met his king a crippled shade. Why was it that Daedalus in safety plied his wings while Icarus marks with his name the limitless waves? Doubtless because Icarus flew high, the other flew lower; for both had wings not their own. Let me tell thee, he who hides well his life, lives well; each man ought to remain within his proper position. Eumedes would not have been childless, if in folly his son [1] had not had a fancy for the horses of Achilles. Merops would not have seen his son in flames nor his daughters in the form of trees if he had been an adequate father for Phaëthon. Do thou also dread constantly that which is too lofty and furl the sails of thine intent. For thou dost deserve to finish life's race with unstumbling foot, enjoying a fairer lot than mine.

[35] These my prayers for thee are deserved by thy gentle affection and by that loyalty which will cling to me for all time. I saw thee lamenting my fate with such a look as I think my own face must have borne. I saw thy tears fall upon my face—tears which I drank in with thy words of loyalty. Even now thou dost defend with zeal thy banished friends, lightening woes that are scarce in any part

[1] Dolon.

vive sine invidia, mollesque inglorius annos
    exige, amicitias et tibi iunge pares,
45 Nasonisque tui, quod adhuc non exulat unum,
    nomen ama : Scythicus cetera Pontus habet.

IV[b] [1]

Proxima sideribus tellus Erymanthidos Ursae
    me tenet, adstricto terra perusta gelu.
Bosphoros et Tanais superant Scythiaeque paludes
50   vix satis et noti nomina pauca loci.
ulterius nihil est nisi non habitabile frigus.
    heu quam vicina est ultima terra mihi !
at longe patria est, longe carissima coniunx,
    quicquid et haec nobis post duo dulce fuit.
55 sic tamen haec adsunt, ut, quae contingere non est
    corpore, sint animo cuncta videnda meo.
ante oculos errant domus, urbsque et [2] forma locorum,
    acceduntque suis singula facta locis.
coniugis ante oculos, sicut praesentis, imago est.[3]
60   illa meos casus ingravat, illa levat :
ingravat hoc, quod abest ; levat hoc, quod praestat
    amorem
inpositumque sibi firma tuetur onus.
vos quoque pectoribus nostris haeretis, amici,
    dicere quos cupio nomine quemque suo.
65 sed timor officium cautus compescit, et ipsos
    in nostro ponti carmine nolle puto.
ante volebatis, gratique erat instar honoris,
    versibus in nostris nomina vestra legi.

[1] *separant quidam codices Heinsii*
[2] urbs et *corr.* ς   [3] est *om.*

---

[1] The Don.

to be lightened.   Live unenvied, pass years of comfort
apart from fame, unite to thee friends like thyself,
and love thy Naso's name—the only part of him not
as yet in exile : all else the Scythian Pontus possesses.

IV *b*

To hearts that cannot vary
Absence is present.

[47] A land next the stars of the Erymanthian bear
holds me, a region shrivelled with stiffening
cold.   Beyond are the Bosporus and the Tanais [1] and
the Scythian marshes and the scattered names of a
region hardly known at all.   Farther still is nothing
but a cold that forbids habitation.   Alas ! how near
to me is the margin of the world !   But my fatherland
is far away, far my dearest wife, and all that after
these two was once sweet to me.   Yet these
things are so present that, though I cannot touch
them, all are visible to my mind.   Before my eyes flit
my home, the city, the outline of places, the events
too that happened in each place.   Before my eyes is
the image of my wife as though she were
present.   She makes my woes heavier, she makes
them lighter—heavier by her absence, lighter by her
gift of love and her steadfast bearing of the burden
laid upon her.

[63] You too are fast in my heart, my friends, whom I
am eager to mention each by his own name, but
cautious fear restrains the duty and you yourselves
do not wish a place in my poetry, I think.   Of old you
wished it, for it was like a grateful honour to have
your names read in my verse.   Since now 'tis

119

quod quoniam est anceps, intra mea pectora quemque
70 adloquar, et nulli causa timoris ero.
nec meus indicio latitantes versus amicos
    protrahit.[1]   occulte, siquis amabit,[2] amet.
scite tamen, quamvis longa regione remotus
    absim, vos animo semper adesse meo ;
75 et qua quisque potest, aliqua mala nostra levate,
    fidam proiecto neve negate manum.
prospera sic maneat vobis fortuna, nec umquam
    contacti simili sorte rogetis idem.

V

Usus amicitiae tecum mihi parvus, ut illam
    non aegre posses dissimulare, fuit,
nec [3] me complexus vinclis propioribus esses
    nave mea vento, forsan, eunte suo.
 5 ut cecidi cunctique metu fugere ruinae,[4]
    versaque amicitiae terga dedere meae,
ausus es igne Iovis percussum tangere corpus
    et deploratae limen adire domus :
idque recens praestas nec longo cognitus usu,
10   quod veterum misero vix duo tresve mihi.
vidi ego confusos vultus visosque notavi,
    osque madens fletu pallidiusque meo,
et lacrimas cernens in singula verba cadentes
    ore meo lacrimas, auribus illa bibi ;
15 brachiaque accepi presso [5] pendentia collo,
    et singultatis oscula mixta sonis.
sum quoque, care, tuis defensus viribus absens—
    scis carum veri nominis esse loco—

[1] protrahet   [2] amavit *vel* -bat *corr. Housman*   [3] ni: nec ς
         [4] ruinam   [5] maesto

---

[1] Perhaps Carus, *i.e. carus*, "dear."   See Introd. p. xiv.
120

dangerous, within my heart will I address each one
and be cause of fear to none. My verse gives no hint
that forces my friends from their concealment. If
anyone will love me, let him love in secret. Yet
know that though I am removed from you by vast
space, you are ever present to my heart. Let each of
you in what way he can—in some way—lighten my
woes, nor refuse an outcast a trusty hand. So may
good fortune abide for you nor ever may you, visited
with a like fate, make the same request.

V. To One who has been faithful

Slight was my friendly intercourse with you so that
you could without difficulty have denied it, and you
would not have embraced me more closely perhaps, if
my ship had been running before a favouring
wind. At my fall, when all fled in fear of ruin,
turning their backs upon friendship with me, you
dared to touch the corpse Jove's fire had blasted and
to approach the threshold of a house
bemoaned. You, a recent friend, not one known
through long intercourse, give me what scarcely two
or three of my old friends gave in my wretchedness. I
myself saw and marked your look of grief, your face
wet with tears and paler than my own. And as I saw
your tears falling with every word, drinking in
with my lips the tears and with my ears the words,
I felt the clasp of your encircling arms about my neck
and I was aware of your kisses mingled with the
sound of your sobbing. I have had your strong
defence also in my absence, dear one—you know
that "dear one" stands for your real name [1]—and

121

multaque praeterea manifestaque [1] signa favoris
20   pectoribus teneo non abitura meis.
di tibi posse tuos tribuant defendere semper,
   quos in materia prosperiore iuves.
si tamen interea, quid in his ego perditus oris—
   quod te credibile est quaerere—quaeris, agam,
25 spe trahor exigua, quam tu mihi demere noli,
   tristia leniri numina posse dei.
seu temere expecto, sive id contingere fas est,
   tu mihi, quod cupio, fas, precor, esse proba,
quaeque tibi linguae est facundia, confer in illud,
30   ut doceas votum posse valere meum.
quo quisque est maior, magis est placabilis irae,
   et faciles motus mens generosa capit.
corpora magnanimo satis est prostrasse leoni,
   pugna suum finem, cum iacet hostis, habet :
35 at lupus et turpes instant morientibus ursi
   et quaecumque minor nobilitate fera.
maius apud Troiam forti quid habemus Achille ?
   Dardanii lacrimas non tulit ille senis.
quae ducis Emathii fuerit clementia, Porus
40   Dareique docent funeris exequiae.
neve hominum referam flexas ad mitius iras,
   Iunonis gener est qui prius hostis erat.
denique non possum nullam sperare salutem,
   cum poenae non sit causa cruenta meae.
45 non mihi quaerenti pessumdare cuncta petitum
   Caesareum caput est, quod caput orbis erat ;
non aliquid dixi, velandave [2] lingua locuta est,
   lapsave sunt nimio verba profana mero :

[1] manifesta *vel* -i
[2] velata *corr. Santen*

---

[1] Priam begging for Hector's body.

many other clear marks of your affection I still retain that will not leave my heart. The gods grant you always the power to defend your own! May you aid them in more fortunate circumstances than mine!

[23] Yet meanwhile, if you ask—and I believe that you do ask—how in my ruin I fare upon this shore, I am led on by the slender hope—take it not from me—that the harsh will of the god can be softened. Whether my hope is groundless or whether it is vouchsafed me to attain it, do you prove to me, I pray, that my great desire *is* vouchsafed; whatever eloquence you have devote to this—to showing that my prayer can be accomplished. The greater a man is, the more can his wrath be appeased; a noble spirit is capable of kindly impulses. For the noble lion 'tis enough to have overthrown his enemy; the fight is at an end when his foe is fallen. But the wolf, the ignoble bears harry the dying—and so with every beast of less nobility. At Troy what have we mightier than brave Achilles? But the tears of the aged Dardanian [1] he could not endure. The quality of the Emathian leader's [2] mercy is proved by Porus and the funeral ceremony of Darius. And not to dwell upon instances of human wrath turned to milder ends—he is now Juno's son-in-law [3] who was once her foe. In fine 'tis possible for me to hope for some salvation since the cause of my punishment involves no stain of blood; I never sought to wreck everything by assailing the life of Caesar, which is the life of the world. I have said nothing, divulged nothing in speech, let slip no impious words by reason of too much wine: because

[2] Alexander the Great.   [3] Hercules, who married Hebe.

inscia quod crimen viderunt lumina, plector,
50 peccatumque oculos est habuisse meum.
non equidem totam possum defendere culpam,
    sed partem nostri criminis error habet.
spes igitur superest, ut molliat ipse, futurum,[1]
    mutati poenam condicione loci.
55 hos [2] utinam nitidi Solis praenuntius ortus
    afferat admisso Lucifer albus equo!

VI

Foedus amicitae nec vis, carissime, nostrae,
    nec, si forte velis, dissimulare potes.
donec enim licuit, nec to mihi carior alter,
    nec tibi me tota iunctior urbe fuit,
5 isque erat usque adeo populo testatus, ut esset
    paene magis quam tu quamque ego notus, amor;
quique est in caris animi tibi candor amicis—
    cognitus est illi, quem colis ipse,[3] viro.
nil ita celabas, ut non ego conscius essem,
10 pectoribusque dabas multa tegenda meis:
cuique ego narrabam secreti quicquid habebam,
    excepto quod me perdidit, unus eras.
id quoque si scisses, salvo fruerere sodali,
    consilioque forem sospes, amice, tuo.
15 sed mea me in poenam nimirum Parca trahebat,[4]
    omne bonae claudens [5] utilitatis iter.
sive malum potui tamen hoc vitare cavendo,
    seu ratio fatum vincere nulla valet,
tu tamen, o nobis usu iunctissime longo,
    pars desiderii maxima paene mei,

[1] facturum u.m.i.: *corr.* *Heinsius* [2] hoc: *corr.* *Riese*
[3] cognita sunt ipsi . . . iste
[4] fata trahebant: *corr. Palmer* [5] claudunt *s*

[1] Augustus.

124

my unwitting eyes beheld a crime, I am punished, and 'tis my sin that I possessed eyes. I cannot indeed exculpate my fault entirely, but part of it consists in error. So have I still some hope it will turn out that he lightens my punishment by changing its place. Would that such a dawn as this may be brought me by the harbinger of the gleaming sun, fair Lucifer, with his swift steed!

IV. To an old Friend

The bond of our friendship, dear one, you neither wish to hide nor, should you perchance so wish, have you the power, for while it was possible no other was dearer to me than you were, no one in the whole city closer to you than I; that love was so thoroughly attested by everybody that it was almost better known than you or I, and the frankness of your heart towards your dear friends is known to that great man [1] whom you yourself revere. You had no secret such that I was not aware of it, and many things you used to entrust to the guardianship of my heart. To you alone I used to tell all my secrets except that one which ruined me. If you had known that also, you would now be enjoying the safety of your comrade: through your advice I should be safe, my friend. But doubtless my fate was dragging me to punishment, shutting off every road of advantage. Yet whether I could have avoided this evil by taking care or whether no planning can defeat fate, do you, close joined to me by long friendship, you almost the largest part of my longing, remember

sis memor, et siquas fecit tibi gratia vires,
    illas pro nobis experiare, rogo,
numinis ut laesi fiat mansuetior ira,
    mutatoque minor sit mea poena loco,
25 idque ita, si nullum scelus est in pectore nostro,
    principiumque mei criminis error habet.
nec breve nec tutum, quo sint mea, dicere, casu
    lumina funesti conscia facta mali ;
mensque reformidat, veluti sua vulnera, tempus
30   illud, et admonitu fit novus ipse dolor,
et quaecumque adeo possunt afferre pudorem,
    illa tegi caeca condita nocte decet.
nil igitur referam nisi me peccasse, sed illo
    praemia peccato nulla petita mihi,
35 stultitiamque meum crimen debere vocari,
    nomina si facto reddere vera velis.
quae si non ita sunt, alium, quo longius absim,
    quaere—suburbana est haec mihi terra—locum.

VII

VADE salutatum, subito perarata, Perillam,
    littera, sermonis fida ministra mei.
aut illam invenies dulci cum matre sedentem,
    aut inter libros Pieridasque suas.
5 quidquid aget, cum te scierit venisse, relinquet,
    nec mora, quid venias quidve, requiret, agam.
vivere me dices, sed sic, ut vivere nolim,
    nec mala tam longa nostra levata mora;
et tamen ad Musas, quamvis nocuere, reverti,
10   aptaque in alternos cogere verba pedes.

126

me; and if favour has given you any powers, I beg
that you will test them in my behalf to soften the
wrath of the injured deity and that my punishment
may be lessened by changing its place—and this only
on condition that no crime is in my heart but a
mistake is responsible for the beginning of my
sin. 'Tis not a brief tale or safe to say what chance
made my eyes witness a baleful evil. My mind
skrinks in dread from that time, as 'twere from its
own wounds, and the very thought of it renews my
pain; whatever can bring such sense of shame should
be covered and hidden in the darkness of
night. Nothing then will I say except that I have
sinned, but by that sin sought no reward; folly is the
proper name for my crime, if you wish to give the true
title to the deed. If this is untrue, then this land is a
suburb of Rome and you should seek a more distant
place for my exile.[1]

VII. To Perilla

Go, greet Perilla, quickly written letter, and be the
trusty servant of my speech. You will find her
sitting in the company of her sweet mother or amid
books and the Pierian maidens she loves. Whatever
she be doing she will leave it when she knows of your
coming and ask at once why you come or how I
fare. Say that I live, but in such wise that I would
not live; that my misfortunes have not been
lightened by the lapse of so long a time, that
nevertheless I am returning to the Muses despite their
injury, forcing words to fit alternating measures.

[1] *i.e.* my present place of exile is all too near Rome for one
who could be guilty of such untruth.

"tu quoque" dic "studiis communibus ecquid
    inhaeres,
  doctaque non patrio carmina more canis ?
nam tibi cum facie mores natura pudicos
  et raras dotes ingeniumque dedit.
15 hoc ego Pegasidas deduxi primus ad undas,
  ne male fecundae vena periret aquae ;
primus id aspexi teneris in virginis annis,
  utque pater natae duxque comesque fui.
ergo si remanent ignes tibi pectoris idem,
20   sola tuum vates Lesbia vincet opus.
sed vereor, ne te mea nunc fortuna retardet,
  postque meos casus sit tibi pectus iners.
dum licuit, tua saepe mihi, tibi nostra legebam ;
  saepe tui iudex, saepe magister eram :
25 aut ego praebebam factis modo versibus aures,
  aut, ubi cessares, causa ruboris eram.
forsitan exemplo, quo [1] me laesere libelli,
  tu metuis [2] poenae fata secunda [2] meae.
pone, Perilla, metum ; tantummodo femini nulla
30   neve vir a scriptis discat amare tuis.
ergo desidiae remove, doctissima, causas,
  inque bonas artes et tua sacra redi.
ista decens facies longis vitiabitur annis,
  rugaque in antiqua fronte senilis erit,
35 inicietque manum formae damnosa senectus,
  quae strepitus passu non faciente venit ;
cumque aliquis dicet 'fuit haec formosa' dolebis,
  et speculum mendax esse querere tuum.
sunt tibi opes modicae, cum sis dignissima magnis :
40   finge sed inmensis censibus esse pares,

[1] quia *corr. Heinsius*   [2] quoque sis . . . secuta *corr. Hall*

---

[1] *i.e.* Ovid's. See Index *s.v.* Perilla.

Say to her, "Art thou too still devoted to our
common pursuit of singing learned verse, though not
in thy father's [1] fashion? For as well as beauty
nature has given thee modest ways and a rare dower
of native wit. This I was the first to guide to the
stream of Pegasus lest the rill of fertile water
unhappily be lost. I was the first to discern this in
the tender years of thy girlhood when, as a father to
his daughter, I was thy guide and comrade. So if
the same fire still abides in thy breast, only the
Lesbian bard [2] will surpass thy work. But I fear
that my fate may now be trammelling thee, that
since my disaster thy mind may have become
inactive. Whilst I could, I used often to read thy
verse to myself and mine to thee; often was I thy
critic, often thy teacher, now lending my ear to the
verses thou hadst recently composed, now causing
thee to blush when thou wert idle. Perchance from
the example of the injury that verse has done me thou
fearest a repetition of the fate which has brought me
punishment. Lay aside thy fear, Perilla; only let no
woman or any man learn from thy writings how to
love.

[1] "So put aside the cause of sloth, accomplished
girl, return to a noble art and thy sacred offerings.
That fair face will be marred by the long years, the
wrinkles of age will come in time upon thy brow.
Ruinous age that comes with noiseless step will lay
her hand upon thy beauty, and when someone shall
say, 'She once was fair,' thou wilt grieve and com-
plain that thy mirror lies. Thou hast a modest
fortune, though full worthy of a great one; but
imagine it the equal of boundless riches, still assuredly

[2] Sappho.

129

nempe dat id cuicumque [1] libet fortuna rapitque,
    Irus et est subito, qui modo Croesus erat.
singula ne referam, nil non mortale tenemus
    pectoris exceptis ingeniique bonis.
45 en ego, cum caream patria vobisque domoque,
    raptaque sint, adimi quae potuere mihi,
ingenio tamen ipse meo comitorque fruorque :
    Caesar in hoc potuit iuris habere nihil.
quilibet hanc saevo vitam mihi finiat ense,
50   me tamen extincto fama superstes erit,
dumque suis victrix septem [2] de montibus orbem
    prospiciet domitum Martia Roma, legar.
tu quoque, quam studii maneat felicior usus,
    effuge venturos, qua potes, usque rogos ! ''

VIII.

Nunc ego Triptolemi cuperem consistere curru,
    misit in ignotam qui rude semen humum ;
nunc ego Medeae vellem frenare dracones,
    quos habuit fugiens arce, Corinthe, tua ;
5 nunc ego iactandas optarem sumere pennas,
    sive tuas, Perseu, Daedale, sive tuas :
ut tenera nostris cedente volatibus aura
    aspicerem patriae dulce repente solum,
desertaeque domus vultus, memoresque sodales,
10   caraque praecipue coniugis ora meae.
stulte, quid haec frustra votis puerilibus optas,
    quae non ulla tulit [3] fertque feretque dies ?
si semel optandum est, Augusti numen adora,
    et, quem sensisti, rite precare deum.
15 ille tibi pennasque potest currusque volucres
    tradere : det reditum, protinus ales eris.

---

      [1] quodcumque   [2] omnem   [3] tibi

fortune enriches and robs whomever she pleases, and
he becomes suddenly an Irus who was but now a
Croesus. In brief we possess nothing that is not
mortal except the blessings of heart and
mind. Behold me, deprived of native land, of you
and my home, reft of all that could be taken from me ;
my mind is nevertheless my comrade and my joy ;
over this Caesar could have no right. Let any you
will end this life with cruel sword, yet when I am dead
my fame shall survive. As long as Martian Rome
gazes forth victorious from her seven hills over the
conquered world, I shall be read. Do thou too—and
may a happier use of thine art await thee—even shun
what way thou canst the coming pyre ! "

VIII. The Exile's Prayer

Now would I crave to stand in the car of
Triptolemus, who flung the untried seed on ground
that had known it not ; now would I bridle the
dragons that Medea had when she fled thy citadel, O
Corinth ; now would I pray for wings to ply—thine,
Perseus, or thine, Daedalus—that the yielding air
might give way before my rapid flight and I might on
a sudden behold the sweet soil of my native land, the
faces in my lonely home, my loyal friends, and—
foremost of all—the dear features of my wife.

"Fool! why pray in vain like a child for such
things as no day has ever brought or brings or will
bring ? If only you must pray, worship Augustus's
divinity ; petition in due form that god whose might
you have felt. He has power to grant you feathers
and winged cars : let him grant return and forthwith

131

si precer hoc—neque enim possum maiora rogare—
    ne mea sint, timeo, vota modesta parum.
forsitan hoc olim, cum iam satiaverit iram,
20   tum quoque sollicita mente rogandus erit.
quod minus interea est, instar mihi muneris ampli,
    ex his me iubeat quolibet ire locis.
nec caelum nec aquae faciunt nec terra nec aurae ;
    ei mihi, perpetuus corpora languor habet !
25 seu vitiant artus aegrae contagia mentis,
    sive mei causa est in regione mali,
ut tetigi Pontum, vexant insomnia, vixque
    ossa tegit macies nec iuvat ora cibus ;
quique per autumnum percussis frigore primo
30   est color in foliis, quae nova laesit hiems,
is mea membra tenet, nec viribus adlevor ullis,
    et numquam queruli causa doloris abest.
nec melius valeo, quam corpore, mente, sed aegra est
    utraque pars aeque binaque damna fero.
35 haeret et ante oculos veluti spectabile corpus
    astat fortunae forma legenda meae :
cumque locum moresque hominum cultusque
      sonumque
    cernimus, et, qui sim qui fuerimque, subit,
tantus amor necis est, querar et cum Caesaris ira,
40   quod non offensas vindicet ense suas.
at, quoniam semel est odio civiliter usus,
    mutato levior sit fuga nostra loco.

IX.

Hic quoque sunt igitur Graiae—quis crederet ?—
    urbes
    inter inhumanae nomina barbariae ;
132

you will have wings. Were I to pray for this (and I can ask no greater things) I fear my prayer would lack restraint. For this perchance sometimes, when his wrath is sated, I shall have to pray with a heart troubled even then. Meanwhile a smaller thing, but equal to a generous boon for me—let him bid me go anywhere from this place. Neither climate nor water suit me, nor land nor air—ah me! a constant weakness possesses my frame. Whether the contagion of a sick mind affects my limbs or the cause of my ills is this region, since I reached the Pontus, I am harassed by sleeplessness, scarce does the lean flesh cover my bones, food pleases not my lips ; and such a hue is in autumn, when the first chill has smitten them, shows on the leaves that young winter has marred, o'erspreads my body ; no strength brings relief, and I never lack cause for plaintive pain. I am no better in mind than in body ; both alike are sick and I suffer double hurt. Clinging and standing like a visible body before my eyes is the figure of my fate that I must scan ; and when I behold the country, the ways, the dress, the language of the people, when I remember what I am and what I was, I have so great a love of death that I complain of Caesar's wrath, because he avenges not his wrongs with the sword. But since he has once exercised his hatred mildly, let him lighten my exile still further by changing its place.

IX. The Origin of Tomis

Here too then there are Grecian cities (who would believe it ?) among the names of the wild barbarian

133

huc quoque Mileto missi venere coloni,
    inque Getis Graias constituere domos.
5 sed vetus huic nomen, positaque antiquius urbe,
    constat ab Absyrti caede fuisse loco.
nam rate, quae cura pugnacis facta Minervae
    per non temptatas prima cucurrit aquas,
impia desertum fugiens Medea parentem
10   dicitur his remos applicuisse vadis.
quem procul ut vidit tumulo speculator ab alto,
    "hospes," ait, "nosco, Colchide, vela, venit."
dum trepidant Minyae, dum solvitur aggere funis,
    dum sequitur celeres ancora tracta manus,
15 conscia percussit meritorum pectora Colchis
    ausa atque ausura multa nefanda manu;
et, quamquam superest ingens audacia menti,
    pallor in attonitae virginis ore fuit.
ergo ubi prospexit venientia vela "tenemur,"
20   et "pater est aliqua fraude morandus" ait.
dum quid agat quaerit, dum versat in omnia
    vultus,
    ad fratrem casu lumina flexa tulit.
cuius ut oblata est praesentia, "vicimus" inquit:
    "hic mihi morte sua causa salutis erit."
25 protinus ignari nec quicquam tale timentis
    innocuum rigido perforat ense latus,
atque ita divellit divulsaque membra per agros
    dissipat in multis invenienda locis.
neu pater ignoret, scopulo proponit in alto
30   pallentesque manus sanguineumque caput,

---

[1] The Argo.

world; hither also came from Miletus colonists to found among the Getae Grecian homes. But the ancient name, more ancient than the founding of the city, was given to this place, 'tis certain, from the murder of Absyrtus. For in the ship [1] which was built under the care of warlike Minerva—the first to speed through the untried seas –wicked Medea fleeing her forsaken sire brought to a haven her oars, they say, in these waters. Him in the distance the lookout on the lofty hill espied and said, " A stranger approaches from Colchis ; I recognize the sails ! "

[13] While the Minyae [2] are all excitement, while the cable is loosed from the shore, while the anchor is being raised following their nimble hands, the Colchian maid conscious of her guilt smote her breast with a hand that had dared and was to dare many things unspeakable, and though her heart still retained its great boldness, there was a pallor of dismay upon the girl's face.

[19] And so at the sight of the approaching sails, she said, " I am caught ! " and " I must delay my father by some trick ! " As she was seeking what to do, turning her countenance on all things, she chanced to bend her gaze upon her brother. When aware of his presence she exclaimed, "The victory is mine ! His death shall save me ! " Forthwith while he in his ignorance feared no such attack she pierced his innocent side with the hard sword. Then she tore him limb from limb, scattering the fragments of his body throughout the fields so that they must be sought in many places. And to apprise her father she placed upon a lofty rock the pale hands and gory head.

[2] The Argonauts.

ut genitor luctuque novo tardetur et, artus
    dum legit extinctos, triste moretur [1] iter.
inde Tomis [2] dictus locus hic, quia fertur in illo
    membra soror fratris consecuisse sui.

X.

Siquis adhuc istic meminit Nasonis adempti,
    et superest sine me nomen in urbe meum,
suppositum stellis numquam tangentibus aequor
    me sciat in media vivere barbaria.
5 Sauromatae cingunt, fera gens, Bessique Getaeque,
    quam non ingenio nomina digna meo !
dum tamen aura tepet, medio defendimur Histro :
    ille suis liquidus [3] bella repellit aquis.
at cum tristis hiems squalentia protulit ora,
10   terraque marmoreo est candida facta gelu,
nec patitur [4] Boreas et nix habitare sub Arcto,
    tum patet has gentes axe tremente premi.
nix iacet, et iactam ne [5] sol pluviaeque resolvant,[6]
    indurat Boreas perpetuamque facit.
15 ergo ubi deliquit nondum prior, altera venit,
    et solet in multis bima manere locis ;
tantaque commoti vis est Aquilonis, ut altas
    aequet humo turres tectaque rapta ferat.
pellibus et sutis arcent mala frigora bracis,
20   oraque de toto corpore sola patent.
saepe sonant moti glacie pendente capilli,
    et nitet inducto candida barba gelu ;

---

[1] retardet   [2] tomus (thomus) *vel* tomos
[3] liquidis   [4] dum patet et *corr. Hall*
[5] ne] nec   [6] resolvunt *corr. Ehwald*

Thus was the sire delayed by his fresh grief, lingering, while he gathered those lifeless limbs, on a journey of sorrow.

[33] So was this place called Tomis because here, they say, the sister cut to pieces her brother's body.[1]

X. THE RIGOURS OF TOMIS

If there be still any there who remembers banished Naso, if my name without me still survives in the city, let him know that beneath the stars which never touch the sea I am living in the midst of the barbarian world. About me are the Sauromatae, a cruel race, the Bessi, and the Getae, names how unworthy of my talent! Yet while the warm breezes blow we are defended by the interposing Hister; with the flood of his waters he repels wars. But when grim winter has thrust forth his squalid face, and the earth is marble-white with frost, and Boreas and the snow prohibit dwelling beneath the Bear, then 'tis clear that these tribes are hard pressed by the shivering pole. The snow lies continuously, and once fallen, neither sun nor rains may melt it, for Boreas hardens and renders it eternal. So when an earlier fall is not yet meltedanother has come, and in many places 'tis wont to remain for two years. So mighty is the power of Aquilo, when once he is aroused, that he levels high towers to the ground and sweeps away buildings. With skins and stitched breeches they keep out the evils of the cold; of the whole body only the face is exposed. Often their hair tinkles with hanging ice and their beards glisten white with

---

[1] Ovid derives Tomis (Tomi) from τέμνω, " to cut."

nudaque consistunt, formam servantia testae,
  vina, nec hausta meri, sed data frusta bibunt.
25 quid loquar, ut vincti concrescant frigore rivi,
  deque lacu fragiles effodiantur aquae ?
ipse, papyrifero qui non angustior amne
  miscetur vasto multa per ora freto,
caeruleos ventis latices durantibus, Hister
30 congelat et tectis in mare serpit aquis ;
quaque rates ierant, pedibus nunc itur, et undas
  frigore concretas ungula pulsat equi ;
perque novos pontes, subter labentibus undis,
  ducunt Sarmatici barbara plaustra boves.
35 vix equidem credar, sed, cum sint praemia falsi
  nulla, ratam debet testis habere fidem :
vidimus ingentem glacie consistere pontum,
  lubricaque inmotas testa premebat aquas.
nec vidisse sat est ; durum calcavimus aequor,
40 undaque non udo sub pede summa fuit.
si tibi tale fretum quondam, Leandre, fuisset,
  non foret angustae mors tua crimen aquae.
tum neque se pandi possunt delphines in auras
  tollere ; conantes dura coërcet hiems ;
45 et quamvis Boreas iactatis insonet alis,
  fluctus in obsesso gurgite nullus erit ;
inclusaeque gelu stabunt in marmore puppes,
  nec poterit rigidas findere remus aquas.
vidimus in glacie pisces haerere ligatos,
50 sed pars ex illis tum quoque viva fuit.
sive igitur nimii Boreae vis saeva marinas,
  sive redundatas flumine cogit aquas,
protinus aequato siccis Aquilonibus Histro
  invehitur celeri barbarus hostis equo ;

---

[1] *Cf.* the tales of serving whisky in the Klondike "in chunks"!   [2] The Nile.

the mantle of frost.   Exposed wine stands upright,
retaining the shape of the jar, and they drink, not
draughts of wine, but fragments served them ! [1]
[25] Why tell of brooks frozen fast with the cold and
how brittle water is dug out of the pool ?   The very
Hister, not narrower than the papyrus-bearing river, [2]
mingling with the vast deep through many mouths,
freezes as the winds stiffen his dark flood, and winds
its way into the sea with covered waters.   Where ships
had gone before now men go on foot and the waters
congealed with cold feel the hoof-beat of the horse.
Across the new bridge, above the gliding current, are
drawn by Sarmatian oxen the carts of the barbarians.
I may scarce hope for credence, but since there is no
reward for a falsehood, the witness ought to be believed
— I have seen the vast sea stiff with ice, a slippery
shell holding the water motionless.   And seeing is not
enough ; I have trodden the frozen sea, and the surface
lay beneath an unwetted foot.   If thou, Leander,
hadst once had such a sea, thy death would not have
been a charge against the narrow waters.   At such
times the curving dolphins cannot launch themselves
into the air ; if they try, stern winter checks them ;
and though Boreas may roar and toss his wings, there
will be no wave on the beleaguered flood.   Shut in
by the cold the ships will stand fast in the marble
surface nor will any oar be able to cleave the stiffened
waters.   I have seen fish clinging fast bound in the
ice, yet some even then still lived.
[51] So whether the cruel violence of o'ermighty
Boreas congeals the waters of the sea or the full waters
of the river, forthwith when the Hister has been
levelled by the freezing Aquilo the barbarian enemy
with his swift horses rides to the attack—an enemy

55 hostis equo pollens longeque volante sagitta
    vicinam late depopulatur humum.
diffugiunt alii, nullisque tuentibus agros
    incustoditae diripiuntur opes,
ruris opes parvae, pecus et stridentia plaustra,
60   et quas divitias incola pauper habet.
pars agitur vinctis post tergum capta lacertis,
    respiciens frustra rura Laremque suum :
pars cadit hamatis misere confixa sagittis :
    nam volucri ferro tinctile virus inest.
65 quae nequeunt secum ferre aut abducere, perdunt,
    et cremat insontes hostica flamma casas.
tunc quoque, cum pax est, trepidant formidine belli,
    nec quisquam presso vomere sulcat humum.
aut videt aut metuit locus hic, quem non videt,
    hostem ;
70   cessat iners rigido terra relicta situ.
non hic pampinea dulcis latet uva sub umbra,
    nec cumulant altos fervida musta lacus.
poma negat regio, nec haberet Acontius in quo
    scriberet hic dominae verba legenda suae.
75 aspiceres [1] nudos sine fronde, sine arbore, campos :
    heu loca felici non adeunda viro !
ergo tam late pateat cum maximus orbis,
    haec est in poenam terra reperta meam !

XI.

Quisquis es, insultes qui casibus, improbe, nostris,
    meque reum dempto fine cruentus agas,
natus es e scopulis et pastus lacte ferino,
    et dicam silices pectus habere tuum.

[1] aspiceret

strong in steeds and in far flying arrows—and lays
waste far and wide the neighbouring soil.   Some flee,
and with none to protect their lands their unguarded
resources are plundered, the small resources of the
country, flocks and creaking carts—all the wealth the
poor peasant has.   Some are driven, with arms
bound behind them, into captivity, gazing back in
vain upon their farms and their homes ; some fall in
agony pierced with barbed shafts, for there is a stain
of poison upon the winged steel.   What they cannot
carry or lead away they destroy, and the hostile flame
burns the innocent hovels.   Even when peace
prevails, there is timorous dread of war, nor does any
man furrow the soil with down-pressed share.   A
foe this region either sees or fears when it does not
see ; idle lies the soil abandoned in stark
neglect.   Not here the sweet grape lying hidden in
the leafy shade nor the frothing must brimming the
deep vats !   Fruits are denied in this region nor here
would Acontius have anything on which to write the
words for his sweetheart [1] to read.   One may see
naked fields, leafless, treeless—a place, alas ! no
fortunate man should visit.   This then, though the
great world is so broad, is the land discovered for my
punishment !

XI. To an Enemy

Whoever thou art that dost mock, wicked man, at
my misfortunes, endlessly bringing an indictment
against me, thirsting for my blood, born art thou of
crags and fed on the milk of wild beasts, and I will
assert that thy breast is made of flint.   What farther

[1] Cydippe.

5 quis gradus ulterior, quo se tua porrigat ira,
    restat ?   quidve meis cernis abesse malis ?
barbara me tellus et inhospita litora Ponti
    cumque suo Borea Maenalis Ursa videt.
nulla mihi cum gente fera commercia linguae :
10   omnia solliciti sunt loca plena metus.
utque fugax avidis cervus deprensus ab ursis,
    cinctave montanis ut pavet agna lupis,
sic ego belligeris a gentibus undique saeptus
    terreor, hoste meum paene premente latus.
15 utque sit exiguum poenae, quod coniuge cara,
    quod patria careo pignoribusque meis :
ut mala nulla feram nisi nudam Caesaris iram,
    nuda parum nobis Caesaris ira mali est ?
et tamen est aliquis, qui vulnera cruda retractet,
20   solvat et in mores ora diserta meos.
in causa facili cuivis licet esse diserto,
    et minimae vires frangere quassa valent.
subruere est arces et stantia moenia virtus :
    quamlibet ignavi praecipitata premunt.
25 non sum ego qui [1] fueram. quid inanem proteris
    umbram ?
quid cinerem saxis bustaque nostra petis ?
Hector erat tunc cum bello certabat ; at idem
    vinctus ad Haemonios non erat Hector equos.
me quoque, quem noras olim, non esse memento :
30   ex illo superant haec simulacra viro.
quid simulacra, ferox, dictis incessis amaris ?
    parce, precor, Manes sollicitare meos !
omnia vera puta mea crimina, nil sit in illis,
    quod magis errorem quam scelus esse putes,
35 pendimus en profugi—satia tua pectora—poenas
    exilioque graves exiliique loco.

[1] sum ego quod

point remains to which thy anger may extend ? What
dost thou see lacking to my woes ? A barbarous
land, the unfriendly shores of Pontus, and the
Maenalian bear with her companion Boreas behold
me. No interchange of speech have I with the wild
people ; all places are charged with anxiety and fear.
As a timid stag caught by ravenous bears or a lamb
surrounded by the mountain wolves is stricken with
terror, so am I in dread, hedged about on all sides by
warlike tribes, the enemy almost pressing against my
side. Were it a slight punishment that I am
deprived of my dear wife, my native land, and my
loved ones ; were I supporting no ills but the naked
wrath of Caesar, is the naked wrath of Caesar too
small an ill ? Yet, despite this, someone there is to
handle anew my raw wounds, to move eloquent lips
against my character ! In an easy cause anybody
may be eloquent ; the slightest strength is enough to
break what is already shattered. To overthrow
citadels and upstanding walls is valour ; the worst of
cowards press hard upon what is already fallen. I
am not what I was. What dost thou trample on an
empty shadow ? Why attack with stones my ashes
and my tomb ? Hector was alive whilst he fought in
war, but once bound to the Haemonian steeds he was
not Hector. I too, whom thou knewest in former
times, no longer exist, remember ; of that man there
remains but this wraith. Why, cruel man, dost thou
assail a wraith with bitter words ? Cease, I beg, to
harass my shade. Consider all my crimes real, let
there be nothing in them that thou couldst think
rather a mistake than a crime—lo ! a fugitive I am
paying (let this sate thy heart) a penalty heavy
through exile and the place of that exile. To a

143

carnifici fortuna potest mea flenda videri :
    et tamen est uno iudice mersa parum.
saevior es tristi Bursiride, saevior illo,
40   qui falsum lento torruit igne bovem,
quique bovem Siculo fertur donasse tyranno,
    et dictis artes conciliasse suas :
" munere in hoc, rex, est usus, sed imagine maior,
    nec sola est operis forma probanda mei.
45 aspicis a dextra latus hoc adapertile tauri ?
    hac [1] tibi, quem perdes, coniciendus erit.
protinus inclusum lentis carbonibus ure :
    mugiet, et veri vox erit illa bovis.
pro quibus inventis, ut munus munere penses,
50   da, precor, ingenio praemia digna meo."
dixerat.   at Phalaris " poenae mirande repertor,
    ipse tuum praesens imbue " dixit " opus."
nec mora, monstratis crudeliter ignibus ustus
    exhibuit geminos ore gemente sonos.
55 quid mihi cum Siculis inter Scythiamque Getasque ?
    ad te, quisquis is es, nostra querella redit.
utque sitim nostro possis explere cruore,
    quantaque vis, avido gaudia corde feras,
tot mala sum fugiens tellure, tot aequore passus,
60   te quoque ut auditis posse dolere putem.
crede mihi, felix,[2] nobis collatus, Ulixes,
    Neptunique minor quam Iovis ira fuit.
ergo quicumque es, rescindere crimina noli,
    deque gravi duras volnere tolle manus ;
65 utque meae famam tenuent oblivia culpae,
    facta cicatricem ducere nostra sine ;

            [1] hic   [2] si sit *corr. Housman*

---

[1] Perillus.   [2] Phalaris.
[3] *i.e.* at once the screams of a man and the bellowing of
a bull.

hangman my fate might seem pitiful, yet there is one judge who thinks it sunk not deep enough!

[39] Thou art more cruel than harsh Busiris, more cruel than he [1] who heated the artifical bull over a slow fire and gave the bull, they say, to the Sicilian lord [2] commending his work of art with the words: "In this gift, O King, there is profit, greater than appears, for not the appearance alone of my work is worthy of praise. Seest thou on the right that the bull's flank may be opened? Through this thou must thrust whomsoever thou wouldst destroy. Forthwith shut him in and roast him over slow-burning coals: he will bellow, and that will be the voice of a true bull. For this invention pay gift with gift, and give me, I pray thee, a reward worthy of my genius." Thus he spake. But Phalaris said, "Marvellous inventor of punishment, dedicate in person thine own work!" At once roasted by the fires to which he had himself cruelly pointed the way he uttered with groaning lips sounds twofold.[3]

[55] What have I, in Scythia among the Getae, to do with Sicilians? To thee, whoever thou art, my complaint returns. That thou mayst sate thy thirst in my bood and carry as much joy as thou wilt in thy greedy heart, I have endured so many woes by land in my flight, so many by sea, that I think even thou canst feel pain at the hearing of them. Truly, Ulysses was fortunate, compared with me, for Neptune's wrath was less than Jove's has been. So then, whoever thou art, do not open again the charges against me, remove thy hard hands from my dangerous wound, and that forgetfulness may lessen the ill repute of my fault, permit a scar to cover my deed;

humanaeque memor sortis, quae tollit eosdem
    et premit, incertas ipse verere vices.
et quoniam, fieri quod numquam posse putavi,
70   est tibi de rebus maxima cura meis,
non est quod timeas : fortuna miserrima nostra est,
    omne trahit secum Caesaris ira malum.
quod magis ut liqueat, neve hoc ego fingere credar,
    ipse velim poenas experiare meas.

XII.

Frigora iam Zephyri minuunt, annoque peracto
    longior antiquis vim moderatur [1] hiems,
inpositamque sibi qui non bene pertulit Hellen,
    tempora necturnis aequa diurna facit.
5 iam violam puerique legunt hilaresque puellae,
    rustica quae nullo nata serente venit ;
prataque pubescunt variorum flore colorum,
    indocilique loquax gutture vernat avis ;
utque malae matris crimen deponat hirundo
10   sub trabibus cunas tectaque parva facit ;
herbaque, quae latuit Cerealibus obruta sulcis,
    exserit e tepida [2] molle cacumen humo ;
quoque loco est vitis, de palmite gemma movetur :
    nam procul a Getico litore vitis abest ;
15 quoque loco est arbor, turgescit in arbore ramus :
    nam procul a Geticis finibus arbor abest.
otia nunc istic, iunctisque ex ordine ludis
    cedunt verbosi garrula bella fori.
usus [3] equi nunc est, levibus nunc luditur armis,
20   nunc pila, nunc celeri volvitur orbe trochus ;

[1] visa meotis *corr. Vogel*   [2] exit et expandit   [3] lusus

---

[1] The constellation of the Ram—the month of March.
[2] Procne.

remember human fate, which lifts or lowers the same men, and fear for thyself uncertain change. And since—as I never thought possible—thou dost take the greatest interest in my affairs, there is naught for thee to fear : my fate is the very worst, Caesar's wrath draws with it every ill. That this may be clearer and I be not thought to feign it, I pray that in thine own person thou mayst try my punishment.

XII. SPRINGTIME IN TOMIS

The cold is now weakening beneath the zephyrs and at the year's end a winter more endless than those of old curbs its rigour, and he [1] who bore Helle but ill upon his back now makes equal the time of night and day. Now merry boys and girls are plucking the violets that spring up unsown in the fields, the meadows are abloom with many-coloured flowers, the chatty birds from unschooled throats utter a song of spring, and the swallow, to put off the name of evil mother,[2] builds beneath the rafters the tiny house that cradles her young. The grain that lay in hiding beneath the furrows sends forth from the unfrozen soil its tender tips. Wherever grows the vine, the bud is just pushing from the shoot (but the vine grows far from the Getic shore!), and wherever grows the tree, the branches are just budding (but the tree grows far from the Getic shore!). In yonder land there is now rest, and the noisy wars of the wordy forum are giving place to festivals one after another; now there is exercise on horse, now there is play with light arms, with the ball or the

147

nunc ubi perfusa est oleo labente iuventus,
    defessos artus Virgine tinguit aqua.
scaena viget studiisque favor distantibus ardet,
    proque tribus resonant terna theatra foris.
25 o quater et quotiens [1] non est numerare beatum,
    non interdicta cui licet urbe frui !
at mihi sentitur nix verno sole soluta,
    quaeque lacu durae non fodiantur aquae :
nec mare concrescit glacie, nec, ut ante, per Histrum
30   stridula Sauromates plaustra bubulcus agit.
incipient aliquae tamen huc adnare carinae,
    hospitaque in Ponti litore puppis erit.
sedulus occurram nautae, dictaque salute,
    quid veniat, quaeram, quisve quibusve locis.
35 ille quidem mirum ni de regione propinqua
    non nisi vicinas tutus ararit [2] aquas.
41 fas quoque ab ore freti longaeque Propontidos
    undis
42   huc aliquem certo vela dedisse Noto.[3]
37 rarus ab Italia tantum mare navita transit,
    litora rarus in haec portubus orba venit.
sive tamen Graeca scierit, sive ille Latina
40   voce loqui—certe gratior huius erit—
43 quisquis is est, memori rumorem voce referre
    et fieri famae parsque gradusque potest.
45 is, precor, auditos possit narrare triumphos
    Caesaris et Latio reddita vota Iovi,
teque, rebellatrix, tandem, Germania, magni
    triste caput pedibus supposuisse ducis.

---

[1] quantum et *vel* quantum o *vel* quater et
[2] arabit *vel* araret *corr. Heinsius*   [3] 41f *post* 36 *Wilamowitz*

---

[1] From the aqueduct called *Virgo*.

swift circling hoop; now the young men, reeking of slippery oil, are bathing wearied limbs in Virgin water.[1] The stage is full of life, and partizanship ablaze with warring passions, and three theatres roar in the place of three forums.[2] Ah! four times happy—yes, countless times happy—is he who may enjoy the unforbidden city!

[27] But mine it is to feel the snow melted by the spring sun and water which is not dug all hard from the pool. The sea, too, is no longer solid with ice, nor as before does the Sauromatian herdsman drive his creaking wagon across the Ister. Some ships will begin to voyage even as far as here, and soon there will be a friendly bark on Pontus' shore. Eagerly I shall run to meet the mariner and when I've greeted him, shall ask why he comes, who and from what place he is. It will be strange, indeed, if he is not from a neighbouring land—one who has ploughed no seas but those near by. It is possible, too, that from the mouth of the strait and the waters of far Propontis someone has set sail hither with a steady south wind. For rarely does a sailor cross the wide seas from Italy, rarely visit this harbourless shore. Yet if he knows how to speak with the voice of Greek or Roman (this last will surely be the sweeter), whoever he is, he may be one to tell faithfully some rumour, one to share and pass on some report. May he, I pray, have power to tell of Caesar's triumphs and vows paid to Jupiter of the Latins; that thou, rebellious Germany, at length hast lowered thy sorrowing head beneath the foot

[2] The three theatres were those of Pompey, Marcellus, and Balbus; the three forums were the forum Romanum, Iulium, and Augusti.

149

haec mihi qui referet, quae non vidisse dolebo,
50   ille meae domui protinus hospes erit.
ei mihi, iamne domus Scythico Nasonis in orbe est ?
    iamque tuum mihi das pro Lare, Ponte, solum ? [1]
di facite ut Caesar non hic penetrale domumque,
    hospitium poenae sed velit esse meae.

XIII.

Ecce supervacuus—quid enim fuit utile gigni ?—
    ad sua Natalis tempora noster adest.
dure, quid ad miseros veniebas exulis annos ?
    debueras illis inposuisse modum.
5 si tibi cura mei, vel si pudor ullus inesset,
    non ultra patriam me sequerere meam,
quoque loco primum tibi sum male cognitus infans,
    illo temptasses ultimus esse mihi,
iamque relinquenda,[2] quod idem fecere sodales,
10   tu quoque dixisses tristis in urbe "vale."
quid tibi cum Ponto ? num te quoque Caesaris ira
    extremam gelidi misit in orbis humum ?
scilicet expectas soliti tibi moris honorem,
    pendeat ex umeris vestis ut alba meis,
15 fumida cingatur florentibus ara coronis,
    micaque sollemni turis in igne sonet,
libaque dem proprie genitale notantia tempus,
    concipiamque bonas ore favente preces.

[1] suum ... dat ... poena locum *corr. Withof*
[2] inque relinquendo *corr. Heinsius*

---

[1] Tiberius, who took the field against the Germans after the defeat of Varus, A.D. 9.

of our leader.[1] He who tells me such things as
these—things it will grieve me that I have not seen—
shall be forthwith a guest within my home. Ah me!
is Naso's home now in the Scythian world, and dost
thou, Pontus, assign me thy soil as an abode? Ye
gods, give Caesar the will that not here may be my
hearth and home but only the hostelry of my
punishment!

XIII. A Birthday at Tomis

Lo! to no purpose—for what profit was there
in my birth?—my birthday god [2] attends his
anniversary. Cruel one, why hast thou come to
increase the wretched years of an exile? To them
thou shouldst have put an end. Hadst thou any love
for me or any sense of shame, thou wouldst not be
following me beyond my native land, and where first
I was known by thee as an ill-starred child, there
shouldst thou have tried to be my last, and when I
was forced to leave Rome, thou too, like my friends,
shouldst have said in sorrow "Farewell."

"What hast thou to do with Pontus? Is it that
Caesar's wrath sent thee too to the remotest land of
the world of cold? Thou awaitest, I suppose, thine
honour in its wonted guise: a white robe hanging
from my shoulders, a smoking altar garlanded with
chaplets, the grains of incense snapping in the holy
fire, and myself offering the cakes that mark my
birthday and framing kindly petitions with pious

[2] The *genius natalis* to whom the Roman offered sacrifice on
his birthday. The *genius* was believed to be a spiritual
counterpart of the individual.

non ita sum positus, nec sunt ea tempora nobis,
20   adventu possim laetus ut esse tuo.
funeris ara mihi, ferali cincta cupressu,[1]
    convenit et structis flamma parata rogis.
nec dare tura libet nil exorantia divos,
    in tantis subeunt nec bona verba malis.
25 si tamen est aliquid nobis hac luce petendum,
    in loca ne redeas amplius ista, precor,
dum me terrarum pars paene novissima, Pontus,
    Euxinus falso nomine dictus, habet.

XIV.

Cultor et antistes doctorum sancte virorum,
    quid facis, ingenio semper amice meo ?
ecquid, ut incolumem quondam celebrare solebas,
    nunc quoque, ne videar totus abesse, caves ?
5 conficio [2] exceptis ecquid mae carmina solis
    Artibus, artifici quae nocuere suo ?
immo ita fac, quaeso, vatum studiose novorum,
    quaque potes, retine corpus in urbe meum.
est fuga dicta mihi, non est fuga dicta libellis,
10   qui domini poenam non meruere sui.
saepe per externas [3] profugus pater exulat oras,
    urbe tamen natis exulis esse licet.
Palladis exemplo de me sine matre creata
    carmina sunt ; stirps haec progeniesque mea est.
15 hanc tibi commendo, quae quo magis orba parente
      est,
    hoc tibi tutori sarcina maior erit.

[1] cupresso   [2] suscipis   [3] extremas

lips. Not such is my condition, nor such my hours, that I can rejoice at thy coming. An altar of death girdled with funereal cypress is suited to me and a flame made ready for the up-reared pyre. Nor is it a pleasure to offer incense that wins nothing from gods, nor in such misfortunes do words of good omen come to my lips. Yet if I must ask thee something on this day, return thou no more to such a land, I pray, so long as all but the remotest part of the world, the Pontus, falsely called Euxine,[1] possesses me.

XIV. Epilogue—to an unnamed Friend

Cherisher and revered protector of learned men, what doest thou— thou that hast ever befriended my genius ? As thou once wert wont to extol me when I was in safety, now too dost thou take heed that I seem not wholly absent ? Dost thou assemble my verse except only that "Art" which ruined its artificer ? Do so, I pray, thou patron of new bards ; so far as may be, keep my body[2] in the city. Exile was decreed to me, exile was not decreed to my books ; they did not deserve their master's punishment. Oft is a father exiled on a foreign shore, yet may the exile's childpen live in the city. Pallas-fashion[3] were my verses born from me without a mother ; these are my offspring, my family. These I commend to thee ; the more bereft they are, the greater burden will they be to thee their guardian.

---

[1] Euxine means "hospitable," cf. *Tr.* iv. 4. 55 f. ; v. 10. 13 f.
[2] *i.e.* my poems.
[3] Pallas was born from the head of Zeus.

tres mihi sunt nati contagia nostra secuti :
    cetera fac curae sit tibi turba palam.
sunt quoque mutatae, ter quinque volumina, formae,
20   carmina de domini funere rapta sui.
illud opus potuit, si non prius ipse perissem,
    certius a summa nomen habere manu :
nunc incorrectum populi pervenit in ora,
    in populi quicquam si tamen ore meum est.
25 hoc quoque nescio quid nostris appone libellis,
    diverso missum quod tibi ab orbe venit.
quod quicumque leget,—si quis leget—aestimet ante,
    compositum quo sit tempore quoque loco.
aequus erit scriptis, quorum cognoverit esse
30   exilium tempus barbariamque locum :
inque tot adversis carmen mirabitur ullum
    ducere me tristi sustinuisse manu.
ingenium fregere meum mala, cuius et ante
    fons infecundus parvaque vena fuit.
35 sed quaecumque fuit, nullo exercente refugit,
    et longo periit arida facta situ.
non hic librorum, per quos inviter alarque,
    copia : pro libris arcus et arma sonant.
nullus in hac terra, recitem si carmina, cuius
40   intellecturis auribus utar, adest ;
non quo secedam locus est.   custodia muri
    summovet infestos clausaque porta Getas.
saepe aliquod quaero verbum nomenque locumque,
    nec quisquam est a quo certior esse queam.
45 dicere saepe aliquid conanti—turpe fateri !—
    verba mihi desunt dedidicique loqui.

Three of my children [1] have caught pollution from
me: make the rest of the flock openly thy
care. There are also thrice five books on changing
forms,[2] verses snatched from the funeral of their
master. That work, had I not perished beforehand,
might have gained a more secure name from my
finishing hand: but now unrevised it has come upon
men's lips—if anything of mine is on their lips. Add
to my books this humble bit also, which comes to you
dispatched from a far-distant world. Whoever
reads this (if anyone does) let him take account
beforehand at what time, in what place it was
composed. He will be fair-minded to writings which
he knows were composed in time of exile, in the
barbarian world; and amid so many adverse
circumstances he will wonder that I had the heart to
write with sorrowing hand any poem. Misfortunes
have broken my talent whose source was even
aforetime unproductive and whose stream was
meagre. But such as it was, with none to exercise it,
it has shrunken and is lost, dried up by long
neglect. Not here have I an abundance of books to
stimulate and nourish me: in their stead is the rattle
of bows and arms. There is nobody in this land,
should I read my verse, of whose intelligent ear I
might avail myself, there is no place to which I may
withdraw. The guard on the wall and a closed gate
keep back the hostile Getac. Often I am at a loss for
a word, a name, a place, and there is none who can
inform me. Oft when I attempt some utterance—
shameful confession!—words fail me: I have un-
learned my power of speech. Thracian and

---

[1] The three books of the *Ars amatoria*.
[2] The *Metamorphoses*.

OVID

Threïcio Scythicoque fere [1] circumsonor ore,
  et videor Geticis scribere posse modis.
crede mihi, timeo ne Sintia mixta Latinis
50 inque meis scriptis Pontica verba legas.
qualemcumque igitur venia dignare libellum,
  sortis et excusa condicione meae.

[1] fero

Scythian tongues chatter on almost every side, and I think I could write in Getic measure.[1]   O believe me, I fear that Sintic and Pontic language may be mingled with the Latin in my writings.   Such as my book is, then, deem it worthy of indulgence and pardon it because of the circumstances of my fate.

[1] See *Ex P*. iv. 13. 19 ff.

LIBER QUARTUS

I.

Siqua meis fuerint, ut erunt, vitiosa libellis,
    excusata suo tempore, lector, habe.
exul eram, requiesque mihi, non fama petita est,
    mens intenta suis ne foret usque malis.
5 hoc est cur cantet vinctus quoque compede fossor,
    indocili numero cum grave mollit opus.
cantat et innitens limosae pronus harenae,
    adverso tardam qui trahit amne ratem ;
quique refert pariter lentos ad pectora remos,
10   in numerum pulsa brachia iactat [1] aqua.
fessus ubi incubuit baculo saxove resedit
    pastor, harundineo carmine mulcet oves.
cantantis pariter, pariter data pensa trahentis,
    fallitur ancillae decipiturque labor.
15 fertur et abducta Lyrneside tristis Achilles
    Haemonia curas attenuasse lyra.
cum traheret silvas Orpheus et dura canendo
    saxa, bis amissa coniuge maestus erat.
me quoque Musa levat Ponti loca iussa petentem :
20   sola comes nostrae perstitit illa fugae ;

[1] pulsat

---

[1] A flute was often used to mark the time for the rowers.
      [2] Briseis.   [3] Eurydice.

BOOK IV

I. A PLEA FOR INDULGENCE

Whatever faults you may find—and you will find them—in my books, hold them absolved, reader, because of the time of their writing.   I am an exile; solace, not fame, has been my object—that my mind dwell not constantly on its own woes.   This is why even the ditcher, shackled though he be, resorts to song, lightening with untutored rhythm his heavy work.   He also sings who bends forward over the slimy sand, towing against the stream the slow-moving barge; he who pulls to his chest in unison the pliant oars, moves his arms rhythmically [1] as he strikes the water.   The weary shepherd leaning upon his staff or seated upon a rock soothes his sheep with the drone of his reeds.   At once singing, at once spinning her allotted task, the slave girl beguiles and whiles away her toil.   They say too that when the maid [2] of Lyrnesus was taken from him, sad Achilles relieved his sorrow with the Haemonian lyre.   While Orpheus was drawing to him the forests and the hard rocks by his singing, he was sorrowing for the wife [3] twice lost to him.

[19] Me also the Muse comforted while on my way to the appointed lands of Pontus ; she only was the steadfast companion of my flight—the only one who

159

sola nec insidias, Sinti nec [1] militis ensem,
　　nec mare nec ventos barbariamque timet.
scit quoque, cum perii, quis me deceperit error,
　　et culpam in facto, non scelus, esse meo,
25 scilicet hoc ipso nunc aequa, quod obfuit ante,
　　cum mecum iuncti criminis acta rea est.
non equidem vellem, quoniam nocitura fuerunt,
　　Pieridum sacris inposuisse manum.
sed nunc quid faciam ? vis me tenet ipsa sacrorum,
30 　　et carmen demens carmine laesus amo.
sic nova Dulichio lotos gustata palato
　　illo, quo nocuit, grata sapore fuit.
sentit amans sua damna fere, tamen haeret in illis,
　　materiam culpae persequiturque suae.
35 nos quoque delectant, quamvis nocuere, libelli,
　　quodque mihi telum vulnera fecit, amo.
forsitan hoc studium possit furor esse videri,
　　sed quiddam furor hic utilitatis habet.
semper in obtutu mentem vetat esse malorum,
40 　　praesentis casus inmemoremque facit.
utque suum Bacche non sentit saucia vulnus,
　　dum stupet Idaeis exululata modis,
sic ubi mota calent viridi mea pectora thyrso,
　　altior humano spiritus ille malo est.
45 ille nec exilium, Scythici nec litora ponti,
　　ille nec iratos sentit habere deos.
utque soporiferae biberem si pocula Lethes,
　　temporis adversi sic mihi sensus abest.

[1] inter nec : Sinti nec *Ehwald*

---

[1] A tribe mentioned only here by Ovid, but the text is not
certain.

fears neither treachery, nor the brand of the Sintian [1]
soldier, nor sea nor winds nor the world of the
barbarians. She knows also what mistake led me
astray at the time of my ruin,—that there is fault in
my deed, but no crime. Doubtless for this very reason
is she fair to me now because she injured me before,
when she was indicted with me for a joint
crime. Well could I wish, since they were destined
to work me harm, that I had ne'er set hand to the holy
service of the Pierian ones. But now, what am I to
do ? The very power of that holy service grips me ;
madman that I am, though song has injured me, 'tis
still song that I love. So the strange lotos tasted by
Dulichian palates [2] gave pleasure through the very
savour which wrought harm. The lover is oft aware
of his own ruin yet clings to it, pursuing that which
sustains his own fault. I also find pleasure in my
books though they have injured me, and I love the
very weapon that made my wounds.

[37] Perchance this passion may seem madness, but
this madness has a certain profit : it forbids the mind
to be ever gazing at its woes, rendering it forgetful of
present mischance. As the stricken Bacchante feels
not her wound while in ecstasy she shrieks to the
accompaniment of Idaean measures, so when my
heart feels the inspiring glow of the green thyrsus, [3]
that mood is too exalted for human woe ; it realizes
neither exile nor the shores of the Scythian sea nor the
anger of the gods, and just as if I were drinking
slumber-bringing Lethe's draughts, I lose the sense of
evil days.

[2] The comrades of Ulysses are meant.
[3] The ivy-crowned staff of the devotees of Bacchus—often
used as a symbol for poetic inspiration.

iure deas igitur veneror mala nostra levantes,
50   sollicitae [1] comites ex Helicone fugae,
et partim pelago partim vestigia terra
    vel rate dignatas vel pede nostra sequi.
sint, precor, hae saltem faciles mihi! namque
        deorum
    cetera cum magno Caesare turba facit,
55 meque tot adversis cumulant,[2] quot litus harenas,
    quotque fretum pisces, ovaque piscis habet.
vere prius flores, aestu numerabis aristas,
    poma per autumnum frigoribusque nives,
quam mala, quae toto patior iactatus in orbe,
60   dum miser Euxini litora laeva [3] peto.
nec tamen, ut veni, levior fortuna malorum est:
    huc quoque sunt nostras fata secuta vias.
hic quoque cognosco natalis stamina nostri,
    stamina de nigro vellere facta mihi.
65 utque neque insidias capitisque pericula narrem,
    vera quidem, veri [4] sed graviora fide,
vivere quam miserum est inter Bessosque Getasque
    illum, qui populi semper in ore fuit!
quam miserum est, porta vitam muroque tueri,
70   vixque suit tutum viribus esse loci!
aspera militiae iuvenis certamina fugi,
    nec nisi lusura movimus arma manu;
nunc senior gladioque latus scutoque sinistram,
    canitiem galeae subicioque meam.
75 nam dedit e specula custos ubi signa tumultus,
    induimus trepida protinus arma manu.

[1] sollicitas *corr. Scaliger*
[2] cumulat   [3] saeva : laeva ς
[4] veri] vera *vel* vidi *corr. Francius*

---

[1] *i.e.* as one enters the Pontus.   But Ovid may be playing

⁴⁹ 'Tis right then for me to revere the goddesses who lighten my misfortunes, who came from Helicon to share my anxious flight, who now by sea, now by land, deigned to follow my route on ship or afoot. May they at least, I pray, be propitious to me! For the rest of the gods take sides with mighty Caesar, heaping upon me as many ills as the sands of the shore, the fishes of the sea, or the eggs of the fish. Sooner will you count the flowers of spring, the grain-ears of summer, the fruits of autumn, or the snowflakes in time of cold than the ills which I suffered driven all over the world seeking in wretchedness the shores to the left ¹ of the Euxine. Yet no lighter since my coming is the lot of my misfortunes; to this place also fate has followed my path. Here also I recognize the threads of my nativity, threads twisted for me from a black fleece. To say naught of ambushes or of dangers to my life—true they are, yet too heavy for belief in truth—how pitiable a thing is living among Bessi and Getae for him who was ever on the people's lips! How pitiable to guard life by gate and wall, and scarce to be safeguarded by the strength of one's own position! The rough contests of military service I shunned even as a youth and touched arms only with a hand intending to play; but now that I am growing old I fit a sword to my side, a shield to my left arm, and I place a helmet upon my gray head. For when the guard from the lookout has given the signal of a raid, forthwith I don my armour with shaking hands.

on the meaning of Euxine, " hospitable," " propitious," *i.e.* the " hospitable sea, so inhospitable," *cf.* Tr. iii. 13. 28 ; v. 10. 14 ; iv. 8. 42. But *Tr.* iv. 10. 97 supports the translation given in the text.

hostis, habens arcus imbutaque tela venenis,[1]
    saevus anhelanti moenia lustrat equo;
utque rapax pecudem, quae se non texit ovili,
80   per sata, per silvas fertque trahitque lupus,
sic, siquem nondum portarum saepe[2] receptum
    barbarus in campis repperit hostis, habet:
aut sequitur captus coniectaque vincula collo
    accipit, aut telo virus habente perit.
85 hic ego sollicitae iaceo novus incola sedis:
    heu nimium fati tempora longa[3] mei!
et tamen ad numeros antiquaque sacra reverti
    sustinet in tantis hospita Musa malis.
sed neque cui recitem quisquam est mea carmina,
    nec qui
90   auribus accipiat verba Latina suis.
ipse mihi—quid enim faciam?—scriboque legoque,
    tutaque iudicio littera nostra suo est.
saepe tamen dixi "cui nunc haec cura laborat?
    an mea Sauromatae scripta Getaeque legent?"
95 saepe etiam lacrimae me sunt scribente profusae,
    umidaque est fletu littera facta meo,
corque vetusta meum, tamquam nova, vulnera novit,
    inque sinum maestae labitur imber aquae.
cum vice mutata, qui sim fuerimque, recordor,
100   et, tulerit quo me casus et unde, subit,
saepe manus demens, studiis irata sibique,
    misit in arsuros carmina nostra focos.
atque ita,[4] de multis quoniam non multa supersunt,
    cum venia facito, quisquis es, ista legas.
105 tu quoque non melius, quam sunt mea tempora,
    carmen,
    interdicta mihi, consule, Roma, boni.

---

[1] veneno   [2] sede : saepe *s*
[3] lenta   [4] ea : ita *s*

The foe with his bows and with arrows dipped in poison fiercely circles the walls upon his panting steed, and as the sheep which has not found shelter in the fold is carried and dragged through field, through forest by the ravening wolf, so 'tis with him whom the barbarian finds not yet sheltered within the hedge of the gates, but in the fields : that man either follows into captivity and submits to the bonds cast about his throat or he dies by an envenomed missile. This is the place in which, a new colonist in an abode of anxiety, I lie secluded—alas ! too long is the period of my fate !

[87] Nevertheless my Muse has the heart to return to rhythm, to her old-time rites, a friendly guest amid these great misfortunes. But there is none to whom I may read my verses, none whose ears can comprehend Latin words. I write for myself—what else can I do ?—and I read to myself, and my writing is secure in its own criticism. Yet have I often said, " For whom this careful toil ? Will the Sauromatae and the Getae read my writings ? " Often too my tears have flowed as I wrote, my writing has been moistened by my weeping, my heart feels the old wounds as if they were fresh, and sorrow's rain glides down upon my breast.

[99] Again when I bethink me what, through change of fortune, I am and what I was, when it comes over me whither fate has borne me and whence, often my mad hand, in anger with my efforts and with itself, has hurled my verses to blaze upon the hearth. And since of the many not many survive, see thou readest them with indulgence, whoever thou mayst be ! Thou too take in good part verse that is not better than my lot, O Rome forbidden to me !

OVID

II.

Iam fera Caesaribus Germania, totus ut orbis,
    victa potest flexo succubuisse genu,
altaque velentur fortasse Palatia sertis,
    turaque in igne sonent inficiantque diem,
5 candidaque adducta collum percussa securi
    victima purpureo sanguine pulset humum,
donaque amicorum templis promissa deorum
    reddere victores Caesar uterque parent,
et qui Caesareo iuvenes sub nomine crescunt,
10   perpetuo terras ut domus illa regat,
cumque bonis nuribus pro sospite Livia nato
    munera det meritis, saepe datura, deis,
et pariter matres et quae sine crimine castos
    perpetua servant virginitate focos ;
15 plebs pia cumque pia laetetur plebe senatus,
    parvaque cuius eram pars ego nuper eques :
nos procul expulsos communia gaudia fallunt,
    famaque tam longe non nisi parva venit.
ergo omnis populus poterit spectare triumphos,
20   cumque ducum titulis oppida capta leget,
vinclaque captiva reges cervice gerentes
    ante coronatos ire videbit equos,
et cernet vultus aliis pro temporo versos,
    terribiles aliis inmemoresque sui.
25 quorum pars causas et res et nomina quaeret,
    pars referet, quamvis noverit illa parum.

---

[1] Tiberius was in the field against the Germans, *cf*. iii. 12.
45.   Ovid is anticipating the triumph.
[2] Augustus and Tiberius.
[3] Germanicus and the younger Drusus.

166

II. A Triumph over Germany

Already wild Germany, like the whole world, may
have yielded on bended knee to the Caesars; [1]
mayhap the lofty Palatium is decked with garlands
and incense is crackling in the fire, colouring the light
of day, while from the white victim's throat smitten
by the axe's stroke the red blood is pattering upon the
ground, the gifts promised to the temples of the
friendly gods are being made ready for offering by
both Caesars [2] and by the youths [3] who are growing
up under Caesar's name to give that house eternal
sway over the world; with her good daughters [4] Livia
for the safety of her son is perchance offering gifts, as
she will often do, to the deserving gods, and in her
company the matrons also and those who without
stain in eternal virginity keep watch over the heart of
purity; the loyal plebs is rejoicing, and with the loyal
plebs the senate and the knights among whom but
recently I had a humble part: but I driven so far
away miss the common rejoicing and nothing but a
slight rumour penetrates so far.

[10] So then all the people will be able to view the
triumph, reading the names of captured towns and
the titles of leaders, beholding the kings with chains
upon their captive throats marching before the
garlanded horses, seeing some countenances turned
to earth as becomes captives, others grim and
forgetful of their lot. Some of the people will inquire
the causes, the objects, the names, and others will
answer though they know all too little.

[4] Agrippina, wife of Germanicus, and Livilla, wife of
Drusus.

167

"hic, qui Sidonio fulget sublimis in ostro,
    dux fuerat belli, proximus ille duci.
hic, qui nunc in humo lumen miserabile fixit,
30   non isto vultu, cum tulit arma, fuit.
ille ferox et adhuc oculis hostilibus ardens
    hortator pugnae consiliumque fuit.
perfidus hic nostros inclusit fraude locorum,
    squalida promissis qui tegit ora comis.
35 illo, qui sequitur, dicunt mactata ministro
    saepe recusanti corpora capta deo.
hic lacus, hi montes, haec tot castella, tot amnes
    plena ferae caedis, plena cruoris erant.
Drusus in his meruit quondam cognomina terris,
40   quae bene [1] progenies, digna parente, tulit.[2]
cornibus hic fractis viridi male tectus ab ulva
    decolor ipse suo sanguine Rhenus erat.
crinibus en etiam fertur Germania passis,
    et ducis invicti sub pede maesta sedet,
45 collaque Romanae praebens animosa securi
    vincula fert illa, qua tulit arma, manu."
hos super in curru, Caesar, victore veheris
    purpureus populi rite per ora tui,
quaque ibis, manibus circumplaudere tuorum,
50   undique iactato flore tegente vias.
tempora Phoebea lauro cingetur "io" que
    miles "io" magna voce "triumphe" canet.
ipse sono plausuque simul fremituque calentes [3]
    quadriiugos cernes saepe resistere equos.
55 inde petes arcem et delubra faventia votis,
    et dabitur merito laurea vota Iovi.

---

[1] bona *corr. Heinsius*   [2] fuit *corr. Faber*   [3] canentum

[1] These are the "floats"—representations of rivers, etc.,
which the Romans transported in triumphal processions.

²⁷ "This one who gleams aloft in Sidonian purple, was the leader in war, that other his next in command. This who now has fixed his sad gaze upon the ground, had not such countenance when he bore arms. That fierce fellow with hostile eyes still ablaze was at once the instigator and planner of the fight. This traitor here trapped our men in a treacherous place—the one who now conceals his unkempt face with his long hair. That one following him they say was the priest who sacrificed captives to a god who often refused them. This lake, these mountains, these many forts,[1] all the rivers were filled with wild slaughter, filled with gore. Drusus once earned in this land a surname, which his son,[2] one worthy of his father, justly adopted. This thing with broken horns and sorry covering of green sedge was the Rhine himself, discoloured with his own blood. See! even Germany is borne along with streaming locks, seated in grief at the feet of the unconquered leader. Offering her proud neck to the Roman axe she wears chains on that hand in which she carried arms."

⁴⁷ High above them in the car of victory, thou wilt ride, O Caesar, clad in purple before the faces of thy people as old rite bids. Throughout thy course thou wilt be applauded by the hands of thy subjects, from all sides flowers will fall and cover thy path. With their temples all garlanded in the laurel of Phoebus the soldiers will chant "io, io triumphe"[3] in loud voices. Thou wilt thyself often see the four steeds rear in confusion at the song, the applause, and the din all at once. Then thou wilt seek the citadel and shrines that favour prayers and thou wilt give the votive laurel to deserving Jupiter.

² Germanicus   ³ The cry of triumph.

haec ego summotus qua possum mente videbo :
    erepti nobis ius habet illa loci :
illa per inmensas spatiatur libera terras,
60   in caelum celeri pervenit illa fuga [1] ;
illa meos oculos mediam deducit in urbem,
    immunes tanti nec sinit esse boni ;
invenietque animus, qua currus spectet eburnos ;
    sic certe in patria per breve tempus ero.
65 vera tamen capiet populus spectacula felix,
    laetaque erit praesens cum duce turba suo.
at mihi fingendo tantum longeque remotis
    auribus hic fructus percipiendus erit,
aque procul Latio diversum missus in orbem
70   qui narret cupido, vix erit, ista mihi.
is quoque iam serum referet veteremque triumphum :
    quo tamen audiero tempore, laetus ero.
illa dies veniet, mea qua lugubria ponam,
    causaque privata publica maior erit.

III.

Magna minorque ferae, quarum regis altera Graias,
    altera Sidonias, utraque sicca, rates,
omnia cum summo positae videatis in axe,
    et maris occiduas non subeatis aquas,
5 aetheriamque suis cingens amplexibus arcem
    vester ab intacta circulus extet humo,
aspicite illa, precor, quae non bene moenia quondam
    dicitur Iliades transiluisse Remus,
inque meam nitidos dominam convertite vultus,
10   sitque memor nostri necne, referte mihi.

                  [1] via

---

[1] The constellations of the Greater and Lesser Bear.

⁵⁷ All this I, an exile, shall see in my mind's eye—
my only way; for my mind at least has a right to that
place which has been torn from me.   It travels free
through measureless lands, it reaches the heaven in
its swift flight, it leads my eyes to the city's midst, not
allowing them to be deprived of so great a blessing;
and my mind will find a place to view the ivory car,—
thus at least for a brief space I shall be in my native
land.   Yet the real sight will belong to the happy
people, the throng will rejoice in the presence of their
own leader.

⁶⁷ But as for me—in imagination only and with
ears far away I shall have perforce to realize the joy,
and there will scarce be one sent far from Latium to
the opposite side of the world to tell it all to eager
me.   Even he will tell the tale of that triumph late,
when it is already of long standing; yet whenever I
hear of it, I shall be glad.   Then will come a day on
which I may lay aside my gloom; greater than a
private cause will be that of the state.

III. To his Wife

Ye two beasts,¹ great and small, one the guide of
Grecian, the other of Sidonian ships, each unwetted
by the waves, since from your places at the summit
of the pole ye behold all things, never dipping
beneath the westering waters, and since your orbit
girdling heaven's heights in its embrace stands out
above the earth it never touches, regard, I pray,
those walls which once, they say, Remus, Ilia's son,
leaped across to his undoing; turn your bright faces
upon my lady and tell me whether she thinks of me

ei mihi, cur, nimium quae sunt manifesta,
 requiro?
cur labat [1] ambiguo spes mea mixta metu ?
crede, quod est et vis, ac desine tuta vereri,
 deque fide certa sit tibi certa fides,
15 quodque polo fixae nequeunt tibi dicere flammae,
 non mentitura tu tibi voce refer,
esse tui memorem, de qua tibi maxima cura est,
 quodque potest, secum nomen habere tuum.
vultibus illa tuis tamquam praesentis inhaeret,[2]
20 teque remota procul, si modo vivit, amat.
ecquid, ubi incubuit iusto mens aegra dolori,
 lenis ab admonito pectore somnus abit ?
tunc subeunt curae, dum te lectusque locusque
 tangit et oblitam non sinit esse mei,
25 et veniunt aestus, et nox inmensa videtur,
 fessaque iactati corporis ossa dolent ?
non equidem dubito, quin haec et cetera fiant,
 detque tuus maesti signa doloris amor,
nec cruciere minus, quam cum Thebana cruentum
30 Hectora Thessalico vidit ab axe rapi.
quid tamen ipse precer dubito, nec dicere possum,
 affectum quem te mentis habere velim.
tristis es ?   indignor quod sim tibi causa doloris :
 non es ?   at [3] amisso coniuge digna fores.
35 tu vero tua damna dole, mitissima coniunx,
 tempus et a nostris exige triste malis,
fleque meos casus : est quaedam flere voluptas ;
 expletur lacrimis egeriturque dolor.
atque utinam lugenda tibi non vita, sed esset
40 mors mea, morte fores sola relicta mea !

---

[1] latet

[2] praesentibus haeret   [3] ut : at *Bentley*

or not. Ah me! Why am I looking for what is all too plain to see? Why do my hopes falter, blighted by anxious dread? Believe that which is true and what you wish, and cease to fear for what is secure. When faith wavers not, have in it unwavering faith, and what the pole flames cannot tell you, that tell yourself in a voice that will not lie: of you in very truth she thinks—she who is the object of your own great love; she keeps with her the only thing she can, your name. She bends over your face as if you were present, and though far away, if only she is alive, she loves you still.

[21] When thy sick heart broods upon thy just grief, can it be that soft slumber leaves thy mindful breast? Does woe then steal upon thee, while my couch and my place touch thee, not permitting thee to forget me? Does anguish come and the night seem endless, and do the weary bones of thy tossing body ache? I doubt not that these and other things occur, that thy love gives token of sorrow's pain, that thou art tortured not less than the Theban princess [1] when she beheld blood-stained Hector dragged by the Thessalian chariot. [2]

[31] Yet what prayer to utter I know not, nor can I say what feeling I wish thee to have. Art thou sad? I am angry that I am the cause of thy grief. Thou art not sad? Yet, I would have thee worthy of a lost husband. Bewail in very truth thy loss, gentlest of wives, live through a time of sorrow for my misfortunes. Weep for my woe; in weeping there is a certain joy, for by tears grief is sated and relieved. And would that thou hadst to mourn not my life but my death, that by my death thou hadst been left

[1] Andromache.   [2] The car of Achilles.

spiritus hic per te patrias exisset in auras,
    sparsissent lacrimae pectora nostra piae,
supremoque die notum spectantia caelum
    texissent digiti lumina nostra tui,
45 et cinis in tumulo positus iacuisset avito,
    tactaque nascenti corpus haberet humus;
denique, ut et vixi, sine crimine mortuus essem.
    nunc mea supplicio vita pudenda suo est.
me miserum, si tu, cum diceris exulis uxor,
50   avertis vultus et subit ora rubor!
me miserum, si turpe putas mihi nupta videri!
    me miserum, si te iam pudet esse meam!
tempus ubi est illud, quo te iactare solebas
    coniuge, nec nomen dissimulare viri?
55 tempus ubi est, quo te [1]—nisi non vis illa referri—
    et dici, memini, iuvit et esse meam?
utque proba dignum est, omni tibi dote placebam:
    addebat veris multa faventis amor.
nec, quem praeferres—ita res tibi magna videbar—
60   quemque tuum malles esse, vir alter erat.
nunc quoque ne pudeat, quod sis mihi nupta;
       tuusque
    non debet dolor hinc, debet abesse pudor.
cum cecidit Capaneus subito temerarius ictu,
    num legis Euadnen erubuisse viro?
65 nec quia rex mundi compescuit ignibus ignes,
    ipse suis Phaëthon infitiandus erat.
nec Semele Cadmo facta est aliena parenti,
    quod precibus periit ambitiosa suis.
nec tibi, quod saevis ego sum Iovis ignibus ictus,
70   purpureus molli fiat in ore pudor.

[1] illud quo te *vel* illud nisi non vis *vel* illud quo ni (non) fugis *corr.* ⚡

174

alone! This spirit of mine through thy aid would
have gone forth to its native air, loving tears would
have wet my breast, my eyes upon the last day gazing
at a familiar sky would have been closed by thy
fingers, my ashes would have been laid to rest in the
tomb of my fathers and the ground that I touched at
birth would possess my body ; as I lived, in fine, so
should I have died,--without crime. Now my life
must be shamed by its own punishment. Wretched
am I if, when thou art called an exile's wife, thou dost
avert thy gaze and a blush steals over thy
face ! Wretched am I if thou countest it disgrace to
be seen as my bride ! Wretched am I if now thou art
ashamed to be mine ! Where is that time when thou
wert wont to boast of thy husband and not conceal
that husband's name ? Where is that time when—
unless thou wouldst not have such things recalled—
thou wert glad (I remember) to be called and to be
mine ? As becomes a good woman thou wert pleased
with every endowment I possessed and to those
which were real thy partial love added many. There
was no other man for thee to put before me—so
important an object did I seem to thee—nor any
whom thou didst prefer to be thy husband. Even
now be not ashamed that thou art wedded to me ; this
should bring thee grief, but no shame. When fell
rash Capaneus by a sudden stroke, dost thou read
that Euadne blushed for her husband ? Not because
the king of the world quelled fire with fire was
Phaëthon to be denied by his friends. Semele was
not estranged from her father, Cadmus, because she
perished through her ambitious prayers. Nor upon
thy tender face, because I have been smitten by
Jove's flame, let red shame be spread. But rather

sed magis in curam nostri consurge tuendi,
    exemplumque mihi coniugis esto bonae,
materiamque tuis tristem virtutibus imple :
    ardua per praeceps gloria vadit iter.
75 Hectora quis nosset, si felix Troia fuisset ?
    publica virtutis per mala facta via est.
ars tua, Tiphy, iacet, si non sit in aequore fluctus :
    si valeant homines, ars tua, Phoebe, iacet.
quae latet inque bonis cessat non cognita rebus,
80   apparet virtus arguiturque malis.
dat tibi nostra locum tituli fortuna, caputque
    conspicuum pietas quo tua tollat, habet.
utere temporibus, quorum nunc munere facta est [1]
    et patet in laudes area magna tuas.

IV.

O qui, nominibus cum sis generosus avorum,
    exsuperas morum nobilitate genus,
cuius inest animo patrii candoris imago,
    non careat nervis [2] candor ut iste suis,
5 cuius in ingenio est partriae facundia linguae,
    quo prior in Latio non fuit ulla foro—
quod minime volui, positis pro nomine signis
    dictus es : ignoscas laudibus ipse tuis.
nil ego peccavi ; tua te bona cognita produnt.
10   si, quod es, appares, culpa soluta mea est.
nec tamen officium nostro tibi carmine factum
    principe tam iusto posse nocere puto.
ipse pater patriae—quid enim est civilius illo ?—
    sustinet in nostro carmine saepe legi,

[1] ficta est *vel* freta es : facta est *Ehwald*
[2] numeris *ς*

---

[1] Perhaps Messalinus, *cf. Ex P*. i. 7, ii. 2.

rise to the charge of my defence and be thou for me
the model of a noble wife. Flood a sad theme with
thy virtues: glory scales the heights by steepest
paths. Who would know Hector, if Troy had been
happy? By public ills was the way of virtue
builded. Thy skill, Tiphys, lies inert if there be no
wave upon the sea: if men be in health, thy skill,
Phoebus, lies inert.

⁷⁹ The virtue which lies hidden and hangs back
unrecognized in times of prosperity, comes to the fore
and asserts itself in adversity. My fate gives thee
scope for fame and provides a chance for thy loyal
love to raise a conspicuous head. Avail thyself of
the crisis through whose gift a mighty field has been
created, open for thy priase.

IV. To a Noble Friend [1]

O you who through ancestral names have noble
birth yet surpass your birth in nobility of character,
whose mind reflects your father's candour yet so that
it lacks not powers all its own, in whose intellect
resides the eloquence of your father's tongue which
no other in the Latin forum has excelled—I have
addressed you not at all as I wished, with symbols
instead of a name; do you pardon these praises that
are all your own. I have been to blame in naught,
for your virtues are recognized and betray you. If
you appear to be what you really are I am acquitted
of fault.

[11] And yet the homage rendered to you by my verse
cannot, I think, harm you with so just a prince; even
the Father of his Country--for who is milder than
he?—submits to frequent mention in my verse, nor

15 nec prohibere potest, quia res est publica Caesar,
    et de communi pars quoque nostra bono est.
Iuppiter ingeniis praebet sua numina vatum,
    seque celebrari quolibet ore sinit.
causa tua exemplo superorum tuta duorum est,
20   quorum hic aspicitur, creditur ille deus.
ut non debuerim, tamen hoc ego crimen habebo :
    non fuit arbitrii littera nostra tui.
nec nova, quod tecum loquor, est iniuria nostra,
    incolumis cum quo saepe locutus eram.
25 quo vereare minus ne sim tibi crimen amicus,
    invidiam, siqua est, auctor habere potest.
nam tuus est primis cultus mihi semper ab annis—
    hoc certe noli dissimulare—pater,
ingeniumque meum (potes hos meminisse) probabat
30   plus etiam quam me iudice dignus eram ;
deque meis illo referebat versibus ore,
    in quo pars magnae nobilitatis erat.
non igitur tibi nunc, quod me domus ista recepit,
    sed prius auctori sunt data verba tuo.[1]
35 nec [2] data sunt, mihi crede, tamen : sed in omnibus actis
    ultima si demas, vita tuenda mea est.
hanc quoque, qua perii, culpam scelus esse negabis,
    si tanti series sit tibi nota mali.
aut timor aut error nobis, prius obfuit error.
40   a ! [3] sine me Fati non meminisse mei !
neve retractando nondum coëuntia rumpam [4]
    vulnera : vix illis proderit ipsa quies.
ergo ut iure damus poenas, sic afuit omne
    peccato facinus consiliumque meo ;

[1] sed sunt auctori non tua verba tuo
[2] non : nec ς   [3] at   [4] rumpe *vel* rupem

[1] Jupiter and Augustus.

can he prevent it, for Caesar is the state, and of the common good I too have a share. Jupiter offers his divinity of poets' art, permitting himself to be praised by every mouth. Your case is safeguarded by the example of two superhuman beings [1] of whom one in men's sight, the other in their belief, is a god. Even though I have transgressed duty, yet I shall be the one accused, for my letter was not under your control. And 'tis no new wrong that I commit in speaking with you, for in the time of my security I often spoke with you. You need not fear that my friendship will be laid as a charge against you; the odium, if there be any, can be assigned to him who was responsible. For from my earliest years I honoured your father [2]—this at least desire not to conceal—and my talent, you may remember, was approved by him even more than in my own judgment I deserved; of my verse he used to speak with those lips in which lay part of his great renown. Not you then, if your house made me welcome, but your father before you was cheated. Yet cheating there was none, believe me, but in all its acts, if you except the very latest, my life is worthy of protection. Even this fault which has ruined me you will say is no crime, if you should come to know the course of this great evil. Either timidity or a mistake— mistake first—has injured me. Ah, let me not remember my fate ! Let me not handle and break open wounds that are not yet closed ! Scarce will rest itself relieve them.

[43] So then I am justly paying a penalty, but no act or design was connected with my sin. And this the

[2] M. Valerius Messalla—if the noble addressed is Messalinus.

45 idque deus sentit; pro quo nec lumen ademptum,
    nec mihi detractas possidet alter opes.
forsitan hanc ipsam, vivam modo, finiet olim,
    tempore cum fuerit lenior ira, fugam.
nunc precor hinc alio iubeat discedere, si non
50   nostra verecundo vota pudore carent.
mitius exilium pauloque propinquius opto,
    quique sit a saevo longius hoste locus;
quantaque in Augusto clementia, si quis ab illo
    hoc peteret pro me, forsitan ille daret.
55 frigida me cohibent Euxini litora Ponti:
    dictus ab antiquis Axenus ille fuit.
nam neque iactantur moderatis aequora ventis,
    nec placidos portus hospita navis adit.
sunt circa gentes, quae praedam sanguine quaerunt;
60   nec minus infida terra timetur aqua.
illi, quos audis hominum gaudere cruore,
    paene sub eiusdem sideris axe iacent,
nec procul a nobis locus est, ubi Taurica dira
    caede pharetratae spargitur ara deae.
65 haec prius, ut memorant, non invidiosa nefandis
    nec cupienda bonis regna Thoantis erant.
hic pro supposita virgo Pelopeïa cerva
    sacra deae coluit qualiacumque suae.
quo postquam, dubium pius an sceleratus, Orestes
70   exactus Furiis venerat ipse suis,
et comes exemplum veri Phoceus amoris,
    qui duo corporibus mentibus unus erant,
protinus evincti [1] tristem ducuntur ad aram,
    quae stabat geminas ante cruenta fores.

---

[1] evicti

---

[1] Euxinus, "hospitable," Axenos, "inhospitable," *cf. Tr*. iii. 13 (end).

God realizes, and so life was not taken from me nor my wealth stripped away to become the property of another. Perchance this very exile, if only I live, he will sometimes bring to an end when time shall soften his wrath. Now I am begging him to order me to another place, if my prayer lacks not respect and modesty. A milder place of exile, a little nearer home, I pray—a place farther from the fierce enemy ; and such is Augustus's mercy that if one should ask this of him in my behalf, it may be he would grant it.

⁵⁵ The cold shores of the Pontus Euxinus keep me ; by men of old it was called Axenus.¹ For its waters are tossed by no moderate winds and there are no quiet harbours visited by foreign ships. Round about are tribes eager for plunder and bloodshed, and the land is not less to be feared than the treacherous sea. They whom you hear as rejoicing in men's gore almost beneath the axis of the same constellation as myself, and not far away from me is the place where the Tauric altar of the quivered goddess ² is sprinkled with the blood of murder. This in former times, they say, was the realm of Thoas, not envied by the wicked nor desired by the good. Here the Pelopian maid,³ she for whom the doe was substituted, cared for the offerings (whatever their nature! ⁴) to her goddess. Hither came Orestes, whether in loyalty or crime, I know not, driven by his own furies, and his Phocean comrade,⁵ the model of sincere love ; these twain were a single heart in two bodies. Forthwith in bonds they were brought to the harsh altar that stood reeking with blood before

² The Taurian Diana.   ³ Iphigenia.
⁴ Human sacrifices.   ⁵ Pylades.

181

75 nec tamen hunc sua mors, nec mors sua terruit illum ;
    alter ob alterius funera maestus erat.
et iam constiterat stricto mucrone sacerdos,
    cinxerat et Graias barbara vitta comas,
cum vice sermonis fratrem cognovit, et illi
80   pro nece complexus Iphigenia dedit.
laeta deae signum crudelia sacra perosae
    transtulit ex illis in meliora locis.
haec igitur regio, magni paene ultima mundi,
    quam fugere homines dique, propinqua mihi est :
85 aque [1] mea terra [2] prope sunt funebria sacra,
    si modo Nasoni barbara terra sua est.
o utinam venti, quibus est ablatus Orestes,
    placato referant et mea vela deo !

V.

O mihi dilectos inter pars prima sodales,
    unica fortunis ara reperta meis
cuius ab adloquiis anima haec moribunda revixit,
    ut vigil infusa Pallade flamma solet ;
5 qui veritus non es portus aperire fideles
    fulmine percussae confugiumque rati ;
cuius eram censu non me sensurus egentem,
    si Caesar patrias eripuisset opes.
temporis oblitum dum me rapit impetus huius,
10   excidit heu nomen quam mihi paene tuum !
tu tamen agnoscis tactusque cupidine laudis,
    ' ille ego sum ' cuperes dicere posse palam.
certe ego, si sineres, titulum tibi reddere vellem,
    et raram famae conciliare fidem.

----

[1] atque   [2] meam terram

----

[1] Augustus.   [2] *i.e.* when oil is poured upon it.

the double doors. Yet either the one nor the other
feared his own death : each sorrowed for the other's
fate. Already had the priestess taken her stand with
drawn knife, her Grecian tresses bound with a
barbarian fillet, when in their talk she recognized her
brother and in the stead of death Iphigenia gave him
her embrace. In joy she bore away the statue of the
goddess, who detested cruel rites, from that place to a
better.

[83] Such then is the region, almost the farthest in the
vast world, fled by men and gods, that is near
me. Near to my land—if a barbarian land is Naso's
own—are the rites of death. O may the winds which
bore Orestes away, waft my wails also homeward,
under the favour of a god [1] appeased !

V. To a Loyal Friend

O thou who art foremost among my beloved
comrades, who didst prove to be the sole altar for my
fortunes, whose words of comfort revived this dying
soul, as the flame is wont to wake at the touch of
Pallas,[2] thou who didst not fear to open a secure
harbour of refuge for a bark smitten by the
thunderbolt ; through whose means I should not have
felt myself in want had Caesar taken from me my
inherited wealth—while my fervour hurries me on in
forgetfulness of my present state, how nearly, ah me !
have I let slip thy name ? Yet dost thou recognize
it, and touched by desire for praise thou
wouldst wish thou couldst say openly, "I am the
man." Surely if thou wouldst permit, I would
render honour to thee and unite rare fidelity to fame.

15 ne noceam grato vereor tibi carmine, neve
   intempestivus nominis obstet honor.
   quod licet (et [1] tutum est) intra tua pectora gaude
   meque tui memorem teque fuisse pium,
   utque facis, remis ad opem luctare ferendam,
20   dum veniat placido mollior aura deo ;
   et tutare caput nulli servabile, si non
      qui mersit Stygia sublevet illud aqua ;
   teque, quod est rarum, praesta constanter ad omne
      indeclinatae munus amicitiae.
25 sic tua processus habeat fortuna perennes,
      sic ope non egeas ipse iuvesque tuos ;
   sic aequet tua nupta virum bonitate perenni,
      incidat et vestro nulla [2] querella toro ;
   diligat et semper socius te sanguinis illo,
30   quo pius affectu Castora frater amat ;
   sic similisque tibi iuvenis [3] sit natus, et illum
      moribus agnoscat quilibet esse tuum ;
   sic faciat socerum taeda te nata iugali,
      nec tardum iuveni det tibi nomen avi.

VI.

Tempore ruricolae patiens fit taurus aratri,
   praebet et incurvo colla premenda iugo ;
tempore paret equus lentis animosus habenis,
   et placido duros accipit ore lupos ;
5 tempore Poenorum compescitur ira leonum,
   nec feritas animo, quae fuit ante, manet ;
quaeque sui monitis [3] obtemperat Inda magistri
   belua, servitium tempore victa subit.

[1] hoc   [2] nulla] rara   [3] sic iuvenis s.t. *corr. Hall*

But I fear that my grateful verse may do thee hurt,
that the unseasonable honour of renown may stand in
thy light.   This thou mayst do, and 'tis safe : rejoice
within thine own breast that I have remembered
thee, and that thou hast been loyal, and as thou art
doing, strain thine oars to bear me aid until the god is
appeased and a gentler breeze shall come ; save a life
that none can save unless he who submerged it lifts it
from the Stygian waters, and give thyself—a rare
thing it is—to every service of unswerving
friendship.   So may thy fortune make constant
progress, so mayst thou need no aid and mayst thou
aid thine own !   So may thy bride equal her husband
in constant goodness and no complaint befall your
union.   Mayst thou have also the love of him who
shares thy blood, such love as his loyal brother [1] feels
for Castor.   So may thy youthful son be like thee and
may his character cause all to know him as thine
own.   So may the marriage torch of thy daughter
make thee a father-in-law and soon give thee, still in
thy prime, a name of grandsire !

VI. Time brings no Anodyne

By time the peasant's bullock is made submissive
to the plough, offering his neck to the pressure of the
curving yoke ; time renders the mettlesome horse
obedient to the pliant bridle as he receives with gentle
mouth the hard bit ; time quiets the rage of
Phoenician lions so that their former wildness abides
not in their spirits ; the Indian brute,[2] obedient to the
commands of her master, vanquished by time,

<hr>

[1] Pollux.   [2] The elephant.

tempus ut extensis tumeat facit uva racemis,
10 vixque merum capiant grana quod intus habent;
tempus et in canas semen producit aristas,
 et ne sint tristi poma sapore cavet.[1]
hoc tenuat dentem terram renovantis[2] aratri,
 hoc rigidas silices, hoc adamanta terit;
15 hoc etiam saevas paulatim mitigat iras,
 hoc minuit luctus maestaque corda levat.
cuncta potest igitur tacito pede lapsa vetustas
 praeterquam curas attenuare meas.
ut patria careo, bis frugibus area trita est,
20 dissiluit nudo pressa bis uva pede.
nec quaesita tamen spatio patientia longo est,
 mensque mali sensum nostra recentis habet.
scilicet et veteres fugiunt iuga saepe iuvenci,
 et domitus freno saepe repugnat equus.
25 tristior est etiam praesens aerumna priore:
 ut sit enim sibi par, crevit et aucta mora est.
nec tam nota mihi, quam sunt, mala nostra fuerunt;
 nunc[3] magis hoc, quo sunt cognitiora, gravant.
est quoque non nihilum[4] vires afferre recentes,
30 nec praeconsumptum temporis esse malis.
fortior in fulva novus est luctator harena,
 quam cui sunt tarda brachia fessa mora.
integer est melior nitidis gladiator in armis,
 quam cui tela suo sanguine tincta rubent.
35 fert bene praecipites navis modo facta procellas:
 quamlibet exiguo solvitur imbre vetus.
nos quoque vix[5] ferimus (tulimus patientius ante)
 quae mala sunt longa multiplicata die.

---

[1] facit
[2] semoventis *vel* scindentis *vel* patientis : renovantis ς
[3] nunc] sed [4] minimum [5] quae *corr. Luck*

submits to servitude. Time causes the grape to
swell on the spreading clusters until the berries
scarce hold the juice within; time develops the
seed into white ears of grain and takes heed that
fruits be not sour. Time thins the ploughshare as
it renews the soil, it wears away hard flint and
adamant; it gradually softens even fierce anger, it
lessens grief and relieves sorrowing hearts. All
things then can be weakened by the passing of
silent-footed time save my woes. Since I have
been bereft of my native land, twice has the
threshing-floor been smoothed for the grain, twice
has the grape burst apart beneath the pressure of
naked feet. And yet the long time has not given
me fortitude; my mind has the sense of a woe
still fresh.

[23] Assuredly even aged bullocks often shun the
yoke, and the well-broken horse often fights the
bit. My present woe is harsher even than of old,
for though still like itself, it has grown and
increased with time. Nor were my evils so well
known to me as now they are; now that I know
them better, they weigh the more heavily. It is
something also to apply to them strength still fresh
and not to have been worn out beforehand by the
ills of time. Stronger is the fresh wrestler on the
yellow sands than one whose arms are wearied by
slow waiting. Unwounded in shining armour the
gladiator is better than the one whose weapons are
stained red with his own blood. The new-built
ship bears well the headlong blast, even a little
squall breaks up the old one. I too can scarcely
bear (though I bore them bravely once) woes that
have been multiplied by the lapse of time.

credite, deficio, nostrisque,[1] a corpore quantum
40   auguror, accedunt tempora parva malis.
  nam neque sunt vires, nec qui color esse solebat :
    vix habeo tenuem, quae tegat ossa, cutem.
  corpore sed mens est aegro magis aegra, malique
    in circumspectu stat sine fine sui.
45 urbis abest facies, absunt, mea cura, sodales,
    et, qua nulla mihi carior, uxor abest.
  vulgus adest Scythicum bracataque turba Getarum :
    sic me quae video non videoque movent.[2]
  una tamen spes est quae me soletur in istis,
50   haec fore morte mea non diuturna mala.

VII.

Bis me sol adiit gelidae post frigora brumae,
    bisque suum tacto Pisce peregit iter.
  tempore tam longo cur non tua dextera versus
    quamlibet in paucos officiosa fuit ?
5 cur tua cessavit pietas, scribentibus illis,
    exiguus nobis cum quibus usus erat ?
  cur, quotiens [3] alicui chartae sua vincula dempsi,
    illam speravi nomen habere tuum ?
  di faciant ut saepe tua sit epistula dextra
10   scripta, sed e multis reddita nulla mihi.
  quod precor, esse liquet.   credam prius ora Medusae
    Gorgonis anguineis [4] cincta fuisse comis,
  esse canes utero sub virginis, esse Chimaeram,
    a truce quae flammis separet angue leam,

---

[1] nostroque *corr.* ς   [2] nocent
[3] totiens   [4] anguinis ς

I assure you I am failing, and so far as I can prophesy from my bodily strength, but little time remains for my sorrows. For I have neither the strength nor the colour I used to have; my thin skin scarce covers my bones. My body is sick but my mind is worse, engrossed in gazing endlessly upon its suffering. Far from me is the sight of the city, far from me my beloved friends, far from me she who is dearer than all, my wife. Before me is a crowd of Scythians, a trousered throng of Getae. Thus what I behold and what I do not behold affect me. Yet there is one hope that consoles me in all this: my death will prevent these ills from enduring long.

VII. A Reproach

Twice has the sun drawn near me after the cold of icy winter, twice completed his journey by touching the Fish.[1] In so long a time why has not thy hand done its duty and completed even a few lines? Why has thy loyalty failed while they are writing with whom I had but slight companionship? Why, whenever I have removed its bonds from some letter, have I hoped that it contained thy name? May the gods grant that thou hast often written a letter but that not one of the many has been delivered to me. My prayer is true, 'tis clear. I'll sooner believe that the gorgon Medusa's face was garlanded with snaky locks, that there is a maiden with dogs below her middle,[2] that there is a Chimaera, formed of a lioness and a fierce serpent held apart by flame, that there

---

[1] The sun enters the constellation of the Fish in February.
[2] Scylla.

15 quadrupedesque hominis[1] cum pectore pectora iunctos,
    tergeminumque virum tergeminumque canem,
Sphingaque et Harpyias serpentipedesque Gigantas,
    centimanumque Gyen semibovemque virum.
haec ego cuncta prius, quam te, carissime, credam
20   mutatum curam deposuisse mei.
innumeri montes inter me teque viaeque
    fluminaque et campi nec freta pauca iacent.
mille potest causis a te quae littera saepe
    missa sit in nostras rara venire manus;
25 mille tamen causas scribendo vince frequenter,
    excusem ne te semper, amice, mihi.

VIII.

Iam mea cycneas imitantur tempora plumas,
    infict et nigras alba senecta comas.
iam subeunt anni fragiles et inertior aetas,
    iamque parum firmo me mihi ferre grave est.
5 nunc erat, ut posito deberem fine laborum
    vivere, me nullo [2] sollicitante metu,
quaeque meae semper placuerunt otia menti
    carpere et in studiis molliter esse meis,
et parvam celebrare domum veteresque Penates
10   et quae nunc domino rura paterna carent,
inque sinu dominae carisque sodalibus inque
    securus patria consenuisse mea.
haec mea sic quondam peragi speraverat aetas:
    hos ego sic annos ponere dignus eram.
15 non ita dis visum est, qui me terraque marique
    actum [3] Sarmaticis exposuere locis.

---

[1] homines *vel* hominum
[2] cum nullo   [3] iactum

are fourfooted creatures whose breasts are joined to those of a man,[1] a triple man [2] and a triple dog,[3] a Sphinx and Harpies and snaky-footed giants, a hundred-handed Gyes and a man who is half a bull.[4] All these things will I believe rather than that thou, dear one, hast changed and put aside thy love for me. Countless mountains lie between thee and me, and roads, and rivers, and plains, and not a few seas. A thousand reasons can exist why the letters often sent by thee rarely reach my hands. But overcome the thousand reasons by writing often, lest I be forever making my own excuses for thee, my friend.

VIII. An Exile's Declining Years

Already my temples are like the plumage of a swan, for white old age is bleaching my dark hair. Already the years of frailty and life's inactive time are stealing upon me, and already 'tis hard for me in my weakness to bear up. Now 'twere time that I should of right cease my toils and live with no harassing fears, to enjoy the leisure that always pleased my taste, comfortably engaged in my pursuits, devoting myself to my humble house and its old Penates, the paternal fields that are now bereft of their master, peacefully growing old in my lady's embrace, among my dear comrades and in my native land. For such consummation as this did my youth once hope; thus to spend these years did I deserve.

[15] Not so have the gods decreed; they have driven me over land and sea and cast me forth in the region

[1] Centaurs.   [2] Geryon.
[3] Cerberus.   [4] The Minotaur.

in cava ducuntur quassae navalia puppes,
   ne temere in mediis dissoluantur aquis.
ne cadat et multas palmas inhonestet adeptus,[1]
20   languidus in pratis gramina carpit equus.
miles ubi emeritis non est satis utilis annis,
   ponit ad antiquos, quae tulit, arma Lares.
sic igitur, tarda vires minuente senecta,
   me quoque donari iam rude tempus erat.
25 tempus erat nec me peregrinum ducere caelum,
   nec siccam Getico fonte levare sitim,
sed modo, quos habui, vacuum[2] secedere in hortos,
   nunc hominum visu rursus et urbe frui.
sic animo quondam non divinante futura
30   optabam placide vivere posse senex.
fata repugnarunt, quae, cum mihi tempora prima
   mollia praebuerint, posteriora gravant.
iamque decem lustris omni sine labe peractis,
   parte premor vitae deteriore meae ;
35 nec procul a metis, quas paene tenere videbar,
   curriculo gravis est facta ruina meo.
ergo illum demens in me saevire coëgi,
   mitius inmensus quo nihil orbis habet ?
ipsaque delictis victa est clementia nostris,
40   nec tamen errori vita negata meo est,
vita procul patria peragenda sub axe Boreo,
   qua maris Euxini terra sinistra iacet?
hoc mihi si Delphi [3] Dodonaque diceret ipsa,
   esse videretur vanus uterque locus.

---

[1] ademptus *vel* adeptas   [2] vacuos *corr. Heinsius*
[3] delphis *vel* delphos *corr. Scaliger*

---

[1] Gladiators who had finished their service were presented with a wooden sword.

of Sarmatia. Battered ships are drawn into the hollow docks lest to no purpose they go to pieces in the waters' midst. Lest the steed that has won many palms should fall, dishonouring his victories, lazily now he crops the meadow grass. When the soldier after years of service is no longer useful, he lays the arms he has borne before the good old Lares. In this way, since slow old age is lessening my strength, 'twere time for me also to be presented with the wooden sword.[1] 'Twere time for me to breathe no foreign air nor slake my parching thirst with Getic water, but now at my leisure to withdraw into the gardens I once had, now once again to enjoy the sight of men and of the city.

[29] Thus with a mind unprophetic of the future did I once pray for power to live quietly when old. The Fates opposed, for they brought comfort to my early years, to the latter ones distress. Now after I have lived ten lustra unblemished,[2] at a harder time of life I am o'erwhelmed; not far from the goal, which I seemed almost to have within my reach, my car has suffered a heavy fall. Did I then in my madness force him into rage against me who is more gracious than anything the wide world possesses? Has his very mercy been overcome by my sins, and yet has my error not denied me life, a life which I must pass far from my country, beneath the pole of Boreas in the land to the left of the Euxine sea?[3] If this had been told me by Delphi or Dodona herself,[4] both places would have seemed to me unworthy of belief.

---

[2] Ovid was about fifty when he was banished, c. A.D. 8.

[3] See note on *Tr.* iv. 1. 60.

[4] Delphi, the oracle of Apollo; Dodona, the oracle of Zeus.

45 nil adeo validum est, adamas licet alliget illud,
    ut maneat rapido firmius igne Iovis;
nil ita sublime est supraque pericula tendit
    non sit ut inferius suppositumque deo.
nam quamquam vitio pars est contracta malorum,
50   plus tamen exitii numinis ira dedit.
at vos admoniti nostris quoque casibus este,
    aequantem superos emeruisse virum.

IX.

Si licet et pateris, nomen facinusque tacebo,
    et tua Lethaeis acta dabuntur aquis,
nostraque vincetur lacrimis sententia [1] seris,
    fac modo te pateat paenituisse tui;
5 fac modo te damnes cupiasque eradere vitae
    tempora, si possis, Tisiphonaea tuae.
sin minus, et flagrant odio tua pectora nostri,
    induet infelix arma coacta dolor.
sim licet extremum, sicut sum, missus in orbem,
10   nostra suas isto [2] porriget ira manus.
omnia, si nescis, Caesar mihi iura reliquit,
    et sola est patria poena carere mea.
et patriam, modo sit sospes, speramus ab illo:
    saepe Iovis telo quercus adusta viret.
15 denique vindictae si sit mihi nulla facultas,
    Pierides vires et sua tela dabunt.
quod Scythicis habitem longe summotus in oris,
    siccaque sint oculis proxima signa meis,

---

[1] *Alton*: cl(d)ementia   [2] istic *vel* istuc *vel* istinc

---

[1] Augustus.

[45] Nothing is so strong, though it be bound with adamant, as to withstand by greater might the swift thunderbolt of Jupiter; nothing is so lofty or reaches so far above perils that it is not beneath a god and subject to him. For although by fault I drew upon me a part of my ills, yet more ruin has befallen me because of the wrath of a divine power. But be ye warned by my fate also that ye make yourselves worthy of the man [1] who is like unto the gods!

IX. A THREAT

If I may and you allow it, I will keep silent your name and deed, consigning your acts to Lethe's waters, and my opinion will be overcome by tears that are overdue, if only you make it clear that you have repented, if only through self-condemnation you show yourself eager to erase from your life, if but you can, that period of Tisiphone. But if not, if your heart still burns with hate for me, unhappy rage shall don perforce its arms   Though I be banished, as I have been, to the edge of the world, to where you are shall my wrath stretch forth its hands. All my rights, if you know it not, Caesar has left me, and my only punishment is to be parted from my country. Even my country, if only he lives on, I hope as a boon from him; often the oak scorched by the bolt of Jove becomes green once more. In fine if I should have no opportunity for vengeance, the daughters of Pieria will give me strength and their own weapons. What though I dwell so far removed on the Scythian shores with the constellations that are ever dry close

195

nostra per inmensas ibunt praeconia gentes,
20   quodque querar notum qua patet orbis erit.
ibit ad occasum quicquid dicemus ab ortu,
    testis et Hesperiae vocis Eous erit.
trans ego tellurem, trans altas audiar undas,
    et gemitus vox est magna futura mei,
25 nec tua te sontem tantummodo saecula norint :
    perpetuae crimen posteritatis eris.
iam feror in pugnas et nondum cornua sumpsi,
    nec mihi sumendi causa sit ulla velim.
Circus adhuc cessat ; spargit iam torvus [1] harenam
30   taurus et infesto iam pede pulsat humum.
hoc quoque, quam volui, plus est. cane, Musa, receptus,
    dum licet huic nomen dissimulare suum.

X.

Ille ego qui fuerim, tenerorum lusor amorum,
    quem legis, ut noris, accipe posteritas.
Sulmo mihi patria est, gelidis uberrimus undis,
    milia qui novies distat ab urbe decem.
5 editus hic ego sum, nec non, ut tempora noris,
    cum cecidit fato consul uterque pari :
si quid id est, usque a proavis [2] vectus ordinis heres
    non modo fortunae munere factus eques.
nec stirps prima fui ; genito sum fratre creatus,
10   qui tribus ante quater mensibus ortus erat.
Lucifer amborum natalibus affuit idem :
    una celebrata est per duo liba dies ;

[1] tamen acer
[2] si quid (quis) et a proavis usque est

to my eyes, my herald-call shall pass through limitless peoples, my complaint shall be known wherever the world extends. Whatever I say shall pass to the setting sun from its rising and the East shall bear witness to the voice of the West. Across the land, across deep waters I shall be heard, and mighty shall be the cry of my lament. Not alone your own age shall know you guilty; to everlasting posterity you shall be a criminal. Already I am carried into battle though I have not yet taken up arms, and I would I had no cause to take them up. The arena is still quiet, but the grim bull is already tossing the sand, already pawing the ground with angry hoof. Even this is more than I wished: Muse, sound the retreat, while this man still has the power to conceal his name.

X. The Poet's Autobiography [1]

That thou mayst know who I was, I that playful poet of tender love whom thou readest, hear my words, thou of the after time. Sulmo is my native place, a land rich in ice-cold streams, thrice thirty miles from the city. There first I saw the light, and if thou wouldst know the date, 'twas when both consuls fell under stress of like fate. I was heir to rank (if rank is aught) that came from forefathers of olden time—no knight fresh made by fortune's gift. I was not the first born, for my birth befell after that of a brother, thrice four months my senior. The same day-star beheld the birth of us both: one birthday was celebrated by the offering of our two

[1] See Introd. pp. vii ff.

haec est armiferae ¹ festis de quinque Minervae,
 quae fieri pugna prima cruenta solet.
15 protinus excolimur teneri curaque parentis
 imus ad insignes Urbis ab arte viros.
frater ad eloquium viridi tendebat ab aevo,
 fortia verbosi natus ad arma fori;
at mihi iam puero caelestia sacra placebant,
20 inque suum furtim Musa trahebat opus.
saepe pater dixit "studium quid inutile temptas?
 Maeonides nullas ipse reliquit opes."
motus eram dictis, totoque Helicone relicto
 scribere temptabam ² verba soluta modis.
25 sponte sua carmen numeros veniebat ad aptos,
 et quod temptabam scribere ³ versus erat.
interea tacito passu labentibus annis
 liberior fratri sumpta mihique toga est,
induiturque umeris ⁴ cum lato purpura clavo,
30 et studium nobis, quod fuit ante, manet.
iamque decem vitae frater geminaverat annos,
 cum perit, et coepi parte carere mei.
cepimus et tenerae primos aetatis honores,
 eque ⁵ viris quondam pars tribus una fui.
35 curia restabat: clavi mensura coacta est;
 maius erat nostris viribus illud onus.
nec patiens corpus, nec mens fuit apta labori,
 sollicitaeque fugax ambitionis eram,

---

¹ armigerae ² conabar ³ dicere
⁴ humeros ⁵ hecque *vel* deque

---

¹ Offered to the *genius, cf. Tr.* iii. 13. 2.
² The festival of *Quinquatrus* (March 19–23), on the last four days of which combats occurred. The poet was then born on March 20, 43 B.C., when both consuls, Hirtius and Pansa, fell in the battles near Mutina, *cf.* v. 6.

cakes [1]—that day among the five sacred to armed Minerva which is wont to be the first stained by the blood of combat.[2]   While still of tender age we began our training, and through our father's care we came to attend upon men of the city distinguished in the liberal arts.   My brother's bent even in the green of years was oratory : he was born for the stout weapons of the wordy forum.   But to me even as a boy service of the divine gave delight and stealthily the Muse was ever drawing me aside to do her work. Often my father said, "Why do you try a profitless pursuit ?   Even the Maeonian left no wealth."   I was influenced by what he said and wholly forsaking Helicon I tried to write words freed from rhythm, yet all unbidden song would come upon befitting numbers and whatever I tried to write was verse.

[27] Meanwhile as the silent-pacing years slipped past we brothers assumed the toga of a freer life and our shoulders put on the broad stripe of purple while still our pursuits remained as before.   And now my brother had seen but twice ten years of life when he passed away, and thenceforth I was bereft of half myself.   I advanced so far as to receive the first office granted to tender youth, for in those days I was one third of the board of three.[3]   The senate house awaited me, but I narrowed my purple stripe [4] : that was a burden too great for my powers. I had neither a body to endure the toil nor a mind suited to it ; by nature I shunned the worries of an

---

[3] The *tresviri*, minor officials.   See Introd. p. viii.
[4] *i.e.* he chose to remain a simple knight and refrained from the pursuit of offices.

OVID

et petere Aoniae suadebant tuta sorores
40   otia, iudico semper amata meo.
temporis illius colui fovique poëtas,
    quotque aderant vates, rebar adesse deos.
saepe suas volucres legit mihi grandior aevo,
    qaueque nocet [1] serpens, quae iuvat [2] herba, Macer.
45 saepe suos solitus recitare Propertius ignes,
    iure sodalicii, quo mihi iunctus erat.
Ponticus heroo, Bassus quoque clarus iambis
    dulcia convictus membra fuere mei.
et tenuit nostras numerosus Horatius aures,
40   dum ferit Ausonia carmina culta lyra.
Vergilium vidi tantum : nec avara Tibullo
    tempus amicitiae fata dedere meae
(successor fuit hic tibi, Galle, Propertius illi ;
    quartus ab his serie temporis ipse fui).[3]
55 utque ego maiores, sic me coluere minores,
    notaque non tarde facta Thalia mea est.
carmina cum primum populo iuvenalia legi,
    barba resecta mihi bisve semelve fuit.
moverat ingenium totam cantata per urbem
60   nomine non vero dicta Corinna mihi.
multa quidem scripsi, sed, quae vitiosa putavi,
    emendaturis ignibus ipse dedi.
tunc quoque, cum fugerem, quaedam placitura
      cremavi,
    iratus studio carminibusque meis.
65 molle Cupidineis nec inexpugnabile telis
    cor mihi, quodque levis causa moveret, erat.

   [1] necet   [2] iuvet   [3] *dist. Courtney*

---

[1] The Muses.
[2] Or perhaps "melodious," but *cf. Ex P*. iv. 2. 33, and the *numeri innumeri* of Plautus's epitaph.
[3] Vergil and Tibullus died 19 B.C.

ambitious life and the Aonian sisters[1] were ever
urging me to seek the security of a retirement I had
ever chosen and loved.

[41] The poets of that time I fondly reverenced : all
bards I thought so many present gods. Ofttimes
Macer, already advanced in years, read to me of the
birds he loved, of noxious snakes and healing plants.
Ofttimes Propertius would declaim his flaming verse
by right of the comradeship that joined him to me.
Ponticus famed in epic, Bassus also, famed in iambics,
were pleasant members of that friendly circle. And
Horace of the many rhythms[2] held in thrall our
ears while he attuned his fine-wrought songs to the
Ausonian lyre. Vergil I only saw, and to Tibullus
greedy fate gave no time for friendship with me[3]
(Tibullus was thy successor, Gallus, and Propertius
his ; after them came I, fourth in order of time).
And as I reverenced older poets so was I reverenced
by the younger, for my Thalia was not slow to
become renowned. When first I read my youthful
songs in public, my beard had been cut but once or
twice. My genius had been stirred by her who was
sung throughout the city, whom I called, not by a
real name, Corinna.[4] Much did I write, but what I
thought defective I gave in person to the flames for
their revision. Even when I was setting forth into exile
I burned certain verse[5] that would have found favour,
for I was angry with my calling and with my songs.

[65] My heart was ever soft, no stronghold against
Cupid's darts—a heart moved by the slightest

[4] The heroine of Ovid's *Amores*. She was probably chiefly a
creature of his imagination.
[5] Including perhaps the *Metamorphoses, cf. Tr.* i. 7. 13, but
other copies of that work existed.

cum tamen hic essem minimoque accenderer igni,
    nomine sub nostro fabula nulla fuit.
paene mihi puero nec digna nec utilis uxor.
70   est data, quae tempus perbreve nupta fuit.
illi successit, quamvis sine crimine coniunx,
    non tamen in nostro firma futura toro.
ultima, quae mecum seros permansit in annos,
    sustinuit coniunx exulis esse viri.
75 filia me mea bis prima fecunda iuventa,
    sed non ex uno coniuge, fecit avum.
et iam complerat genitor sua fata novemque
    addiderat lustris altera lustra novem.
non aliter flevi, quam me fleturus adempto
80   ille fuit.   matri proxima iusta[1] tuli.
felices ambo tempestiveque sepulti,
    ante diem poenae quod periere meae!
me quoque felicem, quod non viventibus illis
    sum miser, et de me quod doluere nihil!
85 si tamen extinctis aliquid nisi nomina restat,[2]
    et gracilis structos effugit umbra rogos,
fama, parentales, si vos mea contigit, umbrae,
    et sunt in Stygio crimina nostra foro,
scite, precor, causam (nec vos mihi fallere fas est)
90   errorem iussae, non scelus, esse fugae.
Manibus hoc satis est: ad vos, studiosa, revertor,
    pectora, qui vitae quaeritis acta meae.
iam mihi canities pulsis melioribus annis
    venerat, antiquas miscueratque comas,

---

[1] busta *corr. Cuiacius*   [2] restant

---

[1] A *lustrum* = five years.
[2] The court of the lower world in which Minos, Aeacus, and Rhadamanthus were the judges.

impulse. And yet, though such my nature, though I was set aflame by the littlest spark, no scandal became affixed to my name. When I was scarce more than a boy a wife unworthy and unprofitable became mine—mine for but a short space. Into her place came one, blameless, but not destined to remain my bride. And last is she who remained with me till the twilight of my declining years, who has endured to be the mate of an exile husband. My daughter, twice fertile, but not of one husband, in her early youth made me grandsire. And already had my father completed his allotted span adding to nine lustra [1] a second nine. For him I wept no otherwise than he would have wept for me had I been taken. Next for my mother I made the offerings to death. Happy both! and laid to rest in good season! since they passed away before the day of my punishment. Happy too am I that my misery falls not in their lifetime and that for me they felt no grief. Yet if for those whose light is quenched something besides a name abides, if a slender shade escapes the high-heaped pyre, if, O spirits of my parents, report of me has reached you and the charges against me live in the Stygian court,[2] know, I beg you—and you 'tis impious for me to deceive—that the cause of the exile decreed me is an error, and no crime. Be these my words to the shades. To you, fond hearts, that would know the events of my life, once more I turn.

[93] Already had white hairs come upon me driving away my better years and mottling my ageing locks; ten

95 postque meos ortus Pisaea vinctus oliva
     abstulerat deciens praemia victor equus,[1]
  cum maris Euxini positos ad laeva Tomitas
     quaerere me laesi principis ira iubet.
  causa meae cunctis nimium quoque nota ruinae
100   indicio non est testificanda meo.
  quid referam comitumque nefas famulosque nocentes ?
     ipsa[2] multa tuli non leviora fuga.
  indignata malis mens est succumbere seque
     praestitit invictam viribus usa suis ;
105 oblitusque mei ductaeque per otia vitae
     insolita cepi temporis arma manu ;
  totque tuli terra casus pelagoque quot inter
     occultum stellae conspicuumque polum.
  tacta mihi tandem longis erroribus acto
110   iuncta pharetratis Sarmatis ora Getis.
  hic ego, finitimis quamvis circumsoner armis,
     tristia, quo possum, carmine fata levo.
  quod quamvis nemo est, cuius referatur ad aures,
     sic tamen absumo decipioque diem.
115 ergo quod vivo durisque laboribus obsto,
     nec me sollicitae taedia lucis habent,
  gratia, Musa, tibi : nam tu solacia praebes,
     tu curae requies, tu medicina venis.
  tu dux et comes es, tu nos abducis ab Histro,
120   in medioque mihi das Helicone locum ;
  tu mihi, quod rarum est, vivo sublime dedisti
     nomen, ab exequiis quod dare fama solet.
  nec, qui detractat praesentia, Livor iniquo
     ullum de nostris dente momordit opus.

---

[1] eques *corr. Bentley*   [2] ipseque

times since my birth had the victorious horse,
garlanded with Pisan olive, borne away the prize,[1]
when the wrath of an injured prince ordered me to
Tomis on the left of the Euxine sea. The cause of my
ruin, but too well known to all, must not be revealed
by evidence of mine. Why tell of the disloyalty of
comrades, of the petted slaves who injured
me? Much did I bear not lighter than exile
itself. Yet my soul, disdaining to give way to
misfortune, proved itself unconquerable, relying on
its own powers. Forgetting myself and a life passed
in ease I seized with unaccustomed hand the arms
that the time supplied: on sea and land I bore
misfortunes as many as are the stars that lie between
the hidden and the visible pole. Driven through
long wanderings at length I reached the shore that
unites the Sarmatians with the quiver-bearing Getae.
Here, though close around me I hear the din of arms, I
lighten my sad fate with what song I may; though
there be none to hear it, yet in this wise do I employ
and beguile the day. So then this living of mine,
this stand against the hardness of my sufferings, this
bare will to view the daylight's woes, I owe, my
Muse, to thee! For thou dost lend me comfort, thou
dost come as rest, as balm, to my sorrow. Thou art
both guide and comrade: thou leadest me far from
Hister and grantest me a place in Helicon's midst;
thou hast given me while yet alive (how rare the
boon!) a lofty name—the name which renown is wont
to give only after death. Nor has jealousy, that
detractor of the present, attacked with malignant

[1] Ten Olympiads, here periods of five years each, *cf.* v. 78 and
Ex P. iv. 6. 5. The Olympic games were held in the district of
Pisa in Elis.

125 nam tulerint magnos cum saecula nostra poetas,
    non fuit ingenio fama maligna meo,
cumque ego praeponam multos mihi, non minor illis
    dicor et in toto plurimus orbe legor.
si quid habent igitur vatum praesagia veri,
130   protinus ut moriar, non ero, terra, tuus.
sive favore tuli, sive hanc ego carmine famam,
    iure tibi grates, candide lector, ago.

tooth any work of mine. For although this age of
ours has brought forth mighty poets, fame has not
been grudging to my genius, and though I place many
before myself, report calls me not their inferior and
throughout the world I am most read of all. If then
there be truth in poets' prophecies, even though I die
forthwith, I shall not, O earth, be thine. But
whether through favour or by very poetry I have
gained this fame, 'tis right, kind reader, that I render
thanks to thee.

LIBER QUINTUS

I.

Hunc quoque de Getico, nostri studiose, libellum
    litore praemissis quattuor adde meis.
hic quoque talis erit, qualis fortuna poetae:
    invenies toto carmine dulce nihil.
5 flebilis ut noster status est, ita flebile carmen,
    materiae scripto conveniente suae.
integer et laetus[1] laeta et iuvenalia lusi:
    illa tamen nunc me composuisse piget.
ut cecidi, subiti perago praeconia casus,
10   sumque argumenti conditor ipse mei.
utque iacens ripa deflere Caystrius ales
    dicitur ore suam deficiente necem,
sic ego, Sarmaticas longe proiectus in oras,
    efficio tacitum ne mihi funus eat.
15 delicias siquis lascivaque carmina quaerit,
    praemoneo, non est[2] scripta quod ista legat.
aptior huic Gallus blandique Propertius oris,
    aptior, ingenium come, Tibullus erit.
atque utinam numero non nos[3] essemus in isto!
20   ei mihi, cur umquam Musa iocata[4] mea est?

[1] donec eram laetus
[2] nostra *vel* numquam: non est *Gronovius*
[3] ne nos   [4] locuta: iocata *ς*

208

BOOK V

I. A Proem and an Apology

Add this book also to the four I have already sent, my devoted friend, from the Getic shore. This too will be like the poet's fortunes : in the whole course of the song you will find no gladness. Mournful is my state, mournful therefore is my song, for the work is suited to its theme. Unhurt and happy with themes of happiness and youth I played (yet now I regret that I composed that verse) ; since I have fallen I act as herald of my sudden fall, and I myself provide the theme of which I write. As the bird of Cayster [1] is said to lie upon the bank and bemoan its own death with weakening note, so I, cast far away upon the Sarmatian shores, take heed that my funeral rites pass not off in silence.

[15] If any seeks the amusement of wanton verse, I forewarn him, there is no warrant for reading such verse as this. Gallus will be better suited for such a one, or Propertius of the alluring lips, better that winning genius Tibullus. And would I were not counted among them ! Alas ! why did my Muse

---

[1] The swans of the Lydian Cayster were believed to sing their own dirges.

sed dedimus poenas, Scythicique in finibus Histri
    ille pharetrati lusor Amoris abest.
quod superest, numeros [1] pudibunda ad [2] carmina
    flexi, et memores iussi nominis esse sui.[2]
25 si tamen e vobis aliquis tam multa requiret,
    unde dolenda canam, multa dolenda tuli.
non haec ingenio, non haec componimus arte :
    materia est propriis ingeniosa malis.
et quota fortunae pars est in carmine nostrae ?
30   felix, qui patitur quae numerare potest !
quot frutices silvae, quot flavas Thybris harenas,
    mollia quot Martis gramina campus habet,
tot mala pertulimus, quorum medicina quiesque
    nulla nisi in studio est Pieridumque mora.
35 " quis tibi, Naso, modus lacrimosi carminis ? " inquis :
    idem, fortunae qui modus huius erit.
quod querar, illa mihi pleno de fonte ministrat,
    nec mea sunt, fati verba sed ista mei.
at mihi si cara patriam cum coniuge reddas,
40   sint vultus hilares, simque quod ante fui.
lenior invicti si sit mihi Caesaris ira,
    carmina laetitiae iam tibi plena dabo.
nec tamen ut lusit, rursus mea littera ludet :
    sit semel illa ioco luxuriata meo.
45 quod probet ipse, canam, poenae modo parte levata
    barbariam rigidos effugiamque Getas.
interea nostri quid agant, nisi triste, libelli ?
    tibia funeribus convenit ista meis.

---

[1] animos *corr. Ehwald*   [2] ad publica *corr. Hall*   [3] mei

ever jest? But I have paid the penalty, for in the lands of the Scythian Hister he who played with quiver-bearing Love is an exile. For the future I have diverted my elegies to bashful poems and bidden them remember their name. Yet if some-one of you asks why I sing so many grievous things—many grievous things have I borne. This verse I compose not by inspiration, not by art; the theme is filled with inspiration by its own evils. And how small a portion of my lot appears in my verse? Happy he who can count his suffer-ings! As many as the twigs of the forest, as many as the grains of Tiber's yellow sands, as many tender grass-blades as the field of Mars possesses, so many ills have I endured for which there is no cure, no relief save in whiling away my time in devotion to the Pierians.

35 "What limit, Naso, to your mournful song?" you say. The same that shall be the limit to this state of mine. For my complaining that state serves me from a full spring, nor are these words mine; they belong to my fate. But should you restore to me my country and my dear wife, my face would be gay, and I should be what I once was. Should unconquerable Caesar's wrath be milder to me, forthwith will I offer you verse filled with joy. Yet no writings of mine shall again wanton as once they wantoned; let them have rioted with my jests but once! I will compose something which he will himself approve, if only a part of my punishment be removed and I escape the barbarian world and the stern Getae. Meanwhile what should be the theme of my verse except sorrow? Such is the pipe whose notes befit this funeral of mine.

"at poteras" inquis "melius mala ferre silendo,
50   et tacitus casus dissimulare tuos."
exigis ut nulli gemitus tormenta sequantur,
    acceptoque gravi vulnere flere vetas ?
ipse Perilleo Phalaris permisit in aere
    edere mugitus et bovis ore queri.
55 cum Priami lacrimis offensus non sit Achilles,
    tu fletus inhibes, durior hoste, meos ?
cum faceret Nioben orbam Latonia proles,
    non tamen et [1] siccas iussit habere genas.
est aliquid, fatale malum per verba levare :
60   hoc querulam Procnen Halcyonenque facit.
hoc erat, in gelido quare Poeantius antro
    voce fatigaret Lemnia saxa sua.
strangulat inclusus dolor atque exaestuat [2] intus,
    cogitur et vires multiplicare suas.
65 da veniam potius, vel totos tolle libellos,
    si mihi quod prodest hoc [3] tibi, lector, obest.
sed neque obesse potest ulli, nec scripta fuerunt
    nostra nisi auctori perniciosa suo.
"at mala sunt." fateor. quis te mala sumere cogit ?
70   aut quis deceptum ponere sumpta vetat ?
ipse nec emendo,[4] sed ut hic deducta legantur ;
    non sunt illa suo barbariora loco.
nec me Roma suis debet conferre poetis :
    inter Sauromatas ingeniosus eram.
75 denique nulla mihi captatur gloria, quaeque
    ingeniis [5] stimulos subdere fama solet.

[1] et] hanc   [2] cor aestuat
[3] sit (sic) . . . si   [4] hoc mando
[5] ingenii *vel* ingenio

---

[1] When Priam begged for the body of Hector.

[49] " But," you say, " you might better endure your sorrows by keeping silent, and in silence hide your misfortunes." Do you demand that no groans should ensue upon torture, and when a deep wound has been received, do you forbid weeping ? Even Phalaris allowed Perillus within the bronze to utter bellows of torture through the mouth of the bull. When Priam's tears did not offend Achilles,[1] do you, more cruel than an enemy, restrain me from weeping ? Though Latona's children made Niobe childless, yet they did not bid her cheeks be dry. 'Tis something to lighten with words a fated evil ; to this are due the complaints of Procne and Halcyone. This was why the son[2] of Poeas in his chill cave wearied with his outcries the Lemnian rocks. A suppressed sorrow chokes and seethes within, multiplying perforce its own strength.

[65] Indulge me rather, or else away with all my books, if that, reader, which helps me harms you. Yet it cannot harm anyone, for my writings have hurt no one save their own author. " But," you say, " they are poor stuff." I admit it. Who forces you to take up such poor stuff, or who forbids you, when you find yourself deceived, to lay it aside ? Even I do not revise them, but as they have here been written, so let them be read ;[3] they are not more barbarous than the place of their origin. Rome ought not to compare me with her own poets ; 'tis among the Sauromatae that I am a genius !

[75] In fine I court no renown nor that fame which usually sets the spur to talent ; I would not have

[2] Philoctetes.

[3] Perhaps *ipse nec emenda, sed*, etc., " Do you (the addressee) not revise them," etc.

213

nolumus assiduis animum tabescere curis,
  quae tamen inrumpunt quoque vetantur eunt.
cur scribam, docui.   cur mittam, quaeritis, isto [1] ?
80   vobiscum cupio quolibet esse modo.

II.

Ecquid ubi e Ponto nova venit epistula, palles,
  et tibi sollicita solvitur illa manu ?
pone metum, valeo ; corpusque, quod ante laborum
  inpatiens nobis invalidumque fuit,
5 sufficit, atque ipso vexatum induruit usu.
  an magis infirmo non vacat esse mihi ?
mens tamen aegra iacet, nec tempore robora sumpsit,
  affectusque animi, qui fuit ante, manet.
quaeque mora spatioque suo coitura putavi
10   vulnera non aliter quam modo facta dolent.
scilicet exiguis prodest annosa vetustas ;
  grandibus accedunt tempore damna malis.
paene decem totis aluit Poeantius annis
  pestiferum tumido vulnus ab angue datum.
15 Telephus aeterna consumptus tabe perisset,
  si non, quae nocuit, dextra tulisset opem.
et mea, si facinus nullum commisimus, opto,
  vulnera qui fecit, facta levare velit,
contentusque mei iam tandem parte doloris
20   exiguum pleno de mare demat aquae.
detrahat ut multum, multum restabit acerbi,[2]
  parsque meae poenae totius instar erit.
litora quot conchas, quot amoenos Ostia[3] flores,
  quotve soporiferum grana papaver habet,

----

¹ istos: isto *Heinsius*   ² acervi
³ hostia *corr. Housman*

----

¹ Philoctetes.

my soul waste away with continual woes, which nevertheless break in upon me, entering where they are forbidden. Why I write I have told you. Why do I send my writings to you, you ask. I am eager to be with you all in some fashion—no matter how.

II. To His Wife

What? When a fresh letter has come from Pontus, do you grow pale, do you open it with anxious hand? Put aside your fear: I am well, and my frame, which before could endure no toils and had no strength, now bears up and under the very harassings of experience has become hardened—or is it rather that I have no leisure to be weak? But my mind lies ill, nor has time given it strength; my feelings remain the same as of old. The wounds that I thought would close with passing time pain me no otherwise than if they had been freshly made. Yes, little troubles are helped by the flight of years; with great ones time but increases the ruin they cause. For almost ten whole years the son [1] of Poeas nursed the baneful wound given him by the venom-swollen snake. Telephus would have died, destroyed by his eternal disease, had not the hand that harmed him borne him aid. My wounds also, if I have committed no crime, may their maker, I pray, desire to heal, and now at length satisfied with a portion of my suffering, may he draw off a little of the water from a brimming sea. Though he draw much, much bitterness will remain, and a part of my penalty will be as good as the whole. As many as are the shells on the shore, the coloured flowers of Ostia, the seeds of the sleep-producing poppy,

215

25 silva feras quot alit, quot piscibus unda natatur,
    quot tenerum pennis aëra pulsat avis,
tot premor adversis : quae sit comprendere coner,
    Icariae numerum dicere coner aquae.
utque viae casus, ut amara pericula ponti,
30   ut taceam strictas in mea fata manus,
barbara me tellus orbisque novissima magni
    sustinet et saevo cinctus ab hoste locus.
hinc ego traicerer [1]—neque enim mea culpa cruenta
    est—
    esset, quae debet, si tibi cura mei.
35 ille deus, bene quo Romana potentia nixa est,
    saepe suo victor lenis in hoste fuit.
quid dubitas et tuta times ?   accede rogaque :
    Caesare nil ingens mitius orbis habet.
me miserum ! quid agam, si proxima quaeque re-
    linquunt ?
40   subtrahis effracto tu quoque colla iugo ?
quo ferar ?   unde petam lassis solacia rebus ?
    ancora iam nostram non tenet ulla ratem.
videris [2] !   ipse sacram, quamvis invisus, ad aram
    confugiam : nullas summovet ara manus.

Precatio

45 Adloquor en absens absentia numina supplex,
    si fas est homini cum Iove posse loqui.
arbiter imperii, quo certum est sospite cunctos
    Ausoniae curam gentis habere deos,
o decus, o patriae per te florentis imago,
50   o vir non ipso, quem regis, orbe minor—

---

[1] traicerem *vel* transigerer   [22] viderit *codd.*: *corr. Ehwald*

as many beasts as the forest supports, as many as the
fishes that swim in the sea, or the feathers with which
a bird beats the yielding air—by so many sorrows am
I overwhelmed. Should I essay to include them all,
as well essay to tell the tale of the Icarian
waters. The dangers of the road, the bitter perils of
the sea, the hands raised to slay me—to say naught of
these, a barbarian land the most remote in the vast
world, a place girt by cruel enemies, holds me. From
here might I pass—for my fault has no taint of
blood—if you had the love for me which is my
due. That god, on whom the power of Rome hath
found happy stay, to his own enemy hath often been a
gentle victor. Why hesitate and fear what has no
peril? Approach, entreat him! the vast world
holds naught more lenient than Caesar. Wretched
me! What am I to do if all that is nearest abandons
me? Do you too break the yoke and withdraw your
neck? Whither shall I rush? Whence seek com-
fort for my weary lot? No anchor now holds my
bark. You shall see! Even I, hated though I am,
will seek refuge at the holy altar; no hands does the
altar repel.

The Suppliant's Prayer

Lo! I an absent suppliant address an absent
deity, if 'tis right for a human being to have power of
converse with Jupiter.

[47] Lord of the empire, whose safety assures the
protection of all the gods for the Ausonian race, thou
glory, thou image of a fatherland that hath success
through thee, hero not less mighty than the very

sic habites terras et te desideret aether,
    sic ad pacta tibi sidera tardus eas—
parce, precor, minimamque tuo de fulmine partem
    deme! satis poenae, quod superabit, erit.
55 ira quidem moderata tua est, vitamque dedisti,
    nec mihi ius civis nec mihi nomen abest,
nec mea concessa est aliis fortuna, nec exul
    edicti verbis nominor ipse tui :
omnia quae [1] timui, quia me meruisse videbam ;
60   sed tua peccato lenior ira meo est.
arva relegatum iussisti visere Ponti,
    et Scythicum profuga scindere puppe fretum.
iussus ad Euxini deformia litora veni
    aequoris—haec gelido terra sub axe iacet—
65 nec me tam cruciat numquam sine frigore caelum,
    glaebaque canenti semper obusta gelu,
nesciaque [2] est vocis quod barbara lingua Latinae,
    Graecaque quod Getico victa [3] loquella sono est,
quam quod finitimo cinctus premor undique Marte, [4]
70   vixque brevis tutum [5] murus ab hoste facit.
pax tamen interdum est, pacis fiducia numquam :
    sic hic nunc patitur, nunc timet arma locus.
hinc ego dum muter, vel me Zanclaea Charybdis
    devoret aque suis ad Styga mittat aquis,
75 vel rapidae flammis urar patienter in Aetnae,
    vel freta Leucadii mittar in alta dei. [6]
quod petimus, poena est : neque enim miser esse
      recuso,
    sed precor ut possim tutius esse miser.

---

[1] omniaque haec   [2] -que] quam
[3] vincta *vel* iuncta   [4] finitima . . . morte
[5] tutos   [6] leucadio . . . deo

---

[2] See Introd. p. xviii.

world thou rulest (so mayst thou dwell on earth and heaven long for thee, so mayst thou be late in passing to thy promised stars) spare me, I beseech thee, and take but the least part from thy lightning's stroke; sufficient will be the penalty that remains. Thine anger is indeed moderate, for thou hast granted me life, I lack neither the right nor the name of citizen, nor has my fortune been granted to others, and I am not called "exile" by the terms of thy decree. All these things I feared because I saw that I had deserved them, but thy wrath is lighter than my sin. "Relegated"[1] didst thou bid me come to view the fields by the Pontus, cleaving the Scythian sea in a fleeing bark. By thy command I have come to the formless shores of the Euxine water—this land lies beneath the frigid pole—nor am I so much tortured by a climate never free from cold and a soil ever shrivelled by white frost, by the fact that the barbarian tongue knows not a Latin voice and Greek is mastered by the sound of Getic, as that I am surrounded and hard pressed on every side by war close at hand and that a low wall scarce gives me safety from the foe. Yet peace there is at times, confidence in peace never: so does this place now suffer, now fear attack. If I may but exchange this place for another, let even Zanclaean Charybdis swallow me, sending me by her waters to the Styx, or let me be resigned to burn in the flames of scorching Aetna or hurled into the deep sea of the Leucadian god.[2] What I seek is punishment, for I do not reject suffering, but I beg that I may suffer in greater safety!

[2] Malefactors were hurled from the cliff near Apollo's temple on the Leucadian promontory.

III.

Illa dies haec est, qua te celebrare poetae,
    si modo non fallunt tempora, Bacche, solent,
festaque odoratis innectunt tempora sertis,
    et dicunt laudes ad tua vina tuas.
5 inter quos, memini, dum me mea fata sinebant,
    non invisa tibi pars ego saepe fui,
quem nunc suppositum stellis Cynosuridos Ursae
    iuncta tenet crudis Sarmatis ora Getis.
quique prius mollem vacuamque laboribus egi
10   in studiis vitam Pieridumque choro,
nunc procul a patria Geticis circumsonor armis,
    multa prius pelago multaque passus humo.
sive mihi casus sive hoc dedit ira deorum,
    nubila nascenti seu mihi Parca fuit,
15 tu tamen e sacris hederae [1] cultoribus unum
    numine debueras sustinuisse tuo.
an dominae fati quicquid cecinere sorores,
    omne sub arbitrio desinit esse dei ?
ipse quoque aetherias meritis invectus es arces,
20   quo non exiguo facta labore via est.
nec patria est habitata tibi, sed adusque nivosum
    Strymona venisti Marticolamque Geten,
Persidaque et lato spatiantem flumine Gangen,
    et quascumque bibit decolor Indus aquas.
25 scilicet hanc legem nentes fatalia Parcae
    stamina bis genito bis cecinere tibi.
me quoque, si fas est exemplis ire deorum,
    ferrea sors vitae difficilisque premit.

[1] hederae] me de

---

[1] The Small Bear.

III. An Appeal to Bacchus

This is the day, if only I do not mistake the time, on which poets are wont to praise thee, Bacchus, binding their brows with sweet-scented garlands, and singing thy praises over thine own wine.   Among them, I remember, whilst my fate allowed, oft did I play a part not distasteful to thee, but now I lie beneath the stars of the Cynosurian Bear,[1] in the grip of the Sarmatian shore, close to the uncivilized Getae.   I who before led a life of ease, toil-free, amid studies in the band of the Pierians, now far from my country am surrounded by the clash of Getic arms, after many sufferings on the sea, many on land.   Whether chance brought this upon me or the wrath of the gods, or whether a clouded Fate attended my birth, thou at least shouldst have supported by thy divine power one of the worshippers of thine ivy.   Or is it true that whatever the sisters, mistresses of fate, have ordained, ceases wholly to be under a god's power ?   Thou thyself wast borne by thy merit to the citadel of heaven, and the path thither was made by no slight toil   Thou didst not dwell in thy native country, but all the way to snowy Strymon thou hast gone and the Mars-worshipping Getae, Persia, and the broad-flowing Ganges, and all the waters that the swarthy Indian drinks.   Such doubtless was the law twice ordained for thee by the Parcae who spun the fated threads at thy double birth.[2]   I too (if 'tis right to make comparison with the gods) am crushed by an iron and a difficult lot.   I have fallen

[2] Bacchus was born prematurely by Semele, and a second time after proper nourishment in the thigh of Jupiter.

illo nec levius cecidi, quem magna locutum
30 reppulit a Thebis Iuppiter igne suo.
ut tamen audisti percussum fulmine vatem,
    admonitu matris condoluisse potes,
et potes aspiciens circum tua sacra poëtas
    "nescioquis nostri" dicere "cultor abest."
35 fer, bone Liber, opem : sic altera [1] degravet ulmum
    vitis et incluso plena sit uva mero,
sic tibi cum Bacchis Satyrorum gnava iuventus
    adsit, et attonito non taceare sono,
ossa bipenniferi sic sint male pressa Lycurgi,
40 impia nec poena Pentheos umbra vacet,[2]
sic micet aeternum vicinaque sidera vincat
    coniugis in caelo clara corona tuae :
huc ades et casus releves, pulcherrime, nostros,
    unum de numero me memor esse tuo.
45 sunt dis inter se commercia.   flectere tempta
    Caesareum numen numine, Bacche, tuo.
vos quoque, consortes studii, pia turba, poëtae,
    haec eadem sumpto quisque rogate mero.
atque aliquis vestrum, Nasonis nomine dicto,
50 apponat labris [3] pocula mixta suis,
admonitusque mei, cum circumspexerit omnes,
    dicat "ubi est nostri pars modo Naso chori?"
idque ita, si vestrum merui candore favorem,
    nullaque iudicio littera laesa meo est,
55 si, veterum digne veneror cum scripta virorum,
    proxima non illis esse minora reor.
sic igitur dextro faciatis Apolline carmen :
    quod licet, inter vos nomen habete meum.

---

[1] altam   [2] vacet] caret   [3] lacrimis *corr. Ehwald*

---

[1] Capaneus.   [2] *i.e.* two vines instead of one.
[3] Ariadne.

no more lightly than he[1] whom Jupiter, for his overweening utterance, drove back from Thebes with his lightning.   Yet when thou didst hear that a poet had been smitten by the bolt, remembering thy mother, thou mightest have felt sympathy and gazing upon the bards about thine altar thou mightest have said, "Some worshipper of mine is missing."

35 Bring aid to me, kind Liber!   So may a second[2] vine weigh down the elm and the grape-clusters be filled with prisoned wine, so may the Bacchae and the young vigour of the Satyrs attend thee and may their frenzied cries keep not silent thy name; so may the bones of axe-bearing Lycurgus be heavily weighed down, nor may the wicked shade of Pentheus ever be free of punishment, so may the crown of thy spouse[3] bright in the sky glitter for ever, surpassing the stars close at hand—hither come and lighten my misfortunes, fairest of gods, remembering that I am one of thine own.   Gods deal with gods; do thou, O Bacchus, seek to sway Caesar's power divine by thine own.   Do ye, too, O poets who share in my pursuit, loyal throng, take each of you unmixed wine and make this same petition.   And let someone of you, uttering Naso's name, raise a bumper of wine to his lips, and in thought of me, when he has gazed around upon all, let him say, "Where is Naso, who was but now a part of our company?"—and this only if I have earned your approval by my sincerity, if no book was ever injured by verdict of mine, if in deserved reverence for the writings of men of old I yet consider not inferior those most recent.   As then I pray ye may compose under Apollo's favour: keep—for this is lawful—my name among you.

OVID

IV.

Litore ab Euxino Nasonis epistula veni,
    lassaque facta mari lassaque facta via,
qui mihi flens dixit "tu, cui licet, aspice Romam.
    heu quanto melior sors tua sorte mea est!"
5 flens quoque me scripsit, nec qua signabar, ad os est
    ante, sed ad madidas gemma relata genas.
tristitiae causam siquis cognoscere quaerit,
    ostendi solem postulat ille sibi,
nec frondem in silvis, nec aperto mollia prato
10   gramina, nec pleno flumine cernit aquam[1];
quid Priamus doleat, mirabitur, Hectore rapto,
    quidve Philoctetes ictus ab angue gemat.
di facerent utinam talis status esset in illo,
    ut non tristitiae causa dolenda foret!
15 fert tamen, ut debet, casus patienter amaros,
    more nec indomiti frena recusat equi.
nec fore perpetuam sperat sibi numinis iram,
    conscius in culpa non scelus esse sua.
saepe refert, sit quanta dei clementia, cuius
20   se quoque in exemplis adnumerare solet:
nam, quod opes teneat patrias, quod nomina civis,
    denique quod vivat, munus habere dei.
te tamen (o, si quid credis mihi, carior illi
    omnibus) in toto pectore semper habet;
25 teque Menoetiaden, te, qui comitatus Oresten,
    te vocat Aegiden Euryalumque suum.
nec patriam magis ille suam desiderat et quae
    plurima cum patria sentit abesse sibi,
quam vultus oculosque tuos, o dulcior illo
30   melle, quod in ceris Attica ponit apis.

                       [1] aquas

---

[1] Ovid.   [2] Patroclus.   [3] Pylades.   [4] Theseus.

IV. THE POET'S LETTER GREETS A TRUE FRIEND

From the Euxine shore have I come, a letter of Naso's, wearied by the sea, wearied by the road. Weeping he said to me, "Do thou, who art allowed, look on Rome. Alas! how much better is thy lot than mine!" Weeping too he wrote me, and the gem with which I was sealed, he lifted first, not to his lips, but to his tear-drenched cheeks.

[7] Whoever seeks to learn the cause of his sorrow is asking that the sun be shown to him; he sees not the leaves in the wood, the soft grass in the open meadow, or the water in the full stream; he will wonder why Priam grieves at the ravishing of Hector, why Philoctetes groans after the snake has struck. Would that the gods might bring to pass such lot for him[1] that he had no cause of sorrow to lament! Yet spite of all he bears, as he ought, with patience his bitter misfortunes, nor, like an unbroken horse, does he refuse the bit. He hopes that not forever will the god's wrath endure, aware that in his fault there is no crime. Often he recalls how great is the god's mercy, of which he is wont to count himself also as an example; for that he retains his father's wealth, the name of citizen— in fine his very life he holds as a gift of the god.

[23] But thee—O, if thou believest me in anything, dearer than all to him—thee he holds constantly in his whole heart. Thee he calls his Menoetiades,[2] thee his Orestes' comrade,[3] thee his Aegides,[4] or his Euryalus. He longs not more for his country and the many things with his country whose absence he feels, than for thy face and eyes, O thou who art sweeter than the honey stored in the wax by the Attic bee.

225

saepe etiam maerens tempus reminiscitur illud,
    quod non praeventum morte fuisse dolet ;
cumque alii fugerent subitae contagia cladis,
    nec vellent ictae limen adire domus,
35 te sibi cum paucis meminit mansisse fidelem,
    si paucos aliquis tresve duosve vocat.
quamvis attonitus, sensit tamen omnia, nec te
    se minus adversis indoluisse suis.
verba solet vultumque tuum gemitusque referre,
40   et te flente suos emaduisse sinus :
quam sibi praestiteris, qua consolatus amicum
    sis ope, solandus cum simul ipse fores.
pro quibus affirmat fore se memoremque piumque,
    sive diem videat sive tegatur humo,
45 per caput ipse suum solitus iurare tuumque,
    quod scio non illi vilius esse suo.
plena tot ac tantis referetur gratia factis,
    nec sinet ille tuos litus arare boves.
fac modo, constanter profugum tueare : quod ille,
50   qui bene te novit, non rogat, ipsa rogo.

V.

Annuus adsuetum dominae natalis honorem
    exigit : ite manus ad pia sacra meae.
sic quondam festum Laërtius egerat heros
    forsan in extremo coniugis orbe diem.
5 lingua favens adsit, nostrorum oblita malorum,
    quae, puto, dedidicit iam bona verba loqui ;
quaeque semel toto vestis mihi sumitur anno,
    sumatur fatis discolor alba meis ;

---

[1] Ulysses.

Often too in his grief he remembers that time, which to his sorrow was not anticipated by death, when others were fleeing the pollution of sudden disaster, unwilling to approach the threshold of the stricken house, thou with a few others didst remain faithful— if anybody terms three or two "a few." Though sore smitten, yet he realized everything—that thou not less than himself didst grieve over his misfortunes. Thy words, thy face, thy laments he is wont to recall, and his own bosom wet with thy tears; how thou didst support him, with what resource thou didst comfort him, although thou wert thyself at the same time in need of comfort.

[43] For this he assures thee that he will be mindful and loyal, whether he behold the light of day or be covered by earth, swearing it by his own life and by thine which I know he counts not cheaper than his own. Full recompense for these many great acts shall be rendered; he will not suffer thine oxen to plough the shore. Only see thou dost constantly protect the exile! What he, who knows thee well, asketh not, that I ask.

V. My Lady's Birthday

The year has flown and the birthday of my lady exacts its customary honour; go, hands of mine, perform affection's rites. Thus of old did the Laërtian hero [1] pass, perhaps at the world's edge, his wife's gala day. Let me have a tongue of good omen forgetful of my misfortunes (my tongue has, I think, unlearned ere now its utterance of propitious words!) and the garb that I put on only once in the whole year let me now put on—the white garb that

araque gramineo viridis de caespite fiat,
10   et velet tepidos nexa corona focos.
da mihi tura, puer, pingues facientia flammas,
    quodque pio fusum stridat in igne merum.
optime natalis! quamvis procul absumus, opto
    candidus huc venias dissimilisque meo,
15 si quod et instabat dominae miserabile vulnus,
    sit perfuncta meis tempus in omne malis;
quaeque gravi nuper plus quam quassata procella est,
    quod superest, tutum per mare navis eat.
illa domo nataque sua patriaque fruatur
20   —erepta haec uni sit satis esse mihi—
quatenus et non est in caro coniuge felix,
    pars vitae tristi cetera nube vacet.
vivat, ametque virum, quoniam sic cogitur, absens,
    consumatque annos, sed diuturna, suos.
25 adicerem et nostros, sed ne contagia fati
    corrumpant timeo, quos agit ipsa, mei.
nil homini certum est.   fieri quis posse putaret,
    ut facerem in mediis haec ego sacra Getis?
aspice ut aura tamen fumos e ture coortos
30   in partes Italas et loca dextra ferat.
sensus inest igitur nebulis, quas exigit ignis:
    consilio fugiunt aethera, Ponte,[1] tuum.
consilio, commune sacrum cum fiat in ara
    fratribus, alterna qui periere manu,
35 ipsa sibi discors, tamquam mandetur ab illis,
    scinditur in partes atra favilla duas.
hoc, memini, quondam fieri non posse loquebar,
    et me Battiades iudice falsus erat:

              [1] consilium . . . cetera pene *corr. Withof*

---

    [1] Perilla.   [2] Eteocles and Polynices.

matches not my fate. Let there be made a green altar of grassy turf, the warm hearth veiled with a braided garland. Give me incense, boy, that produces rich flame, and wine that hisses when poured in the pious fire.

[13] Best of birthdays! though I am far away, I pray thou mayst come hither bright and unlike my own. If any wretched wound is threatening my lady may she have done with it forever by means of my misfortunes, and may the bark which but recently was more than shaken by a violent blast pass in future over an untroubled sea. May she continue to enjoy her home, her daughter,[1] and her native land (let it suffice that these things have been taken from me alone), and in as much as she is not blessed in the person of her dear husband, may all the other part of her life be free from gloomy cloud. Long life to her! and may she in absence, since to this she is forced, love her husband, and pass—but late!—to the end of her years. I would add my own too, but I fear the pollution of my fate would infect those which she herself is living.

[27] Naught is certain for man. Who would have thought it possible that I should be performing these rites amidst the Getae? Yet look how the breeze wafts the smoke that rises from the incense in the direction of Italy and places of good omen. Sentience, then, resides in the vapour thrown off by the fire; designedly it flees thy sky, O Pontus. Designedly, when the common offering is made on the altar to the brothers who died by each other's hands,[2] the very ashes, in dissension as if at their command, separate blackly into two parts. This, I remember, I once said could not be, and in my opinion Battus'

omnia nunc credo, cum tu non stultus ab Arcto
40   terga, vapor, dederis Ausoniamque petas.
haec ergo lux est, quae si non orta fuisset,
     nulla fuit misero festa videnda mihi.
edidit haec mores illis heroisin [1] aequos,
     quis erat Eëtion Icariusque pater.
45 nata pudicitia est ista [2] probitasque, fidesque,
     at non sunt ista gaudia nata die,[3]
sed labor et curae fortunaque moribus impar,
     iustaque de viduo paene querella toro.
scilicet adversis probitas exercita rebus
50   tristi materiam tempore laudis habet.
si nihil infesti durus vidisset Ulixes,
     Penelope felix sed sine laude foret.
victor Echionias si vir penetrasset in arces,
     forsitan Euadnen vix sua nosset humus.
55 cum Pelia genitae tot sint, cur nobilis una est?
     nempe fuit misero nupta quod una viro.
effice ut Iliacas tangat prior alter harenas,
     Laodamia nihil cur referatur erit.
et tua, quod malles,[4] pietas ignota maneret,
60   implerent venti si mea vela sui.
di tamen et Caesar dis accessure, sed olim,
     aequarint Pylios cum tua fata dies,
non mihi, qui poenam fateor meruisse, sed illi
     parcite, quae nullo digna dolore dolet.

     [1] heroibus *corr. Salmasius*   [2] moris *corr. Kenney*
          [3] die] fide   [4] mallem

[1] Callimachus, who must have touched somewhere upon this myth.
[2] Andromache and Penelope.

son[1] was mistaken. Now I believe all, since thou, O vapour, hast in wisdom turned from Arctos and seekest Ausonia.

[41] This then is the dawn in defect of whose rising there would have been no gala day to be seen by wretched me. This brought forth a character equalling those famed heroines[2] whose fathers were Eëtion and Icarus. Chastity was born on this day and uprightness, and loyalty; but on this day no joys—rather woe and cares and a fortune unfitted to thy character, and a plaint all but just about thy widowed couch. Assuredly uprightness schooled by adversity in time of sorrow affords a theme for praise. Had sturdy Ulysses seen no misfortune, Penelope would have been happy but unpraised. Had her husband[3] pressed victoriously into the citadel[4] of Echion, perchance Euadne would scarce have been known to her own land. Though Pelias had so many daughters, why is one[5] only famed? Doubtless because she alone wedded an ill-starred husband.[6] Let but another be first to touch the sands of Ilium and there will be no reason why Laodamia should be remembered. Thy loyalty, too, as thou wouldst prefer, would remain unknown, if favouring winds filled my sails. Yet, O gods and Caesar destined to be one of the gods—but at that time when thy life shall have equalled the days of the Pylian[7]—spare, not me, who confess that I have deserved a punishment, but her who grieves albeit she deserves not grief.

OVID

VI.

Tu quoque, nostrarum quondam fiducia rerum,
    qui mihi confugium, qui mihi portus eras,
tu quoque suscepti curam dimittis amici,
    officiique pium tam cito ponis onus?
5 sarcina sum, fateor, quam si non[1] tempore nostro[2]
    depositurus eras, non subeunda fuit.
fluctibus in mediis navem, Palinure, relinquis?
    ne fuge, neve tua sit minor arte fides.
numquid Achilleos inter fera proelia fidi
10   deseruit levitas Automedontis equos?
quem semel excepit, numquam Podalirius aegro
    promissam medicae non tulit artis opem.
turpius eicitur, quam non admittitur hospes:
    quae patuit, dextrae firma sit ara meae.
15 nil nisi me solum primo tutatus es; at nunc
    me pariter serva iudiciumque tuum,
si modo non aliqua est in me nova culpa, tuamque
    mutarunt subito crimina nostra fidem.
spiritus hic, Scythica quem non bene ducimus aura,
20   quod cupio, membris exeat ante meis,
quam tua delicto stringantur pectora nostro,
    et videar merito vilior esse tibi.
non adeo toti fatis urgemur iniquis,
    ut mea sit longis mens quoque mota malis.
25 finge tamen motam, quotiens Agamemnone natum
    dixisse in Pyladen improba verba putas?
nec procul a vero est quin vel[3] pulsarit amicum:
    mansit in officiis non minus ille suis.

---

       [1] quamvis sine   [2] nostro] duro   [3] quod vel

---

      [1] Orestes—in the course of his madness.

VI. Be Faithful

Do you too, once the stay of my fortunes, my refuge, my harbour—do you too dismiss your love for the friend you took unto yourself? Do you so speedily lay aside the loyal burden of duty? I am a burden, I confess, but one which you should not have taken up if you meant to put it off at a time unfavourable for me. In the midst of the waves, Palinurus, do you desert the ship? Flee not; let not your faith be inferior to your skill. Did Automedon waver in his faith and abandon in the fierceness of the fight the steeds of Achilles? When once he had accepted the charge never did Podalirius fail to bring to the sick man the promised aid of his healing art. 'Tis baser to thrust forth than not to receive a guest: let the altar, once open, be a steady support for my right hand.

[15] Nothing but myself alone did you at first preserve; but now preserve alike me and your own judgment, if only I have not some new fault and my wrongdoings have not suddenly altered your loyalty. May this breath which I draw not easily in the Scythian air leave my body—this is my desire before your heart is wounded by sin of mine and I seem deservedly cheaper in your sight.

[23] Not so utterly overwhelmed am I by unjust fate that my mind also has been unbalanced by my long continued woes. Yet suppose it unbalanced—how many times, think you, Agamemnon's son [1] uttered violent words against Pylades? Nor is it far from truth that he even struck his friend; yet that friend stood fast in his loyalty. This is the only thing in

233

hoc est cum miseris solum commune beatis,
30   ambobus tribui quod solet obsequium :
ceditur et caecis et quos praetexta verendos
   virgaque cum verbis imperiosa facit.
si mihi non parcis, fortunae parcere debes :
   non habet in nobis ullius ira locum.
35 elige nostrorum minimum minimumque laborum,[1]
   isto, quod reris,[2] grandius illud erit.
quam multa madidae celantur harundine fossae,
   florida quam multas Hybla tuetur apes,
quam multae gracili terrena sub horrea ferre
40   limite formicae grana reperta solent,
tam me circumstat[3] densorum turba malorum.
   crede mihi, vero est nostra querella minor.
his qui contentus non est, in litus harenas,
   in segetem spicas, in mare fundat aquas.
45 intempestivos igitur compesce tumores,[4]
   vela nec in medio desere nostra mari.

VII.

Quam legis, ex illa tibi venit epistula terra,
   latus ubi aequoreis additur Hister aquis.
si tibi contingit cum dulci vita salute,
   candida fortunae pars manet una meae.
5 scilicet, ut semper, quid agam, carissime, quaeris,
   quamvis hoc vel me scire tacente potes.
sum miser ; haec brevis est nostrorum summa malorum,
   quisquis et offenso Caesare vivit, erit.

---

      [1] malorum   [2] illo quo quereris
   [3] circumdat (circumdant) : circumstant *s*
       [4] timores *corr. s*

---

   [1] The garb of the official, bordered with a purple stripe.
   [2] The *fasces* (axes encased in the bundle of rods as a

common between the wretched and the fortunate
that regard is wont to be rendered to both. We
make way both for the blind and for those whom the
praetexta [1] and the imperious rods [2] with their cries
make reverend. If you have no consideration for
me, you ought to show consideration for my fate; in
my case there is no room for anger. Choose the very
least of my woes; it will be greater than what you
imagine. As many as are the reeds which hide the
wet ditches, as many as are the bees which flowery
Hybla guards, as many as are the ants that are wont
to carry by tiny paths to underground stores the
grain they find, so crowded is the throng of woes
about me; believe me, my complaint is short of the
truth. Whoever is not content with these, let him
pour sands upon the shore, grain ears into the field, or
water into the sea. Wherefore restrain your un-
seasonable anger and abandon not my bark in the
midst of the sea.

VII. "Among the Goths"

The letter which you are reading has come to you
from that land where the broad Hister adds his
waters to the sea. If you are blessed with life and the
sweetness of safety, bright is still one spot in my
life. Doubtless you are asking, as ever, dearest one,
how I fare, though this you can know even if I speak
not. I am wretched—this is the brief sum of my woes
—and so will all be who live subject to Caesar's wrath.

symbol of authority) borne by the lictors who by their cries
(*animadvertite*, "give heed!") demanded honour for the
magistrates.

turba Tomitanae quae sit regionis et inter
10   quos habitem mores, discere cura tibi est ?
mixta sit haec quamvis inter Graecosque Getasque,
    a male pacatis plus trahit ora Getis.
Sarmaticae maior Geticaeque frequentia gentis
    per medias in equis itque reditque vias.
15 in quibus est nemo, qui non coryton et arcum
    telaque vipereo lurida felle gerat.
vox fera, trux vultus, verissima mentis[1] imago,
    non coma, non trita[2] barba resecta manu,
dextera non segnis fixo dare vulnera cultro,
20   quem iunctum lateri barbarus omnis habet.
vivit in his heu nunc, lusorum[3] oblitus amorum,
    hos videt, hos vates audit, amice, tuus :
atque utinam vivat, non et[4] moriatur in illis,
    absit ab invisis ut tamen umbra locis.
25 carmina quod pleno saltari nostra theatro,
    versibus et plaudi scribis, amice, meis,
nil equidem feci—tu scis hoc ipse—theatris,
    Musa nec in plausus ambitiosa mea est.
non tamen ingratum est, quodcumque oblivia nostri
30   impedit et profugi nomen in ora refert.
quamvis interdum, quae me laesisse recordor,
    carmina devoveo Pieridasque meas,
cum bene devovi, nequeo tamen esse sine illis,
    vulneribusque meis tela cruenta sequor,
35 quaeque modo Euboicis lacerata est fluctibus, audet
    Graia Capheream currere puppis aquam.[5]

---

[1] mortis *corr. Housman*   [2] ulla *corr. Housman*
[3] nullus eorum *vel* his nullus tenerorum : nunc lusorum
Ehwald

[9] What the people of the land of Tomis are like, amid what customs I live, are you interested to know ? Though upon this coast there is a mixture of Greeks and Getae, it derives more from the scarce pacified Getae. Greater hordes of Sarmatae and Getae go and come upon their horses along the roads. Among them there is not one who does not bear quiver and bow, and darts yellow with viper's gall. Harsh voices, grim faces, surest indication of their minds, neither hair nor beard trimmed by practised hand, rights hands not slow to stab and wound with the knife which every barbarian wears fastened to his side. Among such men, alas ! your bard is living, forgetful of the loves with which he played : such men he sees, such men he hears, my friend. Would he might live and not die among them, so that his shade might yet be free of this hated place !

[25] As for your news that my songs are being presented with dancing [1] in a crowded theatre, my friend, and that my verses are applauded—I have indeed composed nothing (you yourself know this) for the theatre ; my Muse is not ambitious for hand-clappings. Yet I am not ungrateful for anything which hinders oblivion of me, which brings back the exile's name to men's lips. Although at times I curse the poems whose injury to me I recall, and my Pierians, yet when I have cursed them well I cannot live without them ; I still seek the weapons that are bloody from my wounds, and the Grecian bark that but now was shattered by the Euboean waves dares to skim the waters of Caphereus. And yet I do not

[1] Probably scenes adapted from the *Heroides*, etc., to the purposes of ballet and pantomime.

---

[4] et non *corr. Heinsius*   [5] capharea . . . aqua

nec tamen, ut lauder, vigilo curamque futuri
    nominis, utilius quod latuisset, ago.
detineo studiis animum falloque dolores,
40   experior curis et dare verba meis.
quid potius faciam desertis solus in oris,
    quamve malis aliam quaerere coner [1] opem ?
sive locum specto, locus est inamabilis, et quo
    esse nihil toto tristius orbe potest,
45 sive homines, vix sunt homines hoc nomine digni,
    quamque lupi, saevae plus feritatis habent.
non metuunt leges, sed cedit viribus aequum,
    victaque pugnaci iura sub ense iacent.
pellibus et laxis arcent mala frigora bracis,
50   oraque sunt longis horrida tecta comis.
in paucis extant Graecae vestigia linguae,
    haec quoque iam Getico barbara facta sono.
unus in hoc nemo est populo, qui forte Latine
    quamlibet [2] e medio reddere verba queat.
55 ille ego Romanus vates—ignoscite, Musae !—
    Sarmatico cogor plurima more loqui.
et pudet et fateor, iam desuetudine longa
    vix subeunt ipsi verba Latina mihi.
nec dubito quin sint et in hoc non pauca libello
60   barbara : non hominis culpa, sed ista loci.
ne tamen Ausoniae perdam commercia linguae,
    et fiat patrio vox mea muta sono,
ipse loquor mecum desuetaque verba retracto,
    et studii repeto signa sinistra mei.
65 sic animum tempusque traho, memeque [3] reduco
    a contemplatu summoveoque mali.
carminibus quaero miserarum oblivia rerum :
    praemia si studio consequar ista, sat est.

[1] coner] cogar   [2] quaelibet
[3] me sicque *vel* mecumque *corr. Housman*

work o' nights for praise, toiling for the future life of a name which had better have lain unnoticed. I busy my mind with studies beguiling my grief, trying to cheat my cares. What else am I to do, all alone on this forsaken shore, what other resources for my sorrows should I try to seek ? If I look upon the country, 'tis devoid of charm, nothing in the whole world can be more cheerless ; if I look upon the men, they are scarce men worthy the name ; they have more of cruel savagery than wolves. They fear not laws ; right gives way to force, and justice lies conquered beneath the aggressive sword. With skins and loose breeches they keep off the evils of the cold ; their shaggy faces are protected with long locks. A few retain traces of the Greek tongue, but even this is rendered barbarous by a Getic twang. There is not a single man among these people who perchance might express in Latin any words however common. I, the Roman bard— pardon, ye Muses !—am forced to utter most things in Sarmatian fashion. I admit it, though it shames me : now from long disuse Latin words with difficulty occur even to me ! And I doubt not there are even in this book not a few barbarisms, not the fault of the man but of the place. Yet for fear of losing the use of the Ausonian tongue and lest my own voice grow dumb in its native sound, I talk to myself, dealing again with disused words and seeking again the ill-omened currency of my art.

⁶⁵ Thus do I drag out my life and my time, and withdraw myself from the contemplation of my woes. Through song I seek oblivion from my wretchedness. If such be the rewards I win by my pursuit, 'tis enough.

OVID

VIII.

Non adeo cecidi, quamvis abiectus, ut infra
    te quoque sim, inferius quo nihil esse potest.
quae tibi res animos in me facit, improbe ? curve
    casibus insultas, quos potes ipse pati ?
5 nec mala te reddunt mitem placidumque iacenti
    nostra, quibus possint inlacrimare ferae ;
nec metuis dubio Fortunae stantis in orbe
    numen, et exosae verba superba deae.
exigit [1] a dignis [2] ultrix Rhamnusia poenas :
10   inposito calcas quid [3] mea fata pede ?
vidi ego naufragium qui risit [4] in aequore [5] mergi,
    et "numquam" dixi "iustior unda fuit."
vilia qui quondam miseris alimenta negarat,
    nunc mendicato pascitur ipse cibo.
15 passibus ambiguis Fortuna volubilis errat
    et manet in nullo certa tenaxque loco,
sed modo laeta nitet, [6] vultus modo sumit acerbos,
    et tantum constans in levitate sua est.
nos quoque floruimus, sed flos erat ille caducus,
20   flammaque de stipula nostra brevisque fuit.
neve tamen tota capias fera gaudia mente,
    non est placandi spes mihi nulla dei,
vel quia peccavi citra scelus, utque pudore
    non caret, invidia sic mea culpa caret,
25 vel quia nil ingens ad finem solis ab ortu
    illo, cui paret, mitius orbis habet.
scilicet ut non est per vim superabilis ulli,
    molle cor ad timidas sic habet ille preces,

---

        [1] exigis *vel* exiget   [2] at dignes
  [3] qui   [4] naufragiumque viros et *corr. Mencken*
        [5] aequora   [6] manet

VIII. To a Detractor

I have not fallen so low, low though I am, that I am
beneath you too, for beneath you there can be
nothing. What stirs your spirit up against me,
shameless man? Why do you mock at misfortunes
which you yourself may suffer? My woes do not
soften you and placate you towards one who is
prostrate—woes over which wild beasts might weep,
nor do you fear the power of Fortune standing on her
swaying wheel, or the haughty commands of the
goddess who hates. Avenging Rhamnusia [1] exacts a
penalty from those who deserve it; why do you set
your foot and trample upon my fate? I have seen
one drowned in the waves who had laughed at
shipwreck, and I said, "Never were the waters more
just." The man who once denied cheap food to
the wretched now eats the bread of beggary.
Changeable Fortune wanders abroad with aimless steps,
abiding firm and persistent in no place; now she beams
with joy, now she puts on a harsh mien, steadfast
only in her own fickleness. I too had my day, but that
day was fleeting; my fire was but of straw and short-
lived. Nevertheless that you may not fill all your soul
with cruel joy, not wholly gone is my hope of appeasing
the god, because my mistake fell short of crime, and
though my fault is not free from shame, yet 'tis free
from odium, or because the wide world from the rising
sun to its setting holds nothing more merciful than
him whom it obeys. Indeed though no force can over-
come him, yet he has a tender heart for the petitions

[1] Nemesis, one of whose shrines was at Rhamnus in Attica.
She detested and punished overweening words and acts.

exemploque deum, quibus accessurus et ipse est,
30   cum poenae venia plura roganda [1] dabit.[2]
si numeres anno soles et nubila toto,
    invenies nitidum saepius isse diem.
ergo ne nimium nostra laetere ruina,
    restitui quondam me quoque posse puta :
35 posse puta fieri lenito principe vultus
    ut videas media tristis in urbe meos,
utque ego te videam causa graviore fugatum,
    haec sunt a primis proxima vota meis.

IX

O tua si sineres in nostris nomina poni
    carminibus, positus quam mihi saepe fores !
te canerem solum, meriti memor, inque libellis
    crevisset sine te pagina nulla meis.
5 quid tibi deberem, tota sciretur in urbe,
    exul in amissa si tamen urbe legor.
te praesens mitem nosset, te serior aetas,
    scripta vetustatem si modo nostra ferent,
nec tibi cessaret doctus bene dicere lector :
10   hic te servato vate maneret honor.
Caesaris est primum munus, quod ducimus auras ;
    gratia post magnos est tibi habenda deos.
ille dedit vitam ; tu, quam dedit ille, tueris,
    et facis accepto munere posse frui.
15 cumque perhorruerit casus pars maxima nostros,
    pars etiam credi praetimuisse [3] velit,

---

[1] regenda   [2] petam : dabit *Faber*   [3] per- *corr. Burman*

of the timid, and after the example of the gods whom he himself is destined to join, with the remission of my penalty he will grant me further boons. If you count the suns and the clouds throughout a year you will find that the day has more often passed brightly.

[33] So then that you rejoice not overmuch in my ruin, consider that even I may some day be restored ; consider that, if the prince is appeased, it may come to pass that you may be dismayed to see my face in the midst of the city, and I may see you exiled for a weightier cause. This, after that first wish, is the second prayer that I put forth.

IX. In Gratitude

O hadst thou but allowed thy name to be set in my verse, how oft wouldst thou have been named ! Of thee alone would I have sung in memory of thy service ; in my books no page would have been completed without thee. My debt to thee would be known throughout the city—if I, an exile, am still read in the city I have lost. Thy kindness the present, thy kindness later time would know, if only my writings endure age, nor would the accomplished reader cease to bless thee ; this honour would abide with thee for having preserved a poet. Caesar's gift—that I draw breath—comes first ; after the mighty gods it is to thee that I must render thanks. He gave me life ; thou dost preserve the life he gave, lending me power to enjoy the boon I have received. When most men shrank with dread at my fall—some even would have it believed that they had

243

naufragiumque meum tumulo spectarit [1] ab alto,
    nec dederit nanti per freta saeva manum,
seminecem Stygia revocasti solus ab unda.
20   hoc quoque, quod memores possumus esse, tuum
      est.
di tibi se tribuant cum Caesare semper amicos :
    non potuit votum plenius esse meum.
haec meus argutis, si tu paterere, libellis
    poneret in multa luce videnda labor ;
25 nunc quoque se, quamvis est [2] iussa quiescere, quin te
    nominet invitum, vix mea Musa tenet.
utque canem pavidae nactum vestigia cervae
    luctantem [3] frustra copula dura tenet,
utque fores nondum reserati carceris acer
30   nunc pede, nunc ipsa fronte lacessit equus,
sic mea lege data vincta atque inclusa Thalia [4]
    per titulum vetiti nominis ire cupit.
ne tamen officio memoris laedaris amici,
    parebo iussis—parce dimere—tuis.
35 at non parerem, nisi me meminisse putares.
    hoc quod non prohibet vox tua, gratus ero.
dumque—quod o breve sit !—lumen vitale videbo,
    serviet officio spiritus iste tuo.

X.

Ut sumus in Ponto, ter frigore constitit Hister,
    facta est Euxini dura ter unda maris.
at mihi iam videor patria procul esse tot annis,
    Dardana quot Graio Troia sub hoste fuit.

[1] spectaret *corr. Heinsius*
[2] iam quamvis est *vel* q. e. iam *corr. Naugerus* (*s* ?)
[3] latrantem   [4] Thalia] voluntas

---

[1] Ten years.

feared it—and gazed from a safe height upon my shipwreck, extending no hand to him who swam in the savage seas, thou alone didst recall me half lifeless from the Stygian waters. My very power to remember this is due to thee.

[21] May the gods and Caesar ever grant thee their friendship! Prayer of mine could not be fuller than this. These things, if thou wouldst permit, my toil would place in eloquent books in a bright light to be seen of all: even now, though my Muse has been constrained to silence, she scarce refrains from naming thee against thy will. As a hound that has scented the trail of a timorous hind, straining in vain, is held in check by the unyielding leash, as upon the door of the barrier as yet unlocked the eager steed frets now with his hoof, now with his very brow, so my Thalia, fettered and confined by the law thou hast imposed, longs to course o'er the glory of thy forbidden name. Yet that thou mayst not be injured by the homage of a grateful friend, I will obey thy commands, fear not. But I would not obey, if thou didst not think me grateful; this, which thy word does not forbid, I shall be—grateful; and so long as I behold the light of life—and may the time be short! that life shall be a slave to thy service.

X. The Evils of Tomis

Since I have been by the Pontus' shore, thrice has Hister halted with the cold, thrice has the water of the Euxine sea grown hard. Yet already I seem to have been absent from my country as many years [1] as Dardanian Troy was besieged by the Grecian

OVID

5 stare putes, adeo procedunt tempora tarde,
  et peragit lentis passibus annus iter.
nec mihi solstitium quicquam de noctibus aufert,
  efficit angustos nec mihi bruma dies.
scilicet in nobis rerum natura novata est,
10   cumque meis curis omnia longa facit.
an peragunt solitos communia tempora motus,
  stantque[1] magis vitae tempora dura meae,
quem tenet Euxini mendax cognomine litus,[2]
  et Scythici vere terra sinistra freti ?
15 innumerae circa gentes fera bella minantur,
  quae sibi non rapto[3] vivere turpe putant.
nil extra tutum est : tumulus defenditur ipse
  moenibus exiguis ingenioque loci.
cum minime credas, ut aves,[4] densissimus hostis
20   advolat, et praedam vix bene visus agit.
saepe intra muros clausis venientia portis
  per medias legimus noxia tela vias.
est igitur rarus, rus qui[5] colere audeat, isque
  hac arat infelix, hac tenet arma manu.
25 sub galea pastor iunctis pice cantat avenis,
  proque lupo pavidae bella verentur oves.
vix ope castelli defendimur ; et tamen intus
  mixta facit Graecis barbara turba metum.
quippe simul nobis habitat discrimine nullo
30   barbarus et tecti plus quoque parte tenet.
quos[6] ut non timeas, possis odisse videndo
  pellibus et longa corpora tecta coma.

---

[1] suntque *corr. Housman*
[2] litus ς] tellus *vel* tempus *vel* pontus
[3] raptu   [4] avis
[5] qui iam *corr. Heinsius* ; *cf.* qui rus ς   [6] quorum

foe. One would think that time stood still, so slowly does it move, and the year completes its journey with lagging pace. For me the solstice lessens not the nights, and winter shortens not the days. In my case surely nature has been made anew and she makes all things as tedious as my own sorrows. Or does time in general run its wonted course, and is it only for *my* life that time stands cruelly still? For I am held by the shore of the false-named Euxine and the land, in truth ill-omened, of the Scythian sea.[1] Countless tribes round about threaten cruel war, thinking it base to live if not by plunder. Without, nothing is secure: the hill itself is defended by meagre walls and by its skilful site. When least expected, like birds, the foe swarms upon us and when scarce well seen is already driving off the booty. Oft, though the gates be closed, we pick up amidst the streets deadly missiles that come within the walls. Few then venture to till the fields, for the wretch must plough with one hand, and hold arms in the other. The shepherd wears a helmet while he plays upon his pitch-cemented reeds, and instead of a wolf the timorous ewes dread war. Scarce with the fortress's aid are we defended; and even within that the barbarous mob mingled with the Greeks inspires fear. For us dwell without distinction the barbarians, occupying even more than half of the dwellings. Even should you not fear them, you may loathe the sight of their bodies covered with hides and with their long hair. Even

[1] *Sinistra* probably has a double meaning here: (1) "to the left" (as one enters from the Bosporus), (2) "ill-omened," *cf.* notes on *Tr.* iv. 4. 55 and iv. 1. 60.

247

hos quoque, qui geniti Graia creduntur ab urbe,
    pro patrio cultu Persica braca tegit.
35 exercent illi sociae commercia linguae:
    per gestum res est significanda mihi.
barbarus hic ego sum, qui non intellegor ulli,
    et rident stolidi verba Latina Getae;
meque palam de me tuto mala saepe loquuntur,
40   forsitan obiciunt exiliumque mihi.
utque fit, in se [1] aliquid fingi,[2] dicentibus illis
    abnuerim quotiens adnuerimque, putant.
adde quod iniustum [3] rigido ius dicitur ense,
    dantur et in medio vulnera saepe foro.
45 o duram Lachesin, quae tam grave sidus habenti
    fila dedit vitae non breviora meae!
quod patriae vultu vestroque caremus, amici,
    atque hic in Scythicis gentibus esse queror:
utraque poena gravis. merui tamen urbe carere,
50   non merui tali forsitan esse loco.
quid loquor, a! demens? ipsam quoque perdere
    vitam,
Caesaris offenso numine, dignus eram.

XI.

Quod te nescioquis per iurgia dixerit esse
    exulis uxorem, littera questa tua est.
indolui, non tam mea quod fortuna male audit,
    qui iam consuevi fortiter esse miser,
5 quam quod cui minime vellem, sum causa pudoris,
    teque reor nostris erubuisse malis.

---

[1] me *corr. Schenkl*   [2] siquidem *corr. Ellis*   [3] et iustum

---

[1] The original Greek colony of Tomis, *cf. Tr.* iii. 9. 3 f.
[2] The text of the hexameter is by no means certain.

these who are believed to derive their descent from the Greek city [1] wear Persian trousers instead of the dress of their fathers. They hold intercourse in the tongue they share; I must make myself understood by gestures. Here it is I that am a barbarian, understood by nobody; the Getae laugh stupidly at Latin words, and in my presence they often talk maliciously about me in perfect security, perchance reproaching me with my exile. Naturally they think that I am poking fun at them [2] whenever I have nodded no or yes to their speech. And besides unjustly the hard sword dispenses justice, for wounds are often given in the midst of the market-place.

[45] Ah! cruel Lachesis,[3] when my star is so ill-fated, not to have granted my life a shorter thread! That I am separated from the sight of my country and of you, my friends, that I must lament my abode among these Scythian tribes—each is a heavy penalty. Yet I deserved exile from the city; I did not perchance deserve to be in such a place. What am I saying? Madman that I am! Even my very life I deserved to lose by offending the divine will of Caesar.

XI. To his Wife

Someone by way of insult has said that thou art "an exile's wife"—of this thy letter complains. I was hurt, not so much that my fate is spoken of with malice—for I am now used to bear my wretchedness with fortitude—as that I am the cause of shame to thee to whom I would wish it least of all, and to think that thou must have blushed for my misfortunes.

[3] Lachesis, one of the Fates, spun the thread of life.

perfer et obdura ; multo graviora tulisti,
    eripuit cum me principis ira tibi.
fallitur iste tamen, quo iudice nominor exul :
10   mollior est culpam poena secuta meam.
maxima poena mihi est ipsum offendisse, priusque
    venisset mallem funeris hora mihi.
quassa tamen nostra est, non mersa nec obruta navis,
    utque caret portu, sic tamen extat aquis.
15 nec vitam nec opes nec ius mihi civis ademit,
    quae [1] merui vitio perdere cuncta meo.
sed quia peccato facinus non affuit illi,
    nil nisi me patriis iussit abesse focis.
utque aliis, quorum numerum comprendere non est,
20   Caesareum numen sic mihi mite fuit.
ipse relegati, non exulis utitur in me
    nomine : tuta suo iudice causa mea est.
iure igitur laudes, Caesar, pro parte virili
    carmina nostra tuas qualiacumque canunt :
25 iure deos, ut adhuc caeli tibi limina claudant,
    teque velint sine se, comprecor, esse deum.
optat idem populus ; sed, ut in mare flumina vastum,
    sic solet exiguae currere rivus aquae.
at tu fortunam, cuius vocor exul ab ore,
30   nomine mendaci parce gravare meam !

XII.

Scribis, ut oblectem studio lacrimabile tempus,
    ne pereant turpi pectora nostra situ.
difficile est quod, amice, mones, quia carmina laetum
    sunt opus, et pacem mentis habere volunt.

[1] qui

---

[1] See Introd. p. xviii.

Endure, harden thy heart ; much heavier things didst
thou bear when the wrath of the prince tore me from
thee. Yet is that judge mistaken who calls me
"exile": a milder penalty befell my fault. My
greatest penalty consists in having offended Him: I
would the hour of death had come upon me
first! Yet my bark was but shattered, not submerg-
ed and overwhelmed, and though it is deprived of a
harbour, yet even so it floats upon the waters.
Neither life nor property nor civil rights did he take
from me, all of which by my fault I deserved to lose.
But since no deed accompanied my sin, he ordained
naught save that I should leave my native hearth.
As to others, whose number may not be counted, so to
me Caesar's power was mild. He himself uses in my
case the term "relegatus,"[1] not exile. My cause is
secure by reason of him who judged it.

[23] Rightly then, Caesar, do my verses, however
humble, sing to the best of their power thy praises:
rightly do I pray the gods to keep their threshold still
closed to thee, and to will that thou be a god apart
from them. The people offer the same prayer ; but
as rivers run into the wide sea, so runs a brook with its
meagre stream

[29] But thou, whose lips call me "exile," cease to
burden my fate with a lying name.

XI. Once a poet—

You write bidding me amuse my tearful hours with
my pursuit, that my wits be not ruined through
unseemly sloth. My friend, your advice is hard, for
verse, being the work of joy, would have the mind

251

5 nostra per adversas agitur fortuna procellas,
    sorte nec ulla mea tristior esse potest.
exigis ut Priamus natorum funere plaudat,[1]
    et Niobe festos ducat ut orba choros.
luctibus an studio videor debere teneri,
10   solus in extremos iussus abire Getas ?
des licet in valido pectus mihi robore fultum.
    fama refert Anyti quale fuisse reo,[2]
fracta cadet tantae sapientia mole ruinae :
    plus valet humanis viribus ira dei.
15 ille senex, dictus sapiens ab Apolline, nullum
    scribere in hoc casu sustinuisset opus.
ut veniant patriae, veniant oblivia vestri,[3]
    omnis ut amissi sensus abesse queat,
at timor officio fungi vetat ipse [4] quietum :
20   cinctus ab innumero me tenet hoste locus.
adde quod ingenium longa rubigine laesum
    torpet et est multo, quam fuit ante, minus.
fertilis, assiduo si non renovatur [5] aratro,
    nil nisi cum spinis gramen habebit ager.
25 tempore qui longo steterit, male currit [6] et inter
    carceribus missos ultimus ibit equus.
vertitur in teneram cariem rimisque dehiscit,
    siqua diu solitis cumba vacavit [7] aquis.
me quoque despera,[8] fuerim cum parvus et ante,
30   illi, qui fueram, posse redire parem.
contudit ingenium patientia longa malorum,
    et pars antiqui nulla vigoris adest.

---

    [1] ludat   [2] rei *vel* senis   [3] nostri
    [4] esse : ipse *ς*   [5] renovetur *vel* removetur
    [6] curret   [4] vacabit *corr. ς*   [8] despero

---

    [1] Socrates.   The Delphian Oracle declared that nobody was
wiser than Socrates.

at peace. My rate is driven on by hostile blasts; nothing could be more gloomy. You are requiring Priam to give applause at the death of his sons, Niobe in her bereavement to lead a gay dance. Is it mourning or poetry, think you, that should occupy him who was bidden to go alone to the land of the distant Getae ? You may give me a heart supported by the mighty power which they say he [1] possessed who was accused by Anytus, but wisdom will fall with a crash under the mass of such a mighty ruin, for the wrath of a god overpowers human strength. That famous old man, called a sage by Apollo, would have had no power in this misfortune to write a single work. Though forgetfulness of country should come, though forgetfulness of you should come, though all realization of what I have lost could leave me, yet very fear forbids the peaceful performance of the task, for I dwell in a place girt about by countless foes. And besides my talent, injured by long neglect, is dull, much inferior to what it was before. A fertile field, if it is not renewed by constant ploughing, will produce nothing but grass and thorns. The horse which has stood for a long time runs but poorly and will be last among those released from the barrier. [2] Any skiff falls into frail rottenness, yawning with cracks, if it has been long separated from its accustomed waters. For me also feel despair that, little as I was even before, I can become once more the man I was. My talent has been crushed by my long endurance of woes: no part of my former vigour remains. Yet

[2] Before the start of a race the horses were held within barriers.

siqua [1] tamen nobis, ut nunc quoque, sumpta tabella
    est,
  inque suos volui cogere verba pedes,
35 carmina nulla mihi sunt scripta,[2] aut qualia cernis,
    digna sui domini tempore, digna loco.
denique non parvas animo dat gloria vires,
    et fecunda facit pectora laudis amor.
nominis et famae quondam fulgore trahebar,
40   dum tulit antemnas aura secunda meas.
non adeo est bene nunc ut sit mihi gloria curae :
    si liceat, nulli cognitus esse velim.
an quia cesserunt primo bene carmina, suades
    scribere, successus ut sequar ipse meos ?
45 pace, novem, vestra liceat dixisse, sorores :
    vos estis nostrae maxima causa fugae.
utque dedit iustas tauri fabricator aëni,
    sic ego do poenas artibus ipse meis.
nil mihi debebat cum versibus amplius esse,
50   cum fugerem merito naufragus omne fretum.
at, puto, si demens studium fatale retemptem,
    hic mihi praebebit carminis arma locus.
non liber hic ullus, non qui mihi commodet aurem,
    verbaque significent quid mea, norit, adest.
55 omnia barbariae loca sunt vocisque ferinae,
    omniaque hostilis [3] plena timore soni.
ipse mihi videor iam dedidicisse Latine :
    nam didici Getice Sarmaticeque loqui.
nec tamen, ut verum fatear tibi, nostra teneri
60   a componendo carmine Musa potest.
scribimus et scriptos absumimus igne libellos :
    exitus est studii parva favilla mei.
nec possum et cupio non ullos ducere versus :
    ponitur idcirco noster in igne labor,

            [1] siqua *Bentley*] saepe

if, as now, I have taken up some tablet and sought to force words into proper feet, no verses are written by me or only such as you see—worthy of their master's state, worthy of his place. In short desire for fame lends no small strength to the mind, love of praise makes the heart fertile. Once I was drawn on by the glamour of name and fame while the favouring breeze bore on my yards. 'Tis not so well with me now that I care for renown; if 'twere possible I would have none know of me.

[43] Or is it because at first my verse went well that you advise me to write—to follow up my success? By your leave, sisters nine, would I say it: you are the chief cause of my exile. As the maker [1] of the bronze bull paid the just penalty, so I am paying the penalty for my art. I ought to have nothing more to do with verse, but once shipwrecked I rightly shun every sea. But, forsooth, if I should be mad enough to try once more the fatal pursuit, will this place afford me the equipment for song! There is not a book here, not a man to lend ear to me, to know what my words mean. All places are filled with barbarism and cries of wild animals, all are filled with the fear of a hostile sound. I myself, I think, have already unlearned my Latin, for I have learned how to speak Getic and Sarmatian.

[59] And yet, to confess the truth to you, my Muse cannot be restrained from composing verses. I write poems which once written I consume in the fire; a few ashes are the result of my toil. I cannot and yet I long to refrain from writing verse; hence

[1] Perillus.

---

[2] carmina sunt mihi scripta aut nulla *vel* carmina scripta mihi sunt nulla   [3] hostilis *Merkel*] possint *vel* possunt

65 nec nisi pars casu flammis erepta dolove
 ad vos ingenii pervenit usque [1] mei.
sic utinam, quae nil metuentem tale magistrum
 perdidit, in cineres Ars mea versa foret!

XIII.

Hanc tuus e Getico mittit tibi Naso salutem,
 mittere si quisquam, quo caret ipse, potest.
aeger enim traxi contagia corpore mentis,
 libera tormento pars mihi ne qua vacet,
5 perque dies multos lateris cruciatibus uror,
 saeva quod [2] immodico frigore laesit hiems.
si tamen ipse vales, aliqua nos parte valemus:
 quippe mea est umeris fulta ruina tuis.
quid,[3] mihi cum dederis ingentia pignora, cumque
10 per numeros omnes hoc tueare caput,
quod tua me raro solatur epistula, peccas,
 remque piam praestas, sed [4] mihi verba negas?
hoc, precor, emenda! quod si correxeris unum,
 nullus in egregio corpore naevus erit.
15 pluribus accusem, fieri nisi possit, ut ad me
 littera non veniat, missa sit illa tamen.
di faciant, ut sit temeraria nostra querella,
 teque putem falso non meminisse mei.
quod precor, esse liquet: neque enim mutabile robur
20 credere me fas est pectoris esse tui.
cana prius gelido desint absinthia Ponto,
 et careat dulci Trinacris Hybla thymo,
inmemorem quam te quisquam convincat amici.
 non ita sunt fati stamina nigra mei.

[1] ulla *corr. Gilbert*   [2] sed quod in *corr. Schrader*
          [3] qui   [4] si: sed ς

---

[1] The *Ars amatoria.*
[2] The under surface of the leaves is white.

my labour is placed in the fire, and nothing but a bit of my effort, saved by chance or by craft, reaches you. In such wise I would that my "Art," [1] which ruined a master who feared nothing of the kind, had been turned to ashes!

XIII. SICK AND REPROACHFUL

This "Health" thy Naso sends thee from the Getic land, if anyone can send what he himself has not. For being sick at heart I drew the contagion into my body—that no part of me may be free from torture!—and for many days I have suffered from an aching side which the excessive cold of the bitter winter has brought me. Yet if thou art well, I am well in some degree, for my ruin was supported by thy shoulders. Why, when thou hast given me mighty proofs of love, when thou dost in every fashion guard this life of mine, dost thou err in rarely comforting me with a letter, supplying me the fact of loyalty but denying me the words £ Correct this, I beg of thee; if thou amend one thing, there will be no blemish on the perfect body.

[15] I should bring more accusations against thee were it not possible that though no letter reaches me, yet that one has been sent. God grant that my complaint be groundless—that I am wrong in believing thou hast forgotten me. What I pray for is true, 'tis clear; for it is not right for me to believe the steadfast strength of thy heart can change. Sooner would the white [2] wormwood fail the icy Pontus, sooner would Trinacrian Hybla lack its sweet thyme than anyone could convict thee of forgetting a friend. Not so black as that are the threads of my fate. But

25 tu tamen, ut possis falsae quoque pellere culpae
    crimina, quod non es, ne videare, cave.
  utque solebamus consumere longa loquendo
    tempora. sermoni [1] deficiente die,
  sic ferat ac referat tacitas nunc littera voces,
30   et peragant linguae charta manusque vices.
  quod fore ne nimium videar diffidere, sitque
    versibus hoc paucis admonuisse satis,
  accipe quo semper finitur epistula verbo—
    aque meis distent ut tua fata !—" vale."

XIV.

  Quanta tibi dederim nostris monumenta libellis,
    o mihi me coniunx carior, ipsa vides.
  detrahat auctori multum fortuna licebit,
    tu tamen ingenio clara ferere meo ;
5 dumque legar, mecum pariter tua fama legetur,
    nec potes in maestos omnis abire rogos ;
  cumque viri casu possis miseranda videri,
    invenies aliquas, quae, quod es, esse velint,
  quae te, nostrorum cum sis in parte malorum,
10   felicem dicant invideantque tibi.
  non ego divitias dando tibi plura dedissem :
    nil feret ad Manes divitis umbra suum.[2]
  perpetui fructum donavi nominis idque,
    quo dare nil potui munere maius, habes.
15 adde quod, ut [3] rerum sola es tutela mearum,
    ad te non parvi venit honoris onus,
  quod numquam vox est de te mea muta tuique
    indiciis debes esse superba viri.

  [1] sermone   [2] suos *corr. Sh. Bailey*   [3] et : ut *Heinsius*

that thou mayst repel the charge (false though it is) of fault, beware of seeming what thou art not. As we were wont to pass long hours in converse, till daylight failed our talk, so now should our letters bring and return our voiceless words, and the paper and our hands should perform the office of our tongues. Lest I seem to distrust overmuch that this shall be so (and may a few lines suffice to have given this reminder), receive that word with which every letter is ended— that thy fate may differ from mine!—the word "farewell"![1]

XIV. To his Wife

What a memorial I have reared to thee in my books, O my wife, dearer to me than myself, thou seest. Though fate may take much from their author, thou at least shalt be made illustrious by my powers. As long as men read me thy fame shall be read along with me; nor canst thou utterly pass away into the sad pyre. Although thy husband's fate may cause thee to seem worthy of pity, thou wilt find some who wish to be what thou art, who in that thou dost share my woes, will call thee fortunate and envy thee. Not by giving thee riches could I have given thee more: naught of himself will the rich man's shade carry to the dead. I gave thee enjoyment of an immortal name, and thou hast a boon than which I could give none greater. And besides, as thou art the sole guardian of my fortunes, an honour of no small moment has come to thee, for my voice is never silent about thee and thou shouldst be proud of thy

[1] *Vale* has a double meaning: (1) goodbye, (2) "fare you well" (literally). (2) explains the clause *atque . . . fata.*

quae ne quis possit temeraria dicere, persta,
20   et pariter serva meque piamque fidem.
nam tua, dum stetimus, turpi sine crimine mansit,
    et tantum [1] probitas inreprehensa fuit.
area de [2] nostra nunc est tibi facta ruina ;
    conspicuum virtus hic tua ponat opus.
25 esse bonam facile est, ubi, quod vetet esse, remotum
        est,
    et nihil officio nupta quod obstet habet.
cum deus intonuit, non se subducere nimbo,
    id demum est pietas, id socialis amor.
rara quidem virtus, quam non Fortuna gubernet,
30   quae maneat stabili, cum fugit illa, pede.
siqua tamen pretium sibi virtus [3] ipsa petitum,
    inque parum laetis ardua rebus adest,
ut tempus numeres, per saecula nulla tacetur,
    et loca mirantur qua patet orbis iter.
35 aspicis ut longo teneat laudabilis aevo
    nomen inextinctum Penelopaea fides ?
cernis ut Admeti cantetur et Hectoris uxor
    ausaque in accensos Iphias ire rogos ?
ut vivat fama coniunx Phylaceïa, cuius
40   Iliacam celeri vir pede pressit humum ?
morte nihil opus est pro me, sed amore fideque :
    non ex difficili fama petenda tibi est.
nec te credideris, quia non facis, ista moneri :
    vela damus, quamvis remige navis eat.
45 qui monet ut facias, quod iam facis, ille monendo
    laudat et hortatu comprobat acta suo.

[1] tanta   [2] par (*vel* per) eadem : area de *Withof*
[3] merces : virtus *Ehwald*

husband's testimony. That none may think it
rashly given, stand thou firm ; preserve me and thy
loyal devotion alike.   For thy goodness, whilst I
stood secure, remained free from accusation's taint,
at best uncriticized,[1] but now by my fall a space has
been cleared for thee ; here let thy virtue build a
structure clear to see.   'Tis easy to be good when
that which forbids it has been removed and a wife has
nothing opposing her duty.   When the god thun-
ders, not to avoid the cloud—that is loyalty indeed,
that is wedded love.   Rare indeed is the virtue not
piloted by Fortune, which remains on steady feet
when Fortune flees.   Yet whenever virtue is herself
her own coveted reward and remains upright in
adversity, though you count all time, she is passed
over in silence by no age and is given homage
wherever the world's highway extends.   Seest thou
how Penelope's faith is praised in the long reaches of
time and how her name never dies ?   How Admetus'
wife[2] and Hector's[3] are sung, and the daughter of
Iphis,[4] who dared to mount the lighted pyre ?   How
the wife of the hero[5] of Phylacos lives, whose
husband touched with his swift foot the soil of
Ilium ?   I need not thy death, but thy love, thy
faith ; not by hard ways hast thou to seek for
fame.   Nor believe that I am reminding thee because
thou art not acting : I am but giving sails to a ship that
is already using the oars.   He who reminds thee to do
what thou art already doing, by so reminding praises
thy acts and by his very exhortation approves them.

---

[1] *i.e.* it was only (*tantum*) nothing evil that was said of you ;
now you have a chance to win a positive fame.
[2] Alcestis.   [3] Andromache.   [4] Evadne.
[5] Protesilaus, whose wife was Laodamia.

The following analyses have been proposed:

Book 1 (Dickinson 161)

A 1 Prologue

B 2 Storm at sea
     3 Last night in Rome
     4 Storm at sea

C 5 To a friend
D 6 To his wife
C 7 To a friend
     8 To a traitor
     9 To a friend

B 10 Ovid's route

A 11 Epilogue

Book 4 (Dickinson 180; Evans 89)

A 1 Prologue

B 2 Triumph in Rome
     3 To his wife
     4 To a noble friend
     5 To a loyal friend

C 6 Ovid's desire of death
     7 To a lapsed friend
     8 Old age in exile
     9 To an enemy

A 10 Epilogue (autobiography)

Book 3 (Dickinson 175; Evans 72)

A 1 Prologue
B 2 Hardship of exile

C 3 To wife
     4a To friend
     4b To friends
     5 To friend
     6 To friend
D 7 To Perilla
C 8 The exile's prayer
     9 Name of Tomis
     10 Winter in Tomis
     11 A harsh country
     12 Spring in Tomis

B 13 Birthday in exile
A 14 Epilogue

Book 5 (Evans 107)

A 1   Prologue
B 2   Wife
     3,4   Friends

     5   Wife

     6, 7   Friends
C 8   Enemy

B 9, 10 Friends

     11   Wife
     12, 13 Friends
     14   Wife

EPISTULAE EX PONTO

EX PONTO LIBER PRIMUS

I.

Naso Tomitanae iam non novus incola terrae
   hoc tibi de Getico litore mittit opus.
si vacat, hospitio peregrinos, Brute, libellos
   excipe, dumque aliquo, quolibet abde loco.[1]
5 publica non audent intra[2] monimenta venire,
   ne suus hoc illis clauserit auctor iter.
a! quotiens dixi "certe nil turpe docetis:
   ite, patet castis versibus ille locus!"
non tamen accedunt, sed, ut aspicis ipse, latere
10   sub Lare privato tutius esse putant.
quaeris ubi hos possis nullo componere laeso?
   qua steterant Artes, pars vacat illa tibi.
quid[3] veniant, novitate roges fortasse sub ipsa.
   accipe, quodcumque est, dummodo non sit amor.
15 invenies, quamvis non est miserabilis index,
   non minus hoc illo triste, quod ante dedi.
rebus idem, titulo differt; et epistula cui sit
   non occultato nomine missa docet.
nec vos hoc vultis, sed nec prohibere potestis,
20   Musaque ad invitos officiosa venit. -

---

      [1] loco] modo   [2] inter   [3] qui

---

   [1] *i.e.* a public library.
   [2] Most of the *Tristia* are addressed to individuals who are not named.

EX PONTO—BOOK I

I. To Brutus

Naso, no recent dweller now in the land of Tomis, sends to you this work from the Getic shore. If you have leisure, entertain and harbour, Brutus, these poems from a foreign land; hide them away where you will, yet somewhere. They venture not to enter a public memorial [1] for fear their master has closed for them this way. Ah, how often have I said, "Surely *you* give no base instruction! Go! Clean verse may freely enter that place!" Yet these verses go not thither, but as you see they deem it safer to lie in the seclusion of a private household. Do you ask where you can lay them without injuring anybody? Where once stood my "Art" there you have a vacant space.

[13] What they come for, perchance you may ask while their novelty is still fresh. Take them, whatever it is, so only it be not love. You will find, though the title implies no sorrow, that this work is not less sad than that which I sent before—in theme the same, in title different, and each epistle reveals the recipient without concealing his name.[2] You are all averse to this but cannot prevent it; my Muse comes to you with homage even against your will. What-

265

quicquid id est, adiunge meis.　nihil impedit ortos
　　exule servatis legibus urbe frui.
quod metuas non est.　Antoni scripta leguntur,
　　doctus et in promptu scrinia [1] Brutus habet.
25　nec me nominibus furiosus confero tantis :
　　saeva deos contra non tamen arma tuli.
denique Caesareo, quod non disiderat ipse,
　　non caret e nostris ullus honore liber.
si dubitas de me, laudes admitte deorum,
30　et carmen dempto nomine sume meum.
adiuvat in bello pacatae ramus olivae :
　　proderit auctorem pacis habere nihil ?
cum foret Aeneae cervix subiecta parenti,
　　dicitur ipsa viro flamma dedisse viam :
35　fert liber Aeneaden, et non iter omne patebit ?
　　at patriae pater hic, ipsius ille fuit.
ecquis ita est audax, ut limine cogat abire
　　iactantem Pharia tinnula sistra manu ?
ante deum Matrem cornu tibicen adunco
40　cum canit, exiguae quis stipis aera negat ?
scimus ab imperio fieri nil tale dearum [2] :
　　unde tamen vivat, vaticinator habet.
ipsa movent animos superorum numina nostros,
　　turpe nec est tali credulitate capi.
45　en ego pro sistro Phrigiique foramine buxi
　　gentis Iuleae nomina sancta fero.

　　　　　　[1] scrinia] carmina　　　　　[2] Dianae *corr. Madvig*

---

[1] M. Junius Brutus, the conspirator.
[2] Augustus prided himself on restoring and maintaining
peace.　　　　　　　[3] Anchises.
[4] *i.e.* Augustus, who is borne by Ovid's book, is as father of his
country much more important than Anchises, who was father
only of the man who bore him.
[5] The sistrum was an instrument used in the worship of

ever it be then, add it to my writings. Nothing
hinders an exile's offspring, if they observe the law,
from enjoying the city. There is naught for you to
fear; Antony's writings are still read, and the
accomplished Brutus [1] finds book-cases in readiness
for him. I am not so mad as to compare myself with
such great names, yet I have borne no hostile arms
against the gods. In fine Caesar, though he needs it
not, lacks not homage in any book of mine. If about
me you doubt, admit a eulogy of the gods : receive my
song after removing the name. In war the peaceful
olive branch is useful; shall it profit me nothing
that my song contains the author of peace [2] ?
When Aeneas bore a father [3] upon his shoulders,
the very flames, they say, made a path for the hero.
If a book bears upon its pages the descendant of
Aeneas, shall not every path be open to it ? Yet
the one is the father of his country, the other only of
his bearer ! [4]

[37] Is there any so brazen as to force from his door
one who shakes the ringing sistra [5] of Pharos in his
hand ! When before the mother [6] of the gods the
piper plays upon his curved horn, who denies him a
few coppers ? We know this [7] occurs not by order of
the goddesses, yet the prophet has the wherewithal
to live. The very power of the celestials stirs our
hearts and there is nothing disgraceful in yielding
to such credulity. Lo, I, in place of sistrum or
hollow shaft of Phrygian boxwood, come bearing the

Isis which made a sharp metallic click. Pharos, an island near
Alexandria, represents this Egyptian cult.
 [6] Cybele.
 [7] i.e. as that alms should be given to prophets.

vaticinor moneoque.   locum date sacra ferenti !
   non mihi, sed magno poscitur ille deo.
nec quia vel merui vel sensi principis iram,
50   a nobis ipsum [1] nolle putate coli.
vidi ego linigerae [2] numen violasse fatentem
   Isidis Isiacos ante sedere focos.
alter, ob huic similem privatus lumine culpam,
   clamabat media se meruisse via.
55 talia caelestes fieri praeconia gaudent,
   ut sua quid valeant numina teste probent.
saepe levant poenas ereptaque lumina reddunt,
   cum bene peccati paenituisse vident.
paenitet, o ! si quid miserorum creditur ulli,
60   paenitet, et facto torqueor ipse meo.
cumque sit exilium, magis est mihi culpa dolori ;
   estque pati poenam, quam meruisse, minus.
ut mihi di faveant, quibus est manifestior ipse,
   poena potest demi, culpa perennis erit.
65 mors faciet certe, ne sim, cum venerit, exul :
   ut [3] non peccarim mors quoque non faciet.
non igitur mirum, si mens mea tabida facta
   de nive manantis more liquescit aquae.
estur ut occulta vitiata teredine navis,
70   aequorei scopulos ut cavat unda salis,
roditur ut scabra positum robigine ferrum
   conditus ut tineae carpitur ore liber,
sic mea perpetuos curarum pectora morsus,
   fine quibus nullo conficiantur, habent.

[1] ipsum] illum   [2] lanigerae
[3] nec *vel* ne : ut *C² Owen*

---

[1] The form is a complimentary reference to the descent of the
Julii from Iulus, son of Aeneas, *cf. Ex. P.* ii. 5. 49.
` A mollusk which weakens timber by boring holes in it.

holy names of the Iulean [1] race. I am a prophet, a
monitor! Give place to one who bears holy
objects! Not by me, but by a mighty god that place
is claimed. Because I have earned or felt the
Prince's wrath, do not suppose that I would not
worship the Prince himself. I have seen one who
confessed to have outraged the deity of linen-wearing
Isis sitting before Isis's shrine. Another bereft of
sight for a like cause was crying out in the midst of the
street that he had deserved it. The gods rejoice in
such heraldings that witnesses may attest their
power. Often do they mitigate penalties and restore
the sight they have taken away when they behold
sincere repentance for sin. I too repent! O, if any
wretched man is believed in anything, I too
repent! I feel the torture of my own
deed! Though exile is anguish, greater anguish is
my fault and it is a smaller thing to suffer the
punishment than to have deserved it. What though
the gods and he who is more conspicuous than the
gods should favour me, my punishment can be
removed, my fault will remain forever. Death at
least by his coming will put an end to my exile, my sin
even death will not remove.

[67] 'Tis then no marvel if my heart has softened and
melts as water runs from snow. It is gnawed as a
ship is injured by the hidden borer,[2] as the briny sea
water hollows out the crags, as stored iron is eaten by
corroding rust, as the book when laid away is nibbled
by the worm's teeth, so my heart feels the constant
gnawing of sorrow which will finish its work

75 nec prius hi mentem stimuli quam vita relinquet,
  quique dolet, citius quam dolor ipse, cadet.
hoc mihi si superi, quorum sumus omnia, credent,[1]
  forsitan exigua dignus habebor ope,
inque locum Scythico vacuum mutabor ab arcu.
80   plus isto, duri, si precer, oris ero.

II.

Maxime, qui tanti mensuram nominis imples,
  et geminas animi nobilitate genus,
qui nasci ut posses, quamvis cecidere trecenti,
  non omnes Fabios abstulit una dies,
5 forsitan haec a quo mittatur epistula quaeras,
  quisque loquar tecum, certior esse velis.
ei mihi, quid faciam ? vereor ne nomine lecto
  durus et aversa cetera mente legas.
videris.[2]   audebo[3] tibi me scripsisse fateri
10   .   .   .   .[4]
qui, cum me poena dignum graviore fuisse
  confitear, possum vix graviora pati.
hostibus in mediis interque pericula versor,
  tamquam cum patria pax sit adempta mihi :
15 qui, mortis saevo geminent ut vulnere causas,
  omnia vipereo spicula felle linunt.
his eques instructus perterrita moenia lustrat
  more lupi clausas circueuntis oves :
et[5] semel intentus nervos levis arcus equino
20   vincula semper habens inresoluta manet.
tecta rigent fixis veluti velata[6] sagittis,
  portaque vix firma summovet arma sera.

---

[1] credant   [2] viderit *corr. Heinsius*
[3] audebo] haec siquis   [4] *om. AC : spuria habent cett.*
       [5] at   [6] vallata

—never! These stings will not leave my mind sooner than life; he who suffers will perish more quickly than the suffering itself. If the celestials, to whom in all things I belong, believe me in this, perchance I shall be deemed worthy of a little succour and they will change my abode to one free from the Scythian bow; should I pray for more than that, my lips will be bold indeed.

II. To Maximus

Maximus, you who fill out the measure of a mighty name doubling nobility of birth by that of soul, you for whose birth, though three hundred fell, one day did not destroy all the Fabii [1]—perchance you may ask by whom this letter is sent and wish to be told who am I that talk with you. Ah me! what am I to do? I fear that when you read the name you will grow stern and read what remains with heart averse. Look you to that. I shall venture the confession that I have written to you. . . . I, who admitting that I have deserved a worse punishment, can scarce endure one worse. I live in the midst of enemies, in the midst of perils—as if, with my native land, peace had been taken from me—enemies who, to double with a cruel wound the causes of death, smear every dart with viper's gall. Equipped with these the horseman circles the frightened walls as a wolf runs about the fenced sheep. The light bow once bent with its horsehair string remains with its bonds ever unrelaxed. The roofs bristle with implanted arrows as if shrouded in a veil, and the gate scarce repels attack with sturdy bar.

[1] In a battle with the Veientes, more than 300 Fabii are said to have fought, and only one escaped, *cf.* Livy ii. 48.

adde loci faciem nec fronde nec arbore tecti,[1]
    et quod iners hiemi continuatur hiems.
25 hic me pugnantem cum frigore cumque sagittis
    cumque meo fato quarta fatigat hiems.
fine carent lacrimae, nisi cum stupor obstitit illis:
    et similis morti pectora torpor habet.
felicem Nioben, quamvis tot funera vidit,
30   quae posuit sensum saxea facta mali!
vos quoque felices, quarum clamantia fratrem
    cortice velavit populus ora novo![1]
ille ego sum, lignum qui non admittor [2] in ullum:
    ille ego sum, frustra qui lapis esse velim.
35 ipsa Medusa oculis veniat licet obvia nostris,
    amittet vires ipsa Medusa suas.
vivimus ut numquam sensu careamus amaro,
    et gravior longa fit mea poena mora.
sic inconsumptum Tityi semperque renascens
40   non perit, ut possit saepe perire, iecur.
at, puto, cum requies medicinaque publica curae
    somnus adest, solitis nox venit orba malis.
somnia me terrent veros imitantia casus,
    et vigilant sensus in mea damna mei.
45 aut ego Sarmaticas videor vitare sagittas,
    aut dare captivas ad fera vincla manus.
aut ubi decipior melioris imagine somni,
    aspicio patriae tecta relicta meae.
et modo vobiscum, quos sum veneratus, amici,
50   et modo cum cara coniuge multa loquor.
sic ubi percepta est brevis et non vera voluptas,
    peior ab admonitu fit status ipse boni.
sive dies igitur caput hoc miserabile cernit,
    sive pruinosi Noctis aguntur equi,

---

[1] laeti   [2] admittar *corr.* ς

[1] The sisters of Phaëthon.

[23] Add to this the aspect of a land protected by neither leaf nor tree, and that lifeless winter without break runs into winter. Here am I fighting with cold, with arrows, with my own fate, in the weariness of the fourth winter. My tears are limitless save when a lethargy checks them, and a deathlike stupor possesses my breast. Happy Niobe, though she saw so many deaths, for she lost the ability to feel pain when she was turned to stone. Happy you [1] also whose lips, in the act of calling upon your brother, the poplar clothed with new bark. I am one who am transformed into no wood, I am one who in vain wish to be a stone. Should Medusa herself come before my eyes, even Medusa will lose her power. My life is such that I never lose the bitterness of sensation and my punishment becomes worse through its long duration. So Tityus's liver unconsumed and ever growing anew perishes not, in order that it may have the power to be ever perishing.

[41] "But," I suppose, "when rest and sleep, the common healer of cares, attend me, night comes free from the usual woes!" Dreams affright me that mimic real dangers, and my senses wake to my own hurt. Either I think myself avoiding Sarmatian arrows or offering a captive's hands to cruel bonds or, when I am beguiled by the semblance of a happier dream, I behold the buildings of the native city I have left, I hold long converse now with you, my friends, whom I once revered, now with my dear wife. Thus when I have had this short and unreal joy, the remembrance of happiness renders this state of mine all the worse.

[53] So whether day beholds this wretched being or whether Night is driving her frosty steeds, my heart

273

55 sic mea perpetuis liquefiunt [1] pectora curis,
  ignibus admotis ut nova cera solet.
  saepe precor mortem, mortem quoque deprecor idem,
  ne mea Sarmaticum contegat ossa solum.
  cum subit Augusti quae sit clementia, credo
60 mollia naufragiis litora posse dari.
  cum video quam sint mea fata tenacia, frangor,
  spesque levis magno victa timore cadit.
  nec tamen ulterius quicquam sperove precorve,
  quam male pacato [2] posse carere loco.
65 aut hoc, aut nihil est, pro me temptare modeste
  gratia quod salvo vestra pudore queat.
  suscipe, Romanae facundia, Maxime, linguae,
  difficilis causae mite patrocinium.
  est mala, confiteor, sed te bona fiet agente,
70 lenia pro misera fac modo verba fuga.
  nescit enim Caesar, quamvis deus omnia norit,
  ultimus hic qua sit condicione locus.
  magna tenent illud rerum molimina numen :
  haec est caelesti pectore cura minor.
75 nec vacat, in qua sint positi regione Tomitae,
  quaerere, finitimo vix loca nota Getae,
  aut quid Sauromatae faciant, quid Iazyges acres
  cultaque Oresteae Taurica terra deae,
  quaeque aliae gentes, ubi frigore constitit Hister,
80 dura meant celeri terga per amnis equo.
  maxima pars hominum nec te, pulcherrima, curat,
  Roma, nec Ausonii militis arma timet.
  dant illis animos arcus plenaeque pharetrae
  quamque libet longis cursibus aptus equus,
85 quodque sitim didicere diu tolerare famemque,
  quodque sequens nullas hostis habebit aquas.

---

[1] liquescunt   [2] mutato *corr. Bentley*

melts from unending sorrows as fresh wax is wont to do when fire is brought near. Often I pray for death, yet I even beg off from death for fear that the Sarmatian soil may cover my bones. When I remember Augustus's mercy, I believe it possible that a kindly shore may be offered for my shipwreck. When I see how persistent is my fate, I break down and my slight hope falls away vanquished by a mighty fear. Yet I neither hope nor pray for anything further than the opportunity to escape from this uncivilised place. 'Tis either this or nothing that your favour can attempt in moderation for me without impairing your self-respect. Maximus, eloquence of the Roman tongue, take upon yourself the merciful pleading of a difficult case. A bad case, I admit, but it will become a good one if you plead it; only utter some words of sympathy in behalf of a wretched exile. For Caesar knows not, though a god knows all things, the nature of this remote place. Great undertakings engross his divine mind; this is a matter too small for his godlike heart. He has no leisure to inquire where the Tomitae are situated, a region hardly known to the neighbouring Getan; or what the Sauromatae are doing, or the fierce Iazyges, and the Tauric land watched over by Orestes' goddess,[1] or what other tribes, when cold halts the Hister's flow, wind along the icy back of the stream on swift horses. The most of these people neither care for thee, fair Rome, nor fear the arms of Ausonian soldiery. Bows and full quivers lend them courage, and horses capable of marches however lengthy and the knowledge how to ensure for long both thirst and hunger, and that a pursuing enemy will

[1] Diana.

ira viri mitis non me misisset in istam,
    si satis haec illi nota fuisset humus.
nec me nec quemquam Romanum gaudet ab hoste,
90   meque minus, vitam cui dabat [1] ipse, capi.
noluit, ut [2] poterat, minimo me perdere nutu.
    nil opus est ullis in mea fata Getis.
sed neque, cur morerer, quicquam mihi comperit
        actum,
    et minus infestus, quam fuit, esse potest.
95 tunc quoque nil fecit nisi quod facere ipse coëgi :
    paene etiam merito parcior ira meo est.
di faciant igitur, quorum iustissimus ipse est,
    alma nihil maius Caesare terra ferat,
utque diu sub eo, sic sit sub Caesare semper,[3]
100   perque manus huius tradita gentis eat.
at tu tam placido, quam nos quoque sensimus illum,
    iudice pro lacrimis ora resolve meis.
non petito [4] ut bene sit, sed uti male tutius, utque
    exilium saevo distet ab hoste meum,
105 quamque dedere mihi praesentia numina vitam,
    non adimat stricto squalidus ense Getes :
denique, si moriar, subeam pacatius arvum,
    ossa nec a Scythica nostra premantur humo,
nec male compositos, ut scilicet exule dignum,
110   Bistonii cineres ungula pulset equi,
et ne, si superest aliquis post funera sensus,
    terreat et Manes Sarmatis umbra meos.
Caesaris haec animum poterant audita movere,
    Maxime, movissent si tamen ante tuum.
115 vox, precor, Augustas pro me tua molliat aures,
    auxilio trepidis quae solet esse reis,

---

[1] dedit *vel* dabit *corr. Merkel*   [2] at   [3] terra *corr. Housman*
[4] petis *vel* pete *corr. Daumius*

have no water. The wrath of a merciful man would
not have sent me to such a land if he had known it
well. Nor is he pleased that I or any Roman be
taken by an enemy—I least of all, to whom he himself
granted life. He would not, as he could have done,
destroy me with the slightest nod. There is no need
of any Getae to bring about my death. But he found
no act on my part worthy of death, and 'tis possible
that he is less incensed against me than he
was. Even then he did nothing save what I forced
him to do ; his wrath is almost more moderate than I
deserve. May then the gods, of whom he is himself
the most just, cause the nourishing earth to bring
forth nothing greater than Caesar, and as it has been
long under his sway, so may it ever be under a
Caesar's, passing on through the hands of his family.

[101] But do you open your lips in behalf of my tears
at a time when the judge is as mild as I found
him. Ask not that I may be happy, but that I may
be safer in my unhappiness, that my place of exile
may be distant from the cruel enemy ; that the life
granted me by a very present deity may not be taken
from me by the drawn sword of some filthy Getan ; in
fine, if I should die, that I may be buried in a more
peaceful land and my bones be not crushed down by
Scythian soil, nor my ashes, meanly buried, as
doubtless an exile deserves, be trampled by the hoof
of a Bistonian horse ; and if there be some feeling that
survives after death, that no Sarmatian shade terrify
even my spirit.

[113] This tale, Maximus, might move the soul of
Caesar, yet only if it had first moved yours. Let your
voice, I pray, soften in my behalf the ears of Caesar,
for it is wont to aid frightened defendants, and with

adsuetaque tibi doctae dulcedine linguae
    aequandi superis pectora flecte viri.
non tibi Theromedon crudusque rogabitur Atreus,
120   quique suis homines pabula fecit equis,
    sed piger ad poenas princeps, ad praemia velox,
        quique dolet, quotiens cogitur esse ferox,
    qui vicit semper, victis ut parcere posset,
        clausit et aeterna civica bella sera,
125 multa metu poenae, poena [1] qui pauca coërcet,
        et iacit invita fulmina rara manu.
ergo tam placidas orator missus ad aures,
    ut propior patriae sit fuga nostra roga.
ille ego sum, qui te colui, quem festa solebat
130   inter convivas mensa videre tuos:
ille ego, qui duxi vestros Hymenaeon ad ignes,
    et cecini fausto carmina digna toro,
cuius te solitum memini laudare libellos,
    exceptis domino qui nocuere suo,
135 cui tua nonnumquam miranti scripta legebas:
    ille ego de vestra cui data nupta domo est.
hanc probat et primo dilectam semper ab aevo
    est inter comites Marcia censa suas,
inque suis habuit matertera Caesaris ante:
140   quarum iudicio siqua probata, proba est.
ipsa sua melior fama, laudantibus istis,
    Claudia divina non eguisset ope.
nos quoque praeteritos sine labe peregimus annos:
    proxima pars vitae transilienda meae.

---

[1] et qui multa metu sed poena *vel* multa metu cohibet poena

[1] Diomedes, king of the Bistones.

The usual sweetness of your accomplished tongue influence the heart of a hero whom we must liken to the gods. You will have to appeal to no Theromedon, no cruel Atreus, or to him [1] who made human beings fodder for his horses, but to a prince, slow to punish, quick to reward, who sorrows whenever he is forced to be severe, who has ever conquered that he might have power to spare the conquered, who has shut in civil war with an everlasting bar, who controls many things by the fear of punishment, few by punishment itself, hurling the thunderbolt rarely and with unwilling hand.

[127] So then since you are sent to plead in such merciful ears ask that my place of exile may be nearer my native land. I am he who attended upon you, whom the festal board used to see among your guests, I am he who led Hymenaeus to your wedding torches and sang a lay worthy of your propitious union, whose books, I remember, you used to praise with the exception of those which harmed their master; who used to admire the writings that you sometimes read to him, to whom a bride [2] was given from your household. She has the respect of Marcia,[3] who has loved her from her early years and given her a place among her companions; earlier still Caesar's aunt [4] so regarded her, and any woman approved in their judgment is indeed approved. Even she who was better than her own fame, even Claudia, had such women praised her, would have needed no divine aid.

[143] I, too, lived the years that are past without a blemish; the most recent part of my life must be passed over in silence. But to say naught of myself,

---

[2] Ovid's third wife, perhaps a Fabia.   [3] The wife of Maximus.
[4] Atia minor, wife of L. Marcius Philippus.

145 sed de me ut sileam,[1] coniunx mea sarcina vestra est :
  non potes hanc salva dissimulare fide.
confugit haec ad vos, vestras amplectitur aras
  —iure venit cultos ad sibi quisque deos—
flensque rogat, precibus lenito Caesare vestris,
150 busta sui fiant ut propiora viri.

III.

Hanc tibi Naso tuus mittit, Rufine, salutem,
  qui miser est, ulli si suus esse potest.
reddita confusae nuper solacia menti
  auxilium nostris spemque tulere malis.
5 utque Machaoniis Poeantius artibus heros
  lenito medicam vulnere sensit opem,
sic ego mente iacens et acerbo saucius ictu
  admonitu coepi fortior esse tuo,
et iam deficiens sic ad tua verba revixi,
10 ut solet infuso vena redire mero.
non tamen exhibuit tantas facundia vires,
  ut mea sint dictis pectora sana tuis.
ut multum demas nostrae[2] de gurgite curae,
  non minus exhausto quod superabit erit.
15 tempore ducetur longo fortasse cicatrix :
  horrent admotas vulnera cruda manus.
non est in medico semper relevetur ut aeger :
  interdum docta plus valet arte malum.
cernis ut e molli sanguis pulmone remissus
20 ad Stygias certo limite ducat aquas.
afferat ipse licet sacras Epidaurius herbas,
  sanabit nulla vulnera cordis ope.

[1] taceam   nostro corpore (pectore)

280

my wife is a charge upon you; you cannot deny her
and maintain your loyalty. She flees to you for
refuge, embracing your altar (rightly does each come
to the gods whom he himself worships) and in tears
she begs that you may soften Caesar by your prayers
and bring the tomb of her husband nearer.

III. To Rufinus

This greeting, Rufinus, your friend Naso sends
you—if a wretched man can be anyone's friend.
[3] The consolation that but now you sent to my
distressed heart brought aid and hope to my
woes. As the Poeantian hero [1] through the art of
Machaon felt in his soothed wound the healing aid, so
I, prostrate in soul and wounded by a bitter blow,
began to grow stronger through your admonition
when I was just on the point of failing; I was as much
restored by your words as the pulse is wont to revive
when wine is administered. Yet your eloquence had
not such power that my heart is whole through your
words. You may take much from my flood of woe,
but there will remain not less than you have drained
away. Perhaps in long time a scar will form, a raw
wound quivers at the touch of a hand. 'Tis not
always in a physician's power to cure the sick; at
times the disease is stronger than trained art. You
see how the blood emitted from a tender lung leads by
an unerring path to the waters of the Styx. Let the
Epidaurian [2] in person bring holy herbs, he will have
no skill with which to heal wounds in the heart. The

---

[1] Philoctetes.
[2] Aesculapius, whose greatest temple was at Epidaurus.

tollere nodosam nescit medicina podagram,
   nec formidatis auxiliatur aquis.
25 cura quoque interdum nulla medicabilis arte est—
   aut, ut sit, longa est extenuanda mora.
cum bene firmarunt animum praecepta iacentem,
   sumptaque sunt nobis pectoris arma tui
rursus amor patriae ratione valentior omni,
30   quod tua fecerunt scripta, retexit opus.
sive pium vis hoc seu vis muliebre vocari,
   confiteor misero molle cor esse mihi.
non dubia est Ithaci prudentia, sed tamen optat
   fumum de patriis posse videre focis.
35 nescioqua natale solum dulcedine cunctos
   ducit et inmemores non sinit esse sui.
quid melius Roma ?   Scythico quid frigore peius ?
   huc tamen ex illa [1] barbarus urbe fugit.
cum bene sit clausae cavea Pandione natae,
40   nititur in silvas illa redire suas.
adsuetos tauri saltus, adsueta leones—
   nec feritas illos impedit—antra petunt.
tu tamen exilii morsus e pectore nostro
   fomentis speras cedere posse tuis.
45 effice vos ipsi ne tam mihi sitis amandi,
   talibus ut levius sit caruisse malum.
at, puto, qua genitus fueram, tellure carenti
   in tamen humano contigit esse loco.
orbis in extremi iaceo desertus harenis,
50   fert ubi perpetuas obruta terra nives.
non ager hic pomum, non dulces educat uvas,[2]
   non salices ripa, robora monte virent,
neve fretum laudes terra magis, aequora semper
   ventorum rabie solibus orba tument.

                 [1] ista   [2] herbas

[1] Ulysses.   [2] Philomela, the nightingale.

healing art knows not how to remove crippling gout,
it helps not the fearful dropsy. Sorrow too can find
at times no skill that will cure it or else to be cured it
must be worn away by long time. When your
admonitions have strengthened my prostrate soul
and I have put on the armour of your heart, once
again my love for the fatherland, stronger than any
reasoning, undoes the work that your writings have
wrought. Whether you call this loyal or womanish,
I admit that in my wretchedness my heart is soft.
None doubt the Ithacan's [1] wisdom, but yet he prays
that he may see the smoke from his native
hearth. By what sweet charm I know not the native
land draws all men nor allows them to forget
her. What is better than Rome? What worse than
the cold of Scythia ? Yet hither the barbarian flees
from that city. Though Pandion's daughter [2] may
be well off in her cage, she strives to return to her own
forests. Bullocks seek their familiar pastures, lions
in spite of their wild nature their familiar lairs.
Nevertheless you hope that the gnawing pangs of
exile can be made by your soothing to leave my
breast. See to it that you and yours be not
yourselves so dear to me ; so will it be a slighter
misfortune to be deprived of you. "But," I sup-
pose, "though I am separated from the land of my
birth, I have yet had the good fortune to be in a place
where men dwell ! " At the edge of the world I lie
abandoned on the strand, where the buried earth sup-
ports constant snows.   No fields here produce fruit,
nor sweet grapes, no willows are green upon the bank,
no oaks upon the hill. Nor can you praise the sea
more than the land, for the sunless waters ever heave
beneath the madness of the winds. Wherever you

55 quocumque aspicies,[1] campi cultore carentes
    vastaque, quae nemo vindicat, arva iacent.
hostis adest dextra laevaque a parte timendus,
    vicinoque metu terret utrumque latus.
altera Bistonias pars est sensura sarisas,
60   altera Sarmatica spicula missa manu.
i nunc et veterum nobis exempla virorum
    qui forti casum mente tulere refer,
et grave magnanimi robur mirare Rutili
    non usi reditus condicione dati.
65 Smyrna virum tenuit, non Pontus et hostica tellus,
    paene minus nullo Smyrna petenda loco.
non doluit patria cynicus procul esse Sinopeus,
    legit enim sedes, Attica terra, tuas.
arma Neoclides qui Persica contudit armis,
70   Argolica primam sensit in urbe fugam.
pulsus Aristides patria Lacedaemona fugit,
    inter quas dubium, quae prior esset, erat.
caede puer facta Patroclus Opunta reliquit,
    Thessalicamque adiit hospes Achillis humum.
75 exul ab Haemonia Pirenida cessit ad undam,
    quo duce trabs Colchas sacra cucurrit aquas.
liquit Agenorides Sidonia moenia Cadmus,
    poneret ut muros in meliore loco.
venit ad Adrastrum Tydeus Calydone fugatus,
80   et Teucrum Veneri grata recepit humus.
quid referam veteres Romanae gentis, apud quos
    exulibus tellus ultima Tibur erat ?
persequar ut cunctos, nulli datus omnibus aevis
    tam procul a patria est horridiorve locus.

---

[1] aspicias

[1] P. Rutilius Rufus, an opponent of Marius, who went into voluntary exile at Smyrna.

gaze, lie plains with no tillers, vast steppes which no man claims. Close at hand on the right and left is a dreaded enemy terrifying us with imminent fear on both sides. One side is on the eve of feeling the Bistonian spears, the other the darts sped by the hand of the Sarmatian. Now then go and cite for me the example of men of old who bore danger with strong mind; admire the impressive strength of great-souled Rutilius [1] who would not avail himself of the proffered offer of return home! Smyrna held him, not the Pontus or a hostile land—Smyrna, than which scarce any place is more to be desired. It grieved not the cynic [2] of Sinope to be far from his native city, for he chose a home in the land of Attica. Neocles' son,[3] who with arms beat down the arms of Persia, first experienced exile in the city of Argos. Aristides expelled from his native city found refuge in Sparta—and it was doubtful which of these two excelled. Young Patroclus, having slain a man, left Opus and became the guest of Achilles in Thessaly. From Haemonia to Pirene's spring fled the exile [4] under whose guidance the sacred ship skimmed the waters of Colchis. Agenor's son Cadmus left the battlements of Sidon to establish walls in a better place.[5] Tydeus came to Adrastus[6] when exiled from Calydon, Teucer found refuge in the land [7] that Venus loves. Why need I tell of the men of olden Roman race with whom the remotest land of exile was Tibur [8]? Though I should enumerate every exile, none in any age has ever been assigned to a more forbidding place so far from his native land.

[2] Diogenes. [3] Themistocles. [4] Jason.
[5] Thebes. [6] At Argos. [7] Cyprus.
[8] About eighteen miles from Rome.

85 quo magis ignoscat sapientia vestra dolenti
    qui[1] facit ex dictis, non ita multa, tuis.
nec tamen infitior, si possint nostra coire
    vulnera, praeceptis posse coire tuis.
sed vereor ne me frustra servare labores
90   nec iuver admota perditus aeger ope.
nec loquor haec, quia sit maior prudentia nobis,
    sed sum quam medico notior ipse mihi.
ut tamen hoc ita sit, munus tua grande voluntas
    ad me pervenit consuliturque boni.

IV.

Iam mihi deterior canis aspergitur aetas,
    iamque meos vultus ruga senilis arat :
iam vigor et quasso languent in corpore vires,
    nec, iuveni lusus qui placuere, iuvant.
5 nec, si me subito videas, agnoscere possis,
    aetatis facta est tanta ruina meae.
confiteor facere hoc annos, sed et altera causa est,
    anxietas animi continuusque labor.
nam mea per longos siquis mala digerat annos,
10   crede mihi, Pylio Nestore maior ero.
cernis ut in duris—et quid bove firmius ?—arvis
    fortia taurorum corpora frangat opus.
quae numquam vacuo solita est cessare novali,
    fructibus assiduis lassa senescit humus.
15 occidet, ad Circi siquis certamina semper
    non intermissis cursibus ibit equus.
firma sit illa licet, solvetur in aequore navis,
    quae numquam liquidis sicca carebit aquis.

[1] quae *corr. Faber*

[85] And so let your wisdom pardon an unhappy man if he does not do much that is in accord with your words. Yet I do not deny that could my wounds heal, 'tis through your teaching they could heal. But I fear that it is in vain you strive to save me, and that I shall not be helped in my desperate sickness by the aid you bring. And this I say, not because I have the greater wisdom, but I know myself better than any doctor can. Yet in spite of this, your good will has come to me as a great boon and I take it in good part.

IV. To his Wife

Now is the worse period of life upon me with its sprinkling of white hairs, now the wrinkles of age are furrowing my face, now energy and strength are weakening in my shattered frame. On a sudden shouldst thou see me, thou couldst not recognize me; such havoc has been wrought with my life. I admit that this is the work of the years, but there is yet another cause—anguish and constant suffering. For should my misfortunes be distributed by anybody through a long series of years, I shall be older, I assure thee, than Pylian Nestor.

[11] Thou sees how in the stubborn fields the sturdy bullocks—and what is stronger than a bullock?—are broken in body with toil. The land which has never been wont to rest as idle fallow, grows weary and old with constant production. That horse will fall which enters every contest of the Circus without omission. Strong though she be, the ship will break up in the sea which never is hauled from the clear waters to

287

me quoque debilitat series inmensa malorum,[1]
20   ante meum tempus cogit et esse senem.
otia corpus alunt, animus quoque pascitur illis:
    inmodicus contra carpit utrumque labor.
aspice, in has partis quod venerit Aesone natus,
    quam laudem a sera posteritate ferat.
25 at labor illius nostro leviorque minorque est,
    si modo non verum nomina magna premunt.
ille est in Pontum Pelia mittente profectus,
    qui vix Thessaliae fine timendus erat.
Caesaris ira mihi nocuit, quem solis ab ortu
30   solis ad occasus utraque terra tremit.
iunctior Haemonia est Ponto, quam Roma, Sinistro,[2]
    et brevius, quam nos, ille peregit iter.
ille habuit comites primos telluris Achivae:
    at nostram cuncti destituere fugam.
35 nos fragili ligno vastum sulcavimus aequor:
    quae tulit Aesoniden, densa carina[3] fuit.
nec mihi Tiphys erat rector, nec Agenore natus
    quas fugerem docuit quas sequererque vias.
illum tutata est cum Pallade regia Iuno:
40   defendere meum numina nulla caput.
illum furtivae iuvere Cupidinis artes;
    quas a me vellem non didicisset Amor.
ille domum rediit: nos his moriemur in arvis,
    perstiterit laesi si gravis ira dei.
45 durius est igitur nostrum, fidissima coniunx,
    illo, quod subiit Aesone natus, opus.[4]
te quoque, quam iuvenem discedens urbe reliqui,
    credibile est nostris insenuisse malis.
o, ego di faciant talem te cernere possim,[5]
50   caraque mutatis oscula ferre comis,

---

      [1] laborum   [2] sit histro *corr. Burmann*
        [3] sacra carina (sa carina) *vel* firma carina

dry. I too am weakened by the measureless series of my woes and am perforce an old man before my time.

[21] Leisure nourishes the body, the mind too feeds upon it, but excessive toil impairs both. Behold what praise the son [1] of Aeson, because he came to this region, receives from late posterity. Yet his toil was lighter and smaller than mine, if only mighty names do not keep down the truth. He set forth to Pontus dispatched by Pelias who was scarce dreaded as far as the bounds of Thessaly. Caesar's anger wrought my ruin at whom the world of sunrise and of sunset alike tremble. Haemonia is closer to ill-omened Pontus than Rome, and he completed a shorter journey than I. He had as comrades the leaders of the Achaean land, but I was abandoned of all on my journey. In a frail bark I ploughed the vast sea; the one that carried Aeson's son was a staunch ship. I had no Tiphys for a pilot nor did Agenor's son [2] teach me what ways to avoid and what to follow. He was safeguarded by Pallas and queenly Juno; no deities defended my life. He was aided by the wily arts of Cupid; would that Love had not learned them from me! He came back to his home, I shall die in this land, if the weighty wrath of the injured god persists. Harder then is my task, my faithful wife, than that which Aeson's son endured.

[47] Thou too, whom I left in youth when I set out from the city, doubtless hast aged in consequence of my misfortunes. O, may the gods grant that I can see thee thus, lovingly kiss thy altered locks, and folding

---

[1] Jason.   [2] Phineus.

---

[4] onus   [5] possem : possim *s*

amplectique meis corpus non pingue lacertis,
    et " gracile hoc fecit " dicere " cura mei,"
et narrare meos flenti flens ipse labores,
    sperato numquam conloquioque frui
55 turaque Caesaribus cum coniuge Caesare digna,
    dis veris, memori debita ferre manu !
Memnonis hanc utinam lenito principe mater
    quam primum roseo provocet ore diem !

V.

Ille tuos quondam non ultimus inter amicos,
    ut sua verba legas, Maxime, Naso rogat.
in quibus ingenium desiste requirere nostrum,
    nescius exilii ne videare mei.
5 cernis ut ignavum corrumpant otia corpus,
    ut capiant vitium,[1] ni moveantur, aquae.
et mihi siquis erat ducendi carminis usus,
    deficit estque minor factus inerte situ.
haec quoque, quae legitis, siquid mihi, Maxime, credis,
10   scribimus invita vixque coacta manu.
non libet in talis animum contendere curas,
    nec venit ad duros Musa vocata Getas.
ut tamen ipse vides, luctor deducere versum :
    sed non fit fato mollior ille meo.
15 cum relego, scripsisse pudet, quia plurima cerno
    me quoque, qui feci, iudice digna lini.
nec tamen emendo.   labor hic quam scribere maior,
    mensque pati durum sustinet aegra nihil.
scilicet incipiam lima mordacius uti,
20   et sub iudicium singula verba vocem ?

---

[1] capeant vitio

thy slender body in my arms say, "Love for me hath wasted thee so," and amid mutual tears tell thee of my sufferings, enjoying a talk I have never hoped for, and offering to the Caesars and the wife who is worthy of Caesar, true gods, the incense due from my grateful hand. Would that Memnon's mother,[1] when the Prince is softened, might with rosy lips call forth this day as soon as may be!

V. TO MAXIMUS

'Tis he who was once not last among your friends— 'tis Naso, asks you, Maximus, to read his words. Seek not in them my native wit lest you seem unaware of my banishment. You see how inactivity spoils an idle body, how water acquires a taint unless it is in motion. For me, too, whatever skill I had in shaping song is failing, diminished by inactive sloth. Even this that you read, Maximus, if in anything you believe me, I write forcing it with difficulty from an unwilling hand. There is no pleasure in straining the mind to such a task, nor does the Muse come at one's call to the stern Getae. Yet, as you see, I am struggling to weave verses, but the fabric is not softer than my fate. When I read it over I am ashamed of my work because I note many a thing that even in my own, the maker's judgment, deserves to be erased. Yet I do not correct it. This is a greater labour than the writing, and my sick mind has not the power to endure anything hard. Am I forsooth to use the file more bitingly, subjecting single words to criticism? Does fortune indeed

[1] Aurora.

torquet enim fortuna parum, nisi Lixus in Hebrum
    confluat, et frondes Alpibus addat Atho [1]?
parcendum est animo miserabile vulnus habenti.
    subducunt oneri colla perusta boves.
25 at, puto, fructus adest, iustissima causa laborum,
    et sata cum multo faenore reddit ager?
tempus ad hoc nobis, repetas licet omnia, nullum
    profuit—atque utinam non nocuisset!—opus.
cur igitur scribam, miraris?   miror et ipse,
30   et tecum quaero saepe quid inde petam.
an populus vere sanos negat esse poëtas,
    sumque fides huius maxima vocis ego,
qui, sterili totiens cum sim deceptus ab arvo,
    damnosa persto condere semen humo?
35 scilicet est cupidus studiorum quisque suorum,
    tempus et adsueta ponere in arte iuvat.
saucius eiurat pugnam gladiator, et idem
    inmemor antiqui vulneris arma capit.
nil sibi cum pelagi dicit fore naufragus undis,
40   et ducit remos qua modo navit aqua.
sic ego constanter studium non utile servo,
    et repeto, nollem quas coluisse, deas.
quid potius faciam? non sum, qui segnia ducam
    otia : mors nobis tempus habetur iners.
45 nec iuvat in lucem nimio marcescere vino,
    nec tenet incertas alea blanda manus.
cum dedimus somno quas corpus postulat horas,
    quo ponam vigilans tempora longa modo?
moris an oblitus patrii contendere discam
50   Sarmaticos arcus, et trahar arte loci?

                [1] athos

torture me too little without my making the Lixus
flow into the Hebrus and Athos add leaves to the
Alps? One must spare a soul that has a wretched
wound; oxen withdraw their chafed necks from a
burden. "But," I suppose, "a reward is at hand,
the most justifiable reason for toil, and the field is
returning the seed with much usury!" To the
present no work of mine, though you enumerate them
all, has brought me profit—would that none had
harmed me!

[29] Why then do I write, you wonder? I too
wonder, and with you I often ask what I seek from
it. Or do the people say true that poets are not sane
and am I the strongest proof of this maxim—I who
though so many times deceived by the barrenness of
the soil, persist in sowing my seed in ground that
ruins me? Clearly each man shows a passion for his
own pursuits, taking pleasure in devoting time to his
familiar art. The wounded gladiator forswears the
fight, yet forgetting his former wound he dons his
arms. The shipwrecked man declares that he will
have nothing to do with the waves of the sea, yet plies
the oar in the water in which but recently he swam.
In the same way I continually hold to a profitless
pursuit, returning to the goddesses whom I would I
had not worshipped. What rather shall I do? I am
not one to lead a life of idle leisure; I regard idleness as
death. I take no pleasure in steeping myself in wine
until daylight, and the alluring dice attract not my
shaking hands. When I have devoted to sleep what
hours my frame demands, how am I to spend the
long period of wakefulness? Forgetting the ways
of my native land shall I learn how to bend the
Sarmatian bow, attracted by the accomplishment

hoc quoque me studium prohibent adsumere vires,
    mensque magis gracili corpore nostra valet.
cum bene quaesieris quid agam, magis utile nil est
    artibus his, quae nil utilitatis habent.
55 consequor ex illis casus oblivia nostri :
    hanc messem satis est si mea reddit humus.
gloria vos acuat, vos, ut recitata probentur
    carmina, Pieriis invigilate choris.
quod venit ex facili, satis est componere nobis,
60   et nimis intenti causa laboris abest.
cur ego sollicita poliam mea carmina cura ?
    an verear ne non approbet illa Getes ?
forsitan audacter faciam, sed glorior Histrum
    ingenio nullum maius habere meo.
65 hoc, ubi vivendum est, satis est, si consequor arvo,
    inter inhumanos esse poëta Getas.
quo mihi diversum fama contendere in orbem ?
    quem fortuna dedit, Roma sit ille locus.
hoc mea contenta est infelix Musa theatro :
70   sic merui, magni sic voluere dei.
nec reor hinc istuc nostris iter esse libellis,
    quo Boreas pinna deficiente venit.
dividimur caelo, quaeque est procul urbe Quirini,
    aspicit hirsutos comminus Ursa Getas.
75 per tantum terrae, tot aquas vix credere possum
    indicium studii transiluisse mei.
finge legi, quodque est mirabile, finge placere :
    auctorem certe res iuvat ista nihil.
quid tibi, si calidae, prosit, laudere Syenae,[1]
80   aut ubi Taprobanen Indica tinguit aqua ?

      [1] calidae . . . syene *etc. corr. Riese*

of the country ? Even this pursuit my strength
prevents me from adopting, for my mind is stronger
than my slender body.

⁵³ When you have pondered well what I am to do,
nothing is more useful than this art which has no
use. From it I win forgetfulness of my misfortune;
this harvest is enough if my ground but yields it. As
for you—your goad may be renown; to read your
poems and win approval, devote your wakeful hours
to the Pierian band. 'Tis enough for me to compose
what comes easily; I lack a reason for too earnest
toil. Why should I refine my verse with anxious
labour ? Should I fear that the Getan will not
approve them ? Perchance 'tis bold of me, and yet I
boast that the Hister has no greater talent than
mine. In this land where I must live 'tis enough if I
succeed in being a poet among the uncivilized
Getae. Why should I attempt to reach with fame
the opposite side of the world ? Let that place be
Rome which fortune has given me. With this
theatre my unhappy Muse is content: so have I
deserved, so have the great gods willed.

⁷¹ And I think that my books cannot journey from
this place to your region whither Boreas comes on
failing wing. We are separated by the heavens' space,
and the She Bear who is far from the city of Quirinus
gazes close at hand upon the shaggy Getae. Over so
vast a stretch of land, so many waters I can scarce
believe it possible that a hint of my work has
leaped. Suppose it is read, and—marvellous indeed—
suppose it finds favour; that fact surely helps its
author not at all. What profit to you if you should
be praised in hot Syene,[1] or where the Indian waves

[1] Assuan, far up the Nile at the bounds of the empire.

altius ire libet ? si te distantia longe
  Pleïadum laudent signa, quid inde feras ?
sed neque pervenio scriptis mediocribus istuc,
  famaque cum domino fugit ab urbe suo.
85 vosque, quibus perii, tunc cum mea fama sepulta est,
  nunc quoque de nostra morte tacere reor.

VI.

Ecquid, ut audisti—nam te diversa tenebat
  terra—meos casus, cor tibi triste fuit ?
dissimules metuasque licet, Graecine, fateri,
  si bene te novi, triste fuisse liquet.
5 non cadit in mores feritas inamabilis istos,
  nec minus a studiis dissidet illa tuis.
artibus ingenuis, quarum tibi maxima cura est,
  pectora mollescunt asperitasque fugit.
nec quisquam meliore fide complectitur illas,
10   qua sinit officium militiaeque labor.
certe ego cum primum potui sentire quid essem
  —nam fuit attoniti [1] mens mea nulla diu—
hoc quoque fortunam [2] sensi, quod amicus abesses,
  qui mihi praesidium grande futurus eras.
15 tecum tunc aberant aegrae solacia mentis,
  magnaque pars animi consiliique mei.
at nunc, quod superest, fer opem, precor, eminus
    unam,
  adloquioque iuva pectora nostra tuo,
quae, non mendaci si quicquam credis amico,
20   stulta magis dici quam scelerata decet.
nec breve nec tutum peccati quae sit origo
  scribere ; tractari vulnera nostra timent.

---

       [1] attonito *corr. Ehwald*   [2] fortunae ς

              [1] Ceylon.

dye Tabropanes [1] ? Would you go further ? If the
far distant stars of the Pleiads should praise you,
what would you gain ? But I do not penetrate by
virtue of my commonplace writings to that place of
yours ; the author's fame was banished with him from
his own city. And you in whose eyes I died when my
fame was buried, now also, I think, are silent about
my death.[2]

VI. To Graecinus

Is it true that when you heard of my disaster, for
you were then in a different land, your heart was
sad ? You may try to hide it and shrink from the
admission, Graecinus, but if I know you well, 'tis
certain it was sad. Revolting cruelty does not
square with your character and is no less at variance
with your pursuits. The liberal arts, for which you
care above all things, soften the heart and expel
harshness. Nobody embraces them with greater
faith than you—so far as duty and the toil of a
soldier's life permit. For my part as soon as I
realized what I was—for long was I stunned and had
no powers of thought—I felt in this also my fate that
you, my friend, were absent,—you who were sure to
be my great support. With you at that time were
absent all that solaces a sick mind, and a great part of
my courage and my counsel.

[17] But as it is, for this alone remains, bring me one
aid, I beseech you, from afar ; help with your
comforting words a heart which, if you believe at all a
friend who does not lie, should be called foolish rather
than wicked. It would be long and not safe to tell
the story of my sin, and my wounds fear to be

[2] *i.e.* they had ceased even to talk about his living death in exile.

qualia quoque [1] modo mihi sint ea facta, rogare
 desine : non agites, siqua coire velis.
25 quicquid id est, ut non facinus, sic culpa vocanda
 est.
 omnis an in magnos culpa deos scelus est ?
 spes igitur menti poenae, Graecine, levandae
 non est ex toto nulla relicta meae.
 haec dea, cum fugerent sceleratas numina terras,
30 in dis invisa sola remansit humo.
 haec facit ut vivat fossor quoque compede vinctus,
 liberaque a ferro crura futura putet.
 haec facit ut, videat cum terras undique nullas,
 naufragus in mediis brachia iactet aquis.
35 saepe aliquem sollers medicorum cura reliquit,
 nec spes huic vena deficiente cadit.
 carcere dicuntur clausi sperare salutem,
 atque aliquis pendens in cruce vota facit.
 haec dea quam multos laqueo sua colla ligantis
40 non est proposita passa perire nece !
 me quoque conantem gladio finire dolorem
 arcuit [2] iniecta continuitque manu,
  "quid" que "facis ? lacrimis opus est, non
  sanguine" dixit,
 "saepe per has flecti principis ira solet."
45 quamvis est igitur meritis indebita nostris,
 magna tamen spes est in bonitate dei.
 qui ne difficilis mihi sit, Graecine, precare,
 confer et in votum tu quoque verba meum.
 inque Tomitana iaceam tumulatus harena,
50 si te non nobis ista vovere liquet.
 nam prius incipient turris vitare columbae,
 antra ferae, pecudes gramina, mergus aquas,

---

  [1] qualiacumque *corr. Housman*   [2] arguit

touched. Ask not the nature of those wounds nor
how I got them : disturb them not, if you wish them to
heal. Whatever that is, though it does not deserve
the term "crime," yet it should be called a
"fault." Or is every fault against the great gods a
crime ?

²⁷ Hope therefore of lessening my punishment,
Graecinus, has not altogether forsaken my
soul. That goddess, when all other deities aban-
doned the wicked earth, remained alone on the god-
detested place. She causes even the ditcher to live in
spite of his shackles and to think that his limbs will be
freed from the iron. She makes the shipwrecked
man, seeing no land on any side, move his arms in the
midst of the waves. Oft has a man been abandoned
by the skill and care of physicians, but hope leaves
him not though his pulses fail. Those who are shut
in prison hope for release, they say, and many a one
hanging on the cross still prays. How many this
goddess has prevented in the act of fastening the
noose about their throats from perishing by the death
they had purposed ! Me also as I was attempting to
end my grief with the sword she held back, checking
me with a touch of her hand and saying, "What are
you about ? There is need of tears, not blood , often
by tears the wrath of a prince may be turned
aside." And so although I do not deserve it, yet I
have strong hope in the kindness of the god. Pray,
Graecinus, that he be not hard for me to win ; add too
some words of your own to my supplication. May I
lie entombed in the sands of Tomis if it is not clear
that you are a suppliant in my behalf. For sooner
will the pigeons avoid the towers, the wild beasts
the forest glades, the cattle the grass, and the

OVID

quam male se praestet veteri Graecinus amico.
    non ita sunt fatis omnia versa meis.

VII.

Littera pro verbis tibi, Messaline, salutem
    quam legis, a saevis attulit usque Getis.
indicat auctorem locus ? an, nisi nomine lecto,
    haec me Nasonem scribere verba latet ?
5 ecquis in extremo positus iacet orbe tuorum,
    me tamen excepto, qui precor esse tuus ?
di procul a cunctis, qui te venerantur amantque
    huius notitiam gentis habere [1] velint.
nos satis est inter glaciem Scythicasque sagittas
10   vivere, si vita est mortis habenda genus.
nos premat aut bello tellus, aut frigore caelum,
    truxque Getes armis, grandine pugnet [2] hiems :
nos habeat regio nec pomo feta nec uvis,
    et cuius nullum cesset ab hoste latus.
15 cetera sit sospes cultorum turba tuorum,
    in quibus, ut populo, pars ego parva fui.
me miserum, si tu verbis offenderis istis
    nosque negas ulla parte fuisse tuos !
idque sit ut verum, mentito ignoscere debes :
20   nil demit laudi gloria nostra tuae.
quis se Caesaribus notus non fingit amicum ?
    da veniam lasso : tu mihi Caesar eras. [3]
nec tamen inrumpto quo non licet ire, satisque est
    atria si nobis non patuisse negas.

       [1] abesse   [2] pulset ς   [3] eris

gull the waters than Graecinus will weakly support an
old friend. Not so utterly have all things been
changed by my fate.

VII. To Messalinus

Letters, instead of spoken words, Messalinus, have
brought you the greeting which you read all the way
from the fierce Getae. Is the place a token of the
author? Or unless you have read the name are you
unaware that I who write these words am
Naso? Does any one of your friends except
myself—who pray that I am your friend—lie at the
very edge of the world? May the gods will that all
who show you respect and love may have no
knowledge of this race! Enough that *I* should live
midst ice and Scythian arrows—if a kind of death
must be considered life. Let me be hard pressed by
war on the earth or by the chill of heaven, the wild
Getae fighting with arms and the winter with its hail;
let me be held in a country that produces neither fruit
nor grape, that has no side free from an enemy: but
safe be all the other throng of your clients, among
whom, as mid a host, I was but one of many. Alas
for me if you take offence at such words as these and
deny that I have been connected with you in any re-
spect. For even though that were true, you ought to
pardon my falsehood; your praise loses nothing through
this boast of mine. What acquaintance of the
Caesars does not imagine himself a friend! Pardon one
who is worn out; to me you have ever been a Caesar.
And yet I do not force my way where I am not allow-
ed to go, and 'tis enough if you do not deny that your
halls were open to me. Though you had nothing

301

25 utque tibi fuerit mecum nihil amplius, uno
  nempe salutaris, quam prius, ore minus.
nec tuus est genitor nos infitiatus amicos,
  hortator studii causaque faxque mei:
cui nos et lacrimas, supremum in funere munus,
30 et dedimus medio scripta canenda foro.
adde quod est frater, tanto tibi iunctus amore,
  quantus in Atridis Tyndaridisque fuit:
is me nec comitem nec dedignatus amicum est:
  si tamen haec illi non nocitura putas.
35 si minus, hac quoque me mendacem parte fatebor:
  clausa mihi potius tota sit ista domus.
sed neque claudenda est, et nulla potentia vires
  praestandi, ne quid peccet amicus, habet.
et tamen ut cuperem culpam quoque posse negari,
40 sic facinus nemo nescit abesse mihi.
quod nisi delicti pars excusabilis esset,
  parva relegari poena futura fuit.
ipse sed hoc vidit, qui pervidet omnia, Caesar,
  stultitiam dici crimina posse mea:
45 quaque ego permisi, quaque est res passa, pepercit,
  usus et est modice fulminis igne sui.
nec vitam nec opes nec ademit posse reverti,
  si sua per vestras victa sit ira preces.
at graviter cecidi.   quid enim mirabile, si quis
50 a Iove percussus non leve vulnus habet?
ipse suas etiam[1] vires inhiberet Achilles,
  missa gravis ictus Pelias hasta dabat.
iudicium nobis igitur cum vindicis adsit,
  non est cur tua me ianua nosse neget.
55 culta quidem, fateor, citra quam debuit, illa est:
  sed fuit in fatis hoc quoque, credo, meis.

---

[1] etiam] quamvis

more to do with me, surely you are saluted by one
voice less than of old.   Your father did not deny my
friendship, he who was at once the encourager, the
cause, and the guiding light of my pursuit.   For him
I gave tears which are the final meed of death, and I
wrote verses to be chanted in the midst of the
forum.   You have also a brother united to you with
as great a love as that which joined the Atridae [1] or
the Tyndaridae [2] : he has not disdained me as
companion or as friend, yet only if you deem these
words will not harm him.   Else will I confess a
falsehood in this particular also ; rather let that whole
house be closed to me.   Yet it ought not to be closed
to me, for no power has strength to guarantee that a
friend will do no wrong.   And yet even as I could
crave the power to deny my fault, so everybody
knows that mine is no crime.   And unless a part of
my sin were pardonable, exile would have been a
small punishment.   But he himself saw this, he who
sees all things—Caesar—that my crimes might be
termed folly.   So far as I permitted, so far as cir-
cumstances allowed, he spared me, making but a mild
use of his flaming thunderbolt.   He took from me
neither life nor property nor the possibility of return —
if his wrath should be conquered by your prayers.

[49] Yet heavy was my fall.   What wonder if one
smitten by Jupiter has no slight wound ?   Even
should Achilles restrain his power, the Pelian spear he
hurled dealt heavy strokes.   Inasmuch then as I
have the judgment of him who punishes me in my
favour, there is no reason why your doorway should
deny knowledge of me.   I admit I paid less court to it
than I ought, but that too was fated for me, I

[1] Agamemnon and Menelaus.   [2] Castor and Pollux.

303

nec tamen officium sensit domus altera nostrum :
  hic illic vestro sub Lare semper eram.
quaeque tua est pietas, ut te non excolat ipsum,
60 ius aliquod tecum fratris amicus habet.
quid quod, ut emeritis referenda est gratia semper,
  sic est fortunae promeruisse tuae ?
quod si permittis nobis suadere quid optes,
  ut des quam reddas plura precare deos.
65 idque facis, quantumque licet meminisse, solebas
  officii causam pluribus ipse dare.[1]
quo libet in numero me, Messaline, repone,
  sim modo pars vestrae non aliena domus :
et mala Nasonem, quoniam meruisse videtur,
70 si non ferre doles, at meruisse dole.

VIII.

A tibi dilecto missam Nasone salutem
  accipe, pars animae magna, Severe, meae.
neve roga quid agam.   si persequar omnia, flebis ;
  summa sat est[2] nostri si tibi nota mali.
5 vivimus assiduis expertes pacis in armis,
  dura pharetrato bella movente Geta.
deque tot expulsis sum miles in exule solus :
  tuta, nec invideo, cetera turba latet.
quoque magis nostros venia dignere libellos,
10 haec in procinctu carmina facta leges.
stat vetus urbs, ripae vicina binominis Histri,
  moenibus et positu vix adeunda loci.

----

[1] esse dari *corr. Madvig*
[2] satis *corr. Bentley*

----

[1] *i.e.* at your home or your brother's (Cotta Maximus).
[2] *Noblesse oblige.*

believe. Yet no other house received my attentions : whether here or there [1] I was constantly beneath the protection of your common Lar, and such is your loyalty that though he court not you in person, your brother's friend has on you some claim. What too of this that as thanks should be rendered to those who have done service so it becomes your position to deserve them ? [2] And if you permit us to advise what you should desire, pray that you may give more than you repay. This you are doing and, as I remember, you used to provide many with a reason for their attentions. In whatever class you will, Messalinus, place me, if only I be no alien member of your household. As for Naso's misfortunes—since it seems that he has deserved them—if you are not grieved that he endures them, yet grieve that he has deserved them.

VIII. To Severus

Severus, my soul's larger part, receive the greeting sent by Naso whom you used to love, nor ask how I fare. Should I tell the whole tale, it will bring you tears ; 'tis enough if you know the sum of my misfortune. I live deprived of peace amid constant strife while the quiver-bearing Getan rouses stern war. Of so many exiled I alone am both exile and soldier ; the rest—nor do I grudge it them—are safe in their retirement. And that you may grant my work greater indulgence, you will read here verses composed on the field of battle. An old city [3] lies hard by the bank of Hister of the double name, scarce accessible because of its walls and the site. Aegisos,

[3] Aegisos, cf. Ex P. iv. 7. 21 and 53. The Danube had a "double name" : Hister and Danuvius.

Caspios Aegisos, de se si credimus ipsis,
    condidit, et proprio nomine dixit opus.
15 hanc ferus, Odrysiis inopino Marte peremptis,
    cepit et in regem sustulit arma Getes.
ille memor magni generis, virtute quod auget,
    protinus innumero milite cinctus adest.
nec prius abscessit, merita quam caede nocentum
20   [audaces animos contuderat [1] populi.[2]]
at tibi, rex aevo, detur, fortissime nostro,
    semper honorata sceptra tenere manu.
teque, quod et praestat—quid enim tibi plenius
      optem ?
Martia cum magno Caesare Roma probet.
25 sed memor unde abii, queror, o iucunde sodalis,
    accedant [3] nostris saeva quod arma malis.
ut careo vobis, Stygias [4] detrusus in oras,
    quattuor autumnos Pleïas orta facit.
nec tu credideris urbanae commoda vitae
30   quaerere Nasonem, quaerit et illa tamen.
nam modo vos animo dulces reminiscor, amici,
    nunc mihi cum cara coniuge nata subit :
aque domo rursus pulchrae loca vertor ad urbis,
    cunctaque mens oculis pervidet usa suis.
35 nunc fora, nunc aedes, nunc marmore tecta theatra,
    nunc subit aequata porticus omnis humo.
gramina nunc Campi pulchros spectantis in hortos,
    stagnaque et euripi Virgineusque liquor.

---

[1] -erit *BC* : *corr. Riese*   [2] *sic BC, sed versum om. A*
[3] accedunt   [4] scythicas

the Caspian, if we may believe the native tale, founded it and gave it his own name. The wild Getae took it after they had destroyed the Odrysii in a warfare of surprise, and raised their arms against the king. He, mindful of the mighty race which his own valour enhances, at once approached with a following of countless warriors. Nor did he depart until with deserved slaughter of the guilty [he beat down the presumptuous spirit of the people.] May it be granted thee, bravest monarch of our time, ever to sway the sceptre with thy honoured hand. Mayst thou, even as she grants it now—for what fuller prayer could I make for thee—find approval with warlike Rome along with mighty Caesar.

[25] But mindful of my beginning, my dear comrade, I complain of the addition of cruel warfare to my misfortunes. Since I have been separated from you, thrust down to the very shores of the Styx, the rising of the Pleiads is now bringing on the fourth autumn. Yet believe not thou that 'tis the joys of city life that Naso seeks—and yet even them he seeks—for at times I have memories of you, my pleasant friends, at times thoughts of my daughter and my dear wife steal over me, and from my own house I am once again visiting the localities of the beautiful town, my mind surveying everything with eyes of its own. Now the fora, now the temples, now the theatres sheathed in marble, now every portico with its levelled ground comes before me; now the greensward of the Campus that looks towards the lovely gardens, the pools, the canals, and the water of the Virgo.[1]

---

[1] The aqueduct Virgo, cf. Tr. iii. 12. 22.

at, puto, sic urbis misero est erepta voluptas,
40   quolibet ut saltem rure frui liceat!
non meus amissos animus desiderat agros,
    ruraque Paeligno conspicienda solo,
nec quos piniferis positos in collibus hortos
    spectat Flaminiae Clodia iuncta viae.
45 quos ego nescio cui colui, quibus ipse solebam
    ad sata fontanas, nec pudet, addere aquas:
sunt ubi,[1] si vivunt, nostra quoque consita quaedam,
    sed non et nostra poma legenda manu.
pro quibus amissis utinam contingere possit
50   hic saltem profugo glaeba colenda mihi!
ipse ego pendentis, liceat modo, rupe capellas,
    ipse velim baculo pascere nixus oves;
ipse ego, ne solitis insistant pectora curis,
    ducam ruricolas sub iuga curva boves,
55 et discam Getici quae norunt verba iuvenci,
    adsuetas illis adiciamque minas.
ipse manu capulum pressi moderatus aratri
    experiar mota spargere semen humo.
nec dubitem longis purgare ligonibus herbas,
60   et dare iam sitiens quas bibat hortus aquas.
unde sed hoc nobis, minimum quos inter et hostem
    discrimen murus clausaque porta facit?
at tibi nascenti, quod toto pectore laetor,
    nerunt fatales fortia fila deae.
65 te modo Campus habet, densa modo porticus umbra,
    nunc, in quo ponis tempora rara, forum.
Umbria nunc revocat, nec non Albana petentem
    Appia ferventi ducit in arva rota.

[1] ibi

---

[1] Probably an estate near Alba.

³⁹ But, I suppose, the delights of the city have been
taken from me in my wretchedness in such fashion
that I may have at least what country joys I will ! It
is not for the fields lost to me that my heart longs, the
fair lands in the Paelignian country, nor for those
gardens lying on the pine-clad hills which the Clodian
and Flaminian roads survey—them I tilled for I
know not whom, in them I used in person to guide
(nor am I ashamed to say it) the spring water upon
the plants ; somewhere, if they still live, there are
certain trees also planted by my hand, but never is
my hand destined to gather their fruit. For all these
losses would that it could be my lot even here to have
in my exile a plot to till ! I would in person, if only I
might, pasture the goats as they hang upon the crags,
I would pasture the sheep as I leaned upon my staff ;
that my breast might not dwell upon its usual cares I
would myself lead the plough-oxen beneath the
curving yoke, teaching myself the words which the
Getic bullocks know, hurling at them the familiar
threats. In person would I control the handle of
the down-pressed plough and try to scatter seed in
the furrowed earth. I would not shrink from
clearing away the weeds with the long hoe and
supplying the water for the thirsty garden to
drink. But whence shall all this come to me
between whom and the enemy there is only the
breadth of a wall and a closed gate ? For you at
birth—my whole heart rejoices at this—the fateful
goddesses spun strong threads. You may stroll
now in the Campus, now in the dusky shade of some
portico, now in the forum, though you spend but
little time there ; Umbria now calls you home, or as
you seek your Albana,¹ the Appian road takes you

forsitan hic optes, ut iustam supprimat iram
70   Caesar, et hospitium sit tua villa meum.
a ! nimium est, quod, amice, petis : moderatius opta,
      et voti quaeso contrahe vela tui.
terra velim propior nullique obnoxia bello
      detur : erit [1] nostris pars bona dempta malis.

IX.

Quae mihi de rapto tua [2] venit epistula Celso,
      protinus est lacrimis umida facta meis ;
quodque nefas dictu, fieri nec posse putavi,
      invitis oculis littera lecta tua est.
5 nec quicquam ad nostras pervenit acerbius aures,
      ut sumus in Ponto, perveniatque precor.
ante meos oculos tamquam praesentis imago
      haeret, et extinctum vivere fingit amor.
saepe refert animus lusus gravitate carentes,
10   seria cum liquida saepe peracta fide.
nulla tamen subeunt mihi tempora densius illis,
      quae vellem vitae summa fuisse meae,
cum domus ingenti subito mea lapsa ruina
      concidit in domini procubuitque caput.
15 adfuit ille mihi, cum me pars magna reliquit,
      Maxime, fortunae nec fuit ipse comes.
illum ego non aliter flentem mea funera [3] vidi,
      ponendus quam si frater in igne foret.
haesit in amplexu consolatusque iacentem est,
20   cumque meis lacrimis miscuit usque suas.
o quotiens vitae custos invisus amarae
      continuit promptas in mea fata manus !

to the country on glowing wheels. There perchance you may wish that Caesar would abate his just wrath and that your villa may entertain me. Alas! 'tis too much that you ask, my friend; utter a more modest wish, furl the sails of your prayer, I beg. My wish is for a land nearer home, one not exposed to war; then a large part of my woes will be removed.

IX. To Maximus

Your letter with its news of Celsus' death was forthwith wetted by my tears: and though 'tis an impious thing to say and, as I thought, impossible, a letter of yours was read with unwilling eyes. Nothing more grievous has reached my ears since I have been in the Pontus, and I pray that nothing more bitter will come. His image lingers before my eyes as if he were present; he is gone, but love imagines him still alive. Often my heart recalls his gaiety freed from solemnity, often his serious tasks performed with transparent fidelity. But no hours come to my mind more frequently than those—would they had been the latest of my life—when my house on a sudden collapsed in utter ruin and fell upon its master's head. He stood by me when the greater part abandoned me, Maximus, and when he was not a partner in my fate. I saw him weeping my death as if perforce he had to lay his own brother in the flames. He clung to my embrace, he consoled me as I lay prostrate, he mingled his tears constantly with mine. How often did he, the then hated guardian of my bitter life, check the hands ready to bring about my

311

o quotiens dixit " placabilis ira deorum est :
    vive nec ignosci tu tibi posse nega " !
25 vox tamen illa fuit celeberrima, " respice, quantum
    debeat auxilium Maximus esse tibi.
Maximus incumbet, quaque est pietate, rogabit,
    ne sit ad extremum Caesaris ira tenax ;
cumque suis fratris vires adhibebit, et omnem,
30   quo levius doleas, experietur opem."
haec mihi verba malae minuerunt taedia vitae.
    quae tu ne fuerint, Maxime, vana cave.
huc quoque venturum mihi se iurare solebat
    non nisi te longae ius sibi dante viae.
35 nam tua non alio coluit penetralia ritu,
    terrarum dominos quam colis ipse deos.
crede mihi, multos habeas cum dignus amicos,
    non fuit e multis quolibet ille minor,
si modo non census nec clarum nomen avorum
40   sed probitas magnos ingeniumque facit.
iure igitur lacrimas Celso libamus adempto,
    cum fugerem, vivus [1] quas dedit ille mihi :
carmina iure damus raros testantia mores,
    ut tua venturi nomina, Celse, legant.
45 hoc est, quod possum Geticis tibi mittere ab arvis :
    hoc solum est istic quod licet esse meum.
funera non potui comitare nec ungere corpus,
    aque tuis toto dividor orbe rogis.
qui potuit, quem tu pro numine vivus habebas,
50   praestitit officium Maximus omne tibi.
ille tibi exequias et magni funus honoris
    fecit et in gelidos versit [2] amoma sinus,

          [1] vivo *corr.* ς   [2] vertit *corr. Heinsius*

death! How often did he say, "The wrath of the
gods may be appeased. Live, and do not say that
you cannot be pardoned"! But his most frequent
words were, "Think how great a help Maximus ought
to be to you. Maximus will make every effort and,
such is his loyalty, will beg that Caesar's wrath
persists not to the end. Together with his own
power he will employ that of his brother; he will try
every resource to lighten your pain."

³¹ These words diminished the weariness I felt in
my unfortunate life. Maximus, see to it that they
were not empty. He was wont to swear that he
would come to me even here and that no other but
yourself would afford him the right to make the long
journey. For he revered your house not otherwise
than you worship the gods who are lords of the
world. Believe me, although you possess deservedly
many friends, he was in no degree inferior to any of
them, if only 'tis true that not property nor the
illustrious names of ancestors, but uprightness and
character render men great.

⁴¹ Rightly then do I grant the meed of tears to
Celsus dead which he in life granted to me as I set
forth to exile. Rightly do I bestow verses bearing
witness to a rare character that those about to come
may read of thy name, Celsus. This is all that I can
send thee from the Getic land, this is the only thing in
Rome that I may have for mine. I had not the power
to follow thy funeral or anoint thy body: I am
separated by the whole world from thy tomb. He
who had the power, that Maximus whom thou didst in
life regard as a god, bestowed upon thee every
service. He conducted for thee a funeral with
ceremonials of great honour, pouring the balsam upon

diluit et lacrimis maerens unguenta profusis
    ossaque vicina condita texit humo.
55 qui quoniam extinctis, quae debet, praestat amicis,
    et nos extinctis adnumerare potest.

X.

Naso suo profugus mittit tibi, Flacce, salutem,
    mittere rem siquis, qua caret ipse, potest.
longus enim curis vitiatum corpus amaris
    non patitur vires languor habere suas.
5 nec dolor ullus adest, nec febribus uror anhelis,
    et peragit soliti vena tenoris iter.
os hebes est positaeque movent fastidia mensae,
    et queror, invisi cum venit hora cibi.
quod mare, quod tellus, adpone quod educat aër,
10   nil ibi, quod nobis esuriatur, erit.
nectar et ambrosiam, latices epulasque deorum,
    det mihi formosa nava [1] Iuventa manu,
non tamen exacuet torpens sapor ille palatum,
    stabit et in stomacho pondus inerte diu.
15 haec ego non ausim, cum sint verissima, cuivis
    scribere, delicias ne mala nostra vocet.
scilicet is status est, ea rerum forma mearum,
    deliciis etiam possit ut esse locus!
delicias illi precor has contingere, siquis
20   ne mihi sit levior Caesaris ira timet.
is quoque, qui gracili cibus est in corpore, somnus,
    non alit officio corpus inane suo.
sed vigilo vigilantque mei sine fine dolores,
    quorum materiam dat locus ipse mihi.

---

[1] nava] grata

[1] *i.e.* show me the same devotion which in my case may result
in help.   [2] Hebe.

thy cold breast. In grief he mingled with the unguents falling tears, laying thy bones to rest in the protection of neighbouring ground. He, since to dead friends he pays the debt he owes, may reckon me also with the dead.[1]

X. To Flaccus

Exiled Naso sends you a "Health," Flaccus, if one can send a thing that he himself lacks. For long continued lassitude has impaired my frame with bitter cares and suffers it not to possess its proper strength. I have no pain, I do not burn and gasp with fever, my pulse continues its normal beat. But my mouth lacks taste, I feel aversion for the courses set before me, and complain whenever the hour for hateful eating comes. Serve me with any product of sea or land or air; nothing will excite my hunger. Let nectar and ambrosia, the food and drink of the gods, be offered me by the shapely hand of busy Juventas,[2] yet that savour will not stimulate my sluggish palate and a weight will long remain in my inactive stomach.

[15] All this I should not venture to write to everybody, despite its truth, lest he should term my woes mere daintiness. Such in sooth is my condition, such is the nature of my circumstances that there is even the possibility of being dainty! I pray such daintiness as this may be the lot of any who fears that Caesar's wrath may rest too lightly upon me!

[21] Even that sleep which is food to a slender frame does not support as it should my impoverished body, but I am wakeful, my endless woes are wakeful too, for the place in which I am supplies them with

25 vix igitur possis visos agnoscere vultus,
  quoque ierit quaeras qui fuit ante color.
 parvus in exiles sucus mihi pervenit artus,
  membraque sunt cera pallidiora nova.
 non haec inmodico contraxi damna Lyaeo:
30 scis mihi quam solae paene bibantur aquae.
 non epulis oneror: quarum si tangar amore,
  est tamen in Geticis copia nulla locis.
 nec vires adimit Veneris damnosa voluptas:
  non solet in maestos illa venire toros.
35 unda locusque nocent et causa valentior istis,
  anxietas animi, quae mihi semper adest.
 hanc [1] nisi tu pariter simili cum fratre levares,
  vix mens tristitiae nostra tulisset onus.
 vos estis fracto tellus non dura phaselo,
40 quamque negant multi, vos mihi fertis opem.
 ferte, precor, semper, quia semper egebimus illa,
  Caesaris offensum dum mihi numen erit.
 qui meritam nobis minuat, non finiat, iram,
  suppliciter vestros quisque rogate deos.

[1] haec

material. Scarce could you recognize my features should you see them, and you would ask what has become of my former colour. But little vigour pervades my emaciated limbs; I am paler than fresh wax. These troubles I have not brought upon myself by immoderate drinking—you know that water is almost my only drink—nor do I overload myself with food; even if I had a passion for it, there is no opportunity in the Getic country. My strength is not impaired by Venus' ruinous passion; she is not wont to approach the couch of sorrow. 'Tis the water and the country that injure me together with a cause still stronger—the mental worry which ever attends me.

[37] Unless you and, like you, your brother were mitigating this worry, scarce would my mind have borne the burden of my sorrow. You are like a kindly land to a shattered boat; you bring me the aid which many deny. Give it me always, I beseech you, for I shall always need it as long as divine Caesar shall feel anger against me. That he may lessen, not end, his deserved wrath, let each of you as suppliants implore your gods.

LIBER SECUNDUS

I.

Huc quoque Caesarei pervenit fama triumphi,
    languida quo fessi vix venit aura Noti.
nil fore dulce mihi Scythica regione putavi :
    iam minus hic odio est, quam fuit ante, locus.
5 tandem aliquid pulsa curarum nube serenum
    vidi, fortunae verba dedique meae.
nolit ut ulla [1] mihi contingere gaudia Caesar,
    velle potest cuivis haec tamen una dari.
di quoque, ut a cunctis hilari pietate colantur,
10   tristitiam poni per sua festa iubent.
denique, quod certus furor est audere fateri,
    hac ego laetitia, si vetet ipse, fruar.
Iuppiter utilibus quotiens iuvat imbribus agros,
    mixta tenax segeti crescere lappa solet.
15 nos quoque frugiferum sentimus inutilis herba
    numen, et invita saepe iuvamur ope.
gaudia Caesareae gentis [2] pro parte virili
    sunt mea : privati nil habet illa domus.
gratia, Fama, tibi, per quam spectata triumphi
20   incluso mediis est mihi pompa Getis.

---

[1] noluit illa   [2] mentis *corr. Heinsius*

---

[1] Germanicus won the triumphal insignia (with Tiberius)

318

BOOK II

I. To Germanicus Caesar

Even to this place has the fame of Caesar's triumph [1] penetrated, whither scarce comes the weak breath of weary Notus. No pleasant news have I ever looked for in the Scythian land, but now this place is less hateful than it was before. At last the clouds of care have burst asunder and I have glimpsed a bit of clear sky; I have cheated my fate. E'en though Caesar may be unwilling that any joys befall me, yet this one joy it may be he wishes to have granted to everybody. Even the gods, to secure joyous worship from all, command men to lay aside sorrow throughout their feast days. In fine, though 'tis outright madness to dare the confession, this is a joy that I would make my own were he in person to forbid it.

[10] Whenever Jupiter floods the fields with helpful showers the tough burs are wont to grow mingled with the crops. I, too, useless weed though I am, feel the fructifying power, and am often benefited against his will. The joys of Caesar's family are mine to the extent of my capacity; that house has nothing that is private. Thanks, Fame, to thee through whom I, prisoned among the Getae, have seen the

against the Dalmatians, A.D. 9, but the actual celebration was postponed because of the defeat of Varus.

indice te didici nuper visenda coisse
    innumeras gentes ad ducis ora sui :
quaeque capit vastis inmensum moenibus orbem,
    hospitiis Romam vix habuisse locum.
25 tu mihi narrasti, cum multis lucibus ante
    fuderit assiduas nubilus Auster aquas,
numine caelesti solem fulsisse serenum,
    cum populi vultu conveniente die,
atque ita victorem cum magnae vocis honore
30   bellica laudatis dona dedisse viris,
claraque sumpturum pictas insignia vestes
    tura prius sanctis inposuisse focis,
iustitiamque sui caste [1] placasse parentis,
    illo quae [2] templum pectore semper habet,
35 quaque ierit felix adiectum plausibus omen,
    saxaque roratis erubuisse rosis ;
protinus argento versos imitantia muros
    barbara cum pictis [3] oppida lata viris,
fluminaque et montes et in altis proelia [4] silvis,
40   armaque cum telis in strue mixta sua,
deque tropaeorum, quod sol incenderit,[5] auro
    aurea Romani tecta fuisse fori,
totque tulisse duces captivis [3] addita collis
    vincula, paene hostis quot satis esse fuit.
45 maxima pars horum vitam veniamque tulerunt,
    in quibus et belli summa caputque Bato. [7]
cur ego posse negem minui mihi numinis iram,
    cum videam mitis hostibus esse deos ?
pertulit hic idem nobis, Germanice, rumor,
50   oppida sub titulo nominis isse [8] tui.

---

[1] castae *vel* castos *vel* iustos *corr. Scaliger*   [2] quo *corr. Scal.*
[3] victis   [4] proelia *Merkel*] proflua *vel* pascua
[5] incenderet *vel* incenderat : incenderit *s*
[6] captivos : captivis *s*   [7] Bato] fuit *vel* tenet   [8] esse

splendour of the triumph. By thy evidence I
learned that recently countless races assembled to see
their leader's face; and Rome, that embraces the
measureless world within her vast walls, scarce had
room for her guests. Thou didst tell me how, though
for many days before the cloudy Auster poured forth
constant rain, the sun through heavenly power shone
bright, the day matching the looks of the people; how
the victor, honouring them with a loud voice,
bestowed the warlike gifts upon the heroes he
praised; how as he was about to don the embroidered
vestments, the marks of glory, first he sprinkled
incense on the sacred hearth, appeasing in purity the
justice of his father which ever has a shrine in that
breast; how wherever he went, he received the happy
omen of applause and the pavement blushed with
dewy roses. Before him, silver counterparts of the
conquered walls, barbarian towns were carried with
pictured men upon them, rivers and mountains and
battles in deep forests, shields and spears in a
confused pile, and from the gold of the trophies
kindled by the sun, the buildings of the Roman forum
turned to gold. So many chieftains bore chains
upon their vanquished necks that they could almost
suffice to be the enemy. The greater part received
life and pardon, among them even Bato, head and
front of the war. Why should *I* deny that for me the
wrath of the deity could diminish when I see the gods
merciful to an enemy?

⁴⁹ The same report told me, Germanicus, that
towns [1] moved on under the title of thy name; that

---

[1] Models or "floats" representing the towns. See note on
Tr. iv. 2. 37.

atque ea te contra nec muri mole nec armis
    nec satis ingenio tuta fuisse loci.
di tibi dent annos, a te nam cetera sumes,
    sint modo virtuti tempora longa tuae.
55 quod precor, eveniet : sunt quiddam [1] oracula vatum :
    nam deus optanti prospera signa dedit.
te quoque victorem Tarpeias scandere in arces
    laeta coronatis Roma videbit equis ;
maturosque pater nati spectabit honores,
60   gaudia percipiens, quae dedit ipse suis.
iam nunc haec a me, iuvenum belloque togaque
    maxime, dicta tibi vaticinante nota.
hunc quoque carminibus referam fortasse triumphum,
    sufficiet nostris si modo vita malis,
65 imbuero Scythicas si non prius ipse sagittas,
    abstuleritque ferox hoc caput ense Getes.
quae si me salvo dabitur tua laurea templis,
    omina bis dices vera fuisse mea.

II.

Ille domus vestrae primis venerator ab annis,
    pulsus ad Euxini Naso sinistra freti,
mittit ab indomitis hanc, Messaline, salutem,
    quam solitus praesens est tibi ferre, Getis.
5 ei mihi, si [2] lecto vultus tibi nomine non est
    qui fuit, et dubitas cetera perlegere !
perlege, nec mecum pariter mea verba relega :
    urbe licet vestra versibus esse meis.
non ego concepi, Si Pelion Ossa tulisset,
10   clara mea tangi sidera posse manu,

---

       [1] quaedam *corr. Heinsius*   [2] si] quid

  [1] This prophecy was fulfilled A.D. 18, when Germanicus triumphed over the Germans.

against thee they had been secure neither by massive walls nor arms nor skilful site. God grant thee years! Thou thyself wilt supply all else, so but time enough be vouchsafed thy worth. My prayer shall be fulfilled; the prophecies of poets are of some worth, for the god has given favourable sign in answer to my prayer. Thou too shalt climb as victor[1] the Tarpeian citadel, a joyful sight for Rome, with garlanded steeds. Thy father shall see the ripe honours of his son, himself feeling the joy that he has given to his own. Even now, greatest of our youth in war and peace, mark these words of prophecy from me. That triumph also perchance I shall relate in song if only my life proves equal to my misfortunes, if I do not first stain Scythian arrows with my blood, if a fierce Getan does not take life from me with the sword. In my lifetime should thy laurel be dedicated in the temple thou wilt say that my prophecies have twice[2] come true.

II. To Messalinus

He who revered your house from his earliest years, Naso, the exile on Euxine's left-hand shore,[3] sends to you, Messalinus, from the land of the unconquered Getae this greeting which he used to offer face to face. Alas! if at the reading of his name you have not the countenance you had of old and hesitate to read what remains. Yet read to the end, nor banish my words along with myself; my verses are permitted to dwell in your city. I never imagined that should Ossa uphold Pelion, my hand could touch the

[2] *i.e.* Germanicus' triumph and the poet's promised eulogy, *cf.* v. 63.   [3] *Cf. Tr.* iv. 1. 60 *n.*

nec nos Enceladi dementia castra secuti
   in rerum dominos movimus arma deos,
nec, quod Tydidae temeraria dextera fecit,
   numina sunt telis ulla petita meis.
15 est mea culpa gravis, sed quae me perdere solum
   ausa sit, et nullum maius adorta nefas.
nil nisi non sapiens possum timidusque vocari :
   haec duo sunt animi nomina vera mei.
esse quidem fateor meritam post Caesaris iram
20   difficilem precibus te quoque iure meis ;
quaeque tua est pietas in totum nomen Iuli,
   te laedi, cum quis laeditur inde, putas.
sed licet arma feras et vulnera saeva mineris,
   non tamen efficies ut timeare mihi.
25 puppis Achaemeniden Graium Troiana recepit,
   profuit et Myso Pelias hasta duci.
confugit interdum templi violator ad aram,
   nec petere offensi numinis horret opem.
dixerit hoc aliquis tutum non esse.   fatemur.
30   sed non per placidas it mea puppis aquas.
tuta petant alii : fortuna miserrima tuta est,
   nam timor eventus deterioris abest.
qui rapitur *praeceps torrenti fluminis unda* [1]
   porrigit ad spinas duraque saxa manus,
35 accipitremque timens [2] pennis trepidantibus ales
   audet ad humanos fessa venire sinus,
nec se vicino dubitat committere tecto,
   quae fugit infestos territa cerva canes.
da, precor, accessum lacrimis, mitissime, nostris,
40   nec rigidam timidis vocibus obde forem,

---

[1] *Archetype defective here : sense supplied by Housman*
[2] accipitrem metuens

bright stars; I have not joined the mad camp of
Enceladus and aroused war against the gods who rule
the world; I have not, like the rash hand of Tydeus'
son,[1] aimed my spear against the gods. My fault is
heavy, but 'tis one which has dared to destroy me
alone, attempting no greater crime. No term save
" senseless " and " timid " can be applied to me; these
are the two true words for my soul. It is indeed, I
admit, after I deserved Caesar's anger, with justice
that you are hard to my entreaties; such is your
devotion to all of the Iulean[2] name that you are
injured too if you think any of them is injured. But
though you take arms and threaten me with cruel
wounds, yet will you not make me fear you. The ship
of a Trojan succoured Achaemenides, Greek though
he was; the Pelian spear helped the Mysian
chieftain.[3] Sometimes the violator of a temple takes
refuge at the altar, not dreading to seek the aid of the
angered god. Someone may say this is not safe. I
admit it; but it is not through calm waters that my
bark sails. Let safety be the quest of others;
uttermost misery is safe, for it lacks fear of an
outcome still worse. One who is *swept away by a
river in flood* stretches out his arms and grasps at
thorns and hard rocks; in fear of the hawk a bird on
trembling wings ventures in weariness to come to
man's protection; the doe hesitates not to trust
herself to a house hard by when she flees in terror
from her enemies, the hounds.

[39] Grant, I beseech you, gentle friend, comfort to
my tears, shut not an unyielding door upon my timid

---

[1] Diomed, who wounded both Mars and Venus.
[2] The Julii claimed descent from Iulus, son of Aeneas.
[3] Telephus.

verbaque nostra favens Romana ad numina perfer,
    non tibi Tarpeio culta Tonante minus,
mandatique mei legatus suscipe causam :
    nulla meo quamvis nomine causa bona est.
45 iam prope depositus, certe iam frigidus aeger.
    servatus per te, si modo servor, ero.
nunc tua pro lassis nitatur gratia rebus,
    principis aeterni quam tibi praestat amor.
nunc tibi et eloquii nitor ille domesticus adsit.
50   quo poteras trepidis utilis esse reis.
vivit enim in vobis facundi lingua parentis,
    et res heredem repperit illa suum.
hanc ego, non ut me defendere temptet, adoro :
    non est confessi causa tuenda rei.
55 num tamen excuses erroris origine factum,
    an nihil expediat tale movere, vide.
vulneris id genus est quod, cum sanabile non sit.
    non contrectari tutius esse puto
lingua, sile !   non est ultra narrabile quicquam.
60   posse velim cineres obruere ipse meos.
sic igitur, quasi me nullus deceperit error,
    verba fac, ut vita, quam dedit ipse,[1] fruar ;
cumque serenus erit vultusque remiserit illos,
    qui secum terras imperiumque movent,
65 exiguam ne me praedam sinat esse Getarum,
    detque solum miserae mite, precare, fugae.
tempus adest aptum precibus.   valet ille videtque
    quas fecit vires, Roma, valere tuas.
incolumis [2] coniunx sua pulvinaria servat ;
70   promovet Ausonium filius imperium ;

---

          [1] ipse] ille   [2] incolumi

plea, favour me and carry my words to the Roman
gods whom you worship no less than the Tarpeian
thunderer; be the envoy of my message and
undertake my cause, though no cause in my name is
good.   Already nearly dead, at least a sick man who
already feels death's chill, I shall be saved by you if
only I am saved at all.   Now in behalf of weakness let
that influence struggle which the love of the eternal
Prince bestows upon you.   Now employ the brilliant
eloquence of your house with which you have been
able to bring aid to trembling accused.   For in you
both [1] lives the eloquent tongue of your father, which
has found in you its heir.   To this I turn, not that it
may try to defend me; one should not defend the
cause of an accused who makes confession.   Yet
consider whether you may palliate my act through
the source of my mistake or if it would be well to stir
up no such matter.   The wound is of such sort that,
since it is past healing, I deem it safer that it be not
touched.   Silence, tongue!   Nothing further can be
told!   Would I could bury my own ashes!

[61] So then, as if I had been beguiled by no mistake,
frame your plea that I may enjoy the life he granted
me.   When he is serene, when there is peace upon
those lineaments whose motion stirs the empire and
the world, beg him not to permit me to be a poor spoil
for the Getae, to grant a peaceful land for my
wretched exile.   A fitting time is at hand for
petitions: well is he and well, he sees, is it with the
work of his hands—thy strength, O Rome.   In
safety his consort guards her divine couch; his son [2] is
pushing out the bounds of the Ausonian empire;

---

[1] *i.e.* Messalinus and his brother Cotta Maximus.
[2] Tiberius.

praeterit ipse suos animo Germanicus annos,
    nec vigor est Drusi nobilitate minor.
adde nurum neptemque[1] pias natosque nepotum
    ceteraque Augustae membra valere domus;
75 adde triumphatos modo Paeonas, adde quieti
    subdita montanae brachia Dalmatiae.
nec dedignata est abiectis Illyris armis
    Caesareum famulo vertice ferre pedem.
ipse super currum placido spectabilis ore
80   tempora Phoebea virgine nexa tulit.
quem pia vobiscum proles comitavit euntem,
    digna parente suo nominibusque datis,
fratribus adsimiles,[2] quos proxima templa tenentis
    divus ab excelsa Iulius aede videt.
85 his Messalinus, quibus omnia cedere debent,
    primum laetitiae non negat esse locum.
quicquid ab his superest, venit in certamen amoris:
    hac hominum nulli parte secundus erit.
hanc colet ante diem qua, quae[3] decreta merenti,
90   venit honoratis laurea digna comis.
felices, quibus, o,[4] licuit spectare triumphos
    et ducis ore deos aequiperante frui!
at mihi Sauromatae pro Caesaris ore videndi
    terraque pacis inops undaque vincta[5] gelu.
95 si tamen haec audis et vox mea pervenit istuc,[6]
    sit tua mutando gratia blanda loco.

[1] neptesque   [2] adsimilis
[3] quamque *vel* qua quam (quamquam): qua quae *Owen*
[4] o] hos   [5] iuncta   [6] illuc, *sed cf*. istae *A*

---

[1] Drusus, son of Tiberius.
[2] Livilla, as wife first of the adopted Gaius Caesar (d. A.D. 4)
and later of the younger Drusus, and Agrippina, wife of
Germanicus, respectively.

the spirit of Germanicus outruns his years, and the
energy of Drusus[1] is not unequal to his noble
birth. Add too that his loyal daughter-in-law and
granddaughter[2], the sons of his grandsons, and all
the members of the Augustan house are well. Add
the triumph over Paeonia,[3] add the right arms
of mountainous Dalmatia constrained to peace.
Illyria has not disdained to throw aside her arms and
submit her enslaved head to a Caesar's foot. He
himself,[4] conspicuous with calm aspect in his car,
bore his temples garlanded by Phoebus' maid.[5] His
loyals sons[6] in your[7] company attended him as he
advanced, worthy of their parent and of the names
conferred upon them, like unto the brethren[8]
dwelling in the neighbouring temple whom the divine
Julius beholds from his lofty shrine. To these[9] to
whom all things ought to yield Messalinus refuses not
the foremost place in rejoicing : all that these do not
claim is matter for affection's rivalry ; therein to no
man will he take second place. Before all else he will
venerate this day on which the laurel decreed for
merit has been worthily placed upon honoured locks.

[91] Oh happy they to whom it has been vouchsafed
to view the triumph, to enjoy the godlike countenance
of the general! But I must gaze upon the Sauroma-
tae in place of Caesar's face, upon a land devoid of
peace, and waters in the bonds of frost. Yet if you
hear my words, if my voice can reach so far, let your
winning influence work to change my abode. This is

[3] *i.e.* Pannonia.
[4] Tiberius, the Caesar just mentioned. [5] Daphne, the laurel.
[6] Germanicus (adopted son) and Drusus.
[7] *i.e.* Messalinus and Cotta Maximus, *cf.* 1. 51.
[8] Castor and Pollux. [9] *i.e.* the emperor and his house.

329

hoc pater ille tuus primo mihi cultus ab aevo,
    siquid habet sensus umbra diserta, petit.
hoc petit et frater, quamvis fortasse veretur
100   servandi noceat ne tibi cura mei.
tota domus rogat hoc, nec tu potes ipse negare
    et nos in turbae parte fuisse tuae.
ingenii certe, quo nos male sensimus usos,
    Artibus exceptis, saepe probator eras.
105 nec mea, si tantum peccata novissima demas,
    esse potest domui vita pudenda tuae.
sic igitur vestrae vigeant penetralia gentis,
    curaque sit superis Caesaribusque tui :
mite, sed iratum merito mihi, numen adora,
110   eximat[1] ut Scythici me[2] feritate loci.
difficile est, fateor, sed tendit in ardua virtus,
    et talis meriti gratia maior erit.
nec tamen Aetnaeus vasto Polyphemus in antro
    accipiet voces Antiphatesve tuas,
115 sed placidus facilisque parens veniaeque paratus,
    et qui fulmineo saepe sine igne tonat.
qui cum triste aliquid statuit, fit tristis et ipse,
    cuique fere poenam sumere poena sua est.
victa tamen vitio est huius clementia nostro,
120   venit et ad vires ira coacta suas.
qui quoniam patria toto sumus orbe remoti,
    nec licet ante ipsos procubuisse deos,
quos colis, ad superos haec fer mandata sacerdos,
    adde sed et proprias ad mea verba preces.
125 sic tamen haec tempta, si non nocitura putabis.
    ignosces.   timeo naufragus omne fretum.

---

[1] eximar   [2] me *om.: add.* s

the request of your famed father whom I worshipped
from my earliest youth, if his shade, still eloquent,
has aught of sentience. This is the request of your
brother too, though perchance he may fear that care
in saving me may bring you harm. All your house
ask this, nor can you yourself say that I too was not
once a member of your throng. At least my talent,
which, as I have learned to feel, I have used but ill,
was oft, except only my "Art," the subject of your
praise. Nor can my life, so you but take away its
latest sins, bring shame upon your house. So,
therefore, may the home of your race thrive, so may
those above, together with the Caesars, watch over
you—on condition that you implore that deity, so
merciful yet justly angry with me, to remove me from
the wildness of the Scythian land. 'Tis hard, I
admit, yet virtue aims at what is hard, and gratitude
for such a service will be all the greater. No
Polyphemus in the lonely caverns of Aetna, no
Antiphates will receive your words, but a calm and
lenient father ready to pardon, who often thunders
without the aid of the fiery lightning, who after a
harsh decision is himself saddened, who usually lays a
penalty upon himself whenever he exacts one. Yet
his mercy was defeated by my fault, his wrath by
compulsion reached its full strength. But I am
separated from my country by the whole world's
span, I cannot throw myself before the deity's
feet. You worship him: be my priest and carry to
him my message, but add your own prayers to my
words. Yet try this only if you feel it will not injure
me. Pardon! I am a shipwrecked man who fears
every sea.

OVID

III.

Maxime, qui claris nomen virtutibus aequas,
  nec sinis ingenium nobilitate premi,
culte mihi—quid enim status hic a funere differt ?—
  supremum vitae tempus adusque meae,
5 rem facis, afflictum non aversatus amicum,
  qua non est aevo rarior ulla tuo.
turpe quidem dictu, sed, si modo vera fatemur,
  vulgus amicitias utilitate probat.
cura, quid expediat, prior[1] est, quam quid sit honestum,
10 et cum fortuna statque caditque fides.
nec facile invenias multis in milibus unum,
  virtutem pretium qui putet esse sui.
ipse decor recte facti, si praemia desint,
  non movet, et gratis paenitet esse probum.
15 nil[2] nisi quod prodest carum est : i,[3] detrahe menti
  spem fructus avidae, nemo verendus[4] erit.
at reditus iam quisque suos amat, et sibi quid sit
  utile, sollicitis supputat articulis.
illud amicitiae quondam venerabile nomen
20 prostat et in quaestu pro meretrice sedet.
quo magis admiror, non, ut torrentibus undis,
  communis vitii te quoque labe trahi.
diligitur nemo, nisi cui fortuna secunda est :
  quae, simul intonuit, proxima quaeque fugat.
25 en ego, non paucis quondam munitus amicis,
  dum flavit velis aura secunda meis,
ut fera nimboso tumuerunt aequora vento,
  in mediis lacera nave relinquor aquis ;
cumque alii nolint etiam me nosse videri,
30 vix duo proiecto tresve tulistis opem.

----

[1] prius   [2] nil] et
[3] sed *corr. Heinsius*   [4] petendus *corr. Madvig*

III. To Maximus

Maximus, you who match your name with illustrious virtues nor permit your nature to be eclipsed by your noble birth, I have revered you—for in what does my condition differ from death ?—even unto my life's latest day.   In not disowning an unfortunate friend you perform an act than which none is rarer in the age in which you live.   Shameful it is to say, yet the common herd, if only we admit the truth, value friendships by their profit.   They care more for advantage than for honour, and their loyalty stands or falls with fortune : nor can one easily find among many thousands a single man who considers virtue its own reward.   The very glory of a good deed, if it lacks rewards, affects men not ; unrewarded uprightness brings them regret. Nothing but profit is prized ; so take from the greedy mind hope of gain and nobody will be the object of respect.   Nowadays everybody loves his own income and reckons on anxious fingers what is of service to himself.   That once revered name of friendship is exposed for sale, awaiting gain like a courtesan.

So my admiration is the greater that you too are not carried away, as by a torrent, by the corruption of a common vice.   There is love for none except him whom fortune favours ; when once she thunders she puts all around to flight.   Behold me ! once supported by many friends—while a favouring breeze filled my sails—now that the wild seas have been swelled by the stormy wind, I am abandoned on a shattered bark in the midst of the waters.   While others would not even seem to know me, there were but two or three of you who aided me when I was

333

quorum tu princeps.   neque enim comes esse, sed
    auctor,
  nec petere exemplum, sed dare dignus eras.
te, nihil exactos [1] nisi nos [2] peccasse fatentem,
  sponte sua probitas officiumque iuvat.
35 iudice te mercede caret per seque petenda est
  externis virtus incomitata bonis.
turpe putas abigi,[3] quia sit miserandus, amicum,
  quodque sit infelix, desinere esse tuum.
mitius est lasso digitum supponere mento,
40 mergere quam liquidis ora natantis aquis.
cerne quid Aeacides post mortem praestet amico :
  instar et hanc vitam mortis habere puta.
Pirithoum Theseus Stygias comitavit ad undas :
  a Stygia quantum mors mea distat aqua ?
45 adfuit insano iuvenis Phoceus Orestae :
  et mea non minimum culpa furoris habet.
tu quoque magnorum laudes admitte virorum,
  utque facis,[4] lapso quam potes affer opem.
si bene te novi, si, qui [5] prius esse solebas,
50 nunc quoque es, atque animi non cecidere tui,
quo Fortuna magis saevit, magis ipse resistis,
  utque decet, ne te vicerit illa, caves ;
et bene uti pugnes, bene pugnans efficit hostis.
  sic eadem prodest causa nocetque mihi.
55 scilicet indignum, iuvenis carissime, ducis
  te fieri comitem stantis in orbe deae.
firmus es, et quoniam non sunt ea, qualia velles,
  vela regis quassae qualiacumque ratis.

---

[1] ex acto : exactos *Ehwald*   [2] nos] non *vel* vos
       [3] abici   [4] ut facis et
     [5] qui, *cf.* quid *A*] quis : quod ς

cast forth. And you were foremost; for you were
suited not to be their comrade, but their leader, not to
seek an example, but to offer one. You who admit
that I, the exiled one, did naught but "err," take
pleasure in uprightness and duty for their own sakes.
In your judgment worth is dissevered from reward
and is to be sought for herself, even unaccompanied
by outward goods. You think it base to drive away
a friend because he is to be pitied, to forbid him your
friendship because he is ill-starred. 'Tis more merci-
ful to support his weary chin even with a finger than
to thrust the swimmer's face beneath the clear waves.

41 See what the scion [1] of Aeacus does for his friend [2]
after death, and remember that this life of mine also is
like unto death! Pirithous had Theseus' company
to the waves of the Styx; how far is my death from
the Stygian water? Crazed Orestes was helped by
the Phocean youth [3]; my fault too involves no little
madness. Do you also accept the praise meet for
mighty heroes and, as you are doing, bring what aid
you can to one who is fallen. If I know you well, if
even now you are what you used to be, and your
courage has not failed you, the greater Fortune's
rage, the more do you resist her, taking care, as is
fitting, that she does not conquer you; and your own
fight is rendered strong by the strong battling of the
foe. Thus the same thing both helps and injures
me. Yea, 'tis an unworthy thing in your sight, dear
youth, to become a companion of the goddess who
stands on the sphere. You are steadfast and since the
sails of the battered ship are not what you would wish,
you control them, such as they are. The craft is so

---

[1] Achilles.　　　[2] Patroclus.　　　[3] Pylades.

quaeque ita concussa est, ut iam casura putetur,
60   restat adhuc umeris fulta ruina tuis.
ira quidem primo fuerat tua iusta, nec ipso
    lenior, offensus qui mihi iure fuit.
quique dolor pectus tetigisset Caesaris alti,
    illum iurabas protinus esse tuum.
65 ut tamen audita est nostrae tibi cladis origo,
    diceris erratis ingemuisse meis.
tum tua me primum solari littera coepit
    et laesum flecti spem dare posse deum.
movit amicitiae tum te constantia longae,
70   ante tuos ortus quae mihi coepta fuit,
et quod eras aliis factus, mihi natus amicus,
    quodque tibi in cunis oscula prima dedi.
quod, cum vestra domus teneris mihi semper ab annis
    culta sit, esse vetus me tibi cogit onus.
75 me tuus ille pater, Latiae facundia linguae
    cui [1] non inferior nobilitate fuit,
primus, ut auderem committere carmina famae,
    impulit: ingenii dux fuit ille mei.
nec quo sit primum nobis a tempore cultus
80   contendo fratrem posse referre tuum.
te tamen ante omnis ita sum conplexus, ut unus
    quolibet in casu gratia nostra fores.
ultima me tecum vidit maestisque cadentes
    excepit lacrimas Aethalis Ilva [2] genis:
85 cum tibi quaerenti, num verus nuntius esset,
    attulerat culpae quem mala fama meae,
inter confessum dubie [3] dubieque negantem
    haerebam, pavidas dante timore notas,
exemploque nivis, quam mollit aquaticus Auster,
90   gutta per attonitas ibat oborta genas.

[1] quae *corr. Housman*   [2] aeithali silva *etc. corr. Rutgers*
[3] dubie] medius: *om.* A

shattered that men expect it to founder at once, but
your shoulders still support the wreck. At first
indeed your wrath was just nor milder than his who
was rightly angered against me. The feeling which
had touched the breast of lofty Caesar—that feeling
you swore forthwith was yours. Yet when you
heard the cause of my disaster, they say you groaned
over my mistake. At that time your letter was
the first to comfort me, bringing the hope that the
injured god could be moved. Then you were stirred
by the constancy of long friendship that began
before your birth, because for others you had become,
for me you had been born, a friend, because I gave
you the first kisses in your cradle. This, since I
have constantly revered your house from my earliest
years, makes me perforce a burden of long standing
upon you. That famed father of yours, who
enjoyed an eloquence in Latin as lofty as his
birth, first urged me to venture upon the publi-
cation of my verse: he was the guide of my
genius. Nor can your brother, I maintain,
recall the time of my first honour to him.
But to you above all I clung so close that
you alone, whate'er befell, were my source
of favour. Aethalian Ilva[1] last saw us to-
gether and received the tears as they fell from
our sorrowing cheeks. Then at your question
whether the news was true which the ill repute
of my sin had brought, I wavered between dubious
confession and dubious denial, fear telling the
tale of my timidity, and like the snow which
rainy Auster melts tears of dismay welled
up and coursed along my cheeks. And so as

[1] The modern Elba.

337

haec igitur referens et quod mea crimina primi
    erroris venia posse latere vides,
respicis antiquum lassis in rebus amicum,
    fomentisque iuvas vulnera nostra tuis.
95 pro quibus optandi si nobis copia fiat,
    tam bene promerito commoda mille precer.[1]
sed si sola mihi dentur tua vota, precabor
    ut tibi sit salvo Caesare salva parens.
haec ego, cum faceres altaria pinguia ture,
100   te solitum memini prima rogare deos.

IV.

Accipe conloquium gelido Nasonis ab Histro,
    Attice, iudicio non dubitande meo.
ecquid adhuc remanes memor infelicis amici,
    deserit an partis languida cura suas ?
5 non ita di mihi sunt tristes, ut credere possim
    fasque putem iam te non meminisse mei.
ante oculos nostros posita est[2] tua semper imago,
    et videor vultus mente videre tuos.
seria multa mihi tecum conlata recordor,
10   nec data iucundis tempora pauca iocis.
saepe citae longis visae sermonibus horae,
    saepe fuit brevior quam mea verba dies.
saepe tuas venit factum modo carmen ad auris
    et nova iudicio subdita Musa tuo est.
15 quod tu laudaras, populo placuisse putabam.
    hoc pretium curae dulce recentis[3] erat.
utque meus lima rasus liber esset amici,
    non semel admonitu facta litura tuo est.

---

[1] precor *corr. Heinsius*
[2] posita est] tua est *vel* tua stat *etc.*
[3] regentis

you recall this, seeing that 'tis possible for my sin, by condoning my original mistake, to lie unnoticed, you take thought of your old friend in his misfortunes, you soothe and help my wounds. For this, should full petition be granted me, I should invoke a thousand blessings upon you for your kindly service, but if I be allowed only your own vows, I will pray, after Caesar's weal, for that of your mother. This, when you enriched the altar with incense, you were wont to ask first of all, I remember, of the gods.

IV. To Atticus

Let Naso converse with you from the freezing Hister, Atticus, friend whom my judgment should not doubt. Do you still remain at all mindful of your unhappy friend or has your regard grown weak and abandoned its rôle ? The gods are not so harsh to me that I can believe and deem it just that you no longer think of me. Before my eyes your image ever stands ; I seem in thought to see your features. I recall many serious talks that we have had and not a few hours given over to pleasant jest. Oft did the hours seem too swift for our long talks, oft the day was too short for my words. Oft came to your ears a poem I had just composed ; a new effort was subjected to your criticism. What you had praised I considered had already pleased the public ; this was the pleasant reward of my latest efforts. To have my book touched by the file of a friend I have more than once made an erasure at your suggestion.

nos fora viderunt pariter, nos porticus omnis,
20   nos via, nos iunctis curva theatra locis.
denique tantus amor nobis, carissime, semper,
   quantus in Aeacide Nestorideque fuit.
non ego, si biberes securae pocula Lethes,
   excidere haec credam pectore posse tuo.
25 longa dies citius brumali sidere, noxque
   tardior hiberna solstitialis erit,
nec Babylon aestum, nec frigora Pontus habebit,
   calthaque Paestanas vincet odore rosas,
quam tibi nostrarum veniant oblivia rerum.
30   non ita pars fati candida nulla mei est.
ne tamen haec dici possit fiducia mendax
   stultaque credulitas nostra fuisse, cave,
constantique fide veterem tutare sodalem,
   qua licet et quantum non onerosus ero.

V.

Condita disparibus numeris ego Naso Salano
   praeposita misi verba salute meo.
quae rata sit, cupio, rebusque ut comprobet omen,
   te precor a salvo possit, amice, legi.
5 candor, in hoc aevo res intermortua paene,
   exigit ut faciam talia vota tuus.
nam fuerim quamvis modico tibi iunctus ab usu,
   diceris exiliis indoluisse meis ;
missaque ab Euxino legeres cum carmina Ponto,
10   illa tuus iuvit qualiacumque favor ;
optastique brevem salvi mihi Caesaris iram,
   quod tamen optari, si sciat, ipse sinat.
moribus ista tuis tam mitia vota dedisti,
   nec minus idcirco sunt ea grata mihi.

The fora saw us side by side, every portico, every
street; the hollow theatre found us in adjoining
seats. In short our affection, dear friend, was
always as strong as that of the scions of Aeacus and
Nestor. Not even were you drinking draughts of
care-dispelling Lethe, could I believe that all this
could fall from your heart. Sooner shall the long
days come to pass in winter, sooner shall the nights of
summer be longer than those of winter, Babylon have
no heat, Pontus no cold, sooner shall the lily surpass
the Paestan rose in perfume than you shall forget
your relations with me. Not so black is any part of
my fate. But beware lest this trust of mine be called
fallacious or my belief foolish; with steadfast faith
defend your old comrade in what way you can and in
so far as I shall not be burdensome.

V. To Salanus

A poem framed in unequal numbers I, Naso, send
to my Salanus, prefaced by a wish for his weal. May
this be so, I earnestly desire, and I pray that you, my
friend, to prove the omen in fact, may be able to read
it safe and sound. Your noble nature, a thing almost
at the point of death in this age, requires such prayer
from me. For though I was joined to you by only
moderate association, they say that you have grieved
over my exile; when you read verses sent from the
Euxine Pontus, your kindness helped them whatever
their worth; you wished Caesar's health and a
relaxation of his anger against me, a wish, that if he
knew, he would yet permit. To your character was
due so kind a wish, and it is none the less pleasing

15 quodque [1] magis moveare malis, doctissime, nostris,
   credibile est fieri condicione loci.
   vix hac invenies totum, mihi crede, per orbem,
   quae minus Augusta pace fruatur humus.
   tu tamen hic structos inter fera proelia versus
20   et legis et lectos ore favente probas,
   ingenioque meo, vena quod paupere manat,
   plaudis, et e rivo flumina magna facis.
   grata quidem sunt haec animo suffragia nostro,
   vix sibi cum miseros posse placere putes. [2]
25 dum tamen in rebus temptamus carmina parvis,
   materiae gracili sufficit ingenium.
   nuper, ut huc magni pervenit fama triumphi,
   ausus sum tantae sumere molis opus.
   obruit audentem rerum gravitasque nitorque,
30   nec potui coepti pondera ferre mei.
   illic, quam laudes, erit officiosa voluntas:
   cetera materia debilitata iacent.
   qui si forte liber vestras pervenit ad auris,
   tutelam mando sentiat ille tuam.
35 hoc tibi facturo, vel si non ipse rogarem,
   accedat cumulus gratia nostra levis.
   non ego laudandus, sed sunt tua pectora lacte
   et non calcata candidiora nive:
   mirarisque alios, cum sis mirabilis ipse,
40   nec lateant artes eloquiumque tuum.
   te iuvenum princeps, cui dat Germania nomen,
   participem studii Caesar habere solet.

---

[1] quoque corr. *Magnus*   [2] putas *vel* putat

to me for that reason.   And the fact that you are the
more moved by my woes, learned friend, is credibly
imputed to the character of my place of exile.   You
will scarce find in the whole world, I assure you, a
land that enjoys so little the Augustan Peace.

[19] Yet you are reading here verses composed amid
fierce battles, and when you have read, your
favouring lips approve them.   My talent, trickling
now in so impoverished a stream, wins your applause
and from a rivulet you make a mighty river.
Gratifying indeed to my soul is this suffrage of yours,
even though one might think that the wretched can
scarce be pleased with themselves.   Still so long as I
attempt verse on humble themes my talent is equal to
the meagre subject. Recently when the report of a
mighty triumph reached me, I ventured to undertake
a work [1] of great difficulty. My venture was
overwhelmed by the grandeur and splendour of the
theme ; I was not able to bear up under the weight of
my task.   Therein you will find worthy of praise the
will to do my duty; all else lies overpowered by the
subject.   If perchance that composition has reached
your ear, I direct that it may know your protection.
To you, who would do this even if I did not ask it in
person, let your favour to me contribute as a slight
incentive.   I do not deserve your praise, but your
heart is whiter than milk, than untrodden snow ; you
feel admiration for others, though you are worthy of
it yourself since your accomplishments and your
eloquence are open to the view of all.

[41] You are wont to share the studies of the leader of
the youth, that Caesar on whom Germany bestows a

---

[1] Perhaps the elegy to Germanicus (*Ex P*. ii. 1).

tu comes antiquus, tu primis iunctus ab annis
 ingenio mores aequiperante places.
45 te dicente prius fit protinus impetus illi :
 teque habet elicias qui sua verba tuis.
cum tu desisti mortaliaque ora quierunt
 tectaque non longa conticuere mora,
surgit Iuleo iuvenis cognomine dignus,
50 qualis ab Eois Lucifer ortus aquis.
dumque silens adstat, status est vultusque diserti,
 spemque decens doctae vocis amictus [1] habet.
mox, ubi pulsa mora est atque os caeleste solutum,
 hoc superos iures more solere loqui,
55 atque " haec est " dicas " facundia principe digna " :
 eloquio tantum nobilitatis inest.
huic tu cum placeas et vertice sidera tangas,
 scripta tamen profugi vatis habenda putas.
scilicet ingeniis aliqua est concordia iunctis,
60 et servat studii foedera quisque sui :
rusticus agricolam, miles fera bella gerentem,
 rectorem dubiae navita puppis amat.
tu quoque Pieridum studio, studiose, teneris,
 ingenioque faves, ingeniose, meo.
65 distat opus nostrum, sed fontibus exit ab isdem :
 artis et ingenuae cultor uterque sumus.
thyrsus abest a te [2] gustata et [3] laurea nobis,
 sed tamen ambobus debet inesse calor :
utque meis numeris tua dat facundia nervos,
70 sic venit a nobis in tua verba nitor.

---

[1] amicus *corr. Heinsius*
[2] abest a te *Rothmaler*] sublestate (*A*) *vel* ubi est a te *vel* enim
vobis [3] est *corr. Rothmaler*

---

[1] *See note on Ex P*. i. 1. 46.
[2] The Romans laid great stress on the grace and appropriateness of the orator's dress.

name.   You have been for long his companion, you
have been in union with him from his earliest years,
finding favour with him by virtue of a talent that
equals your character.   Under your guidance as a
speaker he forthwith attains fiery eloquence, in you
he has one to lure forth his words by your
own.   When you have finished and mortal lips have
become quiet, closed in silence for a short space, then
arises the youth worthy of the Iulean [1] name, as rises
Lucifer from the eastern waters, and as he stands in
silence, his posture, his countenance are those of an
orator, and his graceful robe gives hope of eloquent
words.[2]   Then after a pause he opens his godlike lips
and one might take oath that the gods above speak in
this fashion.   One might exclaim, "This is eloquence
worthy of a prince," such nobility is in his utterance.

[57] Though you find favour with this youth,
touching the very stars with your head, yet you
consider the writings of an exiled bard worthy of
consideration.   Surely there is some bond of har-
mony between kindred spirits, each keeping the
compacts that belong to his pursuit.   The peasant
loves the farmer, the soldier him who wages war, the
sailor the pilot of the swaying ship.   You too are pos-
sessed with devotion to the Pierians, studious one;
you, talented yourself, look with favour on my talent.
Our work differs, but it derives from the same
sources; we are both worshippers of liberal art.   The
thyrsus and laurel tasted by me are foreign to you;[3]
but we both need fire: as my numbers receive vigour
from your eloquence, so I lend brilliance to your words.

[3] Thyrsus, a symbol of poetic inspiration which was also
thought to be caused by tasting laurel, cf. Juv. vii. 19
laurumque momordit.   But the text is far from certain.

iure igitur studio confinia carmina vestro
  et commilitii sacra tuenda putas.
pro quibus ut maneat, de quo censeris, amicus
  comprecor ad vitae tempora summa tuae,
75 succedatque suis[1] orbis moderator[2] habenis :
  quod mecum populi vota precantur idem.

VI.

Carmine Graecinum, qui praesens voce solebat,
  tristis ab Euxinis Naso salutat aquis.
exulis haec vox est : praebet mihi littera linguam,
  et si non liceat scribere, mutus ero.
5 corripis, ut debes, stulti peccata sodalis,
  et mala me meritis ferre minora doces.[3]
vera facis, sed sera meae convicia culpae :
  aspera confesso verba remitte reo.
cum poteram recto transire Ceraunia velo,
10 ut fera vitarem saxa, monendus eram.
nunc mihi naufragio quid prodest discere[4] facto,
  quam mea debuerit currere cumba viam ?
brachia da lasso potius prendenda natanti,
  nec pigeat mento supposuisse manum.
15 idque facis, faciasque precor : sic mater et uxor,
  sic tibi sint fratres totaque salva domus,
quodque soles animo semper, quod voce precari,
  omnia Caesaribus sic tua facta probes.

---

[1] tuis   [2] moderatus   [3] doles *corr. Faber*
        [4] dicere

By right then you think my poetry connected with your pursuit and you believe that the rites of our common warfare should be preserved. Therefore may the friend through whom you win esteem remain, I pray, yours unto the last moment of your life, and may he come to the control of the world with his own reins. This is at once my prayer and that of the people.

VI. To Graecinus

In verse, Graecinus, that Naso who used to greet you face to face in spoken words, greets you sadly from the Euxine waters. An exile's voice is this; letters furnish me a tongue, and if I may not write, I shall be dumb.

[5] You reprove as in duty bound the sins of your foolish friend, showing me that the evils that I suffer are less than my deserts. You are right, but too late is your reproof of my fault: relax the harshness of your words for an accused who has confessed. At the time when I could have passed Ceraunia with standing sails, so as to avoid the cruel reefs, then it was that I should have had your warning. Now after my shipwreck how does it profit me to learn what course my bark should have run? Rather extend an arm to the weary swimmer's grasp; repent not of supporting his chin with your hand. That you are doing and, I pray, will continue to do: so may your mother and wife, so may your brothers and all your house be free from harm, and—as you are wont to pray with heart, with voice—so for all your acts may you find the Caesars' approval. It will be shame

347

turpe erit in miseris veteri tibi rebus amico
20   auxilium nulla parte tulisse tuum.
turpe referre pedem, nec passu stare tenaci,
    turpe laborantem deseruisse ratem ;
turpe sequi casum et fortunae cedere [1] amicum
    et, nisi sit felix, esse negare suum.
25 non ita vixerunt Strophio atque Agamemnone nati,
    non haec Aegidae Pirithoique fides :
quos prior est mirata, sequens mirabitur aetas,
    in quorum plausus tota theatra sonant.
tu quoque per durum servato tempus amico
30   dignus es in tantis nomen habere viris.
dignus es, et, quoniam laudem pietate mereris,
    non erit officii gratia surda tui.
crede mihi, nostrum si non mortale futurum est
    carmen, in ore frequens posteritatis eris.
35 fac modo permaneas lasso, Graecine, fidelis,
    duret et in longas impetus iste moras.
quae tu cum praestes, remo tamen utor in aura :
    non nocet admisso subdere calcar equo.

VII.

Esse salutatum vult te mea littera primum
    a male pacatis, Attice, missa Getis.
proxima subsequitur, quid agas, audire voluntas,[2]
    et si, quidquid [3] agis, sit tibi cura mei.
5 nec dubito quin sit, sed me timor ipse malorum
    saepe supervacuos cogit habere metus.
da veniam, quaeso, nimioque ignosce timori.
    tranquillas etiam naufragus horret aquas.

---

[1] accedere, *at cf. Tib*. iv. 13. 17   [2] voluptas
    [3] si quid *vel* iam si quid *vel* nunc quicquid

if you do not lift a finger to help an old friend in trouble. Just as it is shame to retire in battle and not stand firm, shame to abandon a labouring ship, so it is shame to follow luck and yield one's friend to fate, and disown him except he be prosperous. Not such was the life of the sons[1] of Strophius and Agamemnon; not such was the loyalty of Aegeus' son[2] and Pirithous. Them past ages have admired, and ages to come will admire; to applaud them the whole theatre roars. You too who have held to your friend through times of stress deserve to have a name among such great men. You deserve it—yes, and since praise is the just reward of your loyalty, my gratitude for your service shall never be dumb. Trust me, if my song is not destined to die, you shall be often on the lips of posterity. Only see that you remain faithful to your weary friend, Graecinus, and let your impulse endure for long. Though you do me this service, yet I use the oar while I have the breeze: it does no harm to spur on the galloping steed.

VII. To Atticus

My letter sent from the scarce pacified Getae wishes first to salute you, Atticus; close follows the wish to hear how you fare and whether, no matter what your occupation, you have any interest in me. I doubt not you have, yet the very dread of misfortunes often forces me to feel empty fears. Grant me indulgence, I pray, pardon my excessive dread: the shipwrecked man shrinks even from calm waters.

---

[1] Pylades and Orestes.   [2] Theseus.

qui semel est laesus fallaci piscis ab hamo,
10   omnibus unca cibis aera subesse putat.
saepe canem longe visum fugit agna lupumque
    credit, et ipsa suam nescia vitat opem.
membra reformidant mollem quoque saucia tactum,
    vanaque sollicitis incutit [1] umbra metum.
15 sic ego Fortunae telis confixus iniquis
    pectore concipio nil nisi triste meo.
iam mihi fata liquet coeptos servantia cursus
    per sibi consuetas semper itura vias :
observare deos, ne quid mihi cedat amice,
20   verbaque Fortunae vix puto posse dari.
est illi curae me perdere, quaeque solebat
    esse levis, constans et bene certa nocet.
crede mihi, si sum veri tibi cognitus oris
    (nec fraus in [2] nostris casibus esse potest),
25 Cinyphiae segetis citius numerabis aristas,
    altaque quam multis floreat Hybla thymis,
et quot aves motis nitantur in aëre pinnis,
    quotque natent pisces aequore, certus eris,
quam tibi nostrorum statuatur summa laborum,
30   quos ego sum terra, quos ego passus aqua.
nulla Getis toto gens est truculentior orbe ;
    sed tamen hi nostris ingemuere malis.
quae tibi si memori coner perscribere versu,
    Ilias est fati longa futura mei.
35 non igitur vereor [3] quo [4] te rear esse verendum,
    cuius amor nobis pignora mille dedit,
sed quia res timida est omnis miser, et quia longo
    est
    tempore laetitiae ianua clausa meae.

---

[1] inmutat *vel* incitat *vel* concitat *corr.* ς   [2] planis
[3] verear   [4] quo] qua *vel* quia *vel* quod

The fish once wounded by the treacherous hook
fancies the barbed bronze concealed in every bit of
food. Ofttimes the lamb flees the distant sight of a
dog in the belief that it is a wolf, unwittingly avoiding
its own protector. A wounded body shrinks from
even a delicate touch ; an empty shadow inspires the
anxious with fear. So I, pierced by the unjust shafts
of Fortune, fashion in my breast naught but gloomy
thoughts. Already it is clear to me that fate,
keeping the course begun, will continue always to run
in a familiar path ; the gods are watching that no kind
concession be made me and I think Fortune can
scarcely be cheated. She is working to destroy me—
she who used to be fickle, is now steadfastly and with
determination injuring me. O believe, if I have
been known to you as a speaker of truth, (and it can-
not be that my misfortunes involve fraud,) [1] you
will more quickly count the ears of a crop by the
Cinyphus, or the many blooms of thyme upon
lofty Hybla, or count the number of birds floating in
air on vibrant wings or the fishes swimming in
the waters, than reckon the sum of woes I have
borne on land, on sea.

[31] No race in the wide world is grimmer than the
Getae, yet they have lamented over my misfortunes.
Should I attempt to a full record of them in verse,
there will be a long Iliad of my fate. I fear, therefore,
not that I think I need have fear of you of whose love I
have received a thousand pledges, but because every
unfortunate is a thing full of fear, because for a
long time the door of joy has been closed for me.

---

[1] The text of 1. 24 is uncertain. The meaning seems to be
that the poet's woes though real are incredible.

iam dolor in morem venit meus, utque caducis
40   percussu crebro saxa cavantur aquis,
sic ego continuo Fortunae vulneror ictu,
    vixque habet in nobis iam nova plaga locum.
nec magis assiduo vomer tenuatur ab usu,
    nec magis est curvis Appia trita rotis,
45 pectora quam mea sunt serie calcata [1] malorum,
    et nihil inveni, quod mihi ferret opem.
artibus ingenuis quaesita est gloria multis :
    infelix perii dotibus ipse meis.
vita prior vitio caret et sine labe peracta est [2] :
50   auxilii misero nil tulit illa mihi.
culpa gravis precibus donatur saepe suorum :
    omnis pro nobis gratia muta fuit.
adiuvat in duris aliquos [3] praesentia rebus :
    obruit hoc absens vasta procella caput.
55 quis [4] non horruerit tacitam [5] quoque Caesaris iram ?
    addita sunt poenis aspera verba meis.
fit fuga temporibus levior : proiectus in aequor
    Arcturum subii Pleïadumque minas.
saepe solent hiemem placidam sentire carinae :
60   non Ithacae puppi saevior unda fuit.
recta fides comitum poterat mala nostra levare :
    ditata est spoliis perfida turba meis.
mitius exilium faciunt loca : tristior ista
    terra sub ambobus non iacet ulla polis.
65 est aliquid patriis vicinum finibus esse :
    ultima me tellus, ultimus orbis habet.
praestat et exulibus pacem tua laurea, Caesar :
    Pontica finitimo terra sub hoste iacet.

[1] caecata   [2] est *om. A*   [3] aliquo
[4] quis *Heinsius*] quae *vel* quem (que) obruerit (-et)
[5] taciti

My grief has already become a habit; as the falling drops by their constant force hollow the rock, so am I wounded by the steady blows of fate until now I have scarce space upon me for a new wound. The ploughshare is not more thinned by constant use, the Appia [1] more worn by the curving wheels than my heart is worn by the hoof-beats of my continuous misfortunes; nothing have I found to bring me aid.

[47] By liberal arts many have sought renown; I, unhappy that I am, have been ruined by my own dower. My earlier life was free from fault, was lived without blemish, but it has brought me no succour in my misfortune. Serious fault is often pardoned to the prayers of one's friends; on my behalf all favour has been mute. Some are helped in their difficulties by the fact that they are present; I was absent when this mighty tempest overwhelmed me. Who would not dread even the unspoken wrath of Caesar? My punishment was enhanced by harsh words. The season makes exile lighter; I, driven forth upon the sea, endured Arcturus and the Pleiads' threats. Ships are often wont to experience a mild winter; not the Ithacan ship [2] had a fiercer sea. The upright loyalty of comrades could have alleviated my misfortunes, but a treacherous crowd grew rich on my spoils. Places render exile milder; a more dismal land than this lies not under either pole. 'Tis something to be near the confines of one's native land; the remotest land, the remotest world possesses me. Thy laurel, Caesar, assures peace even to exiles; the Pontic land lies exposed to a neighbouring

---

[1] The *via Appia*, the great highway from Rome to Capua.
[2] The ship of Ulysses.

OVID

tempus in agrorum cultu consumere dulce est :
70   non patitur verti barbarus hostis humum.
temperie caeli corpusque animusque iuvatur :
  frigore perpetuo Sarmatis ora riget.
est in aqua dulci non invidiosa voluptas :
  aequoreo bibitur cum sale mixta palus.
75 omnia deficiunt ; animus tamen omnia vincit :
  ille etiam vires corpus habere facit.
sustineas ut onus, nitendum vertice plano[1] est,
  aut, flecti nervos si patiere, cades.
spes quoque posse mora mitescere principis iram,
80   vivere ne nolim deficiamque, cavet.
nec vos parva datis pauci solacia nobis,
  quorum spectata est per mala nostra fides.
coepta tene, quaeso, neque in aequore desere navem,
  meque simul serva iudiciumque tuum.

VIII.

Redditus est nobis Caesar cum Caesare nuper,
  quos mihi misisti, Maxime Cotta, dei ;[2]
utque tuum munus numerum, quem debet, haberet,
  est ibi Caesaribus Livia iuncta suis.
5 argentum felix omnique beatius auro,
  quod, fuerit pretium cum rude, numen habet.
non mihi divitias dando maiora dedisses,
  caelitibus missis nostra sub ora tribus.
est aliquid spectare deos et adesse putare,
10   et quasi cum vero numine posse loqui.

[1] pleno *corr. Richmond*   [2] deos *corr. Hall*

354

foe. 'Tis pleasant to spend one's time in tilling the fields; the barbarian foe permits no sod to be turned. By a mild climate body and mind are helped; eternal cold freezes the Sarmatian coast. There is in sweet water a pleasure that stirs no envy; I drink marshy water mingled with the salt of the sea. I lack all things, but courage conquers all things; it even causes the body to have strength. To support the burden you must take the strain with shoulders level or, if you allow your sinews to yield, you will fall. Even the hope that 'tis possible time may soften the prince's wrath, prevents me from aversion to life and utter breakdown. And you give me no small comfort—the few whose fidelity has been tested by my misfortunes. Keep on as you have begun, I pray, do not abandon the ship upon the sea; preserve me and with me your own conviction.

VIII. To Cotta Maximus

I have recently received a Caesar in company of a Caesar[1]—the gods whom you sent me, Cotta Maximus; and that your gift might be complete, Livia appeared there united with her Caesars. Happy silver! more blessed than any gold! For though but recently rough metal 'tis now divine! Not by the gift of riches could you have given me a greater present than the three deities whom you have sent to my shores.

9 'Tis something to behold gods and think them present, to have the power to speak as it were with a

---

[1] Perhaps a medallion with likenesses of the imperial three: Augustus, Tiberius, and Livia.

quantum ad te,[1] redii, nec me tenet ultima tellus,
    utque prius, media sospes in urbe moror.
Caesareos video vultus, velut ante videbam :
    vix huius voti spes fuit ulla mihi :
15 utque salutabam numen caeleste, saluto.
    quod reduci tribuas, nil, puto, maius habes.
quid nostris oculis nisi sola Palatia desunt ?
    qui locus ablato Caesare vilis erit.
hunc ego cum spectem, videor mihi cernere Romam ;
20   nam patriae faciem sustinet ille suae.
fallor an irati mihi sunt in imagine vultus,
    torvaque nescio quid forma minantis habet ?
parce, vir inmenso maior virtutibus orbe,
    iustaque vindictae supprime lora tuae.
25 parce, precor,[2] saecli decus indelebile [3] nostri,
    terrarum dominum quem tua cura facit.
per patriae nomen, quae te tibi carior ipso est,
    per numquam surdos in tua vota deos,
perque tori sociam, quae par tibi sola reperta est,
30   et cui maiestas non onerosa tua est,
perque tibi similem virtutis imagine natum,
    moribus agnosci qui tuus esse potest,
perque tuos, vel avo dignos, vel patre nepotes,
    qui veniunt magno per tua iussa gradu,
35 parte leva minima nostras et contrahe poenas,
    daque, procul Scythico qui sit ab hoste, locum.
et tua, si fas est, a Caesare proxime Caesar,
    numina sint precibus non inimica meis.
sic fera quam primum pavido Germania vultu
40   ante triumphantis serva feratur equos :

---

[1] quanta meridi (*A*) *vel* quanta (quantum *vel* quando) a te (ad me) redii, *etc. corr. Ehwald*
[2] precor] puer
[3] admirabile *vel* o venerabile

real deity. So far as you could effect it, I have
returned, I am no more in a remote land ; as of old I
am safe in the midst of the city.   I see the faces of the
Caesars as I used before to see them ; of this prayer's
fulfilment I have scarce had any hope.   I salute the
deity of heaven as I used to do : even should I return,
no greater gift, I think, have you to bestow upon
me.   What do my eyes lack save only the Palatine ?
And that place, if Caesar is removed, will be
worthless.   As I gaze on him I seem to look on Rome,
for he embodies the likeness of our fatherland.   Am I
wrong or do the features of his portrait show anger
against me ?   Is his form somehow grim and threat-
ening ?   Spare me, thou who art mightier in thy
virtues than the measureless world, check the reins of
thy just vengeance.   Spare me, thou imperishable
glory of our age, lord of the world because of thine
own care.   By the name of our country which is
dearer to thee than thyself, by the gods who are never
deaf to thy prayers, by thy consort [1] who alone has
been found equal to thee, who feels not thy majesty a
burden, by thy son [2] like thee a model of virtue whose
character causes him to be recognized as thine, by thy
grandsons [3] worthy of their grandsire or their sire,
who advance with mighty stride along the path of thy
command, lighten in but the least degree and restrict
my punishment : grant me an abode far from the
Scythian enemy.

[37] And if 'tis right, O Caesar [2] nearest to Caesar,—
let not thy divinity be hostile to my prayers.   So
may wild Germany soon be borne with fear-stricken
countenance a slave before thy triumphant steeds ;

[1] Livia.   [2] Tiberius.
[3] Germanicus (by adoption) and Drusus sons of Tiberius.

OVID

sic pater in Pylios, Cumaeos mater in annos
    vivant, et possis filius esse diu.
tu quoque, conveniens ingenti nupta marito,
    accipe non dura supplicis aure preces.
45 sic tibi vir sospes, sic sint cum prole nepotes,
    cumque bonis nuribus quod peperere nurus.
sic, quem dira tibi rapuit Germania Drusum,
    pars fuerit partus sola caduca tui.
sic tibi mature fraterni funeris ultor
50   purpureus niveis filius instet equis.
adnuite o! timidis, mitissima numina, votis.
    praesentis aliquid prosit habere deos.
Caesaris adventu tuta [1] gladiator harena
    exit, et auxilium non leve vultus habet.
55 nos quoque vestra iuvat [2] quod, qua licet, ora videmus,
    intrata est superis quod domus una tribus.
felices illi, qui non simulacra, sed ipsos,
    quique deum coram corpora vera vident.
quod quoniam nobis invidit inutile fatum,
60   quos dedit ars, vultus effigiemque colo.
sic homines novere deos, quos arduus aether
    occulit, et colitur pro Iove forma Iovis.
denique, quae mecum est et erit sine fine, cavete,
    ne sit in inviso vestra figura loco.
65 nam caput hoc [3] nostra citius cervice recedet,
    et patiar fossis lumen abire genis,
quam caream raptis, o publica numina, vobis:
    vos eritis nostrae portus et ara fugae.

---

[1] tota; tuto *Owen*   [2] iuvet   [3] e *corr. s*

[1] Nestor.

so may thy father attain the years of the Pylian [1] and thy mother those of the Cumaean [2] and mayst thou be for long a son. Thou, too, spouse suited to a mighty husband, listen with no cruel ear to the prayers of a suppliant. So may thy husband be safe, so thy grandsons and their offspring, so thy good sons' wives and their children. So may that Drusus,[2] whom cruel Germany tore away from thee, be the only one of thy descendants to fall. So in the near future may the avenger of his brother's death drive, in purple clad, the snow-white steeds. Assent to my timorous prayers, ye kind deities! Let it profit me somewhat to have gods present before me. At Caesar's coming the gladiator leaves the arena in safety, for his countenance brings no slight aid. I too am helped because, so far as I am allowed, I gaze upon the features of you all, because three of the celestials have entered one home. Happy they who see not likenesses, but the reality, the real persons of the gods face to face. This has been begrudged me by hostile fate, and so I cherish the countenances and figures which art has produced. Thus it is that men know the gods whom the lofty aether conceals; they worship in Jupiter's stead the likeness of Jupiter. In fine make it your care that these your likenesses, which are with me and shall ever be with me, be not in a hateful place. For my head shall sooner leave my neck, sooner will I gouge out my eyes from my cheeks, than be deprived, O deities of the state, of you. You shall be the harbour, the altar of my exile.

[2] The Cumaean Sibyl who was 700 years old when she prophesied to Aeneas.

[3] The father of Germanicus. He was killed in Germany by a fall from his horse.

OVID

vos ego complectar, Geticis si cingar ab armis,
70　utque meas aquilas, ut mea [1] signa sequar.
aut ego me fallo nimiaque cupidine ludor,
　　aut spes exilii commodioris adest.
nam minus et minus est facies in imagine tristis,
　　visaque sunt dictis adnuere ora meis.
75　vera precor fiant timidae praesagia mentis,
　　iustaque quamvis est, sit minor ira dei.

IX.

Regia progenies, cui nobilitatis origo
　　nomen in Eumolpi pervenit usque, Coty,
fama loquax vestras si iam pervenit ad auris,
　　me tibi finitimi parte iacere soli,
5　supplicis exaudi, iuvenum mitissime, vocem,
　　quamque potes, profugo (nam potes) adfer opem.
me fortuna tibi—de qua quod non queror,[2] hoc est—
　　tradidit, hoc uno non inimica mihi.
excipe naufragium non duro litore nostrum,
10　ne fuerit terra tutior unda tua.
regia, crede mihi, res est succurrere lapsis,
　　convenit et tanto, quantus es ipse, viro.
fortunam decet hoc istam : quae maxima cum sit,
　　esse potest animo vix tamen aequa tuo.
15 conspicitur numquam meliore potentia causa,
　　quam quotiens vanas non sinit esse preces.
hoc nitor iste tui generis desiderat, hoc est
　　a superis ortae nobilitatis opus.
hoc tibi et Eumolpus, generis clarissimus auctor,[3]
　　et prior Eumolpo suadet Ericthonius.

---

　　[1] ut mea] tutaque *vel* vos mea *vel* signa ego vestra, *etc. corr.*
Korn.　　　　　　　　　　　[2] querar

360

You will I embrace when I am circled about by Getic arms; you will I follow as my eagles, as my standards.

[71] Either I am self-deceived or mocked by excessive longing, or else the hope of a more comfortable exile is at hand. For less and less stern are the features of the portrait—the lips seem to consent at my words. I pray that the premonitions of my fearful heart may become the truth, that although the god's wrath is just, it may grow less.

IX. To King Cotys

Cotys, scion of kings, whose noble line extends even to the name of Eumolpus, if talkative report has already come to your ears that I am lying in a neighbouring land, hear the voice of a suppliant, gentle youth, and bear what aid thou canst—and thou hast the power—to an exile. Fortune—of whom in this one thing I complain not—has given me over to thee; in this alone she is not hostile to me. Harbour my shipwreck on no cruel shore; let not the waters prove safer than thy land. 'Tis a royal deed, I assure thee, to help the fallen, it befits a man as mighty as thou art. This becomes thy position which, great though it is, can scarce be equal to thy spirit. Power is never seen in a better cause than when it does not permit prayers to be vain. This that brilliant birth of thine desires, this is the task of a nobility sprung from those above. This Eumolpus, the illustrious founder of thy race, and before Eumolpus Erich-

---

[3] generis . . . auctor] opus hoc tibi saudet erato

hoc tecum commune deo est,[1] quod uterque rogati
  supplicibus vestris ferre soletis opem.
numquid[2] erit, quare solito dignemur honore
  numina, si demas velle iuvare deos ?
25 Iuppiter oranti surdas si praebeat auris,
  victima pro templo cur cadat icta Iovis ?
si pacem nullam pontus mihi praestet eunti,
  irrita Neptuno cur ego tura feram ?
vana laborantis si fallat vota coloni,
30   accipiat gravidae cur suis exta Ceres ?
nec dabit intonso iugulum caper hostia Baccho,
  musta sub adducto si pede nulla fluent.
Caesar ut imperii moderetur frena precamur,
  tam bene quod patriae consulit ille suae.
35 utilitas igitur magnos hominesque deosque
  efficit, auxiliis quoque favente suis.
tu quoque fac prosis intra[3] tua castra iacenti,
  o Coty, progenies digna parente tuo.
conveniens homini est hominem servare voluptas,
40   et melius nulla quaeritur arte favor.
quis non Antiphaten Laestrygona devovet ? aut quis
  munifici mores improbat Alcinoi ?
non tibi Cassandreus pater est gentisve Pheraeae,[4]
  quive repertorem torruit arte sua :
45 sed quam Marte ferox et vinci nescius armis,
  tam numquam, facta pace, cruoris amans.
adde quod ingenuas didicisse fideliter artes
  emollit mores nec sinit esse feros.
nec regum quisquam magis est instructus ab illis,
50   mitibus aut studiis tempora plura dedit.

[1] deos (deis *vel* dei) : deo est *Riese*
[2] namquid   [3] profugus intra
[4] genitorve (gentisque) caphereus (caphareus)

thonius, enjoin. This thou hast in common with a
god : that ye are both wont to aid your
petitioners. Will there be any reason for us to grant
their usual honour to the gods, if one robs them of
their will to help ? If Jupiter should turn deaf ears
to prayer, why should a victim fall in sacrifice before
Jupiter's temple ? If the sea should offer no calm for
my journey, why should I offer vain incense to
Neptune ? Should she cheat the ineffectual prayers
of the toiling husbandman, why should Ceres receive
the entrails of a gravid sow ? The goat will not offer
his throat in sacrifice to unshorn Bacchus, if no must
flows from beneath the tread of feet. We pray that
Caesar may guide the reins of the empire because he
plans so wisely for his fatherland !

[35] Utility, then, renders great both men and gods, if
each bestows in favour his own peculiar aid. Do
thou also avail him who lies within thy camp, Cotys,
son worthy of thy father. 'Tis a fitting pleasure for
man to save man ; there is no better way of seeking
favour. Who does not curse Antiphates the
Laestrygonian ? Who disapproves the character of
generous Alcinous ? Thou hast for a father no
Cassandrean [1] or man of Pheraean race,[2] or him [3] who
burned the inventor by his own craft, but one who
though fierce in war and unacquainted with defeat in
arms, was yet never fond of blood when peace was
made. Note too that a faithful study of the liberal
arts humanizes character and permits it not to be
cruel. No king has been better trained by them or
given more time to humane studies. Thy verse

[1] Apollodorus of Cassandrea, a cruel tyrant.
[2] *i.e.* descended from Alexander, tyrant of Pherae.
[3] Phalaris, see *Tr.* iii. 11. 39 ff.

carmina testantur, quae, si tua nomina demas,
    Threïcium iuvenem composuisse negem ;
neve sub hoc tractu vates foret unicus Orpheus,
    Bistonis ingenio terra superba tuo est.
55 utque tibi est animus, cum res ita postulat, arma
    sumere et hostili tingere caede manum,
atque ut es excusso iaculum torquere lacerto
    collaque velocis flectere doctus equi,
tempora sic data sunt studiis ubi iusta paternis,
60   aque suis numeris [1] forte quievit opus,
ne tua marcescant per inertis otia somnos,
    lucida Pieria tendis in astra via.
haec quoque res aliquid tecum mihi foederis affert :
    eiusdem sacri cultor uterque sumus.
65 ad vatem vates orantia brachia tendo,
    terra sit exiliis ut tua fida meis.
non ego caede nocens in Ponti litora veni,
    mixtave sunt nostra dira venena manu :
nec mea subiecta convicta est gemma tabella
70   mendacem linis imposuisse notam.
nec quicquam, quod lege vetor committere, feci :
    est tamen his gravior noxa fatenda mihi.
neve roges, quae sit, stultam conscripsimus [2] Artem ;
    innocuas nobis haec vetat esse manus.
75 ecquid praeterea peccarim, quaerere noli,
    ut lateat [3] sola culpa sub Arte mea.
quicquid id est, habuit moderatam vindicis iram,
    qui nisi natalem nil mihi dempsit humum.
hac quoniam careo, tua nunc vicinia praestet,
80   inviso possim tutus ut esse loco.

---

[1] humeris *corr. Heinsius*   [2] quae (quam) scripsimus
                [3] pateat *corr.* ς

bears witness; shouldst thou remove thy name, I
should deny that a Thracian youth was the
composer; and that beneath this sky Orpheus might
not be the only bard, by thy talent is the Bistonian
land made proud. As thou hast the courage, when
need arises, to take arms and stain thy hand with
enemy's blood, and as thou hast been trained to hurl
the javelin with a sweep of thine arm, or to guide the
neck of the swift horse, so when just time has been
given to thy sire's pursuits and the task testing thy
might in all its parts has come to rest, that thy leisure
may not waste away in idle sleep, thou dost press on
the Pierian path towards the bright stars.

[63] This also brings me a certain union with thee:
each is a worshipper at the same shrine. As bard to
bard I extend my arms in prayer that thy land may
be loyal to me in exile. I was not guilty of murder
when I came to Pontus' shores, no baneful poison was
mixed by my hand; my seal was not convicted by a
fraudulent tablet of having imprinted on the linen [1] a
lying mark. I have done naught that the law
forbids. Yet must I confess a weightier sin. Ask
not what it is. But I have composed a foolish
"Art"; 'tis this prevents my hands from being clean.
Have I sinned further? Do not inquire— that my
wrongdoing may hide beneath my "Art" alone.
Whatever it is, the avenger's wrath was moderate.
He took from me nothing but my native land. Since
I am deprived of that, let now thy nearness warrant
that I can be secure in a place I hate.

---

[1] *i.e.* the threads with which documents were tied together.

OVID

X.

Ecquid ab impressae cognoscis imagine cerae
  haec tibi Nasonem scribere verba, Macer?
auctorisque sui si non est anulus index,
  cognitane est nostra littera facta manu?
5 an tibi notitiam mora temporis eripit horum,
  nec repetunt oculi signa vetusta tui?
sis licet oblitus pariter gemmaeque manusque,
  exciderit tantum ne tibi cura mei.
quam tu vel longi debes convictibus aevi,
10   vel mea quod coniunx non aliena tibi est,[1]
vel studiis, quibus es, quam nos, sapientius usus,
  utque decet, nulla factus es Arte nocens.
tu canis aeterno quicquid restabat Homero,
  ne careant summa Troica bella manu.
15 Naso parum prudens, artem dum tradit amandi,
  doctrinae pretium triste magister habet.
sunt tamen inter se communia sacra poetis,
  diversum quamvis quisque sequamur[2] iter:
quorum te memorem, quamquam procul absumus
    esse
20   suspicor, et casus velle levare meos.
te duce magnificas Asiae perspeximus urbes:
  Trinacris est oculis te duce visa[3] meis.
vidimus Aetnaea caelum splendescere flamma,
  subpositus monti quam vomit ore Gigans,
25 Hennaeosque lacus et olentis[4] stagna Palici,
  quaque suis Cyanen miscet Anapus aquis,
nec procul hinc nymphen, quae, dum fugit Elidis
    amnem,
  tecta sub aequorea nunc quoque currit aqua.

---

        [1] est *om.*   [2] queramur *vel* sequatur
        [3] nota   [4] olentia *corr. Zinzerling*

X. To Macer

Does any inkling come to you, Macer, from the figure pressed upon the wax that Naso writes these words to you ? If the ring be not an informant of its master, do you recognize the letters formed by my hand ? Or is recognition of these things stolen from you by length of time, and do your eyes not recall the symbols of long ago ? You may forget alike seal and hand if only interest in me has not dropped from your mind. This you owe to the association of long years, to my wife's kinship with you, or to the poetic studies which you have employed more wisely than I ; and (as 'tis fitting), no "Art" has made you guilty. You sing whatever immortal Homer left unsung, that the wars of Troy may not lack the final hand.[1] Naso thoughtlessly imparts the art of love and the teacher has the harsh reward of his teaching. There are, nevertheless, rites common to all poets—though we may each go our own separate way—which I believe in my heart that you remember, even though we are far apart, and wish to lighten my misfortunes. Under your guidance I beheld the splendid cities of Asia, under your guidance I saw the Trinacrian[2] land : you and I saw the sky agleam with Aetna's flame vomited forth by the giant[3] lying beneath the mountain, the lakes of Henna, the pools of sulphurous Palicus, and the spot where Anapus joins Cyane to his own waters, and hard by the nymph[4] who fleeing the Elean stream runs even now covered beneath the

---

[1] *i.e.* the touch that completes and perfects a work of art.
[2] Sicilian.   [3] Typhon.   [4] Arethusa.

hic mihi labentis pars anni magna peracta est.
30   eheu, quam dispar est locus ille Getis!
et quota pars haec sunt rerum, quas vidimus ambo,
    te mihi iucundas efficiente vias!
seu rate caeruleas picta sulcavimus undas,
    esseda nos agili sive tulere rota,
35 saepe brevis nobis vicibus via visa loquendi,
    pluraque, si numeres, verba fuere gradu,
saepe dies sermone minor fuit, inque loquendum
    tarda per aestivos defuit hora dies.
est aliquid casus pariter timuisse marinos,
40   iunctaque ad aequoreos vota tulisse deos,
et modo res egisse simul, modo rursus ab illis,
    quorum non pudeat, posse referre iocos.
haec tibi cum subeant, absim licet,[1] omnibus annis
    ante tuos oculos, ut modo visus, ero.
45 ipse quidem certe cum sim sub cardine mundi,
    qui semper liquidis altior extat aquis,
te tamen intueor quo solo pectore possum,
    et tecum gelido saepe sub axe loquor.
hic es, et ignoras, et ades celeberrimus absens,
50   inque Getas media iussus ab urbe venis.
redde vicem, et, quoniam regio felicior ista est,
    istic me memori pectore semper habe.

XI.

Hoc tibi, Rufe, brevi properatum tempore mittit
    Naso, parum faustae conditor Artis, opus,
ut, quamquam longe toto sumus orbe remoti
    scire tamen possis nos meminisse tui.

---

[1] ipsum licet *vel* hic sim licet

[1] The pole is often compared to a *cardo* (the pivot on which a door turns) or an axle.

waters of the sea. Here it was that I passed the greater part of a quickly gliding year—alas! how unlike that land to this of the Getae! and how small a part are these of the things that we saw together while you made every road pleasant for me! Whether we furrowed the blue waves in a gaily painted boat or drove in a swift-wheeled carriage, often the way seemed short through our interchange of talk, and our words, could you count them, outnumbered our steps; often the day was not long enough for our talk—even the long hours of summer did not suffice. 'Tis something to have feared together the perils of the sea, together to have paid our vows to the water gods, to have done deeds in common and again after those deeds to be free to utter jests which bring no shame. When these thoughts steal upon you, absent though I be, I shall be before your eyes as if you had just seen me. And as for me, though I dwell beneath the pivot of the heavens which is ever high above the clear waters yet I behold you in my heart—my only way—and often talk with you beneath the icy axle.[1] You are here and know it not, you are full often by my side though far away, and you come at my bidding from the midst of the city to the land of the Getae. Make me recompense, and since yours is the happier land, there keep me ever in a remembering heart.

XI. To Rufus

This work, Rufus, hastily composed in a brief space, Naso sends to you—Naso, the author of the ill-starred "Art"—that despite our separation by the whole world's width you may know that I remember you.

5 nominis ante mei venient oblivia nobis,
  pectore quam pietas sit tua pulsa meo :
et prius hanc animam vacuas reddemus in auras,
  quam fiat meriti gratia vana tui.
grande voco lacrimas meritum, quibus ora rigabas
10 cum mea concreto sicca dolore forent :
grande voco meritum maestae solacia mentis,
  cum pariter nobis illa tibique dares.
sponte quidem per seque mea est laudabilis uxor,
  admonitu melior fit tamen illa tuo.
15 namque quod Hermionae Castor fuit, Hector Iuli,
  hoc ego te laetor coniugis esse meae.
quae ne dissimilis tibi sit probitate labrot,
  seque tui vita sanguinis esse probat.
ergo quod fuerat stimulis factura sine ullis,
20 plenius auctorem te quoque nancta facit.
acer et ad palmae per se cursurus honores,
  si tamen horteris, fortius ibit equus.
adde quod absentis cura mandata fideli
  perficis, et nullum ferre gravaris onus.
25 o, referant grates, quoniam non possumus ipsi,
  di tibi ! qui referent, si pia facta vident ;
sufficiatque diu corpus quoque moribus istis,
  maxima Fundani glora, Rufe, soli.

Sooner shall I forget my own name than allow your loyalty to be driven from my mind; sooner shall I give back this life to the empty air than gratitude for your service become as naught. A great service I call the tears which streamed over your face when my own was dry with chilling grief. A great service I call the consolation of my sorrow when you bestowed it at once upon me and upon yourself. By her own will and of herself my wife deserves all praise, yet she is the better because of your admonitions: for what Castor was to Hermione, Hector to Iulus,[1] this you are, I rejoice to say, to my wife. She strives to be not unlike you in probity, she proves herself by her life to be of your blood, and so that which she would have done with no urging, she does more fully because you are her sponsor. The mettlesome steed who will of his own accord race for the honour of the palm will nevertheless, if you urge him, run with greater spirit. And besides you perform with faithful care the directions of one who is absent; there is no burden that you object to carrying. O may the gods recompense you, since I have not the power; and they will recompense if they but see deeds of loyalty. May you long have health to uphold your character, Rufus, chief glory of Fundi's land!

[1] *i.e.* uncle. Creusa, mother of Iulus (Ascanius), was Hector's sister.

LIBER TERTIUS

I.

Aequor Iasonio pulsatum remige primum,
    quaeque nec hoste fero nec nive, terra, cares,
ecquod erit tempus quo vos ego Naso relinquam
    in minus hostili iussus abesse loco ?
5 an mihi barbaria vivendum semper in ista,
    inque Tomitana condar oportet humo ?
pace tua, si pax ulla est tua, Pontica tellus,
    finitimus rapido quam terit hostis equo,
pace tua dixisse velim, tu pessima duro
10   pars es in exilio, tu mala nostra gravas.
tu neque ver sentis cinctum florente corona,
    tu neque messorum corpora nuda vides.
nec tibi pampineas autumnus porrigit uvas :
    cuncta sed inmodicum tempora frigus habet.[1]
15 tu glacie freta vincta tenes,[2] et in aequore piscis
    inclusus tecta saepe natavit aqua.
nec tibi sunt fontes, laticis nisi paene marini,
    qui potus dubium sistat alatne sitim.
rara, neque haec felix, in apertis eminet arvis
20   arbor, et in terra est altera forma maris.

            [1] habent : habet ς   [2] vides

BOOK III

I. To his Wife

O sea first lashed by Jason's oars, O land never free from cruel enemies and snows, will a time ever come when I, Naso, shall leave you, bidden to an exile in a place less hostile ? Or must I ever live in such a barbaric land, am I destined to be laid in my grave in the soil of Tomis ? With peace from thee [1]—if any peace thou hast—O land of Pontus, ever trodden by the swift horses of a neighbouring foe,—with peace from thee would I say : thou art the worse element in my hard exile, thou dost increase the weight of my misfortunes. Thou neither feelest spring girt with wreaths of flowers nor beholdest the reaper's naked bodies ; to thee autumn extends no clusters of grapes ; but all seasons are in the grip of excessive cold. Thou holdest the flood ice-bound, and in the sea the fishes often swim in water enclosed beneath a roof. Thou hast no springs except those almost of sea water ; quaff them, and doubt whether thirst is allayed or increased. Seldom is there a tree—and that unproductive—rising in the open fields, and the land is but the sea

---

[1] A bitter pun on the literal meaning of *pax* and its meaning in the phrase *tua pace*, "by thy leave."

non avis obloquitur, silvis nisi siqua remota [1]
    aequoreas rauco gutture potat aquas.
tristia per vacuos horrent absinthia campos,
    conveniensque suo messis armara loco.
25 adde metus, et quod murus pulsatur ab hoste,
    tinctaque mortifera tabe sagitta madet,
quod procul haec regio est et ab omni devia cursu,
    nec pede quo quisquam nec rate tutus eat.
non igitur mirum, finem quaerentibus horum
30   altera si nobis usque rogatur humus.
te magis est mirum non hoc evincere, coniunx,
    inque meis lacrimas posse tenere malis.
quid facias, quaeris ? quaeras hoc scilicet ipsum,
    invenies, vere si reperire voles.
35 velle parum est : cupias, ut re potiaris, oportet,
    et faciat somnos haec tibi cura breves.
velle reor multos : quis enim mihi tam sit iniquus,
    optet ut exilium pace carere meum ?
pectore te toto cunctisque incumbere nervis
40   et niti pro me nocte dieque decet.
utque iuvent alii, tu debes vincere amicos,
    uxor, et ad partis prima venire tuas.
magna tibi imposita est nostris persona libellis :
    coniugis exemplum diceris esse bonae.
45 hanc cave degeneres.   ut sint praeconia nostra
    vera, vide famae quod tuearis opus.
ut nihil ipse querar, tacito me fama queretur,
    quae debet, fuerit ni tibi cura mei.
exposuit memet populo Fortuna videndum,
50   et plus notitiae, quam fuit ante, dedit.

---

[1] nisi silvis siqua remotis *corr. Ehwald*

in another guise. No note is there of any bird save such as remote in the forests drink the brackish water with raucous throat. Bitter wormwood bristles throughout the empty plains, a crop suited in harshness to its site. Add fears too—the wall assailed by the enemy, the darts soaked in death-dealing corruption, the distance of this spot from all traffic, to which none can penetrate in safety either on foot or by boat.

[29] No wonder then if I seek an end of this and beg constantly for another land. 'Tis a greater wonder that thou, my wife, dost not prevail in this, that thou canst restrain thy tears at my misfortunes. What art thou to do, thou askest? Ask thyself this very question; thou wilt discover, if thou hast true will to find it out. To wish is not enough; thou shouldst have a passion to win thy end, and this care should make thy slumber brief. Many, I think, wish it; for who can be so hard upon me as to desire my place of exile to be severed from peace? With thy whole heart, with every sinew thou shouldst work and strive for me night and day. And to have others aid me thou shouldst win our friends, my wife, and come foremost thyself to support thy part.

[43] Great is the rôle imposed upon thee in my books; thou art called the model of a good wife. Beware thou fallest not from that: that I may have proclaimed the truth, look to the work that fame has wrought and guard it well. Though I myself make no complaint, whilst I am dumb fame will complain, as she ought, shouldst thou not have regard for me. Fortune has set me forth to be viewed of all the people, she has given me more celebrity than I had of yore.

notior est factus Capaneus a fulminis ictu :
　　notus humo mersis Amphiaraus equis.
si minus errasset, notus minus esset Ulixes :
　　magna Philoctetae vulnere fama suo est.
55 si locus est aliquis tanta inter nomina parvis,
　　nos quoque conspicuos nostra ruina facit.
nec te nesciri patitur mea pagina, qua non
　　inferius Coa Bittide [1] nomen habes.
quicquid ages igitur, scaena spectabere magna,
60　　et pia non paucis [2] testibus uxor eris.
crede mihi, quotiens laudaris carmine nostro,
　　qui legit has laudes, an mereare rogat.
utque favere reor plures virtutibus istis,
　　sic tua non paucae carpere facta volent.
65 quarum tu praesta ne livor dicere possit
　　"haec est pro miseri lenta salute viri."
cumque ego deficiam, nec possim ducere currum,
　　fac tu sustineas debile sola iugum.
ad medicum specto venis fugientibus aeger :
70　　ultima pars animae dum mihi restat, ades ;
quodque ego praestarem, si te magis ipse valerem,
　　id mihi, cum valeas fortius ipsa, refer.
exigit hoc socialis amor foedusque maritum :
　　moribus hoc, coniunx, exigis ipsa tuis.
75 hoc domui debes, de qua censeris, ut illam
　　non magis officiis quam probitate colas.
cuncta licet facias, nisi eris laudabilis uxor,
　　non poterit credi Marcia culta tibi.

---

　　　　[1] bit tibi de *etc. corr. Merkel*　　　　　　[2] parvis

---

[1] The house of the Fabii.
[2] The wife of Fabius Maximus, *cf. Ex P.* i. 2. 139.

Capaneus was made more famous by the lightning's shock; Amphiaraus achieved fame when his steeds were swallowed up in the earth. If Ulysses had wandered less, he would have been less famous; Philoctetes' great name is due to his wound. If there is some place among such mighty names for the humble, I too am become a man of mark by reason of my fall.

[57] And thou art not permitted by my pages to be unknown; thou hast a name not inferior to that of Coan Bittis. Whatever therefore thou shalt do, thou shalt be viewed upon a mighty stage, thou shalt be to many witnesses a loyal wife. I assure thee, as often as thou art praised in my verse, he who reads the praise asks whether thou dost deserve it. And just as many, I think, approve such virtues, so women not a few will seek shortcomings in thy deeds. 'Tis for thee to make sure their jealousy can never say, "This is she who is indifferent to her wretched husband's safety!"

[67] Since I am failing, no longer able to draw the car, see that thou dost alone support the weakening yoke. I am a sick man, gazing with failing pulse upon the doctor; while the last of life remains to me, stand by to help; and what I would myself supply, were I stronger than thou, that grant to me since thou art thyself the stronger. This is demanded by our united love and marriage compact; this, my wife, thou dost demand by virtue of thine own character. This thou dost owe to the house [1] by which thou hast thy esteem, that thou mayst cherish it not more in duty than in uprightness. Thou mayst do all things, but unless thou shalt be a praiseworthy wife, it will not be believed that thou hast honoured Marcia.[2]

nec sumus indigni : nec, si vis vera fateri,
80   debetur meritis gratia nulla meis.
redditur illa quidem grandi cum faenore nobis,
    nec te, si cupiat, laedere rumor habet.
sed tamen hoc factis adiunge prioribus unum,
    pro nostris ut sis ambitiosa malis.
85 ut minus infesta iaceam regione labora,
    clauda nec officii pars erit ulla tui.
magna peto, sed non tamen invidiosa roganti :
    utque ea non teneas, tuta repulsa tua est.
nec mihi suscense,[1] totiens, si carmine nostro,
90   quod facis, ut facias, teque imitere, rogo.
fortibus adsuevit tubicen prodesse, suoque
    dux bene pugnantis incitat ore viros.
nota tua est probitas testatque tempus in omne ;
    sit virtus etiam non probitate minor.
95 non tibi Amazonia est pro me sumenda securis,
    aut excisa levi pelta gerenda manu.
numen adorandum est, non ut mihi fiat amicum,
    sed sit ut iratum, quam fuit ante, minus.
gratia si nulla est, lacrimae tibi gratia fient.
100   hac potes aut nulla parte movere deos.
quae tibi ne desint, bene per mala nostra cavetur :
    meque viro flendi copia dives adest ;
utque meae res sunt, omni, puto, tempore flebis.
    has fortuna tibi nostra ministrat[2] opes.
105 si mea mors redimenda tua, quod abominor, esset,
    Admeti coniunx, quam sequereris, erat.
aemula Penelopes fieres, si fraude pudica
    instantis velles fallere nupta procos.

          [1] succense   [2] ministret

---

[1] The shield was shaped somewhat like a crescent, one side
being indented.
[2] Alcestis.

378

[79] Nor am I unworthy, and if thou art willing to confess the truth, some return is owed to my services. That return thou dost indeed make to me with usury, nor could rumour, even if she should wish, injure thee. But none the less add this one thing to thy previous deeds : be the canvasser for my misfortunes. Toil that I may rest in a less hostile region and no part of thy duty will halt. Great is my request, yet not one that brings odium on the petitioner ; shouldst thou not attain it, thy defeat involves no danger. And be not wroth with me if so many times in my song I ask thee to do what thou art already doing and to imitate thyself. The brave have often been helped by the trumpeter, and the general urges on with his own lips men who are fighting well. Thy probity is known and witnessed for all time ; let thy courage too be not inferior to thy probity. Thou hast not to take up in my behalf the Amazon's battle-axe nor bear with thy frail hand the indented [1] target. Thou has to implore a deity, not to become friendly to me, but less angry than heretofore. If grace thou findest not, tears shall win thee grace ; by this or by no means canst thou move the gods. That they will not fail thee is well assured by my misfortunes ; with me as husband of tears thou hast rich store ; and as things are with me thou wilt weep, I think, at all times—these are the means that my fortune renders to thee. If thou hadst to redeem my death at the price of thine own—away with the thought !—Admetus' wife [2] would be a model to follow. Thou wouldst become a rival of Penelope if by chaste deceit thou, a bride, shouldst wish to beguile insistent

si comes extincti Manes sequerere mariti,
110   esse dux facti Laodamia tui.
Iphias ante oculos tibi erat ponenda volenti
  corpus in accensos mittere forte rogos.
morte nihil tibi opus,[1] nihil Icariotide tela.
  Caesaris est coniunx ore precando tuo,
115 quae praestat virtute sua, ne presca vetustas
  laude pudicitiae saecula nostra premat:
quae Veneris formam, mores Iunonis habendo
  sola est caelesti digna reperta toro.
quid trepidas et adire times? non impia Procne
120   filiave Aeëtae voce movenda tua est,
nec nurus Aegypti, nec saeva Agamemnonis uxor,
  Scyllaque, quae Siculas inguine terret aquas,
Telegonive parens vertendis nata figuris,
  nexaque nodosas angue Medusa comas,
125 femina sed princeps, in qua Fortuna videre
  se probat et caecae crimina falsa tulit:
qua nihil in terris ad finem solis ab ortu
  clarius excepto Caesare mundus habet.
eligito tempus captatum saepe rogandi,
130   exeat adversa ne tua navis aqua.
non semper sacras reddunt oracula sortis,
  ipsaque non omni tempore fana patent.
cum status urbis erit, qualem nunc auguror esse,
  et nullus populi contrahet ora dolor,
135 cum domus Augusti, Capitoli more colenda,
  laeta, quod est et sit, plenaque pacis erit,
tum tibi di faciant adeundi copia fiat,
  profectura aliquid tum tua verba putes.

---

[1] nihil opus est *corr. Bentley*

---

[1] Penelope, daughter of Icarius.   [2] Medea.
[3] A Danaïd, *i.e.* one who slew her husband.   [4] Circe.

suitors. If thou shouldst follow thy dead husband to
the shades Laodamia would guide thee in thy
deed. Iphias would have to be kept before thine
eyes, shouldst thou wish to hurl thyself bravely upon
the kindled pyre. But thou hast no need of death,
no need of the Icarian woman's [1] web, thy lips must
pray to Caesar's spouse, who by her virtue gives
surety that the olden time conquers not our age in
praise of chastity; who, with the beauty of Venus, the
character of Juno, has been found alone worthy to
share the divine couch. Why dost tremble and fear
to approach her? No impious Procne nor daughter [2]
of Aeëtes must needs be touched by thy words, nor
daughter-in-law [3] of Aegyptus, nor cruel wife of
Agamemnon, nor Scylla, terrifying with her loins the
waters of Sicily, nor mother [4] of Telegonus, born with
the power to transform human shape, nor Medusa,
with locks bound and snarled with serpents, but the
foremost of women, who proves that Fortune has the
power of sight and has falsely borne the charge of
blindness; than whom the universe holds nothing
more illustrious from the sun's rising to his setting,
save only Caesar. Choose well the time, already oft
essayed, to make thy petition, lest thy bark put forth
into an adverse sea. Not always do oracles give
forth their holy prophecies, not at all times are even
the shrines open. When the condition of the city
shall be such as I divine it now to be, and no sorrow
brings a frown upon the people's brow, when
Augustus's house, to be revered as it were the Capitol,
shall be happy—as now, I pray, and ever—and filled
with peace, then may the gods grant thee an
opportunity to approach, then thou mayst believe
that thy words will be of some avail. If she is busy

siquid aget maius, differ tua coepta caveque
140   spem festinando praecipitare meam.
nec rursus iubeo dum sit vacuissima quaeras :
    corporis ad curam vix vacat illa sui.
omnia . . . .
    per rerum turbam tu quoque oportet eas.
145 cum tibi contigerit vultum Iunonis adire,
    fac sis personae, quam tueare, memor.
nec factum defende meum : mala causa silenda est.
    nil nisi sollicitae sint tua verba preces.
tum lacrimis demenda mora est, summissaque terra [1]
150   ad non mortalis brachia tende pedes.
tum pete nil aliud, saevo nisi ab hoste recedam ;
    hostem Fortunam sit satis esse mihi.
plura quidem subeunt, sed conturbata [2] timore
    haec quoque vix poteris voce tremente loqui.
155 suspicor hoc damno fore non tibi.   sentiet illa
    te maiestatem pertimuisse suam.
nec, tua si fletu scindentur verba, nocebit :
    interdum lacrimae pondera vocis habent.
lux etiam coeptis facito bona talibus adsit
160   horaque conveniens auspiciumque favens.
sed prius imposito sanctis altaribus igni
    tura fer ad magnos vinaque pura deos.
e quibus ante omnis Augustem numen adora
    progeniemque piam participemque tori.
165 sint utinam mites solito tibi more tuasque
    non duris lacrimas vultibus aspiciant.

---

[1] terrae   [2] sunt turbata : conturbata *s*

---

[1] In 1. 143 the good manuscripts preserve only the word
omnia. A stopgap appears in the later ones, *curia cum patribus
fuerit stipata verendis,* " when the senate-house is crowded with
the revered fathers."

with something of greater import, put off thy purpose and beware of ruining my hope through haste. Nor again do I bid thee seek a time when she is wholly idle—she scarce has leisure for the care of her own person . . .[1] thou too shouldst follow amid the throng of affairs.

[145] When it shall befall thee to approach the countenance of Juno, see that thou dost maintain the part thou hast to play. Defend not my deed : an ill cause admits no speech. Let thy words be naught but sorrowing petitions. Then must thou release the barrier of tears, sink to the earth, and stretch forth thy arms towards those immortal feet. Then ask nothing except that I may withdraw from the neighbourhood of a fierce enemy ; let Fortune for me be enemy enough. More comes into my mind, but confused with fear even this thou wilt scarce be able to utter with stammering voice. This I think will not harm thee. She will perceive thy dread of her majesty and if thy words are broken by sobbing it will do no harm ; for tears sometimes have the weight of spoken words.

[159] See also that thou hast a lucky day for such an enterprise and a suitable hour and favouring omens. But first kindle a fire upon the holy altar, offer incense and pure wine to the great gods. Of them all and before all worship the deity of Augustus, his loyal offspring and his consort. May they be propitious to thee in their wonted fashion, and view thy tears with kindly countenances.

II

Quam legis a nobis missam tibi, Cotta, salutem,
    missa sit ut vere perveniatque, precor.
namque meis sospes multum cruciatibus aufers,
    utque[1] sit in[2] nobis pars bona salva facis.
5 cumque labent aliqui iactataque vela relinquant,
    tu lacerae remanes ancora sola rati.
grata tua est igitur pietas.   ignoscimus illis,
    qui cum Fortuna terga dedere fugae.
cum feriant unum, non unum fulmina terrent,
10   iunctaque percusso turba pavere solet:
cumque dedit paries venturae signa ruinae,
    sollicito vacuus fit locus ille metu.
quis non e timidis aegri contagia vitat,
    vicinum metuens ne trahat inde malum?
15 me quoque amicorum nimio terrore metuque,
    non odio, quidam destituere mei.
non illis pietas, non officiosa voluntas
    defuit: adversos extimuere deos.
utque magis cauti possunt timidique videri,
20   sic appelari non meruere mali.
aut[3] meus excusat caros ita candor amicos,
    utque habeant de me crimina nulla, favet.
sint hi contenti venia, iactentque[4] licebit
    purgari factum me quoque teste suum.
25 pars estis pauci melior, qui rebus in artis
    ferre mihi nullam turpe putastis opem.
tunc igitur meriti morietur gratia vestri,
    cum cinis absumpto corpore factus ero.

---

[1] atque   [2] sit in] ut sit *vel* sit ut
[3] aut] ut *vel* at *vel* et
[4] sientque *vel* signentque *vel* fugiantque *corr. Korn*

II. To Cotta

The " Health," [1] Cotta, of my sending which you
read here, may it, I pray, be sent in truth and reach
you. For your weal takes away much from my
sufferings, causing a good part of me to be
well. When many fall away and abandon the storm-
blown sails, you remain the sole anchor of the
shattered bark. Grateful, therefore, is your
loyalty. I pardon those who along with Fortune
have betaken themselves to flight. Though they
smite but one, not one alone do the lightnings
affright, and the throng around the stricken ever
quakes with fear. When a wall has given warning of
its coming fall, anxiety and fear empty the
place. What timid man does not avoid contact with
the sick, fearing lest he contract a disease so near ? I
too because of the excessive dread and alarm of my
friends, not because of their hatred, was abandoned
by some. They lacked not loyalty, nor the will to
duty ; they dreaded the hostile gods. They can be
deemed too cautious and timid, yet they have not
deserved to be called wicked. Or else my charity
pardons friends who are dear to me and favours them
so much that from me they bear no blame. Let them
be content with this indulgence and they shall be free
to boast that their act is justified even by my
testimony.

[25] But you few are a better group, who in my straits
thought it base to offer me no aid. So then will my
gratitude for your merit die when my body shall be

[1] Referring to the regular opening formula of Roman letters :
S.D. (*salutem dicit*) or *S.P.D.* (*salutem plurimam dicit*).

    fallor, et illa meae superabit tempora vitae,
30   si tamen a memori posteritate legar.
    corpora debentur maestis exsanguia bustis :
      effugiunt structos nomen honorque rogos.
    occidit et Theseus et qui comitavit Oresten :
      sed tamen in laudes vivit uterque suas.
35 vos etiam seri laudabunt saepe nepotes,
      claraque erit scriptis gloria vestra meis.
    hic quoque Sauromatae iam vos novere Getaeque,
      et tales animos barbara turba probat.
    cumque ego de vestra nuper probitate referrem
40   (nam didici Getice Sarmaticeque loqui),
    forte senex quidam, coetu cum staret in illo,
      reddidit ad nostros talia verba sonos :
    "nos quoque amicitiae nomen, bone, novimus,
        hospes,
      quos procul a vobis Pontus et Hister [1] habet.
45 est locus in Scythia, Tauros dixere priores,
      qui Getica longe non ita distat humo.
    hac ego sum terra (patriae nec paenitet) ortus :
      consortem Phoebi gens colit illa deam.
    templa manent hodie vastis innixa columnis,
50   perque quater denos itur in illa gradus.
    fama refert illic signum caeleste fuisse :
      quoque minus dubites, stat basis orba dea :
    araque, quae fuerat natura candida saxi,
      decolor adfuso tincta cruore rubet.
55 femina sacra facit taedae non nota iugali,
      quae superat Scythicas nobilitate nurus.
    sacrifici genus est, sic instituere parentes,
      advena virgineo caesus ut ense cadat.

        [1] Pontus et Hister] barbarus ister, *etc*.

consumed to ashes—I am wrong : it will outlive the
span of my life, if after all posterity shall remember
and read me.   The bloodless body is destined for the
mournful tomb ; name and honour escape the high-
built pyre.   Death befell even Theseus and him [1] who
accompanied Orestes, but yet each still lives to his
own renown.   You too shall oft be praised by late-
born descendants and bright shall be your fame by
reason of my writings.   Even here the Sauromatians
and the Getae already know you ; such a spirit as
yours finds favour with the barbarian throng.   And
when of late I was telling of your uprightness (for I
have learned how to speak Getic and Sarmatian), it
chanced that an aged man, standing in the circle,
made this reply upon hearing my words, "We too,
good stranger, are acquainted with friendship's
name—we whom the Pontus and the Hister separate
from you and your people.   There is a place in
Scythia—men before us called it Tauri—not so far
from the Getic soil.   In that land was I born and I am
not ashamed of my country.   The people worship
Phoebus's companion goddess.   The temple exists
to-day with its huge columns ; by two score steps one
enters.   The story goes that there was once an image
of the deity, and, to remove your doubts, still stands
the pedestal bereft of the goddess, and the altar, once
white from the natural colour of the stone, is
discolored and red with stains from outpoured blood.
A woman who has not known the torch of marriage,
offers the sacrifices—who surpasses in birth the
daughters of Scythia.   The nature of the sacrifice—
so our forefathers ordained—is that strangers fall,
slain by the maiden's sword.   Thoas ruled the

[1] Pylades.

387

regna Thoas habuit Maeotide clarus in ora,
60   nec fuit Euxinis notior alter aquis.
sceptra tenente illo liquidas fecisse per auras
   nescioquam dicunt Iphigenian iter.
quam levibus ventis sub nube per aera [1] vectam
   creditur his Phoebe deposuisse locis.
65 praefuerat templo multos ea rite per annos,
   invita peragens tristia sacra manu :
cum duo velifera iuvenes venere carina
   presseruntque suo litora nostra pede.
par fuit his aetas et amor, quorum alter Orestes,
70   alter erat Pylades [2] : nomina fama tenet.
protinus inmitem Triviae ducuntur ad aram,
   evincti geminas ad sua terga manus.
spargit aqua captos lustrali Graia sacerdos,
   ambiat ut fulvas infula longa comas.
75 dumque parat sacrum, dum velat tempora vittis,
   dum tardae causas invenit ipsa morae,
'non ego crudelis, iuvenes, (ignoscite) ' dixit
   ' sacra suo facio barbariora loco.
ritus is est gentis.   qua vos tamen urbe venitis ?
80   quodve parum fausta puppe petistis iter ? '
dixit, et audito patriae pia nomine virgo
   consortes urbis comperit esse suae.
' alter ut e vobis ' inquit ' cadat hostia sacris,
   ad patrias sedes nuntius alter eat.'
85 ire iubet Pylades carum periturus Oresten ;
   hic negat, inque vices pugnat uterque mori.
extitit hoc unum, quo non convenerit illis :
   cetera par [3] concors et sine lite fuit.
dum peragunt pulchri iuvenes certamen amoris
90   ad fratrem scriptas exarat illa notas.

[1] aequora *corr. s*
[2] alter et est pilades *vel* et pylades alter

kingdom, illustrious in the Maeotian land ; no other was better known to the Euxine's waters. Whilst he held the sceptre they say that a certain Iphigenia journeyed through the clear skies. Her, carried by light breezes through the air, beneath the shelter of a cloud, Phoebe established, so it is believed, in this region. Duly had she presided over the temple for many years, carrying out the gloomy rites with unwilling hand, when on a sail-bearing ship two youths arrived and set foot on our shores. Equal they were in youth and love, one Orestes, the other Pylades : fame holds fast their names. Forthwith were they led to Trivia's cruel altar, hands bound behind their backs. With lustral water the Grecian priestess sprinkled the captives that the long fillet might encircle their yellow locks. While she prepared the sacrifice, while she veiled their temples with the bands, while she found pretexts for lingering delay, ' It is not I,' she said, ' youths, who am cruel ; grant me pardon. I perform sacrifices more barbarous than the land to which they belong. 'Tis the rite of the people. Yet—from what city come ye ? On what journey have ye come in your ill-starred ship ? ' Thus spake the pious girl, and when she heard the name of her native land, she discovered that they were dwellers in her own city. ' Let one of you,' she said, ' fall as a victim in these rites, let the other go a messenger to the home of his fathers.' Pylades, bent on death, bade his Orestes go. He refuses, and each in turn fights to die. On this alone they did not agree : on all else those twain were at one and free from dispute. Whilst the fair youths carry on their contest of love, to her brother she traces written

---

³ pars corr. *Naugerius*

ad fratrem mandata da–at, cuique illa dabantur
    (humanos casus aspice!) frater erat.
nec mora, de templo rapiunt simulacra Dianae,
    clamque per inmensas puppe feruntur aquas.
95 mirus amor iuvenum : quamvis abiere tot anni,
    in Scythia magnum nunc quoque nomen habent.''
fabula narrata est postquam vulgaris ab illo,
    laudarunt omnes facta piamque fidem.
scilicet hac etiam, qua nulla ferocior ora est,
100   nomen amicitiae barbara corda movet.
quid facere Ausonia geniti debetis in urbe,
    cum tangant duros talia facta Getas ?
adde quod est animus semper tibi mitis, et altae
    indicium mores nobilitatis habent,
105 quos Volesus patrii cognoscat nominis auctor,
    quos Numa materni [1] non neget esse suos,
adiectique probent genetiva ad nomina Cottae,
    si tu non esses, interitura domus.
digne vir hac serie, lapso succurrere amico
110   conveniens istis moribus esse puta.

III.

Si vacat exiguum profugo dare tempus amico,
    o sidus Fabiae, Maxime, gentis, ades,
dum tibi quae vidi refero, seu corporis umbra
    seu veri species seu fuit ille sopor.
5 nox erat et bifores intrabat luna fenestras,
    mense fere medio quanta nitere solet.
publica me requies curarum somnus habebat,
    fusaque erant toto languida membra toro,

---

[1] materni (*sc*. nominis) *Naugerius* : maternus

letters. To her brother she was sending the missive and he to whom it was given—behold the fate of man!—as in fact her brother!

⁹³ " With no delay they snatch from the temple the statue of Diana, and stealthily they are borne over the trackless waters in their ship. A marvel was the love of the youths: though so many years have passed, in Scythia even now they have a great name."

⁹⁷ After the telling of this well-known tale, all praised acts of loyal devotion. 'Tis clear that even on this shore, than which none is wilder, the name of friendship affects barbarian hearts. What ought ye to do, born in the Ausonian city, when such deeds move the stern Getae? And besides you have ever a gentle soul and, a token of your lofty birth, a character which Volesus, the founder of your father's name, would recognize, which Numa on your mother's side would not refuse to own, and the Cottae, who have been added to your natal name—a line that but for your life would die out. O worthy of such a line, deem it in harmony with such character to succour a fallen friend!

III. To Maximus

If you have a little leisure to devote to an exiled friend, listen, Maximus, star of the Fabian race, while I relate what I have seen, whether it was the shadow of a body, the appearance of a reality, or merely a dream.

⁵ 'Twas night. The moon was entering the double-shuttered windows with all her accustomed mid-month brightness. Sleep, the common rest from cares, possessed me, my inert limbs stretched about

cum subito pinnis agitatus inhorruit aër,
10   et gemuit parvo mota fenestra sono.
territus in cubitum relevo mea membra sinistrum,
    pulsus et e trepido pectore somnus abit.
stabat Amor, vultu non quo prius esse solebat,
    fulcra tenens laeva tristis acerna manu,
15 nec torquem collo, nec habens crinale capillo,
    nec bene dispositas comptus, ut ante, comas.
horrida pendebant molles super ora capilli,
    est visa est oculis horrida pinna meis,
qualis in aeriae tergo solet esse columbae,
20   tractatam multae quam tetigere manus.
hunc simul agnovi, neque enim mihi notior alter,
    talibus adfata est libera lingua sonis :
" o puer, exilii decepto causa magistro,
    quem fuit utilius non docuisse mihi,
25 huc quoque venisti, pax est ubi tempore nullo,
    et coit adstrictis barbarus Hister aquis ?
quae tibi causa viae, nisi uti mala nostra videres ?
    quae sunt, si nescis, invidiosa tibi.
tu mihi dictasti iuvenalia carmina primus :
30   apposui senis te duce quinque pedes.
nec me Maeonio consurgere carmine nec me
    dicere magnorum passus es acta ducum.
forsitan exiguas, aliquas tamen, arcus et ignes [1]
    ingenii vires comminuere mei.
35 namque ego dum canto tua regna tuaeque parentis,
    in nullum mea mens grande vacavit opus.
nec satis hoc fuerat. stulto [2] quoque carmine feci,
    Artibus ut posses non rudis esse meis.
pro quibus exilium misero est mihi reddita merces,
40   id quoque in extremis et sine pace locis.

---

    [1] ignis   [2] stultus

the couch, when on a sudden the air was vibrant with
the movement of wings and a slight creaking sound
arose as the window was moved. Startled I raised
myself upon my left elbow, and sleep was driven from
my trembling breast. There stood Love, not with
the face he used to have, sadly resting his left hand
upon the maple post, no necklace on his throat, no
ornament in his hair, his locks not carefully arranged
as of old. Over his unkempt face the soft hair was
drooping; his feathers seemed to my eyes all
unkempt, like those on the back of soaring dove
which many hands have touched and handled. As
soon as I recognized him—and none other is better
known to me—my tongue became free and addressed
him in these words. "Boy, cause of thy master's
exile, whom it had been better for me not to teach,
hast thou come even hither where peace exists at no
time, where the waters of the wild Hister feel the
bonds of frost? What reason hast thou for thy
journey except to view my misfortunes? These, if
thou knowest it not, bring reproach upon thee.
Thou wert the first to dictate my youthful verse to
me; it was under thy guidance that I set five feet after
six. Thou didst not allow me to reach the height of
Maeonian song [1] or to sing the deeds of mighty
chieftains. Slight perhaps, yet something, was the
strength of my talent, but thy bow and thy fires
brought weakness. For whilst I sang thy sway and
that of thy mother, my mind had room for no great
work. Nor was this all: by a foolish poem as well, by
my "Art," I caused thee to lose thy inexperience.
For this the reward of exile was meted out to
wretched me, and that too in a land far away and

[1] Epic.

393

at non Chionides Eumolpus in Orphea talis,
    in Phryga nec Satyrum talis Olympus erat,
praemia nec Chiron ab Achille talia cepit,
    Pythagoraeque ferunt non nocuisse Numam.
45 nomina neu referam longum collecta per aevum,
    discipulo perii solus ab ipse meo.
dum damus arma tibi, dum te, lascive, docemus,
    haec te discipulo dona magister habet.
scis tamen, et liquido iuratus dicere possis,
50   non me legitimos sollicitasse toros.
scripsimus haec illis, quarum nec vitta pudicos
    contingit crines nec stola longa pedes.
dic, precor, ecquando didicisti fallere nuptas,
    et facere incertum per mea iussa genus ?
55 an sit ab his omnis rigide summota libellis,
    quam lex furtivos arcet habere viros ?
quid tamen hoc prodest, vetiti si lege severa
    credor adulterii composuisse notas ?
at tu, sic habeas ferientes cuncta sagittas,
60   sic numquam rapido lampades igne vacent,
sic regat imperium terrasque coërceat omnis
    Caesar, ab Aenea qui tibi fratre tuus,[1]
effice, sit nobis non inplacabilis ira,
    meque loco plecti commodiore velit.''
65 haec ego visus eram puero dixisse volucri,
    hos visus nobis ille dedisse sonos :
'' per mea tela, faces, et per mea tela, sagittas,
    per matrem iuro Caesareumque caput,
nil nisi concessum nos te didicisse magistro,
70   Artibus et nullum crimen inesse tuis.

               [1] tuus] nepos

---

[1] Orpheus instructed Eumolpus in the Eleusinian mysteries.
  [2] Marsyas, who taught Olympus to play the pipes.

never at peace.   Not so did Chionian Eumolpus treat
Orpheus,[1] nor Olympus treat the Phrygian Satyr,[2]
nor did Chiron receive such a reward from Achilles,
and they say that Nd no harm to Pythagoras.   Not
to repeat the names amassed through the long ages—
I am the only one who has been ruined by his own
pupil.   Whilst I give arms to thee, whilst I teach
thee, wanton one, this is the reward, with thee as
pupil, that thy master has.   Yet thou knowest, and
thou couldst swear it with a clear conscience, that I
have not disturbed lawful wedlock.   This I wrote for
those who have no modest locks to be touched with
the fillet nor a long stole descending to their
feet.[3]   Speak, I beg thee—hast thou at any time
learned to deceive brides, rendering descent un-
certain by my precepts ?   Or has not every woman
been strictly excluded from these books whom the
law protects from stealthy paramours ?   Yet of what
avail is this if men believe that I have composed
directions for that adultery which is forbidden by
stern laws ?   But do thou—so mayst thou possess
arrows that smite all, so may thy torches never lose
their swift flame, so may Caesar, who through thy
brother Aeneas is thy kin, guide his realm and control
all lands—cause his wrath to be not implacable
against me, cause him to be willing that I be punished
in a better place."

[65] Thus methought I spoke to the winged boy, in
these words methought he answered me, "By my
weapons, the torch and arrows, by my mother I
swear, and by Caesar's head, that I have learned
naught but what is lawful from thy mastership, that
there resides no crime in thine 'Art.'   As I defend

[3] *i.e.* for courtesans, not matrons, *cf. Tr.* ii. 245 ff.

utque hoc, sic utinam defendere cetera possem [1] !
  scis aliud, quod te laeserit, esse, magis.
quicquid id est (neque enim debet dolor ipse referri,
  nec potes a culpa dicere abesse tua)
75 tu licet erroris sub imagine crimen obumbres,
  non gravior merito vindicis [2] ira fuit.
ut tamen aspicerem consolarerque iacentem,
  lapsa per inmensas est mea pinna vias.
haec loca tum primum vidi, cum matre rogante
80   Phasias est telis fixa puella meis.
quae nunc cur iterum post saecula longa revisam,
  tu facis, o castris miles amice meis.
pone metus igitur : mitescet Caesaris ira,
  et veniet votis mollior aura tuis.
85 neve moram timeas, tempus, quod quaerimus, instat,
  cunctaque laetitiae plena triumphus habet.
dum domus et nati, dum mater Livia gaudet,
  dum gaudes, patriae magne ducisque pater,
dum sibi gratatur populus, totamque per urbem
90   omnis odoratis ignibus ara calet,
dum faciles aditus praebet venerabile templum, [3]
  sperandum est nostras posse valere preces.''
dixit, et aut ille est tenues dilapsus in auras,
  coeperunt sensus aut vigilare mei.
95 si dubitem, faveas quin his, o Maxime, dictis,
  Memnonio cycnos esse colore putem.
sed neque mutatur [4] nigra pice lacteus humor,
  nec, quod erat candens, fit terebinthus ebur.

---

[1] posses   [2] iudicis
[3] templum] tempus *vel* numen   [4] fuscatur

[1] Medea.
[2] The triumph of Tiberius over Germany, Jan. 16, A.D. 13.
[3] Memnon as an Ethiopian was conceived to be black.

thee on this score, would I could on the rest! Thou
knowest there is another thing that has injured thee
more. Whatever this is (for neither should the
painful tale itself be repeated nor canst thou say that
thou art free from guilt), though *thou* dost veil thy
crime under the guise of 'error' the avenger's wrath
was not too severe. However, to look upon thee, to
console thee downcast, my wings have glided over
measureless ways. This region I first saw when at my
mother's request I pierced the Phasian maiden [1] with
my darts. The reason for my second visit, now, after
long ages, is in thee, friendly soldier of my own
camp. So put aside thy fears; Caesar's wrath will
soften, a gentler breeze will be wafted upon
thy prayers. Fear not delay; the time we seek is
close at hand; the triumph [2] fills everything with
joy. While the house and the children, while their
mother Livia rejoices, while thou, great father of
our land and of our leader, dost rejoice, while
the people congratulate themselves, and through-
out the city every altar burns with fragrant
flames, while the holy temple affords an easy
approach, we may hope that our prayers can have
some effect.''

[93] He spoke and glided away into thin air or else my
own senses began to awaken.

[95] Were I to doubt your favour for these words,
Maximus, I should believe that swans are the colour
of Memnon.[3] But milk is not changed to black pitch
nor does shining ivory become terebinth.

conveniens animo genus est tibi, nobile namque
100　　pectus et Herculeae simplicitatis habes.
livor, iners vitium, mores non exit in altos,
　　utque latens ima vipera serpit humo.
mens tua sublimis supra genus eminet ipsum,
　　grandius ingenio nec tibi nomen inest.
105 ergo alii noceant miseris optentque timeri,
　　tinctaque mordaci spicula felle gerant:
at tua supplicibus domus est adsueta iuvandis,
　　in quorum numero me, precor, esse velis.

IV

Haec tibi non vanam portantia verba salutem
　　Naso Tomitana mittit ab urbe tuus,
utque suo faveas mandat, Rufine, Triumpho,
　　in vestras venit si tamen ille manus.
5 est opus exiguum vestrisque paratibus inpar :
　　quale tamen cumque est, ut tueare, rogo.
firma valent per se, nullumque Machaona quaerunt.
　　ad medicam dubius confugit aeger opem.
non opus est magnis placido lectore poëtis :
10　　quamlibet[1] invitum difficilemque tenent.
nos, quibus ingenium longi minuere labores,
　　aut etiam nullum forsitan ante fuit,
viribus infirmi, vestro candore valemus :
　　quem[2] mihi si demas, omnia rapta putem.
15 cunctaque cum mea sint propenso nixa favore,
　　praecipuum veniae ius habet ille liber.

---

　　　　　　[1] quemlibet *corr.* ς　　　　[2] quod

---

[1] The Fabii claimed descent from Hercules, the protector of
the oppressed.
[2] Perhaps *Ex P*. ii. 1, the poem on the triumph of Tiberius.

Birth suited to your spirit is yours, for you have a noble breast, with the candour of Hercules.[2] Envy, the vice of cowardice, enters not into lofty character, but creeps like a hidden snake along the ground. Your mind towers aloft above even your birth, for your name is not greater than your character. So let others injure the wretched and desire to be feared; let them carry missiles dipped in corroding poison; your house at least is used to assisting suppliants. In their number, I beseech you, count me also.

IV. To Rufinus

These words that bring no empty greeting your Naso sends from the town of Tomis, and he entrusts to you the fostering of his "Triumph,"[2] Rufinus, if after all it has reached your hands. 'Tis a humble work, not equal to your preparations,[3] yet such as it is, he requests for it your guardianship. Strong things have powers of their own, and need no Machaon[4]; the sick man in his danger has recourse to the art of healing. Great poets need no favouring reader: they hold even the unwilling or him who is hard to please. I, whose talent has been diminished by long sorrows—or perhaps even of old I had no talent—weakened now, am strong in your generosity; if you take that from me, I should deem all else torn away. And though all my work rests upon kindly favour, that poem has a special right of indulgence.

[3] Others are included with Rufinus, cf. vestris (5), vestras (4), vos (23). Great preparations, including poems, were being made to celebrate the triumph, cf. 53 f.

[4] i.e. no physician.

spectatum vates alii scripsere triumphum :
  est aliquid memori visa notare manu.
nos ea vix avidam vulgo captata per aurem
20 scripsimus, atque oculi fama fuere mei.
scilicet adfectus similes, aut impetus idem
  rebus ab auditis conspicuisque venit !
nec nitor argenti, quem vos vidistis, et auri
  quod mihi defuerit, purpuraque illa, queror
25 sed loca, sed gentes formatae mille figuris
  nutrissent carmen proeliaque ipsa meum,
et regum vultus, certissima pignora mentis,[1]
  iuvissent aliqua forsitan illud opus.
plausibus ex ipsis populi laetoque favore
30 ingenium quodvis incaluisse potest :
tamque ego sumpsissem tali clamore vigorem,
  quam rudis audita miles ad arma tuba.
pectora sint nobis nivibus glacieque licebit
  atque hoc, quem patior, frigidiora loco,
35 illa ducis facies in curru stantis eburno
  excuteret frigus sensibus omne meis.
his ego defectus dubiisque auctoribus usus
  ad vestri venio iure favoris opem.
nec mihi nota ducum nec sunt mihi nota locorum
40 nomina.   materiam non habuere manus.
pars quota de tantis rebus, quam fama referre
  aut aliquis nobis scribere posset, erat ?
quo magis, o lector, debes ignoscere, sqiuid
  erratum est illic praeteritumve mihi.
45 adde quod assidue domini meditata querellas
  ad laetum carmen vix mea versa lyra est.
vix bona post tanto quaerenti verba subibant,
  et gaudere aliquid res mihi visa nova est.

[1] mentis] gentis

Other bards have seen the triumph they have described—'tis something to note with faithful hand what one has seen—I have described what I have caught with difficulty in an eager ear from common hearsay; rumour has been for me my eyes. Forsooth the same passion, the same vigour comes from what has been heard and from what has been seen! Not the absence of the gleaming silver or gold that you have seen causes my complaint; but the places, the peoples in a thousand forms, the very battles would have fed my verse—the countenances of the kings, the surest indication of their souls, would have aided, somehow perchance, that work.

[29] From the very applause and glad approval of the people any talent can catch the flame; I should have won vigour from such acclaim even as the raw recruit when he hears the trumpet call to arms. Though my breast be colder than snow or ice—colder even than this land which I endure—the aspect of that general standing in the ivory car would drive all cold from my senses.

[37] Lacking all this and using vague sources, rightly do I resort to the aid of your favour. I know not the names of the chieftains, I know not the names of the places; there was no material for my hands. How small a part of such mighty events could rumour bring me or some friend write! The more then, my reader, ought you to grant me pardon if I have erred or omitted anything therein. Add too that my lyre for ever conning its master's plaints could scarcely turn to a song of rejoicing. Happy words after so long a time responded with difficulty to my quest; to rejoice at anything seemed to me a new thing, and

utque reformidant insuetum lumina solem,
50   sic ad laetitiam mens mea segnis erat.
est quoque cunctarum novitas carissima [1] rerum,
    gratiaque officio, quod mora tardat, abest.
cetera certatim de magno scripta triumpho
    iam pridem populi suspicor ore legi.
55 illa bibit sitiens lector, mea pocula plenus :
    illa recens pota est, nostra tepebit aqua.
non ego cessavi, nec fecit inertia serum :
    ultima me vasti sustinet ora freti.
dum venit huc rumor properataque carmina fiunt
60   factaque eunt ad vos, annus abisse potest.
nec minimum refert, intacta rosaria primus,
    an sera carpas paene relicta manu.
quid mirum, lectis exhausto floribus horto,
    si duce non facta est digna corona suo [2] ?
65 deprecor hoc [3] : vatum [4] contra sua carmina ne quis
    dicta putet ! pro se Musa locuta mea est.
sunt mihi vobiscum communia sacra, poëtae,
    in vestro miseris si licet esse choro.
magnaque pars animae mecum vixistis, amici :
70   hac ego vos absens nunc quoque parte colo.
sint igitur vestro mea commendata favore
    carmina, non possum pro quibus ipse loqui.
scripta placent a morte fere, quia laedere vivos
    livor et iniusto carpere dente solet.
75 si genus est mortis male vivere, terra moratur,
    et desunt fatis sola sepulchra meis.

[1] calidissima   [2] suo : *expl. Housman*
[3] haec *vel* o   [4] vates

as eyes shrink before the sun to which they have been unaccustomed, so towards joyousness my mind moved slowly. Timeliness also is the most precious of all things, and that homage which is delayed receives no favour. Others have vied in writing of the mighty triumph and for a long time now, I suppose, the people have been reading them. These things thirsty readers have drunk; to my bowls they come with thirst already slaked: that drink is fresh, mine will be stale.

⁵⁷ I have not dallied, idleness has not made me slow; I am living on the most remote coast of the vast sea. While news is coming to me and hasty verse is being composed and when composed is travelling to you, a year may pass. It matters not a little whether one is first in the untouched rose-garden or with late hand plucks blooms which have been almost passed by. What wonder, when the flowers are plucked and the garden rifled, if I have twined no garland worthy of the victor for whose brows it was meant?

⁶⁵ This I disavow: let no poet think these words uttered in derogation of his verse; my Muse has but spoken in her own behalf. I have rites in common with you, ye poets—if you allow the unfortunate a place in your guild. Your life with me was a great part of my soul, my friends; even now in absence I continue thus to cherish you. Do you then grant the favour of your commendation to verse for which I cannot plead myself. Writings oft find favour after death, since malice is wont to injure the living, gnawing with unjust tooth. If to live in wretchedness is a kind of death, then earth is a loiterer and my fate lacks only the tomb. In fine

denique opus curae culpetur ut undique nostrae,
    officium nemo qui reprehendat erit.
ut desint vires, tamen est laudanda voluntas:
80   hac ego contentos auguror esse deos.
haec facit ut veniat pauper quoque gratus ad aras,
    et placeat caeso non minus agna bove.
res quoque tanta fuit, quantae subsistere summo
    Aeneadum [1] vati grande fuisset onus.
85 ferre etiam molles elegi tam vasta triumphi
    pondera disparibus non potuere rotis.
quo pede nunc utar, dubia est sententia nobis:
    alter enim de te, Rhene, triumphus adest.
inrita motorum [2] non sunt praesagia vatum:
90   danda Iovi laurus, dum prior illa viret.
nec mea verba legis, qui sum summotus ad Histrum,
    non bene pacatis flumina pota Getis:
ista dei vox est, deus est in pectore nostro,
    haec duce praedico vaticinorque deo.
95 quid cessas currum pompamque perare triumphis,
    Livia? dant nullas iam tibi bella moras.
perfida damnatas Germania proicit hastas.
    iam pondus dices omen habere meum.
crede, brevique fides aderit.   geminabit honorem
100 filius, et iunctis, ut prius, ibit equis.
prome, quod inicias umeris victoribus, ostrum:
    ipsa potest solitum nosse corona caput:
scuta sed et galeae gemmis radientur et auro,
    stentque super vinctos [3] trunca tropaea viros:

    [1] enidos *vel* aenidos *vel* aeneidos *corr. Ehwald*
    [2] votorum *corr. Heinsius*   [3] iunctos *vel* victos

    [1] Vergil.   [2] Tiberius.

though the result of my toil be everywhere disapproved, none will there be to blame my loyalty. Even though I lack the strength, yet the will is praiseworthy; with this, I divine, the gods are content. This it is which makes even the poor man well received when he approaches the altar, and a lamb receives no less favour than a slaughtered ox.

[83] The theme too was great enough to have formed a heavy burden even for the mighty bard [1] of the Aeneadae. Moreover frail couplets could not support the weight of so vast a triumph upon their uneven wheels. What metre I am now to use I am in doubt: for a second triumph is close at hand over thee, O Rhine. The prophecies of inspired bards are not empty: a laurel wreath is destined to be given to Jupiter while that other is still green. 'Tis not my words you read—I am far away by the Hister whose waters the wild Getae drink—'tis the voice of a god: a god is in my breast; under a god's inspiration I make this prophecy. Why dost thou hesitate, Livia, to make ready a car and a procession for a triumph? Already the war grants thee no delay. Traitorous Germany is casting away the spears she has learned to hate. Soon thou wilt say that my prophecy has weight. O believe; soon shall the proof be at hand. Thy son [2] shall double his honour and shall advance, as before, with yoked steeds. Bring forth the purple to throw upon the victor's shoulders; the chaplet of itself can recognize the familiar brow; but let shield and greaves glitter with jewels and gold, and trophies stand upreared [3] above the enchained men. Let towns

[3] *Trunca*, because trophies were originally fastened to a tree whose branches had been lopped.

105 oppida turritis cingantur eburnea muris,
    fictaque res vero more putetur agi.
squalidus inmissos fracta sub harundine crines
    Rhenus et infectas sanguine ploret [1] aquas.
barbara iam capti poscunt insignia reges
110   textaque fortuna divitiora sua,
et quae praeterea virtus invicta tuorum
    saepe parata tibi, saepe paranda facit.
di, quorum monitu sumus eventura locuti,
    verba, precor, celeri nostra probate fide.

V.

Quam legis, unde tibi mittatur epistula, quaeris ?
    hinc, ubi caeruleis iungitur Hister aquis.
ut regio dicta est, succurrere debet et auctor,
    laesus ab ingenio Naso poëta suo.
5 qui tibi, quam mallet praesens adferre salutem,
    mittit ab hirsutis, Maxime Cotta, Getis.
legimus, o iuvenis patrii non degener oris,
    dicta tibi pleno verba diserta foro.
quae quamquam lingua mihi sunt properante per horas
10   lecta satis multas, pauca fuisse queror.
plura sed haec feci relegendo saepe, nec umquam
    non mihi, quam primo, grata fuere magis.
cumque nihil [2] totiens lecta [3] e dulcedine perdant,
    viribus illa suis, non novitate, placent.
15 felices quibus haec ipso cognoscere in actu
    et tam facundo contigit ore frui !
nam, quamquam sapor est adlata dulcis in unda,
    gratius ex ipso fonte bibuntur aquae.

---

[1] portet *corr. Ehwald*   [2] nihil] sua   [3] lecta] nihil

of ivory be girdled with turreted walls, and the pretence be so real as to seem true. Let squalid Rhenus mourn locks trailing beneath broken rushes and waters dyed with blood. Already captive kings are calling for barbarian adornment, for a garb too rich to become their fate, and all the other things which the unconquered valour of thy sons has caused thee often to prepare, and will cause thee often to prepare.

[113] Ye gods, whose admonition inspires my prophecy of events to come, justify my words, I pray, with a speedy proof.

V. To Maximus Cotta

Whence comes the letter that you read, you ask ? From this place where Hister unites with the blue waves. Soon as the place is named the writer too should come before you—he whose own talent injured him, Naso the poet. To you, Maximus Cotta, to whom he would rather offer it face to face, he sends a greeting from the land of the shaggy Getae.

[7] I have read, O youth not untrue to your inherited oratory, the eloquent words you uttered in a crowded forum, and though my hurrying tongue has read them for many an hour, yet is it my complaint that they were few. But I have multiplied them by frequent reading, and ever have they been more pleasing to me than at first, and though they lose by so much reading nothing of their sweetness, 'tis by their force, not their novelty, that they please. Happy they who were vouchsafed to hear them at their delivery, and to enjoy utterance so eloquent ! For albeit water that is brought to one tastes sweet, more grateful is that which is drunk from the spring itself.

407

et magis adducto pomum decerpere ramo
20   quam de caelata sumere lance iuvat.
at nisi peccassem, nisi me mea Musa fugasset,
    quod legi, tua vox exhibuisset opus,
utque fui solitus, sedissem forsitan unus
    de centum iudex in tua verba viris,
25 maior et implesset praecordia nostra voluptas,
    cum traherer dictis adnueremque tuis.
quem quoniam fatum patria vobisque relictis
    inter inhumanos maluit esse Getas,
quod licet, ut videar tecum magis esse, legenda [1]
30   saepe, precor, studii pignora mitte tui,
exemploque meo, nisi dedignaris id ipsum,
    utere, quod nobis rectius ipse dares.
namque ego, qui perii iam pridem, Maxime, vobis,
    ingenio nitor non periisse meo.
35 redde vicem, nec rara tui monimenta laboris
    accipiant nostrae, grata futura, manus.
dic tamen, o iuvenis studiorum plene meorum,
    ecquid ab his ipsis admoneare mei.
ecquid, ubi aut recitas factum modo carmen amicis,
40   aut, quod saepe soles, exigis ut recitent,
quaeror, ut interdum tua mens, oblita quid absit,
    nescio quid certe sentit abesse sui,
utque loqui multum de me praesente solebas,
    nunc quoque Nasonis nomen in ore tuo est ?
45 ipse quidem Getico peream violatus ab arcu
    (et sit periuri quam prope poena, vides)
te nisi momentis video paene omnibus absens,
    gratus [2] quod menti quolibet ire licet.

---

[1] legendo *vel* loquendo *corr. Burman*
[2] gratia *corr. Luck*

---

[1] Ovid had been a member of the Centumviral Court, *cf. Tr.* ii. 93 f.

To draw down the branch and pluck the fruit gives more pleasure than to take it from an engraved salver. If I had not erred, if my Muse had never exiled me, your own voice would have delivered to me the work that I have read; as I was wont, I should perchance have sat as one of those hundred judges intent upon your words,[1] and a greater joy would have filled my breast when I was drawn on and with nods approved each phrase. But since Fate has wished rather that I, leaving my country and you, should dwell among the uncivilized Getae, that I may seem the more to be with you— send for my reading (this is possible) continual proofs, I beseech you, of your study; follow my example, unless you disdain it, an example which you yourself with greater right might give to me. For I, Maximus, who have long been dead, strive by my talent to prove myself not to be dead to you. Recompense me, and at no rare intervals let the monuments of your toil come into my hands to give me joy.

[37] But tell me, my youthful friend, you who are inspired with my own studies, if these very studies bring you any remembrance of me. Whenever you read to your friends a poem newly composed or, as you are often wont to do, urge them to read, do you miss me so that at times your mind, though forgetful of what is lacking, yet feels at least some part of it is gone? As you used to talk often of me in my presence, is Naso's name now also on your lips? As for me, may I die outraged by a Getic bow—and you see how close my penalty if I proved false—if I do not see you at almost every moment, absent though I am, but filled with thanks that the heart may go whithersoever it will. When in this way I

hac ubi perveni nulli cernendus in urbem,
50   saepe loquor tecum, saepe loquente fruor.
    tum mihi difficile est, quam sit bene, dicere, quamque
      candida iudiciis illa sit hora meis.
    tum me, siqua fides, caelesti sede receptum
      cum fortunatis suspicor esse deis.
55 rursus ubi huc redii, caelum superosque relinquo,
      a Styge nec longe Pontica distat humus.
    unde ego si fato nitor prohibente reverti,
      spem sine profectu, Maxime, tolle mihi.

VI.

Naso suo (posuit nomen quam [1] paene !) sodali
    mittit ab Euxinis hoc breve carmen aquis.
at si cauta parum scripsisset dextra quis esses,
    forsitan officio parta querella foret.
5 cur tamen, hoc aliis tutum credentibus, unus,
    appellent ne te carmina nostra, rogas ?
quanta sit in media clementia Caesaris ira,
    si nescis, ex me certior esse potes.
huic ego, quam patior, nil possem demere poenae,
10   si iudex meriti cogerer esse mei.
non vetat ille sui quemquam meminisse sodalis,
    nec prohibet tibi me scribere teque mihi.
nec scelus admittas, si consoleris amicum,
    mollibus et verbis aspera fata leves.
15 cur, dum tuta times, facis ut reverentia talis
    fiat in Augustos invidiosa deos ?
fulminis adflatos interdum vivere telis
    vidimus et refici, non prohibente Iove.

[1] quam] cui

have entered the city though none can see me, I often
converse with you, often enjoy your converse. Then
'tis hard to say how happy I am, how bright I think
that hour. Then, if you can credit it, I conceive
myself harboured in heaven's abode, dwelling with
the blessed gods. Again when I have returned
hither I leave behind heaven and the gods above ; the
land of the Pontus is hard by the Styx. If my
struggle to return from it is against the behest of fate,
then, Maximus, take from me a fruitless hope.

VI. To a Friend

Naso sends to his friend—how nearly did he name
him !—this bit of verse from the waters of the
Euxine. But if with too little caution his hand had
written who you were, perchance the tribute would
have earned a complaint. Yet why, when others
believe it safe, do you alone ask me not to address
you in my verse ? How great is Caesar's clemency
even in the midst of wrath, if you know it not, you
may learn from my case. From this punishment
that I suffer I could myself take away naught, were
I forced to be the judge of my own deserts. He
does not forbid anybody to mention a friend nor
does he prevent me from writing to you nor you to
me. You would commit no crime should you
comfort your friend, lightening with gentle
words his harsh fate. Why, fearful where no
fear is, do you by such homage bring discredit
upon the Augustan gods ? Men smitten by
the lightning's bolt we have seen at times live
and recover, nor did Jupiter prevent. Because

nec, quia Neptunus navem lacerarat Ulixis,
20   Leucothee nanti ferre negavit opem.
crede mihi, miseris caelestia numina parcunt,
   nec semper laesos et sine fine premunt.
principe nec nostro deux est moderatior ullus :
   Iustitia vires temperat ille suas.
25 nuper eam Caesar facto de marmore templo,
   iampridem posuit mentis in aede suae.
Iuppiter in multos temeraria fulmina torquet,
   qui poenam culpa non meruere pati.
obruerit cum tot saevis deus aequoris undis,
30   ex illis mergi pars quota digna fuit ?
cum pereant acie fortissima quaeque, vel ipso
   iudice delectus¹ Martis iniquus erit.
at si forte velis in eos² inquirere, nemo est
   quin² se, quod patitur, commeruisse neget.
35 adde quod extinctos vel aqua vel Marte vel igni
   nulla potest iterum restituisse dies.
restituit multos aut poenae parte levavit
   Caesar : et in multis me, precor, esse velit.
at tu, cum tali populus sub principe simus,
40   adloquio profugi credis inesse metum ?
forsitan haec domino Busiride iure timeres,
   aut solito clausos urere in aere viros.
desine mitem animum vano infamare timore.
   saeva quid in placidis sax vereris aquis ?
45 ipse ego quod primo scripsi sine nomine vobis,
   vix excusari posse mihi videor.
sed pavor attonito rationis ademerat usum,
   cesserat omne novis consiliumque malis,

¹ dilectus   ² in nos . . ./qui *corr. Bentley*

412

Neptune had wrecked Ulysses' ship, Leucothea [1] did
not refuse to aid him as he swam. O believe me, the
deities of heaven are merciful to the wretched;
nor do they always and endlessly oppress the
stricken. And no god is milder than our Prince, for
Justice tempers his strength. Her Caesar but
recently installed in a marble temple; long ago he
enshrined her in his heart. Jupiter hurls at hap-
hazard his bolts against many who have by no fault
deserved to suffer a penalty. Albeit the god of the
sea has o'erwhelmed so many in the cruel waves, how
small the number deserving to be drowned! When
the bravest die in battle, Mars' levy will be unjust
even in his own judgment. But if perchance you
wish to question each of them, there is not one but
would deny that he had deserved his suffering. And
those who have died at sea, in war, by fire no day can
restore. But Caesar has restored many or lightened
a part of their punishment; may it be his will that I
too be one of these many.

[39] But you, when we, his people, live under such an
emperor—do you believe that comforting an exile is
dangerous? Perhaps under the dominion of Busiris
you might rightly fear this or under him [2] who was wont
to burn men within the bronze. Cease to defame a
tender heart with idle fear. Why fear cruel reefs
in a calm sea? Even I, for having written at first
to you without your name, think that I can scarcely
be excused. But I was so stunned that fear had
taken away the use of reason, and all power of thought
had given way to the new misfortune; fearful of my

---

[3] The sea goddess who aided Ulysses to reach Phaeacia.

[2] Phalaris.

fortunamque meam metuens, non vindicis iram,
50   terrebar titulo nominis ipse mei.
hactenus admonitus memori concede poëtae [1]
    ponat ut in chartis nomina cara suis.
turpe erit ambobus, longo mihi proximus usu
    si nulla libri parte legere mei.
55 ne tamen iste metus somnos tibi rumpere possit,
    non ultra, quam vis, officiosus ero,
teque tegam, qui sis, nisi cum permiseris ipse :
    cogetur nemo munus habere meum.
tu modo, quem poteras vel aperte tutus amare,
60   si res est anceps ista, latenter ama.

VII.

Verba mihi desunt eadem tam saepe roganti,
    iamque pudet vanas fine carere preces.
taedia consimili fieri de carmine vobis,
    quidque petam cunctos edidicisse reor.
5 nostraque quid portet iam nostis epistula, quamvis
    cera [2] sit a vinclis non labefacta suis. [3]
ergo mutetur scripti sententia nostri,
    ne totiens contra, quam rapit amnis, eam.
quod bene de vobis speravi, ignoscite, amici :
10   talia peccandi iam mihi finis erit.
nec gravis uxori dicar : quae scilicet in me
    quam proba tam timida est experiensque parum.
hoc quoque, Naso, feres : etenim peiora tulisti.
    iam tibi sentiri sarcina nulla potest.
15 ductus ab armento taurus detrectat [4] aratrum,
    subtrahit[5] et duro colla novella iugo :

----

[1] sodali   [2] charta   [3] suis] meis
    [4] detrectet   [5] subtrahat

own fate, not of the avenger's wrath, I was filled with dread by the superscription of my own name.

51 Now that I have admonished you thus far, permit the poet who remembers you to place in his pages names that are dear to him. It will shame us both if you, so close to me through long intimacy, are mentioned nowhere in my book. Yet I would not have your slumbers broken by that dread of yours ; I will not display my devotion beyond your wishes, and I will conceal who you are save when you shall yourself grant leave ; none shall be forced to receive my tribute. Only do you, though you might with safety have loved me openly, if that seems dangerous—love me in secret.

VII. To Friends

Words fail me to make the same request so many times ; and at last it shames me that my idle prayers are endless. You are all weary of my monotonous verses, and my request you have learned by heart, I think. What message my letter bears you know already, although the wax has not been broken from its bonds. So let me change the purport of my writing that my course be not so often against the hurrying stream.

9 For my good hopes of you, pardon me, my friends : of such error now there shall be an end. Nor will I be called a trouble to my wife who in sooth is as true to me as she is timid and backward in her efforts. This also, Naso, thou shalt bear, and thou hast borne worse things ; no burden can affect thee now. The bull when he is taken from the herd objects to the plough and wrenches his inexperienced neck from

nos, quibus adsuevit fatum crudeliter uti,
    ad mala iam pridem non sumus ulla rudes.
venimus in Geticos fines : moriamur [1] in illis,
20   Parcaque ad extremum qua mea coepit eat.
spem iuvat amplecti—quae non iuvat inrita semper—
    et, fieri cupias siqua, futura putes :
proximus huic gradus est bene desperare salutem,
    seque semel vera scire perisse fide.
25 curando fieri quaedam maiora videmus
    vulnera, quae melius non tetigisse fuit.
mitius ille perit, subita qui mergitur unda,
    quam sua qui tumidis brachia lassat [2] aquis.
cur ego concepi Scythicis me posse carere
30   finibus et terra prosperiore frui ?
cur aliquid de me speravi lenius umquam ?
    an fortuna mihi sic mea nota fuit ?
torqueor en gravius, repetitaque forma locorum
    exilium renovat triste recensque facit.
35 est tamen utilius, studium cessare meorum,
    quam, quas admorint, non valuisse preces.
magna quidem res est, quam [3] non audetis, amici :
    sed si quis peteret, qui dare vellet, erat.
dummodo non nobis [4] hoc Caesaris ira negarit,
40   fortiter Euxinis inmoriemur aquis.

VIII.

Quae tibi quaerebam memorem testantia curam
    dona Tomitanus mittere posset ager.

---

      [1] moriemur   [2] iactat *vel* pulsat
        [3] quam] sed   [4] vobis

---

[1] In bitter despair the poet resolves at least to die bravely if Caesar does not deny him even this.

the hard yoke : I, beneath the practised cruelty of fate, have for long found no misfortune with which I am not familiar. I have come to the Getic shores ; let me die there and let my Fate continue to the end the course she has begun. 'Tis good to embrace a hope—though it bring no good and be ever vain—and whatever you long for that you may deem will happen. The next stage is utterly to give up hope of salvation, to know once and for all with full assurance that one is lost. Some wounds are made worse by treatment, as we see : it had been better not to touch them. More merciful is his death who is suddenly overwhelmed by the waters than his who wearies his arms in the heaving seas. Why did I conceive it possible for me to leave the Scythian land and enjoy a happier one ? Why did I ever hope any mercy for myself ? Was it thus that I had come to know my fate ? Lo ! my torture is all the worse, and the repeated description of this place but renews and freshens the harshness of my exile. Yet 'tis better that the zeal of my friends should cease than that the petitions they have brought should have had no weight. Serious indeed, my friends, is the thing you dare not : but if anybody were to ask, there is one who would be willing to grant. If only Caesar's wrath does not deny me this,[1] I shall bravely die on the shores of the Euxine sea.

VIII. To Maximus

I was pondering what gift to witness my unforgetting love of you the land of Tomis could send you

dignus es argento, fulvo quoque dignior auro,
    sed te, cum donas, ista iuvare solent.
5 nec tamen haec loca sunt ullo pretiosa metallo :
    hostis ab agricola vix sinit illa fodi.
purpura saepe tuos fulgens praetexit amictus.
    sed non Sarmatico tingitur illa mari.
vellera dura ferunt pecudes, et Palladis uti
10   arte Tomitanae non didicere nurus.
femina pro lana Cerealia munera frangit,
    suppositoque gravem vertice portat aquam.
non hic pampineis amicitur vitibus ulmus,
    nulla premunt ramos pondere poma suo.[1]
15 tristia deformes pariunt absinthia campi,
    terraque de fructu quam sit amara docet.
nil igitur tota Ponti regione sinistri,
    quod mea sedulitas mittere posset, erat.
clausa tamen misi Scythica tibi tela pharetra :
20   hoste precor fiant illa cruenta tuo.
hos habet haec calamos, hos haec habet ora libellos,
    haec viget in nostris, Maxime, Musa locis !
quae quamquam misisse pudet, quia parva videntur,
    tu tamen haec, quaeso, consule missa boni.

IX.

Quod sit in his eadem sententia, Brute, libellis,
    carmina nescio quem carpere nostra refers :
nil nisi me terra fruar ut propiore rogare,
    et quam sim denso cinctus ab hoste loqui.
5 o, quam de multis vitium reprehenditur unum !
    hoc peccat solum si mea Musa, bene est.

                     [1] suos

Worthy are you of silver, of tawny gold still more, but such things are wont to please you when you are the giver. Nor are these lands enriched by any mine : scarce does the enemy allow the farmer to dig there. Often has the gleam of purple bordered your robe, but there is no such dye as that by the Sarmatian sea. The flocks produce a coarse fleece and the daughters of Tomis have not learned the craft of Pallas. Instead of working the wool they grind Ceres' gifts or carry heavy burdens of water supported on their heads. Here no clustering vines cloak the elms, no fruits bend the branches with their weight. Harsh wormwood is the product of the unsightly plains, and by this fruit the land proclaims its own bitterness.

[17] Nothing there was, then, in the whole region of ill-omened Pontus that all my pains could send. Yet I am sending some Scythian arrows enclosed in their quiver ; may they be stained, I pray, in the blood of your enemies ! Such are the pens on this shore, such the books ! Such is the Muse who flourishes, Maximus, in this place of mine ! I am ashamed to send them because they seem poor gifts ; yet I pray you to take them in good part.

IX. To Brutus

Because these compositions of mine contain the same thought, Brutus, you report that somebody is carping at my verse : nothing (he says) but petitioning that I may enjoy a land nearer home, and talk of the throng of enemies encircling me. Ah, how the critic seizes on but one of many shortcomings ! If this is the only blemish of my Muse, 'tis well. I

ipse ego librorum video delicta meorum,
    cum sua plus iusto carmina quisque probet.
auctor opus laudat : sic forsitan Agrius olim
10   Thersiten facie dixerit esse bona.
iudicium tamen hic nostrum non decipit error,
    nec, quicquid genui, protinus illud amo.
cur igitur, si me video delinquere, peccem,
    et patiar scripto crimen inesse, rogas ?
15 non eadem ratio est sentire et demere morbos ;
    sensus inest cunctis, tollitur arte malum.
saepe aliquod verbum cupiens mutare reliqui,
    iudicium vires destituuntque meum.
saepe piget (quid enim dubitem tibi vera fateri)
20   corrigere et longi ferre laboris onus.
scribentem iuvat ipse labor [1] minuitque laborem,
    cumque suo crescens pectore fervet opus.
corrigere ut [2] res est tanto minus ardua quanto
    magnus Aristarcho maior Homerus erat,
25 sic animum lento curarum frigore laedit,
    ut cupidi cursor [3] frena retentat equi.
atque ita di mites minuant mihi Caesaris iram,
    ossaque pacata nostra tegantur humo,
ut mihi conanti nonnumquam intendere curas
30   fortunae species obstat acerba meae,
vixque mihi videor, faciam qui [4] carmina, sanus,
    inque feris curem corrigere illa Getis.
nil tamen e scriptis magis excusabile nostris,
    quam sensus cunctis paene quod unus inest.
35 laeta fere laetus cecini, cano tristia tristis :
    conveniens operi tempus utrumque suo est.

[1] favor   [2] et *vel* at : ut *Burmann*
[3] cursus *corr. Madvig*   [4] qui] quod *vel* cum

myself perceive the defects of my own books despite
the fact that every man is all too fond of his own
verse.   A creator finds praise for his own work : so
perchance of old Agrius[1] may have called Thersites
fair.   Yet my judgment is not distorted by this
failing : whatever I beget does not forthwith please
me.   Why then, you ask, if I perceive my mistakes,
should I continue to err, permitting faults to remain
in my writing ?   'Tis not the same story to feel and to
cure a disease ; all men can feel, skill must remove the
trouble.   Often when I am desirous of changing some
word I leave it, and my strength forsakes my
judgment.   Often—why should I hesitate to confess
to you the truth ?—it irks me to emend and endure
the burden of long toil.   While writing the very toil
gives pleasure and itself is lessened, and the growing
work glows with the writer's heart.   But while to
emend is as much easier as great Homer was greater
than Aristarchus, nevertheless it wears down the
mind with a slow chill of worry, as a driver restrains
an eager steed.   As truly as I hope that the merciful
gods may lessen Caesar's wrath and allow my bones
to rest in peaceful soil, when I attempt to work
carefully, sometimes the bitter vision of my lot
confronts me and I think myself hardly sane in
composing verses or in troubling to emend them
among the wild Getae.

[33] And yet there is nothing more deserving of excuse
in what I write than that in it all there is one single
thought.   Gay was oft my song when I was gay, sad it
is now that I am sad : each period has a type of work

---

[1] Father of Thersites, *cf. Ex P.* iv. 13. 15 note.

quid nisi de vitio scribam regionis amarae,
    utque loco moriar commodiore precer ?
cum totiens eadem dicam, vix audior ulli,
40   verbaque profectu dissimulata carent.
et tamen haec eadem cum sint, non scripsimus [1] isdem,
    unaque per plures vox mea temptat opem.
an, ne bis sensum lector reperiret eundem,
    unus amicorum, Brute, rogandus eras [2] ?
45 non fuit hoc tanti.   confesso ignoscite, docti :
    vilior est operis fama salute mea.
denique materiam quamvis [3] sibi finxerit ipse,
    arbitrio variat multa poëta suo.
Musa mea est index nimium quoque vera malorum,
50   atque incorrupti pondera testis habet.
nec liber ut fieret, sed uti sua cuique daretur
    littera, propositum curaque nostra fuit.
postmodo collectas utcumque sine ordine iunxi :
    hoc opus electum ne mihi forte putes.
55 da veniam scriptis, quorum non gloria nobis
    causa, sed utilitas officiumque fuit.

[1] scribimus *vel* scribitur   [2] erat
[3] quam quis *corr. Riese*

that befits it. Of what am I to write save the evils of
a bitter country and to pray that I may die in a
pleasanter region? I write so often of the same
things that scarce any listen, and my words, which
they feign not to understand, are without
result. And yet the words are always the same, I
have not written to the same persons : my cry, always
the same, seeks aid through many. Should I—that
some reader might not twice find the same sense—
petition you alone, Brutus, among my friends? It
was not worth the price; pardon the confession, ye
men of taste! Cheaper in my eyes is the reputation
of my work than my own weal. In fine though he
himself may have fashioned the subject, the poet
introduces many a variation when led by his
judgement. My Muse is but too true an index of my
misfortunes ; she has all the weight of an incor-
ruptible witness. Not to produce a book, but to
send a letter to each has been the object of my
care. Later I collected them and put them together
somehow, without order—not to have you think
perchance that for this work I have made selections.
Grant indulgence to my writings, for their purpose
has been not my renown but my advantage, and to do
homage to others.

LIBER QUARTUS

I.

Accipe, Pompei, deductum carmen ab illo,
    debitor est vitae qui tibi, Sexte, suae.
qui seu non prohibes a me tua nomina poni,
    accedet meritis haec quoque summa tuis:
5 sive trahis vultus, equidem peccasse fatebor,
    delicti tamen est causa probanda mei.
non potuit mea mens, quin esset grata, teneri.
    sit precor officio non gravis ira pio.
o,[1] quotiens ego sum libris mihi visus ab[2] istis
10   impius, in nullo quod legerere loco!
o, quotiens, alii cum vellem scribere, nomen
    rettulit in ceras inqcia dextra tuum!
ipse mihi placuit mendis in talibus error,
    et vix invita facta litura manu est.
15 " viderit! ad summam " dixi " licet ipse queratur!
    hanc[3] pudet offensam non meruisse prius."
da mihi, siquid ea est, hebetantem pectora Lethen,
    oblitus potero non tamen esse tui.
idque sinas oro, nec fastidita repellas
20   verba, nec officio crimen inesse putes,
et levis haec meritis referatur gratia tantis:
    si minus, invito te quoque gratus ero.

      [1] o] di   [2] ab] in   [3] hanc] a, *i.e.* a!

BOOK IV

I. To Sextus Pompey

Deign to receive a poem, Sextus Pompey, composed by him who is indebted to you for his life. If you do not prevent me from uttering your name this also will be added to the sum of your deserts: or if you frown, I shall indeed confess my mistake, but its cause must nevertheless win approval. My heart could not be restrained from gratitude; let not your anger be heavy, I beseech you, upon my loyal service. Ah, how often have I thought myself ungrateful in these books because nowhere was your name read! Ah, how often, when I wished to write to another, has my hand all unconsciously placed your name upon the wax! The very mistake I made in such slips gave me pleasure and my hand was scarce willing to make the erasure. "Let him see it!" I said, "though he may indeed complain! Ashamed am I not to have earned this blame earlier!" Give me, if such thing there be, the waters of Lethe that benumb the heart, yet I shall not be able to forget you. I beg you will permit this nor reject in contempt my words, nor think that in my tribute there is a sin. Let this slight gratitude be rendered to all your services; if you do not, I shall be grateful even against your will.

numquam pigra fuit nostris tua gratia rebus,
    nec mihi munificas arca negavit opes.
25 nunc quoque nil subitis clementia territa fatis
    auxilium vitae fertque [1] feretque meae.
unde rogas forsan fiducia tanta futuri
    sit mihi ? quod fecit, quisque tuetur opus.
ut Venus artificis labor est et gloria Coi,
30   aequoreo madidas quae premit imbre comas :
arcis ut Actaeae vel eburna vel aerea [2] custos
    bellica Phidiaca stat dea facta manu :
vindicat ut Calamis laudem, quos fecit, equorum :
    ut similis verae vacca Myronis opus :
35 sic ego pars rerum non ultima, Sexte, tuarum
    tutelaeque feror munus opusque tuae.

II.

Quod legis, o vates magnorum maxime regum,
    venit ab intonsis usque, Severe, Getis :
cuius adhuc nomen nostros tacuisse libellos,
    si modo permittis dicere vera, pudet.
5 orba tamen numeris cessavit epistula numquam
    ire per alternas officiosa vices.
carmina sola tibi memorem testantia curam
    non data sunt.   quid enim, quae facis ipse, darem ?
quis mel Aristaeo, quis Baccho vina Falerna,
10   Triptolemo fruges, poma det Alcinoo ?
fertile pectus habes, interque Helicona colentes
    uberius nulli provenit ista seges.

---

[1] feretque *vel* refertque *vel* referta   [2] aenea : aerea *s*

---

[1] Ovid plays on *gratia* (thanks), *gratus* (grateful), and *gratia* (favour, kindness).

426

[23] Never has your grace [1] been slow to meet my need nor has your coffer ever denied me generous aid. Even now your clemency, not at all deterred by my sudden misfortune, offers and will continue to offer succour to my life. Whence, perchance you ask, have I so much confidence in the future? Every man watches over the work he has wrought. Just as Venus is at once the work and glory of the Coan artist,[2] as she presses her locks damp with the spray of the sea; as the war goddess [3] who guards the Actaean citadel stands in ivory or bronze wrought by the hand of Phidias, as Calamis claims renown for the steeds he has made, as the lifelike cow is Myron's work, so I am not the last of your possessions, Sextus; I am known as the gift, the work of your guardianship.

II. To Severus

That which you are reading, Severus, mightiest bard of mighty kings, comes all the way from the land of the unshorn Getae, and that as yet my books have made no mention of your name if you will permit me to speak the truth brings me shame Yet letters not in metre have never ceased to go on their mission of friendship between us. Verse alone, bearing witness to your thoughtful care, I have not given you: why should I give what you yourself compose? Who would give honey to Aristaeus, Falernian wine to Bacchus, grain to Triptolemus, fruit to Alcinous? You have a productive heart; of those who cultivate Helicon, none displays

[2] Apelles.   [3] Athena.

mittere ad hunc carmen, frondes erat addere silvis,
    haec mihi cunctandi causa, Severe, fuit.
15 nec tamen ingenium nobis respondet, ut ante,
    sed siccum sterili vomere litus aro.
scilicet ut limus venas excaecat inundans,[1]
    laesaque suppresso fonte resistit aqua,
pectora sic mea sunt limo vitiata malorum,
20   et carmen vena pauperiore fluit.
si quis in hac ipsum terra posuisset Homerum,
    esset, crede mihi, factus et ille Getes.
da veniam fasso, studiis quoque frena remisi,
    ducitur et digitis littera rara meis.
25 impetus ille sacer, qui vatum pectora nutrit,
    qui prius in nobis esse solebat, abest.
vix venit ad partes, vix sumptae Musa tabellae
    inponit pigras paene coacta manus.
parvaque, ne dicam scribendi nulla voluptas
30   est mihi, nec numeris nectere verba iuvat.
sive quod hinc fructus adeo non cepimus ullos,
    principium nostri res sit ut ista mali :
sive quod in tenebris numerosos ponere gestus,[2]
    quodque legas nulli scribere carmen, idem est.
35 excitat auditor studium, laudataque virtus
    crescit, et inmensum gloria calcar habet.
hic mea cui recitem nisi flavis scripta Corallis,
    quasque alias gentes barbarus Hister habet ?
sed quid solus agam, quaque infelicia perdam
40   otia materia surripiamque diem ?
nam quia nec vinum, nec me tenet alea fallax,
    per quae clam tacitum tempus abire solet,
nec me, quod cuperem, si per fera bella liceret,
    oblectat cultu terra novata suo,

---

[1] in undis *corr. Madvig*
[2] gressus *s*

a richer crop. To send verse to such a one were to
add leaves to the forest : this has caused my delay,
Severus. Yet my talent does not answer the call as
of old, for I am furrowing a barren shore with an
ineffective plough. Surely just as clogging silt jams
channels and the outraged water halts in the choked
fountain, so my mind has been injured by the silt of
misfortune, and my verse flows with a scantier
vein. If anyone had set in this land Homer himself,
let me assure you, even he would have become a
Getan. Pardon one who confesses, but in my
pursuit I have relaxed the rein, my fingers rarely
trace a letter. That inspired impulse, the nurse of
poets' thoughts, which once was mine, is gone. My
Muse scarce takes her part, and when I have taken up
my tablets scarce does she lay upon them an inert
hand, almost under coercion. I have little pleasure,
or none at all, in writing, no zest in joining words to
metre, whether it is that I have so reaped from it no
profit that this very thing is the source of my
misfortune, or that making rhythmic gestures in the
dark and composing a poem which you may read to
nobody are one and the same thing. A hearer rouses
zeal, excellence increases with praise, and renown
possesses a mighty spur. In this place who is there to
whom I can read my compositions except the yellow-
haired Coralli, or the other tribes of the wild Hister ?
But what shall I do in my loneliness, with what oc-
cupation shall I pass my ill-starred leisure and beguile
the day ? For since neither wine nor treacherous dice
attract me, which oft cause time to steal quietly away,
nor—although I should like it if fierce war permitted—
can I take pleasure in renewing the earth by cultiva-

45 quid, nisi Pierides, solacia frigida, restant,
    non bene de nobis quae meruere deae ?
at tu, cui bibitur felicius Aonius fons,
    utiliter studium quod tibi cedit ama,
sacraque Musarum merito cole, quodque legamus,
50   huc aliquod curae mitte recentis opus.

III.

Conquerar, an taceam ?   ponam sine nomine crimen,
    an notum qui sis omnibus esse velim ?
nomine non utar, ne commendere querella,
    quaeraturque tibi carmine fama meo.
5 dum mea puppis erat valida fundata carina,
    qui mecum velles currere, primus eras.
nunc, quia contraxit vultum Fortuna, recedis,
    auxilio postquam scis opus esse tuo.
dissimulas etiam, nec me vis nosse videri,
10   quisque sit, audito nomine, Naso, rogas.
ille ego sum, quamquam non vis audire, vetusta
    paene puer puero iunctus amicitia :
ille ego, qui primus tua seria nosse solebam
    et tibi iucundis primus adesse iocis :
15 ille ego convictor densoque domesticus usu,
    ille ego iudiciis unica Musa tuis.
ille ego sum, qui nunc an vivam, perfide, nescis,
    cura tibi de quo quaerere nulla fuit.
sive fui numquam carus, simulasse fateris :
20   seu non fingebas, inveniere levis.
aut age, dic aliquam, quae te mutaverit, iram :
    nam nisi iusta tua est, iusta querella mea est.

---

[1] Since Severus wrote epics on contemporary themes (see Index), it is not improbable that he had received some concrete reward.

tion, what remains except the Pierians, a cold solace,—the goddesses who have not deserved well of me? But you, who quaff more happily the Aonian spring, continue your love for the pursuit which yields you profit; [1] worship as is right the cult of the Muses and for my reading send hither some work over which you have recently toiled.

III. To a Faithless Friend

Complaint or silence? Shall I make a nameless charge, or should I wish all to know who you are? I will not employ your name lest my complaint bring you favour and through my verse you win renown. [5] As long as my bark rested firmly upon its keel among all who wished to sail with me you were first. Now that Fortune has frowned you withdraw upon discovering that your assistance is needed. You play the dissembler, too, and wish not to be thought to know me; when you hear the name you ask who Naso is! 'Tis I, although you will not hear it, who have been united to you in friendship almost boy with boy; 'tis I who used first to hear your serious thoughts, first to listen to your pleasant jests; 'tis I who lived in close union with you in the same household; 'tis I who in your judgment was the one and only Muse; 'tis I of whom you know not, traitor, whether I am now alive, about whom you have been at no pains to inquire. If I was never dear to you, you confess pretence; if you were not feigning, you will be proved faithless. Or else come now, tell me of some reason for anger that has altered you; for if your complaint is not just, then mine is

431

quod te nunc crimen similem [1] vetat esse priori ?
  an crimen, coepi quod miser esse, vocas ?
25 si mihi rebus opem nullam factisque ferebas,
  venisset verbis charta notata tribus.
vix equidem credo, sed et [2] insultare iacenti
  te mihi nec verbis parcere fama refert.
quid facis, a ! demens ? cur, si Fortuna recedat, [3]
30   naufragio lacrimas eripis ipse tuo ?
haec dea non stabili, quam sit levis, orbe fatetur,
  quae summum dubio sub pede semper habet.
quolibet est folio, quavis incertior aura :
  par illi levitas, improbe, sola tua est.
35 omnia sunt hominum tenui pendentia filo,
  et subito casu quae valuere, ruunt.
divitis audita est cui non opulentia Croesi ?
  nempe tamen vitam captus ab hoste tulit.
ille Syracosia modo formidatus in urbe
40   vix humili duram reppulit arte famem.
quid fuerat Magno maius ? tamen ille rogavit
  summissa fugiens voce clientis opem.
cuique viro totus terrarum paruit orbis,

  . . . . [4]

45 ille Iugurthino clarus Cimbroque triumpho,
  quo victrix totiens consule Roma fuit,
in caeno Marius iacuit cannaque palustri,
  pertulit et tanto multa pudenda viro

[1] quae te consimilem res nunc (non)
[2] sed et] subito   [3] recedit : recedat ς
[4] om. optimi codd.

---

[1] Fortuna was often depicted standing on a wheel.
[2] Dionysius, the tyrant, who was expelled and kept school at Corinth.

just. What crime of mine prevents you from being
what you once were ? Or do you term it a crime that
I have become unfortunate ? If you brought me no
aid in fact, in deeds, you might have sent me three
words on a sheet of paper. I can scarce believe it—
but rumour says that you are even insulting me in my
fall, that you do not spare words. Ah, why do you
do this, madman ? Why, in case Fortune should
leave you, do you thus rob your own shipwreck of
tears ? She is a goddess who admits by her unsteady
wheel her own fickleness ; she always has its crest
beneath her swaying foot.[1] She is less stable than
any leaf, than any breeze ; to match her fickleness,
base man, there is only yours !

[35] All human affairs hang by a slender thread ;
chance on a sudden brings to ruin what once was
strong. Who has not heard of Croesus's
wealth ? Yet of a truth he was captured and
received his life from an enemy. He[2] who but now
was dreaded in the city of Syracuse, scarce kept
hunger at bay by a lowly calling. What was
mightier than Magnus[3] ? Yet in his flight he
asked with humble voice a client's aid. The
man whom the whole world obeyed . . . .
, . . [4] he who was famed for his triumphs
over Jugurtha and the Cimbri, under whom as consul
Rome was so often victorious, lay, Marius though he
was, in the slime and marsh grass, enduring many
things shameful for so great a man.

---

[3] Pompey. After the battle of Pharsalus he fled to Egypt
where he was treacherously slain.

[4] V. 44 is omitted by the best manuscripts. In the latter
ones appears the spurious line : *indigus effectus omnibus ipse
magis* ("himself came to feel need more than any ").

ludit in humanis divina potentia rebus,
50 et certam praesens vix feret [1] hora fidem.
"litus ad Euxinum " si quis mihi diceret "ibis,
et metues, arcu ne feriare Getae,"
"i, bibe" dixissem "purgantes pectora sucos,
quidquid et in tota nascitur Anticyra."
55 sum tamen haec passus : nec, si mortalia possem,
et summi poteram tela cavere dei.
tu quoque fac timeas, et quae tibi laeta videntur
dum loqueris, fieri tristia posse puta.

IV.

Nulla dies adeo est australibus umida nimbis,
non intermissis ut fluat imber aquis.
nec sterilis locus ullus ita est, ut non sit in illo
mixta fere duris utilis herba rubis.
5 nil adeo fortuna gravis miserabile fecit,
ut minuant nulla gaudia parte malum.
ecce domo patriaque carens oculisque meorum,
naufragus in Getici litoris actus aquas,
qua tamen inveni vultum diffundere causa
10 possim,[2] fortunae nec meminisse meae.
nam mihi, cum fulva solus [3] spatiarer harena,
visa est a tergo pinna dedisse sonum.
respicio, nec erat corpus, quod cernere possem,
verba tamen sunt haec aure recepta mea :
15 "en ego laetarum venio tibi nuntia rerum
Fama, per inmensas aëre lapsa vias.
consule Pompeio, quo non tibi carior alter,
candidus et felix proximus annus erit."

---

[1] feret] habet   [2] possem   [3] solus] tristis

⁴⁹ Divine power plays with human affairs, and sure trust can scarce be placed in the present hour. If anybody had said to me, "You shall go to the Euxine shore and you shall fear wounds from a Getic bow," I would have said, "Go, drink a potion that clears the brain—everything that Anticyra¹ produces." Yet have I suffered this. Though I might have guarded against the weapons of mortals, yet I could not protect myself against those of a supreme god. See that you too feel afraid and remember that what seems happiness to you has power, while you speak, to change into sorrow.

IV. To Sextus Pompeius

No day is so drenching wet from the southern clouds that the rain pours in uninterrupted flood. No place is so barren that it has no useful plant, oft-times intermixed with the tough brambles. Heavy fortune has rendered nothing so wretched that no joys lessen in some part its sorrow. Behold how I, reft from home and country and the sight of my own, driven like a wreck to the waters of the Getic land, have yet found means to brighten my face and to forget my fate. For as I strolled alone upon the yellow sand, behind me, it seemed, wings rustled. I looked back ; there was no form that I could see, but my ear caught these words, "Lo, I come to bear thee a message of gladness ; I am Report, and I have flown through measureless distances of air. Through the consulship of Pompey, who is dearer to you than any other, the coming year will be bright and blessed."

¹ Anticyra produced an abundance of hellebore which was much used as a cure for insanity.

dixit, et ut laeto Pontum rumore replevit,
20   ad gentes alias hinc dea vertit iter.
at mihi dilapsis inter nova gaudia curis
  excidit asperitas huius iniqua loci.
ergo ubi, Iane biceps, longum reseraveris annum,
  pulsus et a sacro mense December erit,
25 purpura Pompeium summi velabit honoris,
  ne titulis quicquam debeat ille suis.
cernere iam videor rumpi paene atria turba,
  et populum laedi deficiente loco,
templaque Tarpeiae primum tibi sedis adiri,
30   et fieri faciles in tua vota deos ;
colla boves niveos certae praebere securi,
  quos aluit campis herba Falisca suis :
cumque deos omnes, tum quos [1] inpensius aequos
  esse tibi cupias, cum Iove Caesar erunt.
35 curia te excipiet, patresque e more vocati
  intendent aures ad tua verba suas.
hos ubi facundo tua vox hilaraverit ore,
  utque solet, tulerit prospera verba dies,
egeris et meritas superis cum Caesare grates
40   (qui causam, facias cur ita saepe, dabit),
inde domum repetes toto comitante senatu,
  officium populi vix capiente domo.
me miserum, turba quod non ego cernar in illa,
  nec poterunt istis lumina nostra frui !
45 quod licet,[2] absentem qua possum mente videbo :
  aspiciet vultus consulis illa sui.

[1] tunc hos
[2] qualibet *unde* quamlibet *Heinsius*

---

[1] January, in which the magistrates entered on their terms.

She spoke, and having filled the Pontus with the glad
tidings the goddess turned her course to other
peoples. But for me care fell away amidst my new
joys, the cruel harshness of this land vanished. And
so, two-faced Janus, when thou hast unsealed the
long year, when December is driven out by the holy
month,[1] Pompey will assume the purple of highest
office that to his titles of honour he may leave no
debt undischarged.[2] Already I seem to behold your
halls almost bursting with the crowd, the people
bruised for lack of space, the temples of Tarpeia's
abode[3] visited by you as your first act, the gods
becoming propitious to your prayers, the snowy oxen
which Falerii has nourished in her own meadows
offering their throats to the unerring axe; and while
from all the gods you will earnestly seek favour, those
of your more eager desire shall be Jupiter and
Caesar. The senate-house will receive you and the
fathers summoned in the wonted fashion will lend
attentive ear to your words. When they have been
delighted by the words that will fall from your
eloquent lips, when according to custom the day shall
offer words of good omen, and you have rendered due
thanks to the gods above and to Caesar, who will give
you cause to repeat them often, you will return home
escorted by the whole senate, the house scarce finding
room for the people's homage. Wretched am I that
I shall not be seen in that throng, that my eyes will
not be able to enjoy that sight! But this I may
do: in your absence I can see you in my mind;
that will behold the features of its loved

[2] As if the series of offices were a score which Pompey would
pay in full when he became consul.
[3] The Capitoline Hill.

di faciant aliquo subeat tibi tempore nostrum
    nomen, et " heu " dicas " quid miser ille facit ? "
haec tua pertulerit si quis mihi verba, fatebor
50   protinus exilium mollius esse meum.

V.

Ite, leves elegi, doctas ad consulis aures,
    verbaque honorato ferte legenda viro.
longa via est, nec vos pedibus proceditis aequis,
    tectaque brumali sub nive terra latet.
5 cum gelidam Thracen et opertum nubibus Haemum
    et maris Ionii transieritis aquas,
luce minus decima dominam venietis in urbem,
    ut festinatum non faciatis iter.
protinus inde domus vobis Pompeia petatur :
10   non est Augusto iunctior ulla foro.
siquis, ut in populo, qui sitis et unde requiret,
    nomina decepta quaelibet aure ferat.
ut sit enim tutum, sicut reor esse, fateri,
    verba minus certe ficta timoris habent.
15 copia nec vobis nullo prohibente videndi
    consulis, ut limen contigeritis, erit.
aut reget ille suos dicendo iura Quirites,
    conspicuum signis cum premet altus ebur :
aut populi reditus positam componet ad hastam,
20   et minui magnae non sinet urbis opes :
aut, ubi erunt patres in Iulia templa vocati,
    de tanto dignis consule rebus aget :
aut feret Augusto solitam natoque salutem,
    deque parum noto consulet officio.

---

[1] A spear was set up where the consul was letting contracts,
etc.

consul. May the gods grant that at some moment my name may come into your mind, that you may say, "Alas! what is that miserable man doing now?" If such words of yours be reported to me by any, I shall at once confess that my exile is easier to bear.

V. To Sextus Pompeius

On! light couplets, to the consul's learned ears, and bear a message for the honoured man to read. Long is the way, nor do you advance with even steps, and a mantle of winter snow conceals the land. Crossing frozen Thrace with Haemus hidden in clouds and the waters of the Ionian sea, on the tenth day or before you will reach the imperial city though you make no hurried journey. Forthwith then seek the house of Pompeius; none is closer to the forum of Augustus. If any, as may happen in the crowd, asks who you are and whence you come, beguile his ear with any name you will. For even though it should be safe, as I think it is, to make confession, surely fictitious words involve less danger. Nor will you have the power unhindered to see the consul, even though you reach the threshold: either he will be ruling his citizens by the law's word while he sits high upon an ivory chair splendid with carving, or beside the implanted spear [1] he will be ordering the people's revenues, not allowing the wealth of the mighty city to suffer loss; or when the fathers have been summoned to Julius's temple, he will be debating matters worthy of a great consul; or he will be bringing to Augustus and his son the accustomed greeting, seeking advice about an unfamiliar duty.

439

25 tempus ab his vacuum Caesar Germanicus omne
  auferet : a magnis hunc colit ille deis.
 cum tamen a turba rerum requieverit harum,
  ad vos mansuetas porriget ille manus,
 quidque parens ego vester agam fortasse requiret.
30   talia vos illi reddere verba volo :
  " vivit adhuc vitamque tibi debere fatetur,
  quam prius a miti Caesare munus habet.
 te sibi, cum fugeret, memori solet ore referre
  barbariae tutas exhibuisse vias :
35 sanguine Bistonium quod non tepefecerit ensem,
  effectum cura pectoris esse tui :
 addita praeterea vitae quoque multa tuendae
  munera, ne proprias attenuaret opes.
 pro quibus ut meritis referatur gratia, iurat
40   se fore mancipii [1] tempus in omne tui.
 nam prius umbrosa carituros arbore montes,
  et freta velivolas non habitura rates,
 fluminaque in fontes cursu reditura supino,
  gratia quam meriti possit abire tui."
45 haec ubi dixeritis, servet sua dona rogate.
  sic fuerit vestrae causa peracta viae.

VI.

 Quam legis, ex illis tibi venit epistula, Brute,
  Nasonem nolles in quibus esse locis.
 sed tu quod nolles, voluit miserabile fatum.
  ei mihi ! plus illud quam tua vota valet.
5 in Scythia nobis quinquennis Olympias acta est :
  iam tempus lustri transit in alterius.
 perstat enim fortuna tenax, votisque malignum
  opponit nostris insidiosa [2] pedem.

---

[1] mancipium . . . tuum   [2] invidiosa

All the time left from these offices Germanicus Caesar will claim : him he reverences next after the great gods.

[27] Yet when he finds rest from this crowd of affairs, he will extend to you his kindly hands, and he will ask perhaps how I, your parent, am faring. In such words as these I wish you to reply: "He still lives, confessing that he owes the life to you which first he holds as the gift of Caesar's mercy. He is wont to say with grateful lips that upon his journey to exile you made the ways of the barbarian world safe for him : that his blood stained no Bistonian sword was owing to your heartfelt care ; that you gave him besides many gifts to preserve his life that his own resources might not be impaired. To thank you for these services he swears to be your slave for all time. For the mountains will sooner be stripped of their shady trees and the seas of their sailing ships, the rivers will turn and flow backward to their sources before he can cease to be grateful for your service."

[45] When you have spoken thus, ask him to preserve his own gift ; so will the purpose of your journey be accomplished.

VI. To Brutus

The letter that you are reading, Brutus,[1] has come from that land in which you would not wish Naso to be. Yet what you would not wish, wretched fate has willed for me. Alas! fate is stronger than your prayers. In Scythia I have passed the five years of an Olympiad ; the time is now passing to a second lustrum. For obstinate fortune persists and craftily opposes a malicious foot to my desires. Thou,

---

[1] A close friend of Ovid's otherwise unknown, *cf.* i. 1.

certus eras pro me, Fabiae laus, Maxime, gentis,
10   numen ad Augustum supplice voce loqui.
occidis ante preces, causamque ego, Maxime, mortis
(nec fuero tanti) me reor esse tuae.
iam timeo nostram cuiquam mandare salutem :
ipsum morte tua concidit auxilium.
15 coeperat Augustus decepti [1] ignoscere culpae :
spem nostram terras deseruitque simul.
quale tamen potui, de caelite, Brute, recenti
vestra procul positus carmen in ora dedi.
quae prosit pietas utinam mihi, sitque malorum
20   iam modus et sacrae mitior ira domus.
te quoque idem liquido possum iurare precari,
o mihi non dubia cognite Brute nota.
nam cum praestiteris verum mihi semper amorem,
hic tamen adverso tempore crevit amor.
25 quique tuas pariter lacrimas nostrasque videret,
passuros poenam crederet esse duos.
lenem te miseris genuit natura, nec ulli
mitius ingenium, quam tibi, Brute, dedit :
ut qui quid valeas ignoret Marte forensi,
30   posse tuo peragi vix putet ore reos.
scilicet eiusdem est, quamvis pugnare videntur,
supplicibus facilem, sontibus esse trucem.
cum tibi suscepta est legis vindicata severae,
verba velut tinctum singula virus habent.
35 hostibus eveniat quam sis violentus in armis
sentire et linguae tela subire tuae.

----

[1] deceptae *corr. Richmond*

----

[1] *Paullus Fabius Maximus (Introd. p. xii).*
[2] *This poem on the apotheosis of Augustus (cf. also iv. 9. 131)* is not extant. Augustus died A.D. 14, a few months

442

Maximus,[1] glory of the Fabian race, hadst resolved to appeal for me to the deity of Augustus with the voice of a suppliant. Thou didst die before the prayer was uttered, and I count myself, Maximus—though I am not worth so much—the cause of thy death. Now I fear to entrust my salvation to any; help itself has perished with thy death.

[15] Augustus had begun to pardon the fault of one who was misled; my hopes at once and the world he left desolate. Yet from my distant abode I sent for your reading a poem—such poem as I could, Brutus, about the new god.[2] May this act of reverence aid me, let there now be an end to my sorrows, a gentler wrath on the part of the sacred household. I can swear with a clear conscience that you too utter the same prayer, Brutus—you whom I know from indubitable proof. For although you have ever granted me sincere love, yet this love has increased in my time of adversity. One who saw your tears that matched with mine would have believed that both were about to suffer punishment. Nature bore you kind to the wretched; to none, Brutus, has she given a kinder heart, so that he who know not your power in the wars of the forum would scarce suppose that your lips can prosecute defendants. In truth the same man, although such qualities seem to battle with each other, is able to be gentle with suppliants, but harsh to the guilty. When you have taken it upon yourself to champion the strict law, every word is as though it were steeped in poison. May it befall enemies to feel how impetuous you are in arms, to suffer the missiles of your tongue! On these you

after Paulus Fabius Maximus. The present letter, therefore, may be dated in the autumn or winter, A.D. 14–15.

quae tibi tam tenui cura limantur, ut omnes
    istius ingenium corporis esse negent.
at si quem laedi Fortuna cernis iniqua,
40   mollior est animo femina nulla tuo.
hoc ego praecipue sensi, cum magna meorum
    notitiam pars est infitiata mei.
inmemor illorum, vestri non inmemor umquam,
    qui mala solliciti nostra levatis, ero.
45 et prius hic nimium nobis conterminus Hister
    in caput Euxino de mare vertet iter,
utque Thyesteae redeant si tempora mensae,
    Solis ad Eoas currus agetur aquas,
quam quisquam vestrum, qui me doluistis ademptum,
50   arguat ingratum non meminisse sui.

VII.

Missus es Euxinas quoniam, Vestalis, ad undas,
    ut positis reddas iura sub axe locis,
aspicis en praesens, quali iaceamus in arvo,
    nec me testis eris falsa solere queri.
5 accedet voci per te non irrita nostrae,
    Alpinis iuvenis regibus orte, fides.
ipse vides certe glacie concrescere Pontum,
    ipse vides rigido stantia vina gelu ;
ipse vides, onerata ferox ut ducat Iazyx
10   per medias Histri plaustra bubulcus aquas.
aspicis et mitti sub adunco toxica ferro,
    et telum causas mortis habere duas.
atque utinam pars haec tantum spectata fuisset,
    non etiam proprio cognita Marte tibi !

---

[1] The feast at which the flesh of Thyestes' sons was served to
him by Atreus.

use the file with such extreme care that none would recognize in them your real nature. But if you see any injured by unjust Fortune, no woman is more tender than your heart. This I felt above all when the most of my friends denied knowledge of me. I shall forget them, but you I shall never forget, who lighten the woes of my trouble. Sooner shall the Hister, all too near me, turn his march back from the Euxine sea towards its source and, as if the age of Thyestean banquets ¹should return, the chariot of the sun shall sooner be driven towards the eastern waters than that any one of you who have mourned my exile shall call me a forgetful ingrate.

VII. To Vestalis

Seeing that you have been sent to the Euxine waters, Vestalis, to dispense justice to those lands which lie beneath the pole, you behold face to face in what manner of country I am cast and you will bear witness that I am not wont to utter false complaints. My words will receive through you, young scion of Alpine kings, no idle support. You yourself see the Pontus stiffen with ice, you yourself see the wine standing rigid with the frost; you yourself see how the fierce Iazygian herdsman guides his loaded wagon over the middle of Hister's waters. You behold how poison is hurled on the barbed steel and the missile possesses two causes of death. And would that this region had merely met your sight, that you had not also experienced it, in a battle of your own!

15 tendisti [1] ad primum per densa pericula pilum,
    contigit ex merito qui tibi nuper honor.
sit licet hic titulus plenis [2] tibi fructibus ingens,
    ipsa tamen virtus ordine maior erit.
non negat hoc Hister, cuius tua dextera quondam
20   puniceam Getico sanguine fecit aquam.
non negat Aegisos, quae te subeunte recepta
    sensit in ingenio nil opis esse loci.
nam, dubium positu melius defensa manune,
    urbs erat in summo nubibus aequa iugo.
25 Sithonio regi ferus interceperat illam
    hostis et ereptas victor habebat opes,
donec fluminea devecta Vitellius unda
    intulit exposito milite signa Getis.
at tibi, progenies alti fortissima Donni,
30   venit in adversos impetus ire viros.
nec mora, conspicuus longe fulgentibus armis,
    fortia ne possint facta latere caves,
ingentique gradu contra ferrumque locumque
    saxaque brumali grandine plura subis.
35 nec te missa super iaculorum turba moratur,
    nec quae vipereo tela cruore madent.
spicular cum pictis haerent in casside pinnis,
    parsque fere scuti vulnere nulla vacat.
nec corpus cunctos feliciter effugit ictus :
40   sed minor est acri laudis amore dolor.
talis apud Troiam Danais pro navibus Aiax
    dicitur Hectoreas sustinuisse faces.
ut propius ventum est admotaque dextera dextrae,
    resque fero potuit comminus ense geri,

---

[1] tenditis *corr. Merkel*   [2] plenus

Through dense perils you made your way to the first rank,[1] a deserved honour which has recently fallen to your lot. Even though this honour be enhanced with rich rewards for you, yet your worth will be greater than your rank. This the Hister acknowledges, whose water your hand once empurpled with Getic blood. Aegisos acknowledges it, which retaken at your approach, came to know that the nature of its site availed nothing. For 'tis uncertain whether it was better defended by its situation or by force—the city that towered to the clouds upon a lofty ridge. A fierce foe had cut it off from the Sithonian king, and in victory held its captured treasure, until Vitellius, borne adown the stream, disembarked his soldiers and advanced his standards against the Getae. But you, bravest descendant of lofty Donnus, were impelled to rush upon the confronting foe. At once far seen in glittering arms, you take heed that brave acts may not be hidden; with mighty stride you charge the steel, the hill, and stones greater in number than winter's hail. Neither the crowding missiles hurled from above halt you nor those steeped in viper's blood. Arrows with painted feathers cling to your helmet, scarce any part of your shield lacks a wound. Your body has not the luck to escape every stroke, but your pain is less than your keen love of glory. Such at Troy was Danaan Ajax when, they say, in defence of the Grecian ships he bore the brunt of Hector's firebrands. When you came nearer, hand meeting hand, and the battle could be fought at close quarters with the fierce

---

[1] The *primus pilus* was the centurion of highest rank in each legion.

45 dicere difficile est quid Mars tuus egerit illic,
    quotque neci dederis quosque quibusque modis.
 ense tuo factos calcabas victor acervos,
    inpositoque Getes sub pede multus erat.
 pugnat ad exemplum primi minor ordine pili,
50   multaque fert miles vulnera, multa facit.
 sed tantum virtus alios tua praeterit omnes,
    ante citos quantum Pegasus ibit [1] equos.
 vincitur Aegisos, testataque tempus in omne
    sunt tua, Vestalis, carmine facta meo.

VIII.

 Littera sera quidem, studiis exculte Suilli,
    huc tua pervenit, sed mihi grata tamen,
 qua, pia si possit superos lenire rogando
    gratia, laturum te mihi dicis opem.
5 ut iam nil praestes, animi sum factus amici
    debitor, et meritum velle iuvare voco.
 impetus iste tuus longum modo duret in aevum,
    neve malis pietas sit tua lassa meis.
 ius aliquod faciunt adfinia vincula nobis,
10   quae semper maneant inlabefacta precor.
 nam tibi quae coniunx, eadem mihi filia paene est,
    et quae te generum, me vocat illa virum.
 ei mihi, si lectis vultum tu versibus istis
    ducis et adfinem te pudet esse meum !
15 at nihil hic dignum poteris reperire pudore
    praeter Fortunam, quae mihi caeca fuit.
 seu genus excutias, equites ab origine prima
    usque per innumeros inveniemur avos :

[1] ibat

sword, 'tis hard to tell of your martial deeds there,
how many you gave to death, who they were and how
they fell. Upon heaps of dead, the work of your
sword, you trod in victory; many a Getan lay
beneath your planted foot. The soldiers of lesser
rank fought after the model of their centurion,
enduring many wounds, giving many. But your
valour as far surpassed all others as Pegasus distances
a swift steed. Aegisos is conquered, and for all time,
Vestalis, my song bears witness to your deeds.

VIII. To Suillius

Your letter, accomplished Suillius, has been late
in reaching me, yet has it brought me pleasure.
Therein you say that so far as friendly loyalty can
soften the gods by petition you will bring me aid.
Though you should give me nothing more, your
friendly purpose has placed me in your debt, for I
term the will to aid a service. Let only that impulse
of yours endure for long ages and let not your loyalty
be worn out by my misfortunes. Some claim our
bonds of kinship make and I pray that these may ever
last unweakened. For she who is your wife is almost
my daughter; [1] she who calls you son-in-law, calls me
husband. Woe is me if when you read these verses
you frown and feel shame that you are my kinsman!
Yet you will be able to discover in me nothing to
shame you save only Fortune, who to me has proved
blind. If you examine our lineage, we shall be found
knights from our earliest origins all through a line

---

[1] Ovid's step-daughter Perilla, *cf. T.* iii. 7.

sive velis qui sint mores inquirere nostri,
20   errorem misero detrahe, labe carent.
tu modo si quid agi sperabis posse precando,
    quos colis, exora supplice voce deos.
di tibi sunt [1] Caesar iuvenis.   tua numina placa.
    hac certe nulla est notior ara tibi.
25 non sinit illa sui vanas antistitis umquam
    esse preces : nostris hinc pete rebus opem.
quamlibet exigua si nos ea iuverit aura,
    obruta de mediis cumba resurget aquis.
tunc ego tura feram rapidis sollemnia flammis,
30   et valeant quantum numina testis ero.
nec tibi de Pario statuam, Germanice, templum
    marmore : carpsit opes illa ruina meas.
templa domus facient vobis urbesque beatae ;
    Naso, suis opibus, carmine gratus erit.
35 parva quidem fateor pro magnis munera reddi,
    cum pro concessa verba salute damus.
sed qui, quam potuit, dat maxima, gratus abunde est,
    et finem pietas contigit illa suum.
nec quae de parva pauper dis libat acerra
40   tura minus grandi quam data lance valent.
agnaque tam lactens quam gramine pasta Falisco
    victima Tarpeios inficit icta focos.
nec tamen officio vatum per carmina facto
    principibus res est aptior ulla viris.
45 carmina vestrarum peragunt praeconia laudum,
    neve sit actorum fama caduca cavent.
carmine fix vivax virtus, expersque sepulchri
    notitiam serae posteritatis habet.
tabida consumit ferrum lapidemque vetustas,
50   nullaque res maius tempore robur habet.

---

[1] sint

[1] Germanicus.

of countless ancestors, or if you wish to ask what is my character, remove my blunder and my character is spotless.

[21] Do you, if you hope that anything can be accomplished by petition, beseech with a suppliant's prayer the gods you worship. Your gods are—the young Caesar.[1] Propitiate your divinity. No altar surely is more familiar to you than this. That altar never permits the supplications of its priest to be in vain : seek from it succour for my fate. No matter how slight the breeze with which it aids me, my bark now o'erwhelmed will rise once more from the midst of the waters. Then will I offer to the devouring flames holy incense bearing witness to the power of the divinity. I will rear no temple of Parian marble for thee, Germanicus; that disaster tore away my wealth ; temples will be built for thee and thine by rich houses and cities ; Naso will show gratitude with verse, his only wealth. Poor indeed, I confess, is the gift that is rendered for great service, if I give words in return for the grant of salvation. But he who gives his utmost, is lavishly grateful and that loyal service has reached its goal. The incense offered by the poor man from his humble censer has not less effect than that given from a huge platter. The nursling lamb as well as the victim fed on Faliscan grass dyes in sacrifice the Tarpeian altar. Yet than the proffered tribute of poets' verse naught else more befits the leaders of men. Verse heralds abroad your praises and sees to it that the glory of your deeds falls not to the ground. By verse virtue lives on and, avoiding the tomb, becomes known to late posterity. Wasting time consumes both steel and stone; no thing has a strength greater than that

scripta ferunt annos.   scriptis Agamemnona nosti,
  et quisquis contra vel simul arma tulit.
quis Thebas septemque duces sine carmine nosset,
  et quicquid post haec, quidquid et ante fuit ?
55 di quoque carminibus, si fas est dicere, fiunt,
  tantaque maiestas ore canentis eget.
sic Chaos ex illa naturae mole prioris
  digestum partes scimus habere suas :
sic adfectantes caelestia regna Gigantas
60   ad Styga nimbifero vindicis igne datos :
sic victor laudem superatis Liber ab Indis,
  Alcides capta traxit ab Oechalia.
et modo, Caesar, avum, quem virtus addidit astris,
  sacrarunt aliqua carmina parte tuum.
65 siquid adhuc igitur vivi, Germanice, nostro
  restat in ingenio, serviet omne tibi.
non potes officium vatis contemnere vates :
  iudicio pretium res habet ista tuo.
quod nisi te nomen tantum ad maiora vocasset,
70   gloria Pieridum summa futurus eras.
sed dare materiam nobis quam carmina mavis :
  nec tamen ex toto deserere illa potes.
nam modo bella geris, numeris modo verba coërces,
  quodque aliis opus est, hoc tibi lusus erit.
75 utque nec ad citharam nec ad arcum segnis Apollo
    est,
  sed venit ad sacras nervus uterque manus,
sic tibi nec docti desunt nec principis artes,
  mixta sed est animo cum Iove Musa tuo.
quae quoniam nec nos unda summovit ab illa,
80   ungula Gorgonei quam cava fecit equi,

---

[1] Hercules.   [2] Germanicus dabbled in poetry.
  [3] Hippocrene (on Helicon), created by the hoof-beat of
Pegasus.

of time. But writing endures the years. Through writing you know Agamemnon and everyone who bore arms with him or against him. Who would know of Thebes and the seven leaders, were it not for verse, or of all that went before and after ? Even the gods, if 'tis right to say this, are created by verse; their mighty majesty needs the bard's voice. By this it is that we know that Chaos became separated from that mass of earlier nature and took on his divisions; by this that the Giants aiming at the sovereignty of heaven were hurled to the Styx by the cloud-bearing thunderbolt of the avenger; by this that victorious Liber won renown from the conquering of the Indies, Alcides [1] from the capture of Oechalia. And but now, O Caesar, thy grandsire, whom his virtue has sent to the starry heaven, owed in some measure his sanctity to verse. If there be still any life, Germanicus, in my genius, it shall wholly serve thee. Thou canst not as a poet [2] despise the tribute of a poet, for that has a value in thy judgment. Wherefore if a great name had not called thee to greater things, thou wert destined to be the supreme glory of the Pierians. But thou preferest to furnish themes for us rather than verse; yet verse thou canst not wholly leave neglected. Now thou art waging war, now to numbers thou art confining words; what is toil for others will for thee be play. Just as Apollo is no sluggard either with lyre or bow but either string is obedient to his sacred hands, so thou lackest the arts neither of the scholar nor the prince, but in thy mind the Muse and Jupiter are wedded. And since the Muse has not removed me from that spring [3] which the hollow hoof of the Gorgonean steed created, may it profit me and aid

453

prosit opemque ferat communia sacra tueri,
  atque isdem studiis inposuisse manum :
litora pellitis nimium subiecta Corallis
  ut tandem saevos effugiamque Getas :
85 clausaque si misero patria est, ut ponar in ullo,[1]
  qui minus Ausonia distet[2] ab urbe, loco,
unde tuas possim laudes celebrare recentes
  magnaque quam minima facta referre mora.
tangat ut hoc votum caelestia, care Suilli,
90 numina, pro socero paene precare tuo.

IX.

Unde licet, non unde iuvat, Graecine, salutem
  mittit ab Euxinis hanc tibi Naso vadis,
missaque di faciant Auroram occurrat ad illam,
  bis senos fasces quae tibi prima dabit :
5 ut, quoniam sine me tanges Capitolia consul
  et fiam turbae pars ego nulla tuae,
in domini subeat partes et praestet amici
  officium iusso littera nostra die.
atque ego si fatis genitus melioribus essem
10 et mea sincero curreret axe rota,
quo nunc nostra manus per scriptum fungitur, esset
  lingua salutandi munere functa tui,
gratatusque darem cum dulcibus oscula verbis,
  nec minus ille meus quam tuus esset honor.
15 illa, confiteor, sic essem luce superbus,
  ut caperet fastus vix domus ulla meos :
dumque latus sancti cingit tibi turba senatus,
  consulis ante pedes ire iuberer eques ;

---

[1] illo : ullo s   [2] distat : distet s

[1] The consulship.

454

me that I maintain the same rites as thyself, that I
have set my hand to the same pursuit. This shore all
too exposed to the skin-clad Coralli and the savage
Getae—may I at last escape it ; and if my country is
closed against such a wretch, may I be set in any place
less distant than this from the Ausonian city, whence
I can celebrate thy fresh praises and relate thy
mighty deeds with least delay.

[89] That this petition, dear Suillius, may touch the
heavenly powers, utter a prayer for him who is all but
the father of thy wife.

IX. To Graecinus

Whence he may, not whence he would, Graecinus,
this greeting Naso sends you from the Euxine
waters. 'Tis sent, and the gods grant that it may
come to you on that dawn which shall first bring to
you the twice six fasces. For since without my
presence you will reach the Capitol as consul, and I
shall form no part of your retinue, let my missive take
its master's place and bestow the homage of a friend
on the appointed day. Had I been born with a
better fate, did my wheels run on a true axle, that
duty of greeting which my hand now performs in
writing my tongue would have performed ; and along
with pleasant words of congratulation I should give
you kisses, nor would that honour [1] be less mine than
yours. On that day, I confess, I should be so proud
that scarce any house would contain my haughtiness.
While the throng of holy senators surrounded you, I
as a knight would be bidden to go before you, and

455

et quamquam cuperem semper tibi proximus esse,
20   gauderem lateris non habuisse locum.
nec querulus, turba quamvis eliderer, essem :
    sed foret a populo tum mihi dulce premi.
aspicerem gaudens, quantus foret agminis ordo,
    densaque quam longum turba teneret iter.
25 quoque magis noris, quam me vulgaria tangant,
    spectarem, qualis purpura te tegeret.
signa quoque in sella nossem formata curuli
    et totum Numidae sculptile dentis opus.
at cum Tarpeias esses deductus in arces,
30   dum caderet iussu victima sacra tuo,
me quoque secreto grates sibi magnus agentem
    audisset media qui sedet aede deus ;
turaque mente magis plena quam lance dedissem,
    ter quater imperii laetus honore tui.
35 hic ego praesentes inter numerarer amicos,
    mitia ius urbis [1] si modo fata darent,
quaeque mihi sola capitur nunc mente voluptas,
    tunc oculis etiam percipienda foret.
non ita caelitibus visum est, et forsitan aequis :
40   nam quid me poenae causa negata iuvet ?
mente tamen, quae sola loco non exulat, usus [2]
    praetextam fasces aspiciamque tuos.
haec modo te populo reddentem iura videbit,
    et se decretis [3] finget adesse tuis :
45 nunc longi reditus hastae supponere lustri
    credet, et exacta cuncta locare fide :
nunc facere in medio facundum verba senatu,
    publica quaerentem quid petat utilitas :

[1] verbis *vel* si nobis ius *corr. Itali*
[2] utar *corr. Heinsius*   [3] secretis *corr. Korn*

---

[1] See *Ex P*. iv. 5. 19 note.

though I should be very eager to be always near you, I should rejoice to have no place at your side. Nor should I complain, though I were bruised by the crowd; at such time 'twere pleasant to feel the crush of the populace. I should behold with joy the long line of the procession and the dense throng on its long route. And that you may know how trivial things interest me—I should examine the texture of your mantling purple. I should inspect even the outline of the figures on your curule chair all the carved work of Numidian ivory. And after you had been escorted to the Tarpeian rock, while the consecrated victim was falling at your command, me also as I rendered him thanks in secret would the mighty god have heard who is enthroned in the middle of the temple. I would have offered incense with full heart rather than a full censer, thrice and four times rejoicing in your sovereign honour. There should I be counted among your attending friends if only kindly fate granted me of right to be present in the city, and the pleasure which now only my mind can catch would then be wholly grasped by my eyes also.

[39] Not so have the gods decided, and perhaps they are just. For how can the denial of the cause of my punishment aid me ? Yet will I use my mind, which alone is not exiled, to behold your robe and fasces. This shall see you now dispensing justice to the people, and shall fancy itself being present at your decisions ; now it shall believe that you are bringing beneath the spear [1] the revenues of the long lustrum and contracting for everything with minute good faith ; now that you are uttering eloquent words before the senate, seeking what the interest of the

457

nunc pro Caesaribus superis decernere grates,
50   albave opimorum colla ferire boum.
atque utinam, cum iam fueris potiora precatus,
    ut mihi placetur principis ira roges!
surgat ad hanc vocem plena pius ignis ab ara,
    detque bonum voto lucidus omen apex.
55 interea, qua parte licet, ne cuncta queramur,
    hic quoque te festum consule tempus agam.
altera laetitiae est nec cedens causa priori,
    successor tanti frater honoris erit.
nam tibi finitum summo, Graecine, Decembri
60   imperium Iani suscipit ille die.
quaeque est in vobis pietas, alterna feretis
    gaudia, tu fratris fascibus, ille tuis.
sic tu bis fueris consul, bis consul et ille,
    inque domo binus conspicietur honor.
65 qui quamquam est ingens, et nullum Martia summo
    altius imperium consule Roma videt,
multiplicat tamen hunc gravitas auctoris honorem,
    et maiestatem res data dantis habet.
iudiciis igitur liceat Flaccoque tibique
70   talibus Augusti tempus in omne frui.
quod[1] tamen ab rerum cura propiore vacabit,
    vota precor votis addite vestra meis.
et si quem dabit aura sinum, laxate rudentes,
    exeat e Stygiis ut mea navis aquis.
75 praefuit his, Graecine, locis modo Flaccus, et illo
    ripa ferox Histri sub duce tuta fuit.
hic tenuit Moesas[2] gentes in pace fideli,
    hic arcu fisos terruit ense Getas.

---

[1] quod] cum *vel* ut   [2] mysas *corr. Hall*

state demands; now that you are proposing thanks on behalf of the godlike Caesars, or smiting for them the white throats of choice oxen. What that, when you have finished your prayer for more important things, you might ask on my behalf the assuagement of an emperor's wrath! At your words may the holy fire spring up from the full altar and a bright tongue of flame offer a good omen for the prayer.

⁵⁵ Meanwhile so far as I may—let me not complain of everything—even here I will have a festival for your consulship. There is a second cause for joy that yields not to the first; your brother will follow you in so great an honour. For the power which is ended for you with late December he assumes on Janus's day.[1] Such is the affection of you twain that you will receive mutual joy, you in his office and he in yours. Thus you will be twice consul, he twice consul; a double honour will be seen in your household.

⁶⁵ Though mighty the honour and Martian Rome sees no loftier power than that of the supreme consul, yet it is multiplied by the dignity of its sponsor and the gift possesses all the majesty of the giver. Therefore may it be your lot and that of Flaccus to enjoy for all time such verdicts of Augustus. But in his leisure from the more pressing cares of state add both your prayers, I beseech you, to mine, and if the breeze shall belly any sail, loosen the cables that my bark may set forth from the Stygian waters. The commander of this region, Graecinus, was till recently Flaccus, under whose charge the turbulent banks of the Hister were safe. He held the Moesian tribes to loyal peace, he cowed with his sword the Getae who

[1] January 1st.

hic raptam Troesmin [1] celeri virtute recepit,
80   infecitque fero sanguine Danuvium.
quaere loci faciem Scythicique incommoda caeli,
    et quam vicino terrear hoste roga :
sintne litae tenues serpentis felle sagittae,
    fiat an humanum victima dira caput :
85 mentiar, an coëat duratus frigore Pontus,
    et teneat glacies iugera multa freti.
haec ubi narrarit, quae sit mea fama require,
    quoque modo peragam tempora dura roga.
nec sumus hic odio, nec scilicet esse meremur,
90   nec cum fortuna mens quoque versa mea est.
illa quies animi, quam tu laudare solebas,
    ille vetus solito perstat in ore pudor.
sic ego sum longe, sic hic,[2] ubi barbarus hostis,
    ut fera plus valeant legibus arma, facit,
95 rem queat ut nullam tot iam, Graecine, per annos
    femina de nobis virve puerve queri.
hoc facit ut misero faveant adsintque Tomitae :
    haec quoniam tellus testificanda mihi est.
illi me, quia velle vident, discedere malunt :
100   respectu cupiunt hic tamen esse sui.
nec mihi credideris : extant decreta, quibus nos
    laudat et inmunes publica cera facit.
conveniens miseris et quamquam gloria non sit,[3]
    proxima dant nobis oppida munus idem.
105 nec pietas ignota mea est : videt hospita terra
    in nostra sacrum Caesaris esse domo.
stant pariter natusque pius coniunxque sacerdos,
    numina iam facto non leviora deo.

---

[1] troesenen *etc. corr. Korn*   [2] *textus suspectus*   [3] est

trust in the bow. He recovered with swift valour
captured Troesmis, dyeing the Danube with bar-
barian blood. Question him about the face of this
land, the rigours of the Scythian climate; ask him
about the terror that I suffer from the foe so close at
hand—whether the slender arrows are dipped in
serpent's gall, whether the human head becomes a
hideous offering; whether I am a liar or the Pontus
does indeed freeze with the cold and ice covers many
acres of the sea. When he has told you these things,
then ask in what repute I am, how I pass my hours of
suffering. Here I am not hated, and indeed I do not
deserve to be, and my mind has not changed along
with my fate. That tranquillity which you were
wont to praise, that wonted modesty still abides as of
old upon my countenance. Such is my bearing in
this far land, where the barbarian foe causes cruel
arms to have more power than law, that 'tis
impossible now these many years, Graecinus, for
woman or man or child to make complaint of
me. This it is which brings me the kindly attentions
of the Tomitae in my wretchedness—since this land I
must needs call as witness. Because they see that it is
my wish they would like to have me depart; yet for
their own sake are eager to have me remain. And
trust not me for this: there are extant upon the wax
decrees praising me and granting me immunity.[1] And
though it be not fitting for the unfortunate to boast,
the neighbouring towns grant me the same favour. Nor
is my piety unknown : a strange land sees a shrine to
Caesar in my house. Beside him stand the pious son
and priestess wife,[2] deities not less important than him-
self now that he has become a god. To make the

---

[1] *i.e.* from taxes.   [2] Tiberius and Livia.

neu desit pars ulla domus, stat uterque nepotum,
110   hic aviae lateri proximus, ille patris.
his ego do totiens cum ture precantia verba,
    Eoo quotiens surgit ab orbe dies.
tota, licet quaeras, hoc me non fingere dicet
    officii testis Pontica terra mei.
115 Pontica me tellus, quantis hac possumus ara,
    natalem libis [1] scit celebrare dei.
nec minus hospitibus pietas est cognita talis,
    misit in has siquos longa Propontis aquas.
is quoque, quo laevus [2] fuerat sub praeside Pontus,
120   audierit frater forsitan ista tuus.
fortuna est impar animo, talique libenter
    exiguas carpo munere pauper opes.
nec vestris damus haec oculis, procul urbe remoti :
    contenti tacita sed pietate sumus.
125 et tamen haec tangent aliquando Caesaris aures :
    nil illi, toto quod fit in orbe, latet.
tu certe scis haec,[3] superis ascite, videsque,
    Caesar, ut est oculis subdita terra tuis.
tu nostras audis inter convexa locatus
130   sidera, sollicito quas damus ore, preces.
perveniant istuc et carmina forsitan illa,
    quae de te misi caelite facta novo.
auguror his igitur flecti tua numina, nec tu
    inmerito nomen mite Parentis habes.

X.

Haec mihi Cimmerio bis tertia ducitur aestas
    litore pellitos inter agenda Getas.

---

    [1] ludis *corr. Hall*   [2] *laetus*   [3] *hoc*

---

    [1] *Germanicus and Drusus.*   [2] *Tiberius.*

household group complete, both of the grandsons [1]
are there, one by the side of his grandmother, the
other by that of his father. To these I offer incense
and words of prayer as often as the day rises from the
east. The whole land of Pontus—you are free to
inquire—will say that I am not fabricating this and
will bear witness to my devotion. The land of
Pontus knows that on this altar I celebrate with what
offerings I can the birthday of the god, nor is such
service less known to whatsoever strangers the
distant Propontis sends to these waters. Even your
brother, who had charge of ill omened Pontus, may
perhaps have heard of it. My means are unequal to
my wishes, but in such service gladly, though poor, do
I expend my scant resources. Nor do I bring all
these things before your eyes, far removed as I am
from the city, but I am content with an unspoken
loyalty, and nevertheless this shall sometime reach
the ear of Caesar [2] from whom nothing which occurs
in the whole world is hidden. Thou at least knowest
this, O Caesar, now one with the gods, and seest it,
since now the world is placed beneath thine
eyes. Thou hearest from thy place among the stars
of heaven's vault the prayers of my anxious
lips. Perchance even those poems may reach thee
there which I have composed and sent about thee, a
new divinity. And so I prophesy that thy holy will
is yielding to these prayers, for not undeservedly hast
thou the gracious name of "Father."

X. To Albinovanus

Now is the sixth summer wearing away which I
must pass on the Cimmerian shore among the skin-

ecquos tu silices, ecquod, carissime, ferrum
    duritiae confers, Albinovane, meae ?
5 gutta cavat lapidem, consumitur anulus usu,
    atteritur [1] pressa vomer aduncus humo.
tempus edax igitur praeter nos omnia perdet :
    cessat duritia mors quoque victa mea.
exemplum est animi nimium patientis Ulixes,
10   iactatus dubio per duo lustra mari :
tempora solliciti sed non tamen omnia fati
    pertulit, et placidae saepe fuere morae.
an grave sex annis pulchram fovisse Calypso
    aequoreaeque fuit concubuisse deae ?
15 excipit Hippotades, qui dat pro munere ventos,
    curvet ut inpulsos utilis aura sinus.
nec bene cantantes labor est audire puellas :
    nec degustanti lotos amara fuit.
hos ego, qui patriae faciant oblivia, sucos
20   parte meae vitae, si modo dentur, emam.
nec tu contuleris urbem Laestrygonos umquam
    gentibus, obliqua quas obit Hister aqua.
nec vincet Cyclops saevum feritate Piaccen.
    qui quota terroris pars solet esse mei !
25 Scylla feris trunco quod latret ab inguine monstris,
    Heniochae nautis plus nocuere rates.
nec potes infestis conferre Charybdin Achaeis,
    ter licet epotum ter vomat illa fretum.
qui quamquam dextra regione licentius errant,
30 securum latus hoc non tamen esse sinunt.
hic agri infrondes, hic spicula tincta venenis,
    hic freta vel pediti pervia reddit hiems,

---

[1] et teritur *corr. Heinsius*

---

[1] A lustrum was five years.
[2] Aeolus.   [3] The Sirens.

clad Getae. Can you compare any flint, Al-
binovanus, any iron to my endurance? Drops of
water hollow out a stone, a ring is worn thin by use,
the hooked plough is rubbed away by the soil's
pressure. So devouring time will destroy all things
but me: even death keeps aloof defeated by my
endurance. The type of a heart suffering to excess is
Ulysses, who was tossed for two lustra[1] on the
perilous sea. Yet not all his hours were hours of
troubled fate, for oft came intervals of peace. Or
was it a hardship to fondle for six years the fair
Calypso and share the couch of a goddess of the
sea? Hippotes' son[2] harboured him and gave him
the winds, that a favouring breeze might fill and drive
his sails. And 'tis not a sorrow to hear maidens[3]
singing beautifully, nor was the lotos bitter to one
who tasted it. Such juices, which cause forgetful-
ness of one's native land, I would purchase, if only
they were offered, at the price of half my life. Nor
could you compare the city of the Laestrygonian with
the tribes which the Hister touches in its winding
course. Cyclops will not surpass in cruelty
Piacches—and what mere fraction of my dread is he
wont to be! Though Scylla's misshapen loins may
send forth the barkings of cruel monsters, the
Heniochian ships have done more harm to
mariners. You cannot compare Charybdis, though
she thrice drinks in, thrice spews forth the flood,
with the hostile Achaei who though they roam
with larger licence in the eastern lands, yet allow not
this shore to be safe. Here there are lands without
a leaf, here are darts dyed in poison, here the winter
makes even the sea a highway for one on foot, so

ut, qua remus iter pulsis modo fecerat undis,
    siccus contempta nave viator eat.
35 qui veniunt istinc, vix vos ea credere dicunt.
    quam miser est, qui fert asperiora fide!
crede tamen : nec te causas nescire sinemus,
    horrida Sarmaticum cur mare duret hiems.
proxima sunt nobis plaustri praebentia formam
40   et quae praecipuum sidera frigus habent.
hinc oritur Boreas oraeque domesticus huic est
    et sumit vires a propiore loco.
at Notus, adverso tepidum qui spirat ab axe,
    est procul et rarus languidiorque venit.
45 adde quod hic clauso miscentur flumina Ponto,
    vimque fretum multo perdit ab amne suam.
huc Lycus, huc Sagaris Peniusque Hypanisque Cales-
        que
    influit et crebro vertice tortus Halys,
Partheniusque rapax, et volvens saxa Cinases [1]
50   labitur, et nullo tardior amne Tyras,
et tu, femineae Thermodon cognite turmae,
    et quondam Graiis Phasi petite viris,
cumque Borysthenio liquidissimus amne Danapris [2]
    et tacite peragens lene Melanthus iter,
55 quique duas terras, Asiam Cadmique sororem,
    separat et cursus inter utramque facit,
innumerique alii, quos inter maximus omnes
    cedere Danuvius se tibi, Nile, negat.
copia tot laticum, quas auget, adulterat undas,
60   nec patitur vires aequor habere suas.
quin etiam, stagno similis pigraeque paludi,
    caeruleus vix est diluiturque color.

[1] cynapses *corr. Richmond*   [2] dyrapses *corr. Richmond*

---

[1] Probably the Don.   [2] Europa.

that where the oar had but just now beaten a way through the waves, the traveller proceeds dryshod, despising boats.

[35] Those who come from your land report that you scarce believe all this. How wretched is he who endures what is too harsh for credence! Yet believe you must, nor shall I permit you to remain in ignorance of the reason why dread winter freezes the Sarmatian sea. Very near us are the stars having the form of a wain, possessing extreme cold. Here is the source of Boreas; this coast is his home, and he takes on strength from a place nearer to him. On the other hand Notus, whose breath comes warm from the opposite pole, is far away; he comes but rarely and without energy. Moreover, here the rivers mingle in the landlocked Pontus, and the sea loses its own power because of many a stream. Here the Lycus, here the Sagaris, the Penius, the Hypanis, the Cales flow in and the Halys twisting in many an eddy, the destroying Parthenius, and the Cinases glides along tumbling his boulders, and the Tyras inferior to no stream in swiftness, and thou, Thermodon, familiar to the bands of women, and thou, Phasis, sought by Grecian heroes, Borysthenian Dnieper with its clear river, and Melanthus, quietly completing his gentle course, and the river [1] which separates two lands, Asia and Cadmus's sister,[2] making its way between them, and countless others of which mightiest of all the Danube refuses, O Nile, to yield to thee. The wealth of so many waters corrupts the waves which it augments, not allowing the sea to keep its own strength. Nay, like to a still pool or a stagnant swamp its colour is scarce blue and is washed away. The fresh water floats

467

innatat unda freto dulcis, leviorque marina est,
    quae proprium mixto de sale pondus habet.
65 si roget haec aliquis cur sint narrata Pedoni,
    quidve loqui certis iuverit ista modis,
"detinui" dicam "curas tempusque fefelli.
    hunc fructum praesens attulit hora mihi.
afuimus solito, dum scribimus ista, dolore,
70   in mediis nec nos sensimus esse Getis."
at tu, non dubito, cum Thesea carmine laudes,
    materiae titulos quin tueare tuae,
quemque refers, imitere virum.   vetat ille profecto
    tranquilli comitem temporis esse fidem.
75 qui quamquam est factis ingens et conditur a te
    vir tanto quanto debuit ore cani,
est tamen ex illo nobis imitabile quiddam,
    inque fide Theseus quilibet esse potest.
non tibi sunt hostes ferro clavaque domandi,
80   per quos vix ulli pervius Isthmos erat :
sed praestandus amor, res non operosa volenti.
    quis labor est puram non temerasse fidem ?
haec tibi, qui praestas [1] indeclinatus amico,
    non est quod lingua dicta querente putes.

XI.

Gallio, crimen erit vix excusabile nobis,
    carmine te nomen non habuisse meo.
tu quoque enim, memini, caelesti cuspide facta
    fovisti lacrimis vulnera nostra tuis.

---

[1] perstas

---

[1] The robbers on the Isthmus of Corinth whom Theseus
subdued.

upon the flood, being lighter than the sea-water which possesses weight of its own from the mixture of salt.

[65] If somebody ask why I have told all this to Pedo, what profit there has been in speaking so precisely, I would say, "I have given pause to my cares and beguiled the time ; this is the profit the present hour has brought me. I have gained release in writing this from my accustomed grief and have lost the feeling that I am among the Getae."

[71] But you, I doubt not, since you are singing in verse the praises of Theseus, are doing honour to the subject and imitating the hero whom you describe. Surely he forbids fidelity to be the companion only of happy moments. His deeds are great and he is described by you in a vein grand enough for a hero, yet there is one thing in him that we can imitate : in fidelity anybody can be a Theseus. You do not have to subdue with sword and club the foe[1] who rendered the Isthmos scarce passable for anyone, but you must show your love, a thing not hard for one who has the wish. Is it so difficult to refrain from outraging unblemished fidelity ? You, who have unswervingly shown love to your friend, must not think that these words have been uttered by a complaining tongue.

XI. To Gallio

Gallio, it will be a sin which I can scarce palliate if your name proves not to have found a place in my verse. For you too, I remember, when I was smitten by the divine spear, bathed my wounds with your tears.

5 atque utinam rapti iactura laesus amici
  sensisses ultra, quod quererere, nihil!
non ita dis placuit, qui te spoliare pudica
  coniuge crudeles non habuere nefas.
nuntia nam luctus mihi nuper epistula venit,
10 lectaque cum lacrimis sunt tua damna meis.
sed neque solari prudentem stultior ausim,
  verbaque doctorum nota referre tibi:
finitumque tuum, si non ratione, dolorem
  ipsa iam pridem suspicor esse mora.
15 dum tua pervenit, dum littera nostra recurrens
  tot maria ac terras permeat, annus abit.
temporis officium est solacia dicere certi,
  dum dolor in cursu est et petit aeger opem.
at cum long dies sedavit vulnera mentis,
20 intempestive qui movet illa, novat.
adde quod (atque utinam verum tibi venerit omen!)
  coniugio felix iam potes esse novo.

XII.

Quo minus in nostris ponaris, amice, libellis,
  nominis efficitur condicione tui,
aut[1] ego non alium prius hoc dignarer honore—
  est aliquis nostrum si modo carmen honor.
5 lex pedis officio fortunaque nominis obstat,
  quaque meos adeas est via nulla modos.
nam pudet in geminos ita nomen scindere versus,
  desinat ut prior hoc incipiatque minor.

[1] ast

---

[1] *Tūtĭcānus* can be got into elegiac verse in four ways, all
violent: (1) by dividing the name between two lines; by
scanning (2)*Tūtĭcānus* or (3) *Tŭtĭcānus* or (4) *Tūtĭcānus*.

And would that injured by the loss of your ravished
friend you had felt no further blow to stir
lament. Not so has it pleased the gods, for in their
cruelty they have not thought it wrong to despoil you
of your pure wife. I have but just received a letter
which told me your sorrow, and I read of your loss
with tears. But I should not venture in folly to
console one who is wiser than I, to repeat to you the
familiar words of the wise men ; your grief has been
for some time ended, I suppose, if not by reasoning,
then by the lapse of time. While your letter has
been on its way, while mine in answer is traversing so
many lands and seas, a year has passed. The service
of consolation belongs to a definite period while grief
is still in progress and the stricken one is seeking
aid. But after long time has quieted the soul's
wounds, he who touches them out of season, only
reopens them. Moreover—and may this omen be
true when it reaches you !—you may already be
happy through a new marriage.

XII. To Tuticanus

The bar, my friend, that prevents your finding a
place in my verse, is set up by the nature of your
name, else for my part I should deem no other
worthier of the honour—if only my verse involves
any honour. 'Tis my metre's law and your unfortu-
nate name that oppose the compliment, and there is
no method by which you can enter my rhythm. For
I should be ashamed to separate your name between
two lines,[1] ending the first with a part and beginning
the second with another part, and I should be equally

et pudeat, si te, qua syllaba parte moratur,
10   artius adpellem Tuticanumque vocem.
nec [1] potes in versum Tuticani more venire,
    fiat ut e longa syllaba prima brevis,
aut producatur,[2] quae nunc correptius exit,
    et sit porrecta long secunda mora.
15 his ego si vitiis ausim corrumpere nomen,
    ridear et merito pectus habere neger.
haec mihi causa fuit dilati muneris huius,
    quod meus adiecto faenore reddet [3] amor,
teque canam, quacumque nota tibi carmina mittam,
20   paene mihi puero cognite paene puer,
perque tot annorum seriem, quot habemus uterque,
    non mihi, quam fratri frater, amate minus.
tu bonus hortator, tu duxque comesque fuisti,
    cum regerem tenera frena novella manu.
25 saepe ego correxi sub te censore libellos,
    saepe tibi admonitu facta litura meo est,
dignam Maeoniis Phaeacida condere chartis
    cum te Pieriae perdocuere deae.
hic tenor, haec viridi concordia coepta iuventa
30   venit ad albentis inlabefacta comas.
quae nisi te moveant, duro tibi pectora ferro
    esse vel invicto clausa adamante putem.
sed prius huic desint et bellum et frigora terrae,
    invisus nobis quae duo Pontus habet,
35 et tepidus Boreas et sit praefrigidus Auster,
    et possit fatum mollius esse meum,
quam tua sint lasso [4] praecordia dura sodali.
    hic cumulus nostris absit abestque malis.

[1] nec] et *vel* non *corr.* ς
[2] ut ducatur   [3] reddit   [4] lapso

---

[1] Similarly Horace alludes to a town whose name resisted metre (*Sat.* i. 5. 87), Lucilius to a festival (228 f. Marx), and

ashamed if, where a syllable is long, I should shorten it and address you as Tuticănus. Nor can you enter into the verse as Tŭticanus, so that the first long syllable is shortened; or so that the second syllable, which is now short, should be long by extending its time. If by such faults as these I should venture to distort your name, I should be laughed at and they would say rightly that I had no taste.[1]

[17] This was my reason for putting off this service, but my love shall render it with added interest, and I will sing of you, whatever the device I use to address you verses—you whom I knew when we were almost boys, whom through the succession of all the years of our lives I have loved no less dearly than a brother. You gave me kindly encouragement, you were my guide and comrade, whilst with youthful hand I was guiding the novel reins. Often I revised my work in deference to your criticism, often on your advice I made erasures, while you the Pierian goddesses taught to compose a *Phaeacis*[2] worthy of the Maeonian pages. This constancy, this harmony of tastes begun in the green of youth, has continued unweakened to the time when our hair is white. If this should not affect you, I should believe that you had a heart encased in iron or unconquerable adamant. But sooner would this land lack war and cold—the two things which hated Pontus holds for me—sooner would Boreas become warm and Auster chilly, and my fate less harsh, than would your heart be hard to your weary friend. Let this final blow be absent—and it is absent—from my woes.

Critias had trouble with "Alcibiades," *cf.* Bergk-Hiller-Crusius, *Anthol. lyr.* fr. 5, p. 136.
[2] An epic on the sojourn of Ulysses in Phaeacia.

tu modo per superos, quorum certissimus ille est,
40   quo tuus assidue principe crevit honor,
efface constanti profugum pietate tuendo,
    ne sperata meam deserat aura ratem.
quid mandem, quaeris ? peream, nisi dicere vix est ;
    si modo, qui periit, ille perire potest.
45 nec quid agam invenio, nec quid nolimve velimve,
    nec satis utilitas est mihi nota mea.
crede mihi, miseros prudentia prima relinquit,
    et sensus cum re consiliumque fugit.
ipse, precor, quaeras, qua sim tibi parte iuvandus,
50   quoque viam facias ad mea vota vado.

XIII.

O mihi non dubios inter memorande sodales,
    qui quod es, id vere, Care, vocaris, ave !
unde salutaris, color hic tibi protinus index
    et structura mei carminis esse potest.
5 non quia mirifica est, sed quod non publica certe est :
    qualis enim cumque est, non latet esse meam.
ipse quoque, ut titulum chartae de fronte revellas,
    quod sit opus, videor dicere posse, tuum.
quamlibet in multis positus noscere libellis,
10   perque observatas inveniere notas.
prodent auctorem vires, quas Hercule dignas
    novimus atque illi, quem canis ipse,[1] pares.
et mea Musa potest, proprio deprensa colore,
    insignis vitiis forsitan esse suis.
15 tam mala Thersiten prohibebat forma latere,
    quam pulchra Nireus conspiciendus erat.

[1] ipse] esse

---

[1] *Carus*, " dear."
[2] As Thersites was the ugliest, so Nireus was (after Achilles) the most beautiful man in the Greek host at Troy.

[39] Only do you—by the gods of whom He is most
trustworthy under whose lead your honour has stead-
ilyincreased—see to it by watching over an exile with
steadfast devotion that the breeze of hope does not
forsake my bark. What are my directions, you
ask ?   May I die if it is not hard to say—if only he
who is already dead can die.   I find nothing to do or
to wish or not wish, nor do I quite know what is to my
advantage.   Believe me, foresight is the first thing to
abandon the wretched, and along with fortune sense
and reason flee.   Seek in person, I beg you, how
you ought to aid me, and over what shallows
you may construct a way to accomplish my wishes.

XIII. To Carus

To you who must be counted among my undoubted
friends—to you who are in very truth what you are
called, Carus,[1]—greetings   The source of this salut-
ation, the tone of this letter and the structure of the
verse can tell you, not that it is excellent, but 'tis at
least not commonplace ; for whatever be its merit, 'tis
clear to see that it is mine.   I, too, though you should
tear the title from the head of your pages, could tell, I
think, what work is yours.   No matter how many the
books among which you may be placed you
will be recognized, discovered by signs I have
observed.   The author will be betrayed by the
vigour which we know to be worthy of Hercules and
suited to him of whom you yourself sing.   My Muse
too, detected by her own complexion, can perhaps be
distinguished by her very blemishes.   Ugliness
prevented Thersites from escaping notice as much as
beauty made Nireus conspicuous.[2]

nec te mirari, si sint vitiosa, decebit
carmina, quae faciam paene poëta Getes.
a ! pudet, et Getico scripsi sermone libellum,
20   structaque sunt nostris barbara verba modis :
et placui (gratare mihi) coepique poëtae
inter inhumanos nomen habere Getas.
materiam quaeris ? laudes : de Caesare dixi.
adiuta est novitas numine nostra dei.
25 nam patris Augusti docui mortale fuisse
corpus, in aetherias numen abisse domos :
esse parem virtute patri, qui frena rogatus
saepe recusati ceperit imperii :
esse pudicarum te Vestam, Livia, matrum,
30   ambiguum nato dignior anne viro :
esse duos iuvenes, firma adiumenta parentis,
qui dederint animi pignora certa sui.
haec ubi non patria perlegi scripta Camena,
venit et ad digitos ultima charta meos,
35 et caput et plenas omnes movere pharetras,
et longum Getico murmur in ore fuit.
atque aliquis " scribas haec cum de Caesare," dixit
" Caesaris imperio restituendus eras."
ille quidem dixit : sed me iam, Care, nivali
40   sexta relegatum bruma sub axe videt.
carmina nil prosunt.   nocuerunt carmina quondam,
primaque tam miserae causa fuere fugae.
at tu, per studii communia foedera sacri,
per non vile tibi nomen amicitiae
45 (sic vincto ¹ Latiis Germanicus hoste catenis
materiam vestris adferat ingeniis :

------

¹ capto corr. Akrigg

¹ Tiberius.   ² Drusus, the son, and Germanicus, the
nephew and adopted son, of Tiberius.

[17] Nor should you wonder if my verse prove faulty,
for I am almost a Getic poet. Ah! it brings me
shame! I have even written a poem in the Getic
tongue, setting barbarian words to our measures: I
even found favour—congratulate me!—and began to
achieve among the uncivilized Getae the name of
poet. You ask my theme? you would praise it: I
sang of Caesar. My novel attempt was aided by the
god's will. For I told how the body of father
Augustus was mortal, but his spirit had passed to the
abodes of heaven; that equal in virtue to his father
was he [1] who, when importuned, accepted the
guidance of the empire which he had often refused;
that thou, Livia, wert the Vesta of pure matrons, it is
uncertain whether more worthy of thy son or thy
husband; that there were two sons,[2] strong supports
of their father, who had given sure proofs of their
spirit.

[33] When I read all this, written not in the language
of my native Muse, and the last page felt the touch of
my fingers, all moved their heads and their full
quivers, and there was a long murmur on the lips of
the Getae. And one of them said, "Since you write
this about Caesar, it were fitting that you be restored
by Caesar's command." He said this, yes, but,
Carus, already the sixth winter sees me banished
beneath the icy pole. My verse avails me naught;
my verse once wrought me harm and was the first
cause of this wretched exile. But do you, by the
common pledges of our sacred calling, by the name
of friendship which is not cheap in your eyes—
so may Germanicus cast the enemy in Latin chains
and provide a subject for your abilities; so

477

OVID

sic valeant pueri, votum commune deorum,
  quos laus formandos est tibi magna datos),
quanta potes, praebe nostrae momenta saluti,
50 quae nisi mutato nulla futura loco est.

XIV.

Haec tibi mittuntur, quem sum modo carmine questus
  non aptum numeris nomen habere meis,
in quibus, excepto quod adhuc utcumque valemus,
  nil, te [1] praeterea quod iuvet, invenies.
5 ipsa quoque est invisa salus, suntque ultima vota
  quolibet ex istis scilicet ire locis.
nulla mihi cura est, terra quo muter [2] ab ista,
  hac quia, quam video, gratior omnis erit.
in medias Syrtes, mediam mea vela Charybdin
10 mittite, praesenti dum careamus humo.
Styx quoque, si quid ea est, bene commutabitur
      Histro,
  siquid et inferius quam Styga mundus habet.
gramina cultus ager, frigus minus odit hirundo,
  proxima Marticolis quam loca Naso Getis.
15 talia suscensent [3] propter mihi verba Tomitae,
  iraque carminibus publica mota meis.
ergo ego cessabo numquam per carmina laedi,
  plectar et incauto semper ab ingenio ?
ergo ego, ne scribam, digitos incidere cunctor,
20 telaque adhuc demens, quae nocuere, sequor ?
ad veteres scopulos iterum devertor [4] et illas,
  in quibus offendit naufraga puppis, aquas ?

----

[1] me   [2] mittar
    [3] succensent   [4] devertar

----

[1] Probably the sons of Germanicus.   [2] *Ex P*. iv. 12.

478

may the youths [1] be well, the source of universal prayers to the gods, whose training to your great praise has been made your trust—do you to your utmost power advance that weal of mine which I shall never have, unless the place be changed.

XIV. To Tuticanus

These words are sent to you whose name but recently I complained in verse [2] was not suited to my metre: here—except that I am still in some sort well—you will find nothing else to afford you pleasure. My very health is hateful to me, and 'tis my final prayer to go anywhere, be it only from this place. I care not whither I am moved from such a land, because any land will please me better than this upon which I look. Cause me to sail to the midst of the Syrtes, or Charybdis, provided I escape this present soil. Even the Styx, if such thing there be, will be well exchanged for the Hister, or whatever the world has that is lower than the Styx. The tilled field feels less hate for the grass, the swallow for the cold, than Naso hates the region near the war-loving Getae.

[15] For such words the anger of the Tomitae rises against me, the wrath of the town is stirred by my verse. Shall I then never cease to be injured by verse, shall I always suffer from my indiscreet talent ? Do I then hesitate to cut my fingers that I may not write, do I still in madness trail after the weapons which have harmed me ? Am I driven once more upon the old reef and into those waters in which my

479

sed nihil admisi, nulla est mea culpa, Tomitae,
    quos ego, cum loca sim vestra perosus, amo.
25 quilibet excutiat nostri monimenta laboris:
    littera de vobis est mea questa nihil.
frigus et incursus omni de parte timendos
    et quod pulsetur murus ab hoste queror.
in loca, non homines, verissima crimina dixi.
30   culpatis vestrum vos quoque saepe solum.
esset perpetuo sua quam vitabilis Ascra,
    ausa est agricolae Musa docere senis:
et fuerat genitus terra, qui scripsit, in illa,
    intumuit vati nec tamen Ascra suo.
35 quis patriam sollerte magis dilexit Ulixe?
    hoc tamen asperitas indice docta[1] loci est.
non loca, sed mores scriptis vexavit amaris
    Scepsius Ausonios, actaque Roma rea est:
falsa tamen passa est aequa convicia mente,
40   obfuit auctori nec fera lingua suo.
at malus interpres populi mihi concitat iram
    inque novum crimen carmina nostra vocat.
tam felix utinam quam pectore candidus essem!
    extat adhuc nemo saucius ore meo.
45 adde quod Illyrica si iam pice nigrior essem,
    non mordenda mihi turba fidelis erat.
molliter a vobis mea sors excepta, Tomitae,
    tam mites Graios indicat esse viros.
gens mea Paeligni regioque domestica Sulmo
50   non potuit nostris lenior esse malis.
quem vix incolumi cuiquam salvoque daretis,
    is datus a vobis est mihi nuper honor.

[1] dicta nota ς

---

[1] Hesiod.   [2] Metrodorus.
[3] *Niger* means here "slanderous."   [4] *i.e.* unexiled.

bark was wrecked? But I have committed no
crime, I am not at fault, Tomitae, for you I esteem,
though I detest your land. Let anyone you will
examine the memorials of my toil, my letters have
uttered no complaints about you. Of the cold, of the
raids to be feared from every side, of the assaults by
the enemy upon the wall I complain. Against the
land, not the people, I have uttered true charges;
even you often criticize your own soil. How his own
Ascra was constantly to be avoided the old farmer
poet[1] dared to sing, and he who wrote had been born
in that land, yet Ascra grew not angry with her
bard. Who loved his native land more than the wily
Ulysses? Yet its roughness has been learned
through his own evidence. Not the land, but the
ways of Ausonia were attacked in bitter writing by
the Scepsian,[2] and Rome was indicted, yet she bore
the false abuse calmly, and the author's wild tongue
did him no harm. But against me a perverse
interpreter rouses the popular wrath, bringing a new
charge against my verse. Would I were as happy as
my heart is clean! Nobody to this day lives whom
my lips have wounded. And besides if I were now
blacker[3] than Illyrian tar, a loyal people would not
be attacked by me. Your gentle harbouring of my
fate, Tomitae, shows how kindly are men of Grecian
stock. My own people, the Paeligni, my home
country of Sulmo could not have been gentler to my
woes. An honour which you would scarcely grant to
one who was without blemish[4] and secure, that you
have recently granted to me: I am as yet the

solus adhuc ego sum vestris inmunis in oris,
    exceptis, siqui munera legis habent.
55 tempora sacrata mea sunt velata corona,
    publicus invito quam favor inposuit.
quam grata est igitur Latonae Delia tellus,
    erranti tutum quae dedit una locum,
tam mihi cara Tomis, patria quae sede fugatis
60   tempus ad hoc nobis hospita fida manet.
di modo fecissent, placidae spem posset habere
    pacis, et a gelido longius axe foret.

XV.

Siquis adhuc usquam nostri non inmemor extat,
    quidve relegatus Naso, requirit, agam :
Caesaribus vitam, Sexto debere salutem
    me sciat.   a superis hic mihi primus erit.
5 tempora nam miserae complectar ut omnia vitae,
    a meritis eius pars mihi nulla vacat.
quae numero tot sunt, quot in horto fertilis arvi
    Punica sub lento cortice grana rubent,
Africa quot segetes, quot Tmolia terra racemos,
10   quot Sicyon bacas, quot parit Hybla favos.
confiteor : testere licet.   signate Quirites !
    nil opus est legum viribus, ipse loquor.
inter opes et me, parvam rem, pone paternas :
    pars ego sum census quantulacumque tui.
15 quam tua Trinacria est regnataque terra Philippo,
    quam domus Augusto continuata foro,

---

[1] *i.e.* from taxes. It is not known who were exempted
besides Ovid or what imposts are meant.
[2] Lydia.   [3] Sicilian.
[4] *i.e.* in Macedonia.

only one immune[1] upon your shores, those only
excepted who have the boon by law. My brow has
been veiled with a sacred chaplet which the popular
favour placed there all against my will. Wherefore
dear as is to Latona the land of Delos, which alone
offered her a safe place in her wandering, so dear is
Tomis to me ; to me exiled from my native abode it
remains hospitable and loyal to the present
time. Would that the gods had only made it possible
for it to have the hope of calm peace and to be farther
away from the icy pole !

XV. To Sextus Pompeius

If there be still anywhere one who has not forgotten
me or who asks how exiled Naso fares, let him know
that I owe my life to the Caesars, my well-being to
Sextus. After those above he in my eyes should
stand first. For though I should include all the
hours of my wretched life, none is lacking in services
from him. These are as many as in the orchard of a
fertile farm are the seeds of the pomegranate, red
beneath their slow growing husk, as the grain of
Africa, as the grape clusters of the Tmolian land,[2] as
the olives of Sicyon, or the honey-cells of
Hybla. This is my confession ; you may witness it ;
put your seal upon it, Quirites. It needs not the
force of the law ; I myself declare it. Set me too, an
humble chattel, amongst your inherited wealth ; I am
a part, no matter how small, of your estate. As
Trinacrian[3] lands are yours or those once ruled over
by Philip,[4] as the home next the forum of Augustus,

quam tua, rus oculis domini, Campania, gratum,
   quaeque relicta tibi, Sexte, vel empta tenes :
tam tuus en ego sum, cuius te munere tristi
20   non potes in Ponto dicere habere nihil.
atque utinam possis, et detur amicius arvum,
   remque tuam ponas in meliore loco !
quod quoniam in dis est, tempta lenire precando
   numina, perpetua quae pietate colis.
25 erroris nam tu vix est discernere nostri
   sis argumentum maius an auxilium.
nec dubitans oro : sed flumine saepe secundo
   augetur remis cursus euntis aquae.
et pudet et metuo semperque eademque precari,
30   ne subeant animo taedia iusta tuo.
verum quid faciam ? res inmoderata cupido est.
   da veniam vitio, mitis amice, meo.
scribere saepe aliud cupiens delabor eodem :
   ipsa locum per se littera nostra rogat.
35 seu tamen effectus habitura est gratia, seu me
   dura iubet gelido Parca sub axe mori,
semper inoblita repetam tua munera mente,
   et mea me tellus audiet esse tuum.
audiet et caelo posita est quaecumque sub ullo
40   (transit nostra feros si modo Musa Getas)
teque meae causam servatoremque salutis,
   meque tuum libra norit et aere minus.

XVI.

Invide, quid laceras Nasonis carmina rapti ?
   non solet ingeniis summa nocere dies,

---

[1] Apparently Pompey could prove (*argumentum*) that
"error" which Ovid regarded as the beginning of all his woes.

as your Campanian lands, an estate dear to your eyes, or whatever you hold by inheritance, Sextus, or by purchase, so am I yours, and by reason of this sad gift you cannot say that you own naught in the Pontus. Would that you could and that a more pleasant estate might be given you, that you might establish your property in a better place! Since this rests with the gods, try to soften by prayer those deities whom you worship with constant devotion. For 'tis hard to distinguish whether you are more the proof of my mistake or the relief.[1]

[27] Nor do I plead because I doubt; but oft adown the stream the oars hasten the voyage over the flowing waters. I feel shame and apprehension always to be making the same request, lest your heart grow justly weary. But what am I to do? My desire is measureless. Pardon my fault, gentle friend. Though I often wish to write in a different vein, I pass imperceptibly to the same theme; my very letters of their own accord seek the opportunity. Yet whether your influence shall win its end or whether a cruel fate bids me die beneath the freezing pole, I shall always recall your services with unforgetting heart and my land shall hear that I belong to you. It shall be heard by every land under any sky—if only my Muse passes the confines of the wild Getae—that you are the cause and saviour of my weal; that I am yours almost as if the scales and bronze had bought me.

XVI. To an Enemy

Jealous man, why do you wound the verse of ravished Naso? The final day is not wont to injure

famaque post cineres maior venit.   et mihi nomen
   tum quoque, cum vivis adnumerarer, erat :
5 cumque foret Marsus magnique Rabirius oris
   Iliacusque Macer sidereusque Pedo ;
et, qui Iunonem laesisset in Hercule, Carus,
   Iunonis si iam non gener ille foret ;
quique dedit Latio carmen regale Severus,
10   et cum subtili Priscus uterque Numa ;
quique vel imparibus numeris, Montane, vel aequis
   sufficis, et gemino carmine nomen habes ;
et qui Penelopae rescribere iussit Ulixem
   errantem saevo per duo lustra mari,
15 quique suam Troesmin ¹ imperfectumque dierum
   deseruit celeri morte Sabinus opus ;
ingeniique sui dictus cognomine Largus,
   Gallica qui Phrygium duxit in arva senem ;
quique canit domito Camerinus ab Hectore Troiam ;
20   quique sua nomen Phyllide Tuscus habet ;
velivolique maris vates, cui credere posses
   carmina caeruleos composuisse deos ;
quique acies Libycas Romanaque proelia dixit ;
   et Marius scripti dexter in omne genus ;
25 Trinacriusque suae Perseidos auctor, et auctor
   Tantalidae reducis Tyndaridosque Lupus ;
et qui Maeoniam Phaeacida ² vertit, et une ³
   Pindaricae fidicen tu quoque, Rufe, lyrae ;
Musaque Turrani tragicis innixa cothurnis ;
30   et tua cum socco Musa, Melisse, levi ⁴ ;

¹ trisonem *vel* troadem *vel* troezen *etc. corr.* *Ehwald*
² ecateida *vel* aeacida   ³ uni *vel* una   ⁴ levis

genius, and fame is greater after one is ashes. I too had a name even at the time when I was counted with the living, when Marsus [1] lived and Rabirius of the mighty voice, the Ilian Macer, and Pedo towering to the stars, and Carus, who in his *Hercules* had angered Juno if that hero were not already Juno's son-in-law; and he who gave to Latium a regal poem, Severus, and both Prisci together with tasteful Numa; and thou, Montanus, master of metres whether even or uneven, whose fame rests upon two kinds of verse, and he who bade Ulysses write home to Penelope as he wandered for two lustra over the savage sea; Sabinus, who in untimely death abandoned his *Troesmis*, [2] the uncompleted work of many days; Largus, called by the surname of his own genius, who guided the aged Phrygian to the fields of Gaul; and Camerinus who sings of Troy after the vanquishing of Hector; and Tuscus, renowned for his *Phyllis*; the bard [3] of the sail-covered sea, whose verse one might believe composed by the sea-coloured gods; and he who sang of the armies of Libya and Rome's battles; and Marius, skilled in every style of composition, and Trinacrius who wrote of the *Perseid* he knew so well, and Lupus, author of the homecoming of Tyndarus's daughter with the scion of Tantalus; and he [4] who translated the Maeonian *Phaeacis*, and thou too, Rufus, unique player onPindar's lyre; and Turranius's Muse wearing the tragic buskin, and thine, Melissus, with

---

[1] For information concerning the poets in this long list see Index.

[2] Possibly an epic on the recovery of Troesmis, *cf.* iv. 9. 79. See Index.

[3] The poets alluded to in vv. 21–26 are otherwise unknown.

[4] Probably Tuticanus (Index).

cum Varius Gracchusque darent fera dicta tyrannis,
  Callimachi Proculus molle teneret iter,
Tityron antiquas Passerque rediret [1] ad herbas
  aptaque venanti Grattius arma daret ;
35 Naïdas a Satyris caneret Fontanus amatas,
  clauderet imparibus verba Capella modis ;
cumque forent alii, quorum mihi cuncta referre
  nomina longa mora est, carmina vulgus habet ;
essent et iuvenes, quorum quod inedita cura [2] est,
40 adpellandorum nil mihi iuris adest
(te tamen in turba non ausim, Cotta, silere,
  Pieridum lumen praesidiumque fori,
maternos Cottas cui Messallasque paternos,
  Maxime,[3] nobilitas ingeminata dedit)
45 dicere si fas est, claro mea nomine Musa
  atque inter tantos quae legeretur erat.
ergo summotum patria proscindere, Livor,
  desine, neu cineres sparge, cruente, meos.
omnia perdidimus : tantummodo vita relicta est,
50 praebeat ut sensum materiamque mali.
quid iuvat extinctos ferrum demittere [4] in artus ?
  non habet in nobis iam nova plaga locum.

---

[1] Passerque rediret] et erat qui pasceret herbas
[2] causa : cura *s*   [3] maxima
[4] dimittere *corr. Itali*

her light slippers. While Varius and Gracchus
furnished cruel words to tyrants, Proculus followed
the tender path of Callimachus, Passer [1] returned to
Tityrus and the familiar meadows, and Grattius
supplied weapons suited to the hunter; while
Fontanus sang of Naïads beloved by Satyrs, while
Capella prisoned words in unequal measures; and
while there were others all of whose names it were
long for me to mention, whose songs the people
possess; while there were youths also whose work
unpublished gives me no right to name them—yet
amid the throng, of thee, Cotta Maximus, I should
not venture to be silent, light of the Pierians and
guardian of the forum, to whom a twofold noble
lineage has given on thy mother's side the Cottas, on
the father's the Messallas—my Muse was famed, if
'tis right to speak thus, and she was one who was read
among so many of the great.

[47] So, Malice, cease to tear one banished from his
country; scatter not my ashes, cruel one! I have
lost all; life alone remains, to give me the conscious-
ness and the substance of sorrow. What pleasure to
thee to drive the steel into limbs already dead?
There is no space in me now for a new wound.

---

[1] Line 33 has been much emended. I have followed Riese,
Némethy, and Housman, who retain the reading of the best
MSS. and take Passer as a poet's name.

STRUCTURE IN EX PONTO I–III

Cf. Froesch, diss. 1968, p. 137 ; André, ed. p. xxxv ; Evans p. 111.

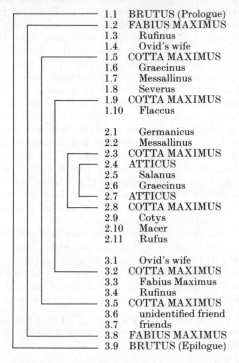

1.1	BRUTUS (Prologue)
1.2	FABIUS MAXIMUS
1.3	Rufinus
1.4	Ovid's wife
1.5	COTTA MAXIMUS
1.6	Graecinus
1.7	Messallinus
1.8	Severus
1.9	COTTA MAXIMUS
1.10	Flaccus
2.1	Germanicus
2.2	Messallinus
2.3	COTTA MAXIMUS
2.4	ATTICUS
2.5	Salanus
2.6	Graecinus
2.7	ATTICUS
2.8	COTTA MAXIMUS
2.9	Cotys
2.10	Macer
2.11	Rufus
3.1	Ovid's wife
3.2	COTTA MAXIMUS
3.3	Fabius Maximus
3.4	Rufinus
3.5	COTTA MAXIMUS
3.6	unidentified friend
3.7	friends
3.8	FABIUS MAXIMUS
3.9	BRUTUS (Epilogue)

It will be noted that the balanced structure suggests that the addressee of 3.8 is Fabius Maximus (Luck, André) rather than Cotta Maximus (Syme) ; and that the transposition of 2.9 *or* 10 *or* 11 to a place between 3.2 and 3.5 would produce a perfect symmetry for the whole.

490

INDEX

The references are to lines of the Latin text. $T.$ = Tristia; $P.$ = Ex Ponto; fl = floruit, "flourished"; c. = circa, "about,"; b. = born; † = died; n. = note. The citations are complete except where etc. is added.]

Thyestes. When Atreus slew Aërope together with Thyestes and his children, the sun turned aside in horror (*T.* ii. 392). According to another story. Atreus slew Thyestes' children and served them to him at a feast. *P.* i. 2. 119

Aeson, father of Jason, *P.* i. 4. 23, 46

Aesonides, son of Aeson, *i.e.* Jason, *P.* i. 4. 36

Aethalis, an adj. applied to Elba, the Greek Αἰθάλη, *P.* ii. 3. 84

Aetna, the great volcano of Sicily, *T.* v. 2. 75

Agamemnon, king of Mycenae, leader of the Greeks of Troy. See Clytaemestra, Orestes, Achilles. *T.* v. 6. 25, etc.

Agenor. See Phineus

Agenorides, son of Agenor, *i.e.* Cadmus, *P.* i. 3. 77

Agrius, father of Thersites, the ugliest man among the Greeks who besieged Troy, *P.* iii. 9. 9

Ajax, son of Telamon, the mightiest Greek warrior at Troy save only Achilles, *P.* iv. 7. 41

Albanus, "Alban," from Alba Longa, a town on the Alban Mount not far from Rome, founded by Ascanius (Iulus), *P.* i. 8. 67

Albinovanus, probably Albino-vanus Pedo, a soldier, who served with Germanicus in Germany, and a poet best known for epigrams (only one fragment of his work is extant), *P.* iv. 10′

Alcathous, son of Pelops and king of Megara, *T.* i. 10. 39

Alcestis, wife of Admetus. She consented to die in her husband's stead, but was saved by Hercules. *T.* v. 14. 37; *P.* iii. 1. 106

Alcides, Hercules — perhaps the hero's earliest name

Alcinous, king of the Phaeacians. He entertained Ulysses, and his orchards were famous, *P.* iv. 2. 10

Alcmene, wife of Amphitryon. She bore Hercules to Jupiter, who in his suit of her had caused the night to be doubled in length *T.* ii. 402

Alexandria, capital of Egypt, founded by Alexander the Great, *T.* i. 2. 79

Althaea, mother of Meleager. She burned the brand on which de-pended the life of her son because he had slain her brother

Amazons, a race of female warriors, *P.* iii. 1. 95

Amor (or Cupido), the god of love, often represented as a winged boy, *T.* v. 1. 22; *P.* iii. 3. 9 ff., etc.

Amphiaraus, one of the seven heroes who attacked Thebes. The earth yawned apart and engulfed him with his chariot. *P.* iii. 1. 52

Anacreon, a famous Greek lyric poet of Teos, Ionia, fl. *c.* 509 B.C.; numerous fragments, T. ii. 364

Anapus, a Sicilian river flowing into the harbour of Syracuse, *P.* ii. 10. 26

Anchialus, a Greek town on the Thracian coast of the Black Sea, south of Tomis, *T.* i. 10. 36

Anchises, father (by Venus) of Aeneas, who bore him from burning Troy upon his shoulders, *T.* ii. 299; *P.* i. 1. 33

Andromache, daughter of Eëtion, king of Cilician Thebes; wife of Hector

Andromeda, daughter of Cepheus, Ethiopian king; rescued by Perseus from a dragon; wife of Perseus, *T.* ii. 401

Anser, an Augustan erotic poet, *T.* ii. 435

Antenor, A Trojan noble, founder of Padua, *P.* iv. 16. 18

Antigone, daughter of Oedipus. She performed burial rites for her brother Polynices although King Creon had forbidden it because Polynices had attacked his native city Thebes. *T.* iii. 3. 67

Antilochus, son of Nestor and the closest friend (after Patroclus) of Achilles, *P.* i. 4. 22

Antimachus, an epic and elegiac poet of Colophon (or Claros), fl. *c.* 400 B.C. His most famous work, written to console himself for the loss of his wife, was the *Lyde*; meagre fragments. *T.* i. 6. 1

Antiphates, king of the Laestrygonians who ate human flesh, *P.* ii. 2. 114, etc.

Antonius (Marcus), the trimuvir, defeated by Augustus at Actium, *P.* i. 1. 23

Anytus, one of the accusers of Socrates, *T.* v. 12. 12

Aonia, originally a district of Boeotia next Phocis, then a poetic term for all Boeotia. Helicon and the Muses are often called "Aonian," *T.* iv 10 39, etc.

Apelles, the famous painter of Cos, 4th cent. B.C., who depicted Venus wringing the sea water from her hair, *P.* iv. 1. 29

Apollo (or Phoebus), god of the sun, of poetry, etc., *T.* i. 2. 5, etc.

Appia (via), the first great Roman road—from Rome to Capua, *P.* i. 8. 68

Aquilo, the Latin name for Boreas, the north wind, *T.* i. 11. 19, etc.

Arctos, the Great Bear (Ursa Maior), a constellation which never sets, *T.* i. 2. 29, etc.

Arcturus, guardian of the Bear, a stormy constellation, *P.* ii. 7. 58

Arethusa, a nymph beloved by the river god Alpheus in Elis Changed into a spring she was pursued by the god beneath the sea to Sicily. *P.* ii. 10. 27

Argo, Jason's ship, built by Athene's aid, *T.* ii. 439

Argolicus, properly "Argive," but a general term for "Greek," *T.* i. 9. 27, etc.

Ariadne, daughter of Minos, king of Crete. She aided Theseus to penetrate the labyrinth and slay the Minotaur, then fled with him but was abandoned on the Isle of Dia and wedded by Bacchus. The god placed her crown in heaven as a constellation—Ariadne's crown, *T.* v. 3. 42

Aristaeus, son of Apollo, patron of dairying, bee culture, etc., *P.* iv. 2. 9

Aristarchus, the famous Homeric critic of Alexandria, 2nd cent. B.C., *P.* iii. 9. 24

Aristides (1) the famous Athenian statesman, exiled 482 B.C., *P* i. 3. 71. (2) The author of the *Milesian Tales*; very meagre fragments of Sisenna's Latin translation survive, *T.* ii. 413, 443

Ars, Ovid's *Ars amatoria* (*Art of Love*). See Introd. p. xix

Ascra, A Boeotian town, where Hesiod was born, *P.* iv. 14. 31

Atalanta (1) daughter of Schoeneus, won by Hippomenes who defeated her in a foot-race by the device of rolling golden apples in her path, *T.* ii. 399. (2) Daughter of Iasos, an Arcadian huntress who disdained love, but was won by Milanion after many hardships

Athos, a lofty promontory of the Macedonian Chalcidice, *P.* i. 5. 22

Atia (minor), aunt of Augustus and wife of L. Marcius Phillippus, *P.* i. 2. 139

Atreus, father of Agamemnon and Menelaus, *P.* i. 2. 119. See Aërope

Atticus, a friend to whom Ovid addresses *P.* ii. 4 and ii. 7; otherwise unknown

Augustus, the Emperor Augustus Caesar, *T.* i. 2. 102, etc ; Ovid's lost poem on A.'s apotheosis, *P.* iv. 6. 18, iv. 9. 131 ; Getic poem on A., *P.* iv. 13. 19. See Introd. p. xxviii. Tiberius also was called Augustus, *P.* iv. 9. 70, etc.

Aurelia, wife of M. Valerius Corvinus Messala, *P.* ii. 3. 98

Ausonia, originally a Greek name for the land of the Aurunci (Αὔσονες) ; later a poetic term for Latium or even Italy, *T.* i. 2. 92, etc.

Auster, the south wind. See Notus. *T.* i. 10. 33, etc.

Automedon, the charioteer of Achilles, *T.* v. 6. 10

Axenus, "inhospitable," and adj. applied to the Black Sea (Pontus), *T*. iv. 4. 56

Azanis, "Arcadian," descended from Azan, son of Arcas: epithet of the Great Bear, *T*. i. 11. 15

Babylon, *P*. ii. 4. 27

Bacche, a Bacchante, *T*. iv. 1. 41, etc.

Bacchus (or Liber, Lyaeus, etc.), god of the vine, poetry, etc., *T*. i. 10. 38, etc.

Ball games, *T*. ii. 485

Bassus, an iambic poet, member of Ovid's circle (*T*. iv. 10. 47); otherwise unkown, although attempts have been made to identify him with Bassus (Propert. i. 4), or with Bassus (Seneca, *Controvers*. x. *Praefat*. xii.)

Basternae, a German (or Celtic?) people dwelling, in Ovid's time, along the Danube from the Carpathians to the Black Sea, *T*. ii. 198

Bato, a Dalmatian chief who fought against Rome, A.D. 6–9. He obtained immunity and was allowed to live at Ravenna. *P*. ii 1. 46

Battiades, "descendant of Battus," *i.e.* Callimachus, T. ii. 367, etc.

Belides, *T*. iii. 1. 62. See Danaïdes

Bellerophon, entertained by Proetus, king of Argos; rejected the advances of Stheneboea, his hostess, who in revenge accused him. The king gave him over to Iobates to slay, but the latter not daring to slay him forced him to fight the fire-breathing Chimaera which he succeeded in killing. *T*. ii. 397

Bessi, A Thracian people dwelling on the Upper Hebrus, *T*. iii. 10. 5, etc.

Birthday, Ovid's (at Tomis), *T*. iii. 13; iv. 10. 11; his wife's, *T*. v. 5

Bistonii, a Thracian people of the Aegean coast. Ovid uses the name as equivalent to "Thracians"; adj. Bistonius, Bistonis. *T*. i. 10. 23, etc.

Bittis, the beloved, probably the wife, of Philetas, *T*. i. 6. 2; *P*. iii. 1. 58

Book, description of a Roman book, *T*. i. 1. 1 ff. n., 106 ff.; iii. 1. 13 ff.

Boötes, Ox-Driver, the star which "drives" the seven oxen of the Wain (Great Bear), later called Arcturus

Boreas, the north wind, adj. Boreus, *T*. i. 2. 29, etc.

Borysthenes, a river flowing into the Black Sea—the Dnieper, *P*. iv. 10. 53

Bosporus, *T*. ii. 298; *cf*. iii. 4. 49

Briseis. See Achilles

Brutus, (1) M. Junius, one of the leaders of the conspiracy against Julius Caesar, and a writer on philosophy and rhetoric, *P*. i. 1. 24; (2) A friend whom Ovid addresses, *P*. i. 1, iii. 9, iv. 6. He acted as Ovid's editor; not otherwise known. See Introd. p. xv

Busiris, an Egyptian king who sacrificed strangers to Jupiter, *T*. iii. 11. 39, etc.

Byzantium, *T*., i. 10. 31

Cadmus, son of Agenor and founder of (Boeotian) Thebes, *T*. iv. 3. 67, etc.

Caesar (1) C. Julius, the Dictator, *P*. iv. 8. 63; (2) Augustus, *T*. i. 1. 30, etc.; (3) Tiberius, *P*. ii. 8. 1, etc.; (4) Germanicus, *T*. ii. 230, etc. Ovid uses Caesares, "the Caesars," of two or more members of the imperial house

Calamis, an Athenian artist (*c*. 460 B.C.), famous for his work in metal, *P*. iv. 1. 33

Cales, probably a Bithynian river (south of Herakleia), *P*. iv. 10. 47

Callimachus, the famous scholar and poet of Alexandria (3rd cent. B.C.), who claimed descent from Battus, founder of Cyrene; a voluminous writer in prose and verse. Numerous epigrams and some hymns survive, but most of his work is now in fragments. Catullus, Propertius, and Ovid

494

greatly admired him. *P*. iv. 16. 32. See also Battiades

Calliope, the muse of elegiac poetry, but often she represents poetry in general, *T*. ii. 568

Callisto, daughter of the Arcadian king, Lycaon. She was changed into the constellation of the Great Bear

Calvus, C. Licinius Macer Calvus (82–46 B.C.), famous orator and poet, friend of Catullus. He was a man of small stature; few fragments, *T*. ii. 431

Calydon, an Aetolian town, *P*. i. 3 79

Calypso, a goddess who fell in love with Ulysses and detained him on her isle, *P*. iv. 10. 13

Camena, a Roman term for Muse, *P*. iv. 13. 33

Camerinus, an Augustan epic poet, *P*. iv. 16. 19; not otherwise known

Campania, *P*. iv. 15. 17

Campus (Martis), just outside Rome (north-west) along the Tiber, the great recreation ground of the Romans, *T*. v. 1. 32, etc.

Canace, daughter of Aeolus, lord of the winds. Her love for her brother Macareus was the theme of Euripides' *Aeolus*. *T*. ii. 384

Capaneus, one of the seven leaders who attacked Thebes; slain by the lightning of Zeus, *T*. iv. 3. 63, etc.

Capella, an Augustan poet who wrote in elegiac verse, *P*. iv. 16. 36; not otherwise known

Caphereus, the northern cape of Euboea on which the Greeks were wrecked as they were returning from Troy, *T*. i. 1. 83

Capitolium, properly the southern summit of the Capitoline Hill, but often used of the whole hill, *T*. i. 3. 29, etc.

Carus, a friend to whom Ovid addresses *P*. iv. 13, perhaps also *T*. iii. 5. He was a poet (*P* iv. 13. 12; 16. 7) and had charge of the education of Germanicus' sons (*P*. iv. 13. 47 f.). See Introd. p. xv

Caspios Aegisos, the founder of Aegisos, *P*. i. 8. 13

Cassandra, daughter of Priam, priestess and prophetess. Agamemnon took her to Mycenae where she was murdered. *T*. ii. 400

Cassandreus, a "Cassandrean," *i.e.* resembling Apollodorus, the cruel lord of Cassandrea in Macedonia, *P*. ii. 9. 43

Castor, son of Jupiter and Leda, twin brother of Pollux, *T*. iv. 5. 30, etc.

Cato (C. Valerius), Roman grammarian and poet, an older contemporary of Catullus, very influential as a teacher, *T*. ii. 436

Catullus (C. Valerius), *c*. 87–*c*. 54 B.C., the greatest Roman lyric poet. His most famous poems are those to Lesbia (Clodia, a sister of P. Clodius). *T*. ii. 427

Celsus, one of Ovid's closest friends, *P*. i. 9. (his death), perhaps also *T*. i. 5. 1–44 and iii. 6. See Introd. p. xvi

Cenchreae, the harbour of Corinth on the Saronic Gulf, *T*. i. 10. 9

Ceraunia (or Acroceraunia), a dangerous promontory on the Adriatic coast of Illyria and Epirus, *P*. ii. 6. 9

Cerberus, the monstrous dog, often depicted as three-headed, which guarded the entrance to Hades, *T*. iv. 7. 16

Ceres, goddess of grain, etc.; adj Cerialis, *T*. ii. 300, etc.

Chaos, *P*. iv. 8. 57

Charybdis, in Homer a whirlpool, later a hungry monster supposed to inhabit the Sicilian Straits, *T*. v. 2. 73, etc.

Chess, *T*. ii. 471 n.

Chimaera, *T*. ii. 397, etc. See Bellerophon

Chiron, a centaur who instructed Achilles, in hunting, lyre-playing etc., *P*., iii. 3. 43

Cimbri, a horde of invading Teutons, defeated by Marius at Vercellae (101 B.C.), *P*. iv. 3. 45

Cimmerii, a people between the Danube and the Don—probably in

Ovid's time not near the Danube although he calls the region of Tomis "Cimmerian," *P*. iv. 10. 1

Cinases, a river in Scythia, cf. Arrian, *Periplus* 7. 5, *P*. iv. 10. 49

Cinna (C. Helvius), a poet and friend of Catullus; few fragments, *T*. ii. 435

Cinyphus, a river of North Africa flowing into the sea near the Syrtes, *P*. ii. 7. 25

Circe, a divine sorceress, mother (by Ulysses) of Telegonus. She transformed some of Ulysses' men into swine. *P*. iii. 1. 123

Circus (Maximus), the huge circus between the Palatine and the Aventine, used for pageants, races, etc., *T*. ii. 283, etc.

Ciziges, *T*. ii. 191

Claudia, a Roman matron accused of unchastity, who, after an oracle had declared that the ship bearing the image of Cybele could be moved from the shoal on which it had grounded only by a pure woman, vindicated herself by seizing the rope and drawing it off, *P*. i. 2. 142

Clodia (via). See *P*. i. 8. 44 n.

Clytaemestra, wife of Agamemnon. During her husband's absence at Troy she became enamoured of Aegisthus and slew her husband on his return. She was in turn slain by her son, Orestes

Colchi, *T*. ii. 191 n.

Colchis. See Medea

Coralli, a Moesian tribe dwelling near the Danube, *P*. iv. 2. 37, etc.

Corinna. See *T*. iv. 10. 60 n.

Corinthus. *T*. iii. 8. 4

Cornificius, a Roman erotic poet; date uncertain; very few fragments, *T*. ii. 436

Cotta, Maximus, *P*. i. 5 and 9; ii. 3 and 8; iii. 2 and 5; cf. iv. 16. 41–44. See introd. p. xii

Cotys, name of several kings of Thrace. The one reigning at the time of Ovid's exile was probably the son of Rhoemetalces First. *P*. ii. 9

Croesus, king of Lydia, famed for his wealth, defeated and captured by Cyrus (6th cent. B.C.), *T*. iii. 7. 42, etc.

Cupido (or Amor), god of love, *T*. ii. 385, etc. See Amor

Cyane, a playmate of Proserpina. Pluto changed her into a spring when she resisted his seizure of Proserpina. *P*. ii. 10. 26

Cyaneae (insulae), Greek Symplegades, the "clashing rocks," *T*. i. 10. 34 n., cf. 47

Cybele (or Rhea), the Great Mother (Magna Mater) of the gods, whose worship was introduced at Rome 204 B.C., *P*. i. 1. 39

Cyclades, the "encircling isles" (with Delos as a centre) in the Aegean, *T*. i. 11. 8

Cyclopes, the Cyclopes, a race of one-eyed giants living in Sicily. One of them, Polyphemus, imprisoned Ulysses and twelve of his men in a cave and devoured six of them. Ulysses saved the rest by making the giant drunk and then blinding him. *P*. iv. 10. 23

Cydippe. See Acontius

Cyzicus, a town on the Asian shore of the Propontis, *T*. i. 10. 30, n.

Daedalus, *T*. iii. 4. 21, etc. See Icarus

Dalmatia, a Roman province bordering the eastern shore of the Adriatic, *P*. ii. 2. 76

Danaë, mother of Perseus, *T*. ii 401

Danaides, the fifty daughters of Danaus (or granddaughters of Belus, Belidae). They wedded the sons of Aegyptus and at the command of their father all save Hypermnestra slew their husbands on the wedding night. See *T*. iii. 1. 62

Danapris, the river Dnieper, *P*. iv. 10. 53

Danaus, "Danaan," originally applied to the people about Argos, later a general term ("Greek"), *P*. iv. 7. 41

Danuvius, the Danube, *T*. ii. 192, etc. Ovid prefers Hister

Dardania a town on the Asian

shore of the Hellespont, *T*. i. 10. 25

Dareus (Third), king of Persia. Alexander gave him rites of burial after he had been murdered by his own kin, *T*. iii. 5. 40

Deianira, daughter of King Oeneus of Aetolia, wife of Hercules, *T*. ii. 405

Deidamia, daughter of Lycomedes, king of the Dolopians in Scyros. She became (by Achilles) mother of Neoptolemus (Pyrrhus). See *T*. ii. 405

Delos (or Delia tellus), the Aegean isle, birthplace of Apollo, *P*. iv. 14. 57

Delphi, the holy town of Phocis in which was the famous oracle of Apollo, *T*. iv. 8. 43

Diana (or Phoebe), goddess of the moon, the hunt, etc., *T*., ii. 105, etc.

Dice. See notes on *T*. ii. 473 ff.

Diogenes, the famous Cynic philosopher (4th cent. B.C.), *P*. i. 3. 67

Diomedes, (1) son of Tydeus; one of the most valiant Greek leaders at Troy, *P*. ii. 2. 13; (1) king of the Bistones, who fed his horses on human flesh, *P*. i. 2. 120

Dionusopolis, a town on the Moesian coast of the Pontus, south of Tomis, *T*. i. 10. 38

Dionysius (the Younger), tyrant of Syracuse. After his expulsion he opened a school at Corinth. *P*. iv. 3. 39

Dirae, Ovid's (lost) dirge for Messalla, *P*. i. 7. 30

Dodona, the oracle of Zeus in Epirus, *T*. iv. 8. 43

Dolon, a Trojan, son of Eumedes. Having served as a spy in the Greek camp he asked as his reward the horses of Achilles. He was slain by Ulysses and Diomed. *T*. iii. 4. 27

Donnus, a Celtic chieftain, ancestor of Vestalis, *P*. iv. 7. 29

Draughts. See notes on *T*. ii. 477 ff.

Drusus (1) surnamed Germanicus, younger son of Livia Augusta by her first husband; father of Germanicus, *T*. iv. 2. 39. (2) Son of Tiberius and Vipsania, cousin and (through adoption of Germanicus by Tiberius) brother of Germanicus, *P*. ii. 2. 72

Dulichium, an isle belonging to Ulysses, hence Ulysses and his comrades are called "Dulichian," *T*. i. 5. 60, etc.

Echionius, "Theban," from Echion, son-in-law of Cadmus, the founder of Thebes, *T*. v. 5. 53

Eëtion, father of Andromache, *T*. v. 5. 44

Electra, daughter of Agamemnon and Clytaemestra and sister of Orestes. She saved Orestes from Aegisthus after the murder of Agamemnon, was ill-treated by him and was forced to marry a man of humble station. She was the subject of tragedies by Sophocles and Euripides; in *T*. ii. 395 that of Euripides is probably meant

Elegi. See Metre

Elis, *P*. ii. 10. 27

Elpenor, a comrade of Ulysses who fell from the roof of Circe's palace and broke his neck. Ulysses saw his shade later in Hades, *T*. iii. 4. 19

Emathius, orginally applied to the Emathian plain, later a poetic term for "Macedonian," *T*. iii. 5. 39 n.

Enceladus, one of the Giants who attempted to storm heaven by piling Mts. Pelion, Ossa, and Olympus on each other. He was overthrown by Pallas. *P*. ii. 2. 11

Endymion, the beautiful youth of Carian Latmos who was loved by Luna (Diana), *T*. ii. 299

Ennius (Quintus), one of the most important of early Roman poets (239–169 B.C.). His chief work was the *Annales*, an epic on the history of Rome; numerous fragments. *T*. ii. 259, 423 f.

497

Eous, (1) the dawn (Eos), *T*. iv. 9. 22; (2) "eastern," *P*. ii. 5. 50, etc.

Epidaurus, a town in Argolis famous for the great precinct of Aesculapius, *P*. i. 3. 21

Erichthonius, the misshapen son of Vulcan, born of that god's attempted outrage of Pallas; brought up by Pallas secretly in her temple; in early times identified with Erechtheus, the mythical king of Athens, *T*. ii. 294, etc.

Erymanthis, "Arcadian," from Mt. Erymanthus in Arcadia, *T*. i. 4. 1, etc.

Eteocles: Eteocles and Polynices, Theban brothers, slew each other in the battle before Thebes. Etocles was one of the seven leaders who defended the city, *T*. v. 5. 34. See Antigone

Euadne, daughter of Iphis and wife of Capaneus. She had herself burned on her husband's funeral pyre. *T*. iv. 3. 64, etc.

Eubius. See *T*. ii. 416 n.

Eumedes, father of Dolon, *T*. iii. 4. 27

Eumolpus, a famous Thracian singer, son of Poseidon and Chione, *P*. ii. 9. 19

Europa, sister of Cadmus, from whom "Europe" is named, *P*. iv. 10. 55

Eurus, the east, or south-east wind, *T*. i. 2. 27

Euryalus. See Nisus

Eurydice. See Orpheus

Euxinus. The Black Sea was called Pontus Euxinus ("hospitable sea") for purposes of good omen. *T*. iii. 13. 28, etc. See Axenus

Fabia, Ovid's third wife, *T*. iv. 10. 73, *P*. i. 2, 136, etc. See Introd. p. xvii

Fabius, Paullus Fabius Maximus. See Maximus and Introd. p. xii

(Falerii). See Falisca herba

Falerna (vina), *P*. iv. 2. 9

Falisca (herba), grass "of Falerii," a town on the Etruscan bank of the Tiber north-west of Rome,

famed for its meadows and cattle, *P*. iv. 4. 32, etc.

Fasti, Ovid's poem on the calendar, *T*. ii. 549

Flaccus (L. Pomponius), brother of Ovid's friend Graecinus. He served in Moesia about A.D. 15 (*cf*. *P*. iv. 9. 75 ff.), and again as governor A.D. 18 or 19. See Introd. p. xiii

Flaminia (via). See *P*. i. 8. 44 n.

Fontanus, an Augustan bucolic poet, *P*. iv. 16. 35

Fortuna, goddess of fortune, *T*. i. 1. 51, etc.

Fundi (Fundanum solum), a town on the Via Appia in southern Latium, *P* ii. 11. 28

Furiae, The Furies, *T*. iv. 4. 70

Gallio (L. Junius), a rhetorician, friend of Ovid's, *P*, iv. 11. See Introd. p. xv

Gallus (C. Cornelius), an Augustan elegist famed for his poems to Lycoris (only one line extant). He incurred the disfavour of Augustus, was exiled, and committed suicide. *T*. ii. 445; iv. 10. 53; v. 1. 17

Ganges, *T*. v. 3. 23

Ganymede, the beautiful Ilian boy who was carried off by Jupiter who had assumed the form of an eagle, *T*. ii. 406

Germania, *T*. ii. 229, etc.

Germanicus, son of the elder Drusus and adopted son of Tiberius; husband of Agrippina (granddaughter of Augustus), *P*. ii. 1. 49, etc. See Introd. pp. xv-xvi

Geryon, a monster with a triple body whose cattle Hercules drove away

Getae (adj. Geticus). See Introd. p. xxvi

Gigantes, the Giants who attempted to storm heaven and were hurled down by Jove's thunderbolt, *T*. ii. 333, etc.

Gorgo, *T*. iv. 7. 12. See Medusa

Gracchus, probably Ti. Sempronius Gracchus, a clever but degenerate

498

descendant of the great Gracchi. He wrote tragedies; few fragments. *P.* iv. 16. 31

Graecinus (P. Pomponius). See Introd. p. xiii

Grattius, an Augustan poet who wrote a poem on hunting (extant) and bucolics (now lost), *P.* iv. 16. 34 ff.

Gyes, one of the Gigantes, *T.* iv 7. 18

Hadria, the Adriatic, *T.* i. 11. 4

Haedi. See *T.* i. 11. 13 n.

Haemon, son of Creon, king of Thebes, He slew himself at the death of Antigone, his betrothed. *T.* ii. 402

Haemonia, Thessaly, from Haemon, father of Thessalos; adj. Haemonius, "Thessalian," *P.* i. 3. 75, etc.

Haemus, a Thracian mountain range, *P.* iv. 5. 5

Halcyone, wife of Ceyx, changed into a bird (a kingfisher, according to Ovid) because she dared to call her husband Jupiter, *T.* v. 1. 60

Halys, a large river flowing through central Asia Minor into the Pontus, *P.* iv. 10. 48

Harpyia, a monster with a bird's body and the head of a maiden, *T.* iv. 7. 17

Hebrus, the chief river of Thrace, *P.* i. 5. 21

Hector, son of Priam, husband of Andromache, and father of Astyanax; best warrior of the Trojans; led the attack on the Greek ships, many of which he burned. He slew Patroclus and was himself slain in vengeance by Achilles, who dragged him behind his chariot, but yielded up his body for burial on the entreaties of Priam. *T.* i. 6. 19, etc.

Helicon, a Boeotian mountain, a favourite abode of the Muses, *T.* iv. 1. 50, etc.

Helle, granddaughter of Aeolus, daughter of Athamas. She fell from the back of the gold-fleeced ram into the waters which were named from her the Hellespont. *T.* i. 10. 15, etc.

Hemitheon, the probable author of the *Sybaritica*, "Tales of Sybaris," *T.* ii. 417

Heniochi, a people—Sarmatian apparently—who practised piracy, *P.* iv. 10. 26

Henna, a town in central Sicily, *P.* ii. 10. 25

Hercules, son of Jupiter (Zeus) and Alcmena; also called Alcides, *T.* ii. 405, etc.

Hermione, daughter of Menelaus and Helen and niece of Castor and Pollux, betrothed at Troy to Neoptolemus, who, returning to Greece, found her betrothed (or married) to Orestes. When Neoptolemus demanded her he was slain by Orestes. *T.* ii. 399, etc.

Hesiodus, the early Greek poet (*c.* 700 B.C.) of Ascra in Boeotia. To him are attributed the *Theogony*, *Works and Days*, and *Shield of Hercules*, *P.* iv. 14. 32, etc.

Hesperius, "of the evening," western, hence Hesperia, the West, often applied to Italy, *T.* iv. 9. 22

Hippocrene, *P.* iv. 8. 80, n.

Hippodamia, daughter of Oenomaus, king of Pisa. Pelops defeated Oenomaus in a chariot race and carried off Hippodamia. *T.* ii. 386

Hippolytus, the son of Theseus. The love of his stepmother Phaedra for him is the theme of Euripides' *Hippolytus.* *T.* ii. 383

Hister, the Danube, also called Danuvius, *T.* ii. 189, etc.

Homerus, the great Greek epic poet, *T.* ii. 379, etc.

Hoop, *T.* ii. 486

Horatius, Q. Horatius Flaccus (65–8 B.C.), one of the greatest of Augustan poets, *T.* iv. 10. 49

Hortensius (Q.), the famous orator and rival of Cicero. He also dabbled in erotic poetry (one word extant). *T.* ii. 441

Hyades, a constellation that caused rain, *T.* i. 11. 16

Hybla, a Sicilian town (near Syracuse) famed for honey, *T*. v. 6. 38

Hylas, a beautiful boy, beloved by Hercules, who was stolen by nymphs when the Argonauts landed near the Ascanius river, *T*. *ii*. 406

Hymenaeus (or Hymen), god of marriage, *P*. i. 2. 131

Hypanis, a Sarmatian river, now the Bug, *P*. iv. 10. 47

Hyrtacides. See Nisus

Iasion, father (by Ceres) of Plutus, *T*. ii. 300

Iazyges, Sarmatian tribe dwelling near the Danube, *P*. i. 2. 77, etc.

Icariotis. See Penelope

Icarius, father of Penelope, *T*. v. 5. 44, etc.

Icarus, son of Daedalus, who perished by falling into the (Icarian) sea as he and Daedalus were flying from Crete on the wings his father had made, *T*. i. 1. 90, etc.

Idaei (modi), so called from Idaeus who founded on Mt. Ida the rites of Cybele, *T*. iv. 1. 42

Ilia (or Rhea Silvia), the Vestal who bore to Mars Romulus and Remus, *T*. ii. 260

Iliacus, "Ilian," hence "Trojan"

Iliades, "son of Ilia," *i.e.* Remus, *T*. iv. 3. 8

Ilias, the *Iliad*, *T*. ii 371, etc.

Illyria (or Illyris), the district along the east coast of the Adriatic, *T*. i. 4. 19, etc.

Ilva, Elba, also called Aethale or Aethalia, *P*. ii. 3. 84

Imbros, an Aegean isle, *T*. i. 10. 18

Indicus (or Indus), "Indian," *P*. i. 5. 80, etc.

Iole, daughter of King Eurytus of Oechalia whom Hercules carried off after slaying her father, *T*. ii. 405

Ionium (mare), the Ionian Sea, between Greece and southern Italy, *T*. i. 4. 3, etc.

Iphias, "daughter of Iphis," *i.e.* Euadne, *P*. iii. 1. 111

Iphigenia, daughter of Agamemnon and sister of Orestes. Agamemnon was ordered to sacrifice her at Aulis in order to appease the gods, but Diana substituted a hind and transported Iphigenia to the land of the Taurians. *T* iv. 4. 63 ff.; *P*. iii. 2. 43 ff.

Irus, the Ithacan beggar with whom Ulysses had a boxing match on his return home in disguise, *T*. iii. 7. 42

Isis, the Egyptian goddess, identified in Ovid with Io, who was beloved by Jupiter and in the form of a heifer was driven about the world by the jealousy of Juno, *T*. ii. 297

Isthmos (of Corinth), *T*. i. 11. 5; *P*. iv. 10. 80

Italia, *T*. i. 4. 20; iii. 12. 37; adj. Italus

Ithace, the isle of Ithaca, home of Ulysses, usually identified with Thiaki, *T*. i. 5. 67

Itys, *T*. ii. 390. See Tereus

Iulus (or Ascanius), son of Aeneas, from whom the Julii claimed descent, *P*. ii. 2. 21; adj. Iuleus

Ivory, *cf.* Numidae dentis, *P*. iv. 9. 28

Janus, god of passage-ways (doors, etc.), beginnings, etc., represented with two faces, *P*. iv. 4. 23, etc.

Jason, son of Aeson, leader of the Argonauts, *P*. i. 4. 36, etc. See Medea

Jugurtha, the Numidian king, conquered by Marius, died in prison at Rome (104 B.C.), *P*. iv 3. 45

Juno, wife of Jupiter and chief among the Olympian goddesses, corresponding to the Greek Hera, *T*. ii. 291, etc.

Jupiter (or Juppiter), ruler of the gods, corresponding to the Greek Zeus, *T*. i. 1. 81, etc. Many epithets, *e.g.* Stator, *T*. iii. 1. 32

Juventa (or -as), an old Roman goddess, later identified (as in Ovid) with the Greek Hebe, the servitor of the gods, *P*. i. 10. 12

500

Lacedaemon (or Sparta), *P.* i. 3. 71

Lachesis. See *T.* v. 10. 45 n.

Laërtes, father of Ulysses, *T.* v. 5. 3

Laestrygon (adj.). The Laestrygonians were a race of cannibals in whose land great disasters befell Ulysses. *P.* ii. 9. 41, etc.

Lampsacus, a town on the Asiatic shore of the Hellespont, *T.* i. 10. 26

Lares, beneficent spirits watching over the fields, the public domain, the household, etc. Each house had a Lararium in which the image of the Lar was kept. The Lares are often mentioned with the Penates (strictly guardians of the larder). Lar often stands for "home." *T.* i. 3. 30, etc.

Largus, an Augustan poet who wrote an epic on Antenor's wanderings, and final settlement near the Po (sometimes identified with Valerius Largus, the accuser of Cornelius Gallus), *P.* iv. 16. 17

Latium, the district in which Rome lies, *T.* iv. 2. 69, etc.

Latona (or Leto), mother (by Jupiter) of Apollo and Diana; adj. Letoïus, *T.* iii. 2. 3, etc.

Laodamia, wife of Protesilaus, the first Greek to fall on Trojan soil. He begged a day's release from Hades in order to be with her, and she slew herself in order to be his companion even in death. *T.* i. 6. 20, etc.

Leander, who perished while swimming the Hellespont from Abydos to his sweetheart Hero at Sestos, *T.* iii. 10. 41

Lemnos, a large island in the Thracian (north Aegean) Sea, *T.* v. 1. 62

Lesbia, Catullus' name for his sweetheart Clodia, *T.* ii. 428

Lesbos, a large island in the north-eastern Aegean near Asia, *T.* ii. 365, etc.

Lethe, a river of Hades, a draught of whose water brought forgetfulness, *T.* iv. 1. 47

Leucadia, a large island in the Ionian Sea near Acharnania, *T.* iii. 1. 42 n.

Leucothee. Ino, wife of Athamas, threw herself into the sea and was changed into the sea goddess Leucothea, *P.* iii. 6. 20

Liber. See Bacchus

Libertas. The Atrium Libertatis (north of the Forum) was where Asinius Pollio established a public library, *T.* iii. 1. 72

Libya, coast district of North Africa, west of Egypt, *T.* i. 3. 19, etc.

Livia (Augusta), the empress (58 B.C.–A.D. 29). Her first husband was Ti. Claudius Nero to whom she bore Tiberius (later emperor) and Drusus (father of Germanicus). She married Octavianus (Augustus) 38 B.C. *T.* ii. 161, etc.

Lixus, a river; location uncertain, *P.* i. 5. 21

Lucifer, the morning-star, *T.* 1. 3. 72, etc.

Lucretius, T. Lucr. Carus (c. 95–c. 54 B.C.), the greatest Roman didactic poet; author of the *De rerum natura*. *T.* ii. 425

Luna, goddess of the moon, *T.* i. 3. 28. See Diana

Lupus, an Augustan poet who wrote on the home-coming of Menelaus and Helen, *P.* iv. 16. 26

Lyaeus. See Bacchus

Lycaon, the Arcadian (Parrhasian) king whose daughter Callisto was changed into the Great Bear; hence the pole is called "Lycaonian" or "Parrhasian," *T.* iii. 2. 2 ; 2. 190

Lycoris, mistress of Cornelius Gallus, *T.* ii. 445. (Probably a pseudonym).

Lycurgus, the Thracian king who tried to cut down the vines introduced by Bacchus and was driven mad by the god so that imagining his own foot to be a vine he hewed it with an axe, *T.* v. 3. 39

Lycus, (1) a river in Bithynia; (2) another in Pontus, *P.* iv. 10. 47.

It is uncertain which Ovid means
Lyde. See Antimachus

Macer, (1) Aemilius M., a poet who wrote of birds, serpents, plants, etc.; he was an old man in Ovid's youth, *T*. iv. 10. 43. (2) Pompeius M., and epic poet who wrote on parts of the Trojan cycle which preceded the action of the *Iliad*; probably the same as the Macer who travelled with Ovid in Sicily and was related to his wife, *P*. ii. 10. 10 ff.; iv. 16. 6

Machaon, *P*. iii. 4. 7. See Podalirius

Maenalis, "Maenalian." The Great Bear is so called from Mt. Maenalus in Arcadia because Callisto (the Bear) was, before her transformation, an Arcadian. *T*. iii. 11. 8

Maeonides, Homer, so called from Maeonia, a name for Lydia, where according to one story he was born, or because his father was Maion; adj. Maeonius, *T*. i. 1. 47, etc.

Maeotia, "Maeotian," a term applied to the kingdom of Thoas from the Maeotes who dwelt near the Sea of Azof, *P*. iii. 2. 59; at *T*. iii. 12. 2 the adjective Maeotis does not scan and must be emended

Manes, the di manes, *i.e.* "good deities," a general term for the gods of the lower world and (later) for the shades of the dead who were regarded as divine, *T*. i. 9. 31, etc.

Marcia, daughter of L. Marcius Philippus, and wife of Paullus Fabius Maximus, *P*. i. 2. 138 n.

Marius, (1) C. Marius, seven times consul conqueror of the Cimbri, Jugurtha, etc. When Sulla entered Rome (88 B.C.) Marius hid in the marshes of Minturnae and later escaped to Africa, *P*. iv. 3. 47. (2) An Augustan poet, otherwise unknown, *P*. iv. 16. 24

Mars, god of war, often used for "war," "battle," *T*. ii. 295, etc.

Marsus (Domitius), an Augustan poet famed chiefly for epigrams, two or three of which survive, *P*. iv. 16. 5

Marsyas, a Phrygian satyr, inventor of the flute and teacher of the famous flute-player Olympus, *P*. iii. 3. 42 n.

Maximus (1) M. Aurelius Cotta Max. See Introd. p. xii. (2) Paullus Fabius Max. See Introd. pp. xii–xiii

Medea, daughter of Aeetes, king of Colchis, fell in love with Jason when he came to Colchis in quest of the Golden Fleece, and aided him by her enchantments to escape with it. Later when Jason abandoned her she slew their two children and fled in a chariot drawn by winged dragons. Ovid's lost tragedy was a *Medea*. *T*. iii. 8. 3, ii. 553, etc.

Medusa, one of the Gorgons, a glance at whose face turned the beholder to stone, *T*. iv. 7. 11, etc.

Melanthus, a river in Pontus (or Sarmatia?), *P*. iv. 10. 54

Melissus (C.), a freedman of Maecenas, grammarian, poet, librarian. He wrote *Trabeatae*, comedies of Roman manners, in which he seems to have dealt with the life of the upper classes, thus developing an Augustan form of the old *Togatae*. *P*. iv. 16. 30

Memmius, probably C. Memm., praetor 58 B.C., to whom Lucretius dedicated the *De rerum natura* and with whom Catullus went to Bithynia (57 B.C.). He wrote love poetry (one line extant). *T*. ii. 433

Memnon, son of Aurora, goddess of the dawn, *P*. i. 4. 57

Menander, an Athenian, the most famous writer of New Comedy († *c*. 292 B.C.), extensive fragments. He was very popular at Rome. *T*. ii. 369

Merops. See Phaëthon

502

Mesembria, a town on the Thracian coast of the Pontus south of Tomis, *T*. i. 10. 37

Messalinus (M. Valerius Messalla Corvinus of Messalinus), older son of the following, *P*. i. 7; ii. 2. See Introd. p. xii

Messalla (M. Valerius Corvinus), the great soldier, statesman, and patron of literature (*c*. 65 B.C.-*c*. A.D. 8), *P*. ii. 3. 73 ff.; i. 7. 27 ff. (Ovid's epicede for him), ii. 2. 51, 97

Metamorphoses, Ovid's hexameter poem on transformation, *T*. i. 7. 13; ii. 63 and 555; iii. 14. 19. See introd. p. xxiv

Metellus, *T*. ii. 438. See Perilla

Metre (elegiac), *T*. i. 1. 16; ii. 220; iii. 1. 11 f.; *P*. ii. 5. 1; iii. 3. 30; iii. 4. 85 f.; iv. 16. 11 f., 36 etc.

Metrodorus, of Skepsis in Mysia; a philosopher and statesman who served Mithradates Eupator (*c*. 100 B.C.). He hated Rome so fiercely that he was called the "Rome Hater." *P*. iv. 14. 38

Mettus (or Mettius) Fufetius, an Alban commander who for his treachery to Rome in the war with Fidenae was bound to teams of horses, at the command of Tullus Hostilius, and torn apart, *T*. i. 3. 75

Milesian tales. See Aristides (2)

Miletus, *T*. iii. 9. 3; i. 10. 41 n.

Mimi, "Mimes," short, farcical dramatic pieces, presented with much gesticulation: often very coarse. They were popular at Rome, but only fragments survive. *T*. ii. 497 ff.

Minerva, Roman counterpart of Pallas Athene, goddess of war, handicraft (weaving, etc.), wisdom, etc. *T*. i. 2. 10, etc.

Minotaur, the monster—half bull, half man—which Minos enclosed in the labyrinth; offspring of Pasiphaë. *T*. iv. 7. 18

Minyae, a name for the Argonauts because many of them were of the race of Minyas in Thessaly and Boeotia. *T*. iii. 9. 13

Montanus, an Augustan epic and elegiac poet—*tolerabilis poëta* (Sen *Ep*. 122); two fragments, *P*. iv. 16. 11

Mulciber, the "Melter," a name of Vulcan, god of fire and the forge, *T*. i. 2. 5

Musae, the Muses, patronesses of poetry, music, etc., nine in all, of whom Ovid mentions in the *T*. and *P*. only Calliope and Thalia. Musa stands often for "poetry," "poetic inspiration," etc.

Myron, of Eleutherae, one of the greatest Greek sculptors (*c*. 450 B.C.); the cow is his most frequently mentioned work. *P*. iv. 1. 34

Mysiae gentes, a name used vaguely in Ovid's time for the tribes along the north side of Mt. Haemus (more often spelled Moesiae), *P*. iv. 9. 77

Mysus (dux). See Telephus

Naïdes, nymphs. *P*. iv. 16. 35

Naso, Ovid always so names himself, *T*. i. 7. 10, etc.

Natalis, the Genius (Genius and Natalis mean the same and are not used in one phrase), the spiritual counterpart of every man who watched over him, worshipped especially on the birthday—the Birthday God. *T*. iii. 13. 2 n.; *cf*. v 5 1 and 13

Neptunus, god of the sea, *T*. i. 2. 9, etc.

Neritus, *T*. i. 5. 57 n.

Nestor, king of Pylos, the oldest of the Greek leaders at Troy, *P* i. 4. 10

Nilus, the Nile, *T*. i. 2. 80; *P*. iv. 10. 58

Niobe, daughter of Tantalus and wife of Amphion, king of Thebes. Proud of her numerous children she ventured to compare herself with Latona who had only two, Apollo and Diana. The angered gods slew Niobe's children, and she herself after many days of weeping was

503

changed to stone. *T.* v. 1. 57, etc.

Nireus, *P.* iv. 13. 16 n.

Nisus, son of Hyrtacus. N. and Euryalus, followers of Aeneas, were famed for their devoted friendship. Having penetrated the camp of Turnus both fell because neither would abandon the other. *T.* i. 5. 24, etc.

Notus, the South wind. The name implies moisture whereas Auster implies heat, but both were used as general terms. *T.* i. 2. 15, etc.

Nox, goddess of night, *P.* i. 2. 54

Numa, (1) the second king of Rome who was said to have been a pupil of Pythagoras, *P.* iii. 3 44, etc. (2) An Augustan poet known only from *P.* iv. 16. 10

Odesos, a town on the Thracian coast of the Pontus, now Varna, *T.* i. 10. 37

Odrysii (or Odrysae), a Thracian people who once held sway as far east as the delta of the Danube, *P.* i. 8. 15

Odyssea, the *Odyssey*, Homer's epic, *T.* ii. 375

Oechalia, the city of King Eurytus, captured by Hercules; site uncertain. *P.* iv. 8. 62 n.

Oedipus, king of Thebes, who unwittingly slew Laïus, his own father, *T.* i. 1. 114

Olympias, an Olympiad, *P.* iv. 6. 5 n.

Olympus, a famous flute-player, *P.* iii. 3. 42. See Marsyas

Ops, goddess of agricultural abundance, *T.* ii. 24

Opus, capital of the Opuntian Locrians, *P.* i. 3. 73

Orestes, son of Agamemnon and Clytaemestra. He slew his mother to avenge his father who she and Aegisthus had murdered, was presecuted by the Furies, and driven over the world until he gained release at the Court of the Areopagus in Athens. Pylades, of Phocis, his faithful friend, shared his wanderings, in the course of which they rescued Iphigenia from her position as priestess among the Taurians. *T.* i. 5. 22, etc.

Orpheus, the famous Thracian bard whose song caused even trees and rocks to follow him. When Eurydice, his wife, died from a serpent's bite, Orpheus visted the lower world and at his entreaty Pluto allowed Eurydice to return to the upper world on condition that Orpheus should not look back at her during the journey. He disobeyed and death a second time claimed Eurydice. *P.* ii. 9. 53, etc.

Ossa, a mountain in Thessaly, *P.* ii. 2. 9

Paeligni, the Italian people in whose capital (Sulmo) Ovid was born, *P.* i. 8. 42 ; iv. 14. 49

Paeones, the Pannonians, a group of Illyrian tribes south and west of the great bend of the Danube; organized as a province *c.* A.D. 10. *P.* ii. 2. 75

Paestum, an old city (the Greek Posidonia) on the Lucanian coast, south of Salernum, *P.* ii. 4. 28

Palatium, the Palatine Hill, on which Augustus resided, *T.* i. 1. 69, etc.

Palicus, one of the guardian deities of sulphurous springs in Sicily, between Syracuse and Henna, *P* ii. 10. 25

Palinurus, the helmsman of Aeneas, who fell into the sea while asleep and was drowned, *T.* v. 6. 7

Pallas. See Minerva

Pandion, *P.* i. 3. 39 n.

Pannonia, *T.* ii. 225. See Paeones

Parcae, the Fates — Clotho, Lachesis, Atropos—who presided over destiny, *T.* v. 3. 14, etc. See Lachesis

Parrhasius. See Lycaon

Parthenius, a river in eastern Bithynia, flows into the Pontus, *P.* iv. 10. 49

Parthus, Parthian, *T.* ii. 228

Passer, an Augustan poet (?), *P*. iv.
16. 33 n.
Patroculus, son of Menoetius and
grandson of Actor, the devoted
friend of Achilles; slain by
Hector. *P*. i. 3. 73, etc.
Pedo. See Albinovanus
Pegasus, the winged steed of
Bellerophon, born from the
Gorgon Medusa's blood. With
a beat of his hoof he created
Hippocrene (the Steed's Spring),
on Mt. Helicon. *T*. iii. 7. 15, etc.
Pelasgi, "Greeks," originally the
name of a Thessalian people, *T*.
ii. 403
Pelias, a Thessalian who took Iolkos
from his half-brother Aeson, and
sent the latter's son Jason in
quest of the golden fleece, *T*. ii.
403, etc.
Pelion, a Thessalian mountain, *P*.
ii. 2. 9. See Gigantes
Pelops, son of Tantalus, whom his
father slew and served up at
table to the gods. The gods
restored him to life giving him
an ivory shoulder in place of that
injured by the bite of Ceres.
Later he carried off Hippodamia,
daughter of King Oenomaus of
Pisa, after he had defeated the
latter in a chariot race. *T*. ii.
385, etc.
Penates. See Lares
Penelope, daughter of Icarius and
wife of Ulysses, *q.v.*
Penius, a river in Colchis, *P*. iv. 10.
47
Pentheus, king of Thebes, who
disturbed the orgies of Bacchus
and was torn to pieces by the
devotees, among whom was his
mother Agave, *T*. v. 3. 40
Perilla, (1) pseudonym of Metella,
mistress of Ticida, *T*. ii. 437–438 n.;
(2) Ovid's stepdaughter, the
daughter of his third wife, *T*. iii.
7 (the name prob. a pseudonym)
Perillus. See Phalaris
Perseis, an epic on Perseus
Perseus, son of Jupiter and Danaë.
He slew the Gorgon Medusa by
the aid of the helmet of invisi-

bility, the winged sandals, etc.,
which he obtained from the
nymphs. *T*. iii. 8. 6
Persia, *T*. v. 3. 23
Phaeacia. See Alcinous and *P*. iv.
12. 27 n.
Phaëthon, son of Helios (Sol, the
sun god), and Clymene (whose
husband was Merops). His father
promised that whatever request
he should make would be grant-
ed and he asked permission to
drive the chariot of the sun. In
spite of the god's warning he
insisted and was hurled into
the Po. His grieving sisters,
the Heliads, were changed into
poplars. *P*. i. 2. 32, etc.
Phalaris, tyrant of Agrigentum, *T*.
iii. 11. 39 ff.
Pharos, *P*, i. 1. 38 n.
Phasis, a river in Colchis, the land
of the Golden Fleece. Medea is
called "the Phasian" (Phasias).
P. iii. 3. 80
Pherae, *P*. ii. 9. 43 n.
Phidias, the famous Athenian
sculptor (5th cent. B.C.) who
made the gold and ivory statue
of Pallas for the Parthenon, *P*.
iv. 1. 32
Philetas, of Cos, a Greek gram-
marian and poet (*c.* 300 B.C. and
later), famed for elegy (few
fragments). His poems (or a
poem) to Bittis, his wife or
sweetheart, were especially cele-
brated. *T*. i. 6. 2, etc.
Philippus I, king of Macedonia,
P. iv. 15, 15
Philoctetes, son of Poeas, the
famous archer, set out for Troy
but was left at Lemnos suffering
from a serpent's bite. He was
brought to Troy in the 10th year
of the war, because the city could
not be captured without his
arrows, and was healed by
Machaon. *T*. v. 1. 61, etc.
Phineus, son of Agenor; freed by
the Argonauts from the Harpies
he gave them advice concerning
their voyage, *P*. i. 4. 37
Phoebe, a name for Diana as the

female counterpart of Phoebus, *P*. iii. 2. 64

Phrygia, the district of north-western Asia Minor in which lay Troy; hence Phrygius means often "Trojan," *P*. i. 1. 45, etc.

Phyllis, (1) a character in Vergil's *Bucolics*, *T*. ii. 537; (2) the title of a poem by Tuscus, *P*. iv. 16. 20

Piacches, a chieftain of some wild tribe near Tomis, *P*. iv. 10. 23

Pierides, the Muses, so called from the Pierian district on Mt. Olympus, one of their favourite haunts; adj. Pierius. *T*. iii. 2. 3, etc.

Pindar, the famous lyric poet of Boeotian Thebes (†after 442 B.C.), *P*. iv. 16. 28

Pirene, the celebrated spring at Corinth, *P*. i. 3. 75

Pirithous. See Theseus

Pisa, the district of Elis in which lay Olympia, often synonymous with Elis, *T*. ii. 386, etc.

Pleiades, a constellation of seven stars whose rising in the spring and setting in the autumn were supposed to mark the beginning and end of navigation each year, *P*. i. 5. 82, etc. See Sterope

Pluto, god of the lower world, *T*. i. 9. 32

Podalirius, son of Aesculapius. He and Machaon were the chief physicians in the Greek host before Troy. See Eteocles

Polyphemus, *P*. ii. 2. 113. See Cyclopes

Pompeius, (1) Cn. Pompeius Magnus, the triumvir, *P*. iv. 3. 41; (2) Sex. Pompeius, a patron of Ovid, *P*. iv. 1, iv. 4, iv. 5, iv. 15. See Introd. p. xiii

Ponticus, an epic poet, member of Ovid's circle; probably the same as the Ponticus of Propert. I. 7 and 9; *T*. iv. 10. 47

Pontus, the Black Sea, originally called inhospitable (ἄξεινος, axenus) because of its storms and the barbarous tribes on its coasts, later hospitable (εὔξεινος, euxinus), an

euphemism. Ovid also calls the region in which Tomis lay, Pontus. *T*. i. 2. 83, etc.

Porus, an Indian chieftain whom Alexander conquered but treated generously, *T*. iii. v. 39

Priamus, king of Troy, *T*. v. 1. 55, etc. See Hector

Priapus, god of fertility, especially honoured at Lampsacus on the Hellespont, *T*. i. 10. 26

Prisci, two Augustan poets referred to in *P*. iv. 16. 10. One was probably Clutorius Priscus who was later (A.D. 21) put to death for having read to a circle of ladies a poem in which he lamented the death of Drusus while Drusus was still alive. The other Priscus is not known from other sources

Procne, *T*. iii. 12. 9, etc. See Tereus

Proculus, an Augustan erotic poet who imitated Callimachus, *P*. iv. 16. 32

Propertius (Sex. Aurelius), one of Rome's best elegiac poets (c. 49–c. 15 B.C.). Ovid often refers to him and considered him his immediate predecessor. *T*. ii. 465; iv. 10. 51 ff. *cf*. 45 f.

Propontis, the Sea of Marmora, *T*. i. 10. 29, etc.

Protesilaus, grandson of Phylacus. See Laodamia

Pylades, of Phocis, son of Strophius, *T*. i. 9. 28, etc. See Orestes

Pylos, the isle of which Nestor was king, *T*. v. 5. 62, etc.

Pyrrhus (or Neoptolemus), son of Achilles and Deidamia, *T*. ii. 405

Pythagoras, the learned sage of Samos (6th cent. B.C.), *T*. iii. 3. 62, etc. See Numa

Quirinus, an ancient Sabine deity, identified with Romulus after the latter's apotheosis, *T*. i. 3. 33, etc.

Rabirius, an Augustan epic poet who wrote of the fate of Antony; few fragments, *P*. iv. 16. 5

Raetia, the district north of Verona from the Alps to Vindelicia on the north, Helvetia on the west and Noricum on the east, *T*. ii. 226

Remus, son of Mars and Ilia—hence Iliades; twin brother of Romulus, *T*. iv. 3. 8

Rhamnusia, Nemesis, *T*. v. 8. 9 n.

Rhenus, the Rhine, *T*. iv. 2. 42, etc.

Rhoemetalces, father of Cotys. He may be referred to *P*. i. 8. 16 ff.; iv. 7. 25 ff., but more probably Cotys is meant. See Cotys

Roma, *T*. i. 1. 57, etc.

Rufinus, a friend whom Ovid addresses, *P*. i. 3; iii. 4. Nothing is known of him from other sources

Rufus, (1) a friend of Ovid's addressed *P*. ii. 11. He was an uncle of the poet's wife and a native of Fundi; (2) an Augustan poet who imitated Pindar; perhaps identical with the Titius of Horace, *Epis*. i. 3. 9. *P*. iv. 16. 28

Rutilius, P. Rutilius Rufus, a friend of Scipio Aemilianus and con. 105 B.C., *P*. i. 3. 63 n.

Rutuli, *T*. i. 5. 23. See Turnus

Sabinus, an Augustan epic and elegiac poet. He wrote answers to some of the love letters of Ovid's Heroïdes, *cf Am*. ii. 18. 19 ff., perhaps a poem of the calendar (*P*. iv. 16. 15 f.), and a Troezania, *cf. P*. iv. 16. 10 n.

Sagaris, a river flowing into the Black Sea; location uncertain, *P*. iv. 10. 47

Salanus, a friend whom Ovid addresses, *P*. ii. 5. He was a friend of Germanicus, and apparently coached that prince in oratory

Same, an island subject to Ulysses, *T*. i. 5. 67

Samos, i.e. Samothrace, *T*. i. 10. 20

Sappho, the famous Lesbian poetess (*c*. 600 B.C.), *T*. ii. 365 f.

Sarmatia, a general name for Europe east of the Carpathians and north of the Black Sea. It included many tribes. Ovid often calls the region of Tomis "Sarmatian." *T*. i. 2. 82, etc.

Saturnia, a name for Juno, daughter of Saturn, *T*. i. 2. 7, etc.

Satyrs, followers of Bacchus, conceived (in Ovid's time) as possessing goatlike ears, hoofs, *T*. v. 3. 37, etc.

Sauromatae, Sarmatians, *T*. ii. 198, etc. (The form is convenient metrically)

Scylla, (1) a monster with six heads and twelve feet who destroyed six of Ulysses' men. Later, as in Ovid, she is a maiden the lower part of whose form is that of a monster girdled with dogs. *T*. iv. 7. 13, etc. (2) daughter of Nisus, king of Megara. She fell in love with Minos while he was besieging Megara and cut from her father's head the purple lock on which the safety of the town depended. Minos then captured the town, but Scylla whom he tried to put to death was changed into a seabird. *T*. ii. 393

Scythia, originally the country from the Danube to the Don, but by Ovid's time the Scythians had been supplanted by Sarmatian and other tribes. Ovid uses "Scythian" as a general term for the region of his exile. *T*. i. 3. 61, etc.

Secular Games (Ludi saeculares), the Centennial Games celebrated (17 B.C.) by Augustus in honour of Apollo and other gods as a symbol of the regeneration of Rome under the new regime. The festival was represented as a revival of ancient custom although none quite like it had ever existed. *T*. ii. 26

Semele, daughter of Cadmus, king of Thebes, and mother (by Jupiter) of Bacchus (Lyaeus). She asked Jupiter (Zeus) to appear to her in full panoply and perished in the flame of his lightning. *T*. iv. 3. 67

507

Servius, an erotic poet—probably of the Republican period, *T.* ii. 441

Sestos, a town on the Thracian shore of the Hellespont, *T.* i. 10. 28

Severus, Cornelius Severus, an epic poet who wrote on the war between Octavian and Sex. Pompey (38–36 B.C.) and perhaps other themes; few fragments. Ovid addresses him, *P.* iv. 2. The Severus of *P.* i. 8, also a poet, is probably the same man. In this case, *P.* iv. 2 was written earlier but published later than i. 8

Sibyl, *P.* ii. 8. 41 n

Sicily, *T.* iii. 11. 55, etc.

Sicyon, a town west of Corinth on the Asopus river, *P.* iv. 15. 10

Sidon, a coast city of Phoenicia famous for its purple dyes, *T.* iv. 2. 27, etc.

Sinope, a coast city of Paphlagonia on the Black Sea, *P.* i. 3. 67

Sinti, a Thracian tribe dwelling near the Strymon river, *T.* iv. 1. 21 n.

Sirens, maidens who lured sailors to death by their song. Ulysses stopped the ears of his men with wax and had himself lashed to the mast, and so heard them in safety, *P.* iv. 10. 17

Sisenna, *T.* ii. 443. See Aristides

Sithonius, referring to the central peninsula of Chalcidice, hence "Thracian," *P.* iv. 7. 25

Smyrna, an important Greek city on the coast of Lydia, *P.* i. 3. 65

Socrates, *T.* v. 12. 12 n.

Sol, Greek Helios, the god of the sun, *T.* i. 8. 2, etc.

Sphinx, a monster with a winged lion's body and the head of a maiden, *T.* iv. 7. 17

Sterope, one of the seven stars of the constellation Pleiades, *T.* i. 11. 4

Steneboea. See Bellerophon, *T.* ii. 398

Strophius, father of Pylades, *P.* ii. 6. 25

Strymon, a river in Thrace, *T.* v 3. 22

Styx, a river of the lower world, *T.* v. 2. 74, etc.

Suillius, P. Suillius Rufus, husband of Ovid's stepdaughter Perilla *P.* iv. 8 11 f. He rose to the proconsulship, A.D. 52 or 53, but was a corrupt judge and administrator, and was twice banished. See Tac. *Ann.* iv. 31; xi. 4 f.; xiii. 42 f.

Sulmo, chief town of the Paeligni, Ovid's birthplace, *T.* iv. 10. 3; *P.* iv. 14. 49

Sybaritica, *T.* ii. 417. See Hemitheon

Syene, a town far up the Nile at the confines of the empire (the modern Assuan), *P.* i. 5. 79 n.

Symplegades, *T.* i. 10. 47. See Cyaneae

Syracuse, the largest city of Sicily, *P.* iv. 3. 39

Syrtes, dangerous waters full of shoals off the coast of Africa between Tunis and Cyrene. Pirates infested the neighbouring coasts. *P.* iv. 14. 9

Tabropanes, Ceylon (?), *P.* i. 5. 80

Tanais, the Don, *T.* iii. 4b. 49, etc.

Tantalus, father of Pelops and great-grandfather of Menelaus who are both called Tantalides. *T.* ii. 385; *P.* iv. 16. 26

Tarpeius. Ovid calls the Capitoline Hill "Tarpeian." Strictly this name belonged to the western cliff—the Tarpeian Rock—so called from Spurius Tarpeius who commanded the citadel in the Sabine war or from his daughter Tarpeia who betrayed the citadel to the Sabines, or from L. Tarpeius whom Romulus caused to be hurled from the rock. *P.* ii. 1. 57, etc.

Tartarus (or Tartara), the lower world (Hades) or (as in Ovid) that part of it in which the wicked were punished, *T.* i. 2. 22

Tauri, a people dwelling in the

Crimea, the Tauric Chersonesus, *P*. iii. 2. 45

Telegonus, son of Ulysses and Circe. He unwittingly slew his own father. *T*. i. 1. 114, etc.

Telephus, a Mysian to whom an oracle had declared that only Achilles who had wounded him could cure his wound. He sought Achilles who healed him with the rust of the spear that he had used in the combat. *T*. v. 2. 15, etc. 2. 19 f.

Tempyra, a town of southern Thrace near the sea, *T*. i. 10. 21

Terence, P. Terentius After (†159 B.C.), one of Rome's best comic poets. He was born at Carthage; six plays extant. *T*. ii. 359

Teretei, *T*. ii. 191 n.

Tereus, king of Daulis who loved his wife's sister Philomela. His wife Procne in vengeance slew his son Itys (Itylus) and served the flesh to the father. Tereus was changed into a hoopoe, Philomela into a nightingale, Procne into a swallow. (In some versions Procne became a nightingale, Philomela a swallow.) *T*. ii. 389. etc.

Teucer, son of Telamon, half-brother of Ajax, a famous archer, driven into exile by his father because he had not avenged Ajax. *P*. i. 3. 80

Teucri, the Trojans, so called from their first king. Teucer, *T*. i. 2. 6

Thalia, the Muse of comedy and light verse, used symbolically for poetic work in general, *T*. iv. 10. 56, etc.

Thebae, Thebes, the chief city of Boeotia, *T*. ii. 319, etc.

Themistocles, son of Neocles; the great Athenian who defeated the Persians at Salamis, exiled *c*. 474–472 B.C., *P*. i. 3. 69

Thermodon, a river in Pontus frequented by Amazons, *P*. iv. 10. 51

Theromedon, a Scythian chieftain who fed lions on human flesh, *P*. i. 2. 119

Thersites, *P*. iii. 9. 10, etc. See Agrius

Theseus, son of Aegeus, king of Athens. He slew the Minotaur after penetrating the labyrinth by means of the clue given him by Ariadne, escaped with her but later abandoned her. His friendship for Pirithous, whom he accompanied to the lower world, was proverbial. *T*. i. 9. 31, etc.

Thessaly, the north-east district of Greece, *P*. i. 4. 28

Thoas (Thoans), *T*. i. 9. 28, etc. See Iphigenia

Thrace, the country extending from Macedonia to the Pontus and from the Danube to the Aegean and Propontis, *P*. iv. 5. 5, etc.

Thybris, the Tiber, *T*. v. 1. 31

Thyestes, *P*. iv. 6. 47 n.

Thyniacus (sinus), the Thynian Bay on the Thracian coast of the Pontus, *T*. i. 10. 35

Tiberius, Ti. Claudius Nero, the Emperor (42 B.C.–A.D. 37), elder son of Livia by her first husband. Augustus adopted him and finally made him his successor. *P*. iv. 9. 70, etc.

Tibullus (Albius), one of Rome's best elegists (*c*. 54–19 B.C.); much admired by Ovid, *T*. ii. 447, etc.

Tibur, the modern Tivoli, about eighteen miles east of Rome, *P*. i. 3. 82

Ticida (or Ticidas), a Roman erotic poet contemporary with Catullus; very few fragments, *T*. ii. 433

Tiphys, the pilot of the Argo, *T*. iv. 3. 77, etc.

Tisiphone, one of the three Furies, a symbol for madness, *T*. iv. 9. 6

Tityrus, a shepherd's name, a symbol for pastoral poetry, *P*. iv. 16. 33

Tityus, attempted to outrage Latona, was punished in the lower world where two vultures fed eternally on his liver which was as eternally renewed, *P*. i. 2. 39

509

Tomis, the Moesian town to which Ovid was banished; Tomitae, the inhabitants. Adj. Tomitanus, *T.* i. 2. 85; iii. 9. 33 n.; v. 7. 9; *P.* iv. 14. 59, etc. See Introd. pp. xxvi ff.

Tonans, the "Thunderer," epithet of Jupiter, *P.* ii. 2. 42

Trinacria, the "three-cornered land," a name of Sicily, *P.* iv. 15. 15

Trinacrius, an Augustan poet who wrote a *Perseis*, probably an epic on Perseus, *P.* iv. 16. 25

Triptolemus, son of Celeus, king of Eleusis. He received from Ceres a car loaded with seeds and instructed men in agriculture. *T.* iii. 8. 1, etc.

Triumphus, the "Triumph," Ovid's poem on the triumph, *P.* iii. 4. 3 n.

Trivia, originally the same as Hecate; later (as in Ovid), often identified with Diana. Hecate was called Trivia (trivia, "three ways") because of her function as goddess of roads, etc. *P.* iii. 2. 71

Troesmis (Troesme?), (1) a Moesian town near the Danube just above the delta, *P.* iv. 9. 79; (2) a poem by Sabinus (if the text is correct) on the capture of the town by Flaccus, *P.* iv. 16. 15

Troia, in north-west Asian Minor, *T.* i. 2. 5, etc.

Turnus, king of the Rutulians in Latium with whom Aeneas engaged in war, *T.* i. 2. 7, etc.

Turranius, an Augustan tragic poet, *P.* iv. 16. 29 (nothing further known)

Tuscus, an Augustan poet who wrote a *Phyllis*, perhaps of the love of Phyllis and Demophoon in which Demophoon may have been a pseudonym for the poet himself, *cf.* Propert. ii. 22. *P.* iv. 16. 20

Tuticanus, a friend to whom Ovid addresses *P.* iv. 12 and 14. He was an epic poet, *cf.* iv. 16. 27, where he is probably meant as the author of a *Phaeacis*—an epic

(or epyllion?) on the sojourn of Ulysses in Phaeacia

Tydeus, father of Diomed and one of the seven leaders who fell in the attack on Thebes. He had been exiled from Calydon because he had slain a relative. *P.* i. 3. 79

Tyndareus, husband of Leda; hence Leda's children, Castor, Pollux, Helen, and Clytaemestra are called Tyndaridae "sons (or daughters) of Tyndareus," *T.* i. 10. 45, etc.

Typhon, one of the Giants, whom Jupiter placed beneath Mt. Aetna, *P.* ii. 10. 24

Tyras, a Sarmatian river—the Dniester, *P.* iv. 10. 50

Tyre, the Phoenician coast city from which came the settlers of Carthage who are often called Tyrians, *T.* ii. 534

Ulysses (Ulixes), the Greek Odysseus, son of Laërtes, king of Ithaca; the most crafty and one of the bravest of Greek leaders before Troy. After ten years of wandering he reached home to find his substance wasted by the suitors of Penelope his faithful wife. He slew the suitors and regained his power. *T.* i. 2. 9, etc.

Umbria, the district of Italy north of Rome extending from Etruria to the Adriatic and north to the Po valley, *P.* i. 8. 67

Varius, L. Varius Rufus, an Augustan poet famed for tragedy and epic; only one certain fragment, *P.* iv. 16. 31

Varro, P. Varro Atacinus, an epic and erotic poet contemporary with Catullus. He wrote an epic on the Argonautic expedition. A few fragments survive. *T.* ii. 439

Venus, goddess of love, often used as a symbol for the passion itself, *T.* i. 2. 6, etc.

Vergilius, P. Vergilius Maro (70–19 B.C.) the greates Roman epic poet, author of the *Aeneid*,

Georgics, Bucolics, and certain minor poems, *T*. iv. 10. 51

Vesta, goddess of the hearth fire. Her cult was administered at Rome by six Vestal Virgins. *T*. ii. 311 ; iii. 1. 29, etc.

Vestalis, son (or grandson ?) of Donnus, a Celtic chieftian. He had taken service with the Romans and had become a centurion and served with Vitellius(?) at the capture of Aegisos. Later he was sent to Thrace on some imperial mission which is not clear. *P*. iv. 7

Victoria, goddess of victory, *T*. ii. 169

Virgo, the aqueduct built by Agrippa (19 B.C.) to supply his baths on the Campus Martis. A maiden (virgo) is said to have pointed out the springs which supplied the water, *T*. iii. 12. 22 ; *P*. i. 8. 38

Vitellius, P. Vitellius, friend of Germanicus, procon. of Bithynia 18 or 19 A.D. He may be the Vitellius to whom Ovid refers as recovering Aegisos. *P*. iv. 7. 27

Volesus, companion of T. Tatius and founder of the Valerian family. Volesus is probably the Sabine form of Valerius. *P*. iii. 2. 105

Zephyrus, the west wind, *T*. i. 2. 28, etc.

Zerinthia (litora), *T*. i. 10. 19 n.

511

THE LOEB CLASSICAL LIBRARY

VOLUMES ALREADY PUBLISHED

Latin Authors

AMMIANUS MARCELLINUS. J. C. Rolfe. 3 Vols.

APULEIUS: THE GOLDEN ASS (METAMORPHOSES). W. Adlington (1566). Revised by S. Gaselee.

ST. AUGUSTINE: CITY OF GOD. 7 Vols. Vol. I. G. E. McCracken. Vols. II and VII. W. M. Green. Vol. III. D. Wiesen. Vol. IV. P. Levine. Vol. V. E. M. Sanford and W. M. Green. Vol. VI. W. C. Greene.

ST. AUGUSTINE, CONFESSIONS. W. Watts (1631). 2 Vols.

ST. AUGUSTINE, SELECT LETTERS. J. H. Baxter.

AUSONIUS. H. G. Evelyn White. 2 Vols.

BEDE. J. E. King. 2 Vols.

BOETHIUS: TRACTS and DE CONSOLATIONE PHILOSOPHIAE. Rev. H. F. Stewart and E. K. Rand. Revised by S. J. Tester.

CAESAR: ALEXANDRIAN, AFRICAN and SPANISH WARS. A. G. Way.

CAESAR: CIVIL WARS. A. G. Peskett.

CAESAR: GALLIC WAR. H. J. Edwards.

CATO: DE RE RUSTICA. VARRO: DE RE RUSTICA. H. B. Ash and W. D. Hooper.

CATULLUS. F. W. Cornish. TIBULLUS. J. B. Postgate. PERVIGILIUM VENERIS. J. W. Mackail. Revised by G. P. Goold.

CELSUS: DE MEDICINA. W. G. Spencer. 3 Vols.

CICERO: BRUTUS and ORATOR. G. L. Hendrickson and H. M. Hubbell.

[CICERO]: AD HERENNIUM. H. Caplan.

CICERO: DE ORATORE, etc. 2 Vols. Vol. I. DE ORATORE, Books I and II. E. W. Sutton and H. Rackham. Vol. II. DE ORATORE, Book III. DE FATO; PARADOXA STOICORUM; DE PARTITIONE ORATORIA. H. Rackham.

CICERO: DE FINIBUS. H. Rackham.

CICERO: DE INVENTIONE, etc. H. M. Hubbell.

CICERO: DE NATURA DEORUM and ACADEMICA. H. Rackham.

CICERO: DE OFFICIIS. Walter Miller.

CICERO: DE RE PUBLICA and DE LEGIBUS. Clinton W. Keyes.

1

NEPOS, CORNELIUS. J. C. Rolfe.

OVID: THE ART OF LOVE and OTHER POEMS. J. H. Mozley. Revised by G. P. Goold.

OVID: FASTI. Sir James G. Frazer. Revised by G. P. Goold.

OVID: HEROIDES and AMORES. Grant Showerman. Revised by G. P. Goold.

OVID: METAMORPHOSES. F. J. Miller. 2 Vols. Revised by G. P. Goold.

OVID: TRISTIA and EX PONTO. A. L. Wheeler. Revised by G. P. Goold.

PERSIUS. Cf. JUVENAL.

PERVIGILIUM VENERIS. Cf. CATULLUS.

PETRONIUS. M. Heseltine. SENECA: APOCOLOCYNTOSIS. W. H. D. Rouse. Revised by E. H. Warmington.

PHAEDRUS and BABRIUS (Greek). B. E. Perry.

PLAUTUS. Paul Nixon. 5 Vols.

PLINY: LETTERS, PANEGYRICUS. Betty Radice. 2 Vols.

PLINY: NATURAL HISTORY. 10 Vols. Vols. I.–V. and IX. H. Rackham. VI.–VIII. W. H. S. Jones. X. D. E. Eichholz.

PROPERTIUS. H. E. Butler.

PRUDENTIUS. H. J. Thomson. 2 Vols.

QUINTILIAN. H. E. Butler. 4 Vols.

REMAINS OF OLD LATIN. E. H. Warmington. 4 Vols. Vol. I. (ENNIUS AND CAECILIUS) Vol. II. (LIVIUS, NAEVIUS PACUVIUS, ACCIUS) Vol. III. (LUCILIUS and LAWS OF XII TABLES) Vol. IV. (ARCHAIC INSCRIPTIONS).

RES GESTAE DIVI AUGUSTI. Cf. VELLEIUS PATERCULUS.

SALLUST. J. C. Rolfe.

SCRIPTORES HISTORIAE AUGUSTAE. D. Magie. 3 Vols.

SENECA, THE ELDER: CONTROVERSIAE, SUASORIAE. M. Winterbottom. 2 Vols.

SENECA: APOCOLOCYNTOSIS. Cf. PETRONIUS.

SENECA: EPISTULAE MORALES. R. M. Gummere. 3 Vols.

SENECA: MORAL ESSAYS. J. W. Basore. 3 Vols.

SENECA: TRAGEDIES. F. J. Miller. 2 Vols.

SENECA: NATURALES QUAESTIONES. T. H. Corcoran. 2 VOLS.

SIDONIUS: POEMS and LETTERS. W. B. Anderson. 2 Vols.

SILIUS ITALICUS. J. D. Duff. 2 Vols.

STATIUS. J. H. Mozley. 2 Vols.

SUETONIUS. J. C. Rolfe. 2 Vols.

TACITUS: DIALOGUS. Sir Wm. Peterson. AGRICOLA and GERMANIA. Maurice Hutton. Revised by M. Winterbottom, R. M. Ogilvie, E. H. Warmington.

TACITUS: HISTORIES and ANNALS. C. H. Moore and J. Jackson. 4 Vols.

TERENCE. John Sargeaunt. 2 Vols.

TERTULLIAN: APOLOGIA and DE SPECTACULIS. T. R. Glover. MINUCIUS FELIX. G. H. Rendall.

3

TIBULLUS. Cf. CATULLUS.
VALERIUS FLACCUS. J. H. Mozley.
VARRO: DE LINGUA LATINA. R. G. Kent. 2 Vols.
VELLEIUS PATERCULUS and RES GESTAE DIVI AUGUSTI. F. W. SHIPLEY.
VIRGIL. H. R. Fairclough. 2 Vols.
VITRUVIUS: DE ARCHITECTURA. F. Granger. 2 Vols.

Greek Authors

ACHILLES TATIUS. S. Gaselee.
AELIAN: ON THE NATURE OF ANIMALS. A. F. Scholfield. 3 Vols.
AENEAS TACTICUS. ASCLEPIODOTUS and ONASANDER. The Illinois Greek Club.
AESCHINES. C. D. Adams.
AESCHYLUS. H. Weir Smyth. 2 Vols.
ALCIPHRON, AELIAN, PHILOSTRATUS: LETTERS. A. R. Benner and F. H. Fobes.
ANDOCIDES, ANTIPHON. Cf. MINOR ATTIC ORATORS Vol. I.
APOLLODORUS. Sir James G. Frazer. 2 Vols.
APOLLONIUS RHODIUS. R. C. Seaton.
APOSTOLIC FATHERS. Kirsopp Lake. 2 Vols.
APPIAN: ROMAN HISTORY. Horace White. 4 Vols.
ARATUS. Cf. CALLIMACHUS.
ARISTIDES: ORATIONS. C. A. Behr.
ARISTOPHANES. Benjamin Bickley Rogers. 3 Vols. Verse trans.
ARISTOTLE: ART OF RHETORIC. J. H. Freese.
ARISTOTLE: ATHENIAN CONSTITUTION, EUDEMIAN ETHICS, VICES AND VIRTUES. H. Rackham.
ARISTOTLE: GENERATION OF ANIMALS. A. L. Peck.
ARISTOTLE: HISTORIA ANIMALIUM. A. L. Peck. Vols. I.–II.
ARISTOTLE: METAPHYSICS. H. Tredennick. 2 Vols.
ARISTOTLE: METEOROLOGICA. H. D. P. Lee.
ARISTOTLE: MINOR WORKS. W. S. Hett. On Colours, On Things Heard, On Physiognomies, On Plants, On Marvellous Things Heard, Mechanical Problems, On Indivisible Lines, On Situations and Names of Winds, On Melissus, Xenophanes, and Gorgias.
ARISTOTLE: NICOMACHEAN ETHICS. H. Rackham.
ARISTOTLE: OECONOMICA and MAGNA MORALIA. G. C. Armstrong (with METAPHYSICS, Vol. II).
ARISTOTLE: ON THE HEAVENS. W. K. C. Guthrie.
ARISTOTLE: ON THE SOUL, PARVA NATURALIA, ON BREATH. W. S. Hett.
ARISTOTLE: CATEGORIES, ON INTERPRETATION, PRIOR ANALYTICS. H. P. Cooke and H. Tredennick.

4

ARISTOTLE: POSTERIOR ANALYTICS, TOPICS. H. Tredennick and E. S. Forster.

ARISTOTLE: ON SOPHISTICAL REFUTATIONS. On Coming-to-be and Passing-Away, On the Cosmos. E. S. Forster and D. J. Furley.

ARISTOTLE: PARTS OF ANIMALS. A. L. Peck; MOTION AND PROGRESSION OF ANIMALS. E. S. Forster.

ARISTOTLE: PHYSICS. Rev. P. Wicksteed and F. M. Cornford. 2 Vols.

ARISTOTLE: POETICS and LONGINUS. W. Hamilton Fyfe; DEMETRIUS ON STYLE. W. Rhys Roberts.

ARISTOTLE: POLITICS. H. Rackham.

ARISTOTLE: PROBLEMS. W. S. Hett. 2 Vols.

ARISTOTLE: RHETORICA AD ALEXANDRUM (with PROBLEMS. Vol. II). H. Rackham.

ARRIAN: HISTORY OF ALEXANDER and INDICA. Rev. E. Iliffe Robson. 2 Vols. New version P. Brunt.

ATHENAEUS: DEIPNOSOPHISTAE. C. B. Gulick. 7 Vols.

BABRIUS and PHAEDRUS (Latin). B. E. Perry.

ST. BASIL: LETTERS. R. J. Deferrari. 4 Vols.

CALLIMACHUS: FRAGMENTS. C. A. Trypanis. MUSAEUS: HERO AND LEANDER. T. Gelzer and C. Whitman.

CALLIMACHUS, Hymns and Epigrams and LYCOPHRON. A. W. Mair; ARATUS. G. R. Mair.

CLEMENT OF ALEXANDRIA. Rev. G. W. Butterworth.

COLLUTHUS. Cf. OPPIAN.

DAPHNIS AND CHLOE. Thornley's translation revised by J. M. Edmonds: and PARTHENIUS. S. Gaselee.

DEMOSTHENES I.: OLYNTHIACS, PHILIPPICS and MINOR ORATIONS I.–XVII. and XX. J. H. Vince.

DEMOSTHENES II.: DE CORONA and DE FALSA LEGATIONE. C. A. Vince and J. H. Vince.

DEMOSTHENES III.: MEIDIAS, ANDROTION, ARISTOCRATES, TIMOCRATES and ARISTOGEITON I. and II. J. H. Vince.

DEMOSTHENES IV.–VI.: PRIVATE ORATIONS and IN NEAERAM. A. T. Murray.

DEMOSTHENES VII.: FUNERAL SPEECH, EROTIC ESSAY, EXORDIA and LETTERS. N. W. and N. J. DeWitt.

DIO CASSIUS: ROMAN HISTORY. E. Cary. 9 Vols.

DIO CHRYSOSTOM. J. W. Cohoon and H. Lamar Crosby. 5 Vols.

DIODORUS SICULUS. 12 Vols. Vols. I.–VI. C. H. Oldfather. Vol. VII. C. L. Sherman. Vol.VIII. C. B. Welles. Vols. IX. and X. R. M. Geer. Vol. XI. F. Walton. Vol. XII. F. Walton. General Index. R. M. Geer.

DIOGENES LAERTIUS. R. D. Hicks. 2 Vols. New Introduction by H. S. Long.

DIONYSIUS OF HALICARNASSUS: ROMAN ANTIQUITIES. Spelman's translation revised by E. Cary. 7 Vols.

DIONYSIUS OF HALICARNASSUS: CRITICAL ESSAYS. S. Usher. 2 Vols.
EPICTETUS. W. A. Oldfather. 2 Vols.
EURIPIDES. A. S. Way. 4 Vols. Verse trans.
EUSEBIUS: ECCLESIASTICAL HISTORY. Kirsopp Lake and J. E. L. Oulton. 2 Vols.
GALEN: ON THE NATURAL FACULTIES. A. J. Brock.
GREEK ANTHOLOGY. W. R. Paton. 5 Vols.
GREEK BUCOLIC POETS (THEOCRITUS, BION, MOSCHUS). J. M. Edmonds.
GREEK ELEGY AND IAMBUS with the ANACREONTEA. J. M. Edmonds. 2 Vols.
GREEK LYRIC. D. A. Campbell. 4 Vols. Vols. I. and II.
GREEK MATHEMATICAL WORKS. Ivor Thomas. 2 Vols.
HERODAS. Cf. THEOPHRASTUS: CHARACTERS.
HERODIAN. C. R. Whittaker. 2 Vols.
HERODOTUS. A. D. Godley. 4 Vols.
HESIOD AND THE HOMERIC HYMNS. H. G. Evelyn White.
HIPPOCRATES and the FRAGMENTS OF HERACLEITUS. W. H. S. Jones and E. T. Withington. 7 Vols. Vols. I.–VI.
HOMER: ILIAD. A. T. Murray. 2 Vols.
HOMER: ODYSSEY. A. T. Murray. 2 Vols.
ISAEUS. E. W. Forster.
ISOCRATES. George Norlin and LaRue Van Hook. 3 Vols.
[ST. JOHN DAMASCENE]: BARLAAM AND IOASAPH. Rev. G. R. Woodward, Harold Mattingly and D. M. Lang.
JOSEPHUS. 10 Vols. Vols. I.–IV. H. Thackeray. Vol. V. H. Thackeray and R. Marcus. Vols. VI.–VII. R. Marcus. Vol. VIII. R. Marcus and Allen Wikgren. Vols. IX.–X. L. H. Feldman.
JULIAN. Wilmer Cave Wright. 3 Vols.
LIBANIUS. A. F. Norman. 2 Vols..
LUCIAN. 8 Vols. Vols. I.–V. A. M. Harmon. Vol. VI. K. Kilburn. Vols. VII.–VIII. M. D. Macleod.
LYCOPHRON. Cf. CALLIMACHUS.
LYRA GRAECA, III. J. M. Edmonds. (Vols. I.and II. have been replaced by GREEK LYRIC I. and II.)
LYSIAS. W. R. M. Lamb.
MANETHO. W. G. Waddell.
MARCUS AURELIUS. C. R. Haines.
MENANDER. W. G. Arnott. 3 Vols. Vol. I.
MINOR ATTIC ORATORS (ANTIPHON, ANDOCIDES, LYCURGUS, DEMADES, DINARCHUS, HYPERIDES). K. J. Maidment and J. O. Burtt. 2 Vols.
MUSAEUS: HERO AND LEANDER. Cf. CALLIMACHUS.
NONNOS: DIONYSIACA. W. H. D. Rouse. 3 Vols.
OPPIAN, COLLUTHUS, TRYPHIODORUS. A. W. Mair.
PAPYRI. NON-LITERARY SELECTIONS. A. S. Hunt and C. C. Edgar. 2 Vols. LITERARY SELECTIONS (Poetry). D. L. Page.

6

PARTHENIUS. Cf. DAPHNIS AND CHLOE.

PAUSANIAS: DESCRIPTION OF GREECE W. H. S. Jones. 4 Vols. and Companion Vol. arranged by R. E. Wycherley.

PHILO. 10 Vols. Vols. I.–V. F. H. Colson and Rev. G. H. Whitaker. Vols. VI.–IX. F. H. Colson. Vol. X. F. H. Colson and the Rev. J. W. Earp.

PHILO: two supplementary Vols. (*Translation only*.) Ralph Marcus.

PHILOSTRATUS: THE LIFE OF APOLLONIUS OF TYANA. F. C. Conybeare. 2 Vols.

PHILOSTRATUS: IMAGINES; CALLISTRATUS: DESCRIPTIONS. A. Fairbanks.

PHILOSTRATUS and EUNAPIUS: LIVES OF THE SOPHISTS. Wilmer Cave Wright.

PINDAR. Sir J. E. Sandys.

PLATO: CHARMIDES, ALCIBIADES, HIPPARCHUS, THE LOVERS, THEAGES, MINOS and EPINOMIS. W. R. M. Lamb.

PLATO: CRATYLUS, PARMENIDES, GREATER HIPPIAS, LESSER HIPPIAS. H. N. Fowler.

PLATO: EUTHYPHRO, APOLOGY, CRITO, PHAEDO, PHAEDRUS. H. N. Fowler.

PLATO: LACHES, PROTAGORAS, MENO, EUTHYDEMUS. W. R. M. Lamb.

PLATO: LAWS. Rev. R. G. Bury. 2 Vols.

PLATO: LYSIS, SYMPOSIUM, GORGIAS. W. R. M. Lamb.

PLATO: REPUBLIC. Paul Shorey. 2 Vols.

PLATO: STATESMAN, PHILEBUS. H. N. Fowler; ION. W. R. M. Lamb.

PLATO: THEAETETUS and SOPHIST. H. N. Fowler.

PLATO: TIMAEUS, CRITIAS, CLEITOPHON, MENEXENUS, EPISTULAE. Rev. R. G. Bury.

PLOTINUS: A. H. Armstrong. 7 Vols.

PLUTARCH: MORALIA. 16 Vols. Vols. I.–V. F. C. Babbitt. Vol. VI. W. C. Helmbold. Vols. VII. and XIV. P. H. De Lacy and B. Einarson. Vol. VIII. P. A. Clement and H. B. Hoffleit. Vol. IX. E. L. Minar, Jr., F. H. Sandbach, W. C. Helmbold. Vol. X. H. N. Fowler. Vol. XI. L. Pearson and F. H. Sandbach. Vol. XII. H. Cherniss and W. C. Helmbold. Vol. XIII. 1 2. H. Cherniss. Vol. XV. F. H. Sandbach.

PLUTARCH: THE PARALLEL LIVES. B. Perrin. 11 Vols.

POLYBIUS. W. R. Paton. 6 Vols.

PROCOPIUS. H. B. Dewing. 7 Vols.

PTOLEMY: TETRABIBLOS. F. E. Robbins.

QUINTUS SMYRNAEUS. A. S. Way. Verse trans.

SEXTUS EMPIRICUS. Rev. R. G. Bury. 4 Vols.

SOPHOCLES. F. Storr. 2 Vols. Verse trans.

STRABO: GEOGRAPHY. Horace L. Jones. 8 Vols.

THEOCRITUS. Cf. GREEK BUCOLIC POETS.

THEOPHRASTUS: CHARACTERS. J. M. Edmonds. HERODAS, etc. A. D. Knox.

7

THEOPHRASTUS: ENQUIRY INTO PLANTS. Sir Arthur Hort, Bart. 2 Vols.

THEOPHRASTUS: DE CAUSIS PLANTARUM. G. K. K. Link and B. Einarson. 3 Vols. Vol. I.

THUCYDIDES. C. F. Smith. 4 Vols.

TRYPHIODORUS. Cf. OPPIAN.

XENOPHON: CYROPAEDIA. Walter Miller. 2 Vols.

XENOPHON: HELLENICA. C. L. Brownson. 2 Vols.

XENOPHON: ANABASIS. C. L. Brownson.

XENOPHON: MEMORABILIA and OECONOMICUS. E. C. Marchant. SYMPOSIUM and APOLOGY. O. J. Todd.

XENOPHON: SCRIPTA MINORA. E. C. Marchant. CONSTITUTION OF THE ATHENIANS. G. W. Bowersock.